PSYCHIANA MAN

Frank Robinson speaking in Spokane, WA. Undated photo. University of Idaho Special Collections.

PSYCHIANA MAN

A Mail-Order PROPHET, His FOLLOWERS, and the POWER of BELIEF in HARD TIMES

BRANDON R. SCHRAND

WSU PRESS

Washington State University Press
Pullman, Washington

WSU PRESS
WASHINGTON STATE UNIVERSITY

Washington State University Press
PO Box 645910
Pullman, Washington 99164-5910
Phone: 800-354-7360
Email: wsupress@wsu.edu
Website: wsupress.wsu.edu

Library of Congress Cataloging-in-Publication Data

Names: Schrand, Brandon R., author.
Title: Psychiana man : a mail-order prophet, his followers, and the power of belief in hard times / Brandon R. Schrand.
Description: Pullman, Washington : Washington State University Press, [2021] | Includes bibliographical references and index.
Identifiers: LCCN 2021058773 | ISBN 9780874224047 (trade paperback)
Subjects: LCSH: Robinson, Frank B. (Frank Bruce), 1886-1948. | Religious leaders--United States--Biography. | Psychiana movement.
Classification: LCC BL2790.R6 S37 2021 | DDC 299/.93 [B]--dc23
LC record available at https://lccn.loc.gov/2021058773

The Washington State University Pullman campus is located on the homelands of the Niimíipuu (Nez Perce) Tribe and the Palus people. We acknowledge their presence here since time immemorial and recognize their continuing connection to the land, to the water, and to their ancestors. WSU Press is committed to promoting education about and fostering understanding of historical issues as well as the current concerns of Native peoples.

Cover design by Brad Norr Design

To Mason and Madeline for all the reasons.

"You don't know me; you never knew my heart. No man knows my history…I shall never understand it. I don't blame anyone for not believing my history. If I had not experienced what I have, I could not have believed it myself."

—Joseph Smith, April 7, 1844

Contents

Part IV: THROUGH WAR TO GOD 1937–1945

Part V: REQUIEM FOR A PROPHET 1945–1952

A Note on the Sources

It was by complete chance that I learned about Frank Bruce Robinson and Psychiana. In 2014, I had decided to write a letter to the editor of my local paper, *The Moscow-Pullman Daily News* about a neighborhood zoning issue. Because I wanted my letter to provide some historical context, I consulted a local history book, *Moscow* (Images of America series) by Julie Monroe. It was in her volume that I first happened upon the photos and brief description about a strange religion and the man who started it.

The story was so bizarre and baffling that it seemed like bad fiction. But it was not. It was all too real. The more I looked into it, the more fascinated I became. My interest in Psychiana did not hang from a religious or ecumenical hook, however. I am not a religious man, and my curiosity seldom runs in that direction. Instead, it was the human perspective that had hooked my interest. The question I asked then, and that I asked throughout the writing of this book, was simple and endlessly (at least to me) profound: why do people believe what they believe? Especially if something seems by all accounts to be specious or suspect, and even if facts fly in the face of the thing or person believed in, why do people hold fast to their convictions?

Initially, I thought I might write an essay about Psychiana, or a magazine piece about Robinson and his religion as a way of addressing some of these ongoing questions. But in a matter of days, I discovered that the story was far too big for an essay or article. It demanded the space of a book.

One of the first texts I read in preparing to write about Robinson and Psychiana was Lawrence Wright's *Going Clear: Scientology, Hollywood & the Prison of Belief*. Wright's book got me thinking about how to tackle a unique and, to many, utterly unknown American religion, and how to do so without alienating the reader. It was important to me that I treat such a mercurial subject as fairly but as truthfully as possible.

To that end, *Going Clear* was especially illuminating in how to write about a wildly unreliable figure—L. Ron Hubbard in his case, and Frank B.

Robinson in my own. Hubbard has been called a charlatan, quack, mystic, genius, visionary, madman, and liar. The same adjectives have been used to describe Robinson. What made Robinson such a satisfying subject to write about was his complexity and often-contradictory traits, so it was critical that I let the readers experience the vast nuances of his personality, and Wright's book provided an apt structural model.

I was particularly interested in how Wright told the story of Scientology through one of its members: Paul Haggis. The insider's perspective, I came to realize, was not only invaluable, but it comprised the beating heart of the entire Psychiana Movement.

Along a similar vein, I consulted Fawn Brodie's foundational biography, *No Man Knows My History: The Life of Joseph Smith*, still the best, most reliable and, I would argue, fair treatment of the Mormon prophet in print (though the book cost Brodie her membership in that church). Like Smith and Hubbard, Robinson was charismatic, charming, driven, brilliant, egomaniacal, and wildly flawed. These seemingly paradoxical traits are precisely what make characters like Robinson so fascinating, but they also provide unique challenges to a writer hoping to paint a balanced portrait of his or her subject.

Like Joseph Smith and L. Ron Hubbard, Frank B. Robinson was a self-invented individual who understood the power of the printed word, and who spent his life writing, revising, and advertising his official life story. And like Smith and Hubbard, Robinson spent much of that same time defending and justifying glaring inconsistencies between the official story that he promulgated about his life, and the evidentiary record that often contradicted the former.

Officially, I had two autobiographies to consult in writing this book: *The Life Story of Frank B. Robinson (Written By Himself)* and *The Strange Autobiography of Frank B. Robinson*. The titles alone, however, are enough to put attentive researchers on guard. As artifacts of record, neither of these works is wholly reliable. Their veracity has less to do with the vagaries of human memory and more to do with the calculations of a gifted ad-man. Still, they are valuable to the researcher for what they do not say as much as for what they do; for what they purport as much as for what they reveal. That said, their internal contradictions, obfuscations, omissions, and prevarications presented real and substantive challenges that demanded constant corroboration. Moreover, the entire narrative thrust of Psychiana is so inextricably tied to Frank Robinson's life story that all of his written work including the Lessons, books, magazines, newsletters, radio programs, broadsides, and advertisements are autobiographical in nature, making the task of writing accurately about his life challenging in the extreme.

Fortunately, I was not the first person who tried to corroborate Robinson's life story. His son, Alfred Robinson, wrote *A Family Trilogy*, an unpublished and thoroughly researched genealogical history and exploration of his father's history and movement. Each of the three manuscript volumes contains scores of documents and records, along with the narrative of his journey in tracking down these sources. Alfred had donated several bound photocopies to the Latah County Historical Society. I would not have been able to write this book had it not been for Alfred Robinson's steadfast work.

Indeed, one aspect that most aptly characterizes the Latah Historical Society's Frank Robinson materials is the intimacy of the documents. Their photographs, trove of personal correspondence, financial statements, and family records reveal an unflinching and often shockingly candid portrait of Frank B. Robinson that is not portrayed anywhere else in his voluminous output of writing. The society's records on Robinson's federal trial and legal troubles were invaluable as I pieced together how his alleged criminal acts were always linked to his origin story. Of particular value, too, were the society's oral histories by Sam Schrager, who in the 1970s interviewed a number of Psychiana employees and individuals who were otherwise familiar with Robinson, his family, and his movement.

The Frank Bruce Robinson Papers at the University of Idaho, on the other hand, are less intimate, perhaps, but are enormously substantive in their scope of operational and organizational materials, including advertisements, publications, flyers, propaganda, books, monographs, promos, audio recordings, company audits, news clippings, draft manuscripts, office memoranda, scrapbooks, telegrams and cables, legal documents, and of course the student letters themselves.

I had spent about a week poring over a fraction of the student correspondence when it became clear to me that I wanted my book to be as much about them and their lives as it would be about Frank Robinson and Psychiana. Taken together, these letters served as a mirror that reflected the perceptions and realities of Psychiana, but also the perceptions and realities of daily life in the Great Depression across America and abroad. Ultimately, I wanted to create a kind of national composite diary, a cross-section of private lives bearing witness to the unraveling of a nation in real time. Little did I realize just how long it would take to read my way through all the correspondence, let alone how difficult it would be to tease out which student letters would best serve the narrative I wanted to write.

Ultimately, I devised four criteria that helped me decide which letters might be included over others. The first criterion was that the student letter had to illuminate some aspect, however small, of Psychiana or Robinson himself. This could entail anything from the mailing process to the exchange of money, Lessons, brochures, or other materials. It could also include the tone or tenor of Robinson's responses to students (or lack of response), or the difference between a genuinely personal reply and a form letter. It entailed, too, the degree to which Robinson became reliant on assistants to answer the deluge of student correspondence. The second criterion was that the letters had to address the concept of belief either implicitly or explicitly. Third, the student had to be "storyable." In other words, I had to find enough of a paper trail on the individual student—vital records, census data, newspaper articles, maps, city directories, along with information on his or her community—to create a serviceable vignette that would offer a window not only into that part of the world at that time, but also into why that average person might find solace in Psychiana.

The final criterion was that the letters had to reflect not just the diversity of Psychiana membership, but more generally the religion's broad appeal during hard times, showing that it was far more mainstream than fringe. It was important to me that readers understood that Psychiana members were not all cut from the same cloth. On the contrary. They ranged from the highly literate and even literary to the barely literate; from atheists to ordained ministers; from the affluent to the destitute; and from cops to criminals. And perhaps most notably, because Psychiana was a mail-based religion, it was truly color-blind, making its membership strikingly racially diverse and all-inclusive for the time.

In the years I spent digging through this trove of correspondence, I expected to read letters from disillusioned students writing in to voice their grievances and demanding their money back, per Robinson's vaunted policy. I kept expecting to find a whistle-blower in the reams of pages, some clarion call denouncing the entire operation. But if such a recalcitrant letter existed, it was not kept or has been lost. What I did find, however, was far more telling. The handful of students who did grumble or grouse about the cost of Lessons, form-letter responses, mailing delays, and the like, still remained faithful—ardently so.

An important text I kept on my desk during the writing of this book was Benjamin Roth's *Great Depression Diary*, edited by James Ledbetter and Daniel B. Roth. So much of what I wanted to capture in this book was the individual's voice trying to make sense of the world in incredibly difficult times. Not only did I find that in Roth's diary, but I also found a voice I could use to compare and contrast with those of Psychiana students, often on the same day.

Likewise, it was imperative that I immersed myself in the history of the Great Depression. One of the go-to texts I also kept on my desk was Robert S. McElvaine's *The Great Depression: America 1929–1941*. Immensely readable, McElvaine's text was instrumental to my work, as it charted the political, social, and economic shifts that tracked parallel to Robinson's establishment of Psychiana and its subsequent success. It was incredibly important too in establishing a broader context for what some of the Psychiana students were going through personally, particularly when it came to labor strikes, Relief Rolls, and the fluctuating prices for everyday goods like meat, coal, and wheat.

Morris Dickstein's *Dancing in the Dark: A Cultural History of the Great Depression* was also helpful, especially as I tried to peer into the daily lives of Psychiana students. When I wanted to know what songs or movies were popular (and why), or what books people were reading, Dickstein's sweeping work was the one I returned to time and again.

As the Great Depression sowed daily uncertainty in America and worldwide, people began turning to self-help books, lessons, and organizations. (It is not entirely coincidental, for instance, that Alcoholics Anonymous was founded in this period.) Indeed, if any one era can be credited for the rise of self-help, it may have been the Great Depression, a period in which people began to distrust the very institutions they had previously relied on: banks, government agencies, even church. To further understand this cultural shift, I turned to Miki McGee's inestimable *Self-Help, Inc.: Makeover Culture in American Life*. McGee shows how movements like New Thought (a "parent" philosophy of Psychiana), founded in the nineteenth century, flourished in the Great Depression. She further points to self-help as not just a byproduct of the Depression-era zeitgeist, but also as an American capitalistic phenomenon. It was her text that provided me with a theoretical framework into which I could ably situate Psychiana.

Her work also alerted me to a number of other writers and thinkers of the period who were working along similar lines as Frank Robinson, many of whom directly influenced him. It was important that I familiarize myself with figures such as Robert Collier (*Secret of the Ages*); Charles Haanel (*The Master Key System*); Bruce Barton (*The Man Nobody Knows*); Ernest Holmes (*The Science of Mind*); and of course Dale Carnegie (*How to Win Friends and Influence People*). The sheer proliferation of these writers and works cropping up out of the Great Depression was, to my thinking, markedly suggestive of deeper cultural moods and temperaments of that particular era when people needed, and sought out, advice.

But if Psychiana came of age in the Great Depression, it also fledged concurrently with the steady rise of fascism worldwide. Because Robinson so explicitly lassoed his Movement to global news and trends for what were clearly reasons of currency and relevancy, Psychiana became as intertwined with the rise of World War II as it was with the Depression itself. Tracking Robinson's Movement in the newspapers became a master class in Hitler's rise to power and the world's ineffectual and tacit response to his and other totalitarian regimes. For help in capturing the simmering mood of this seminal moment in global history, I turned to Erik Larson's *In the Garden of Beasts*. By no means an academic or definitive history of Hitler's ascension, Larson's book nonetheless provides a chilling window into the daily indifference and acquiescence ordinary people seemed to show toward the march of authoritarianism. And because my book was so grounded in the daily perceptions of ordinary people living in extraordinary times, *In the Garden of Beasts* was extremely useful in identifying the machinations of that slow burn.

––––––––––––––– ✦ –––––––––––––––

Of course, there was no better body of work to study than Frank Robinson's own oeuvre. That he was prolific goes without saying. However, much of his work—particularly his later writings—was largely derivative, recycled from previous publications. Robinson's chief talent did not reside in generating original content, but in repackaging extant content in original ways.

That said, Robinson's most original and convincing ideas were laid out in his first set of Psychiana Lessons and in his debut book, *The God Nobody Knows*. In many ways his most cogent work, *The God Nobody Knows* promulgates the fundamentals on which Psychiana would stand for decades to come: a wholesale disavowal of conventional religion, and the Bible specifically; an embrace for a more universal God power, rather than a God entity; and a reliance on daily affirmations and self-empowerment.

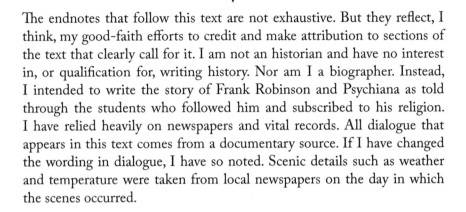

The endnotes that follow this text are not exhaustive. But they reflect, I think, my good-faith efforts to credit and make attribution to sections of the text that clearly call for it. I am not an historian and have no interest in, or qualification for, writing history. Nor am I a biographer. Instead, I intended to write the story of Frank Robinson and Psychiana as told through the students who followed him and subscribed to his religion. I have relied heavily on newspapers and vital records. All dialogue that appears in this text comes from a documentary source. If I have changed the wording in dialogue, I have so noted. Scenic details such as weather and temperature were taken from local newspapers on the day in which the scenes occurred.

Prologue

On the morning of May 16, 1936, a clear-skied Saturday, a tall, handsome, and charismatic man left his stylish brick home on 122 South Howard Street in the somnolent college town of Moscow, Idaho, to drive four blocks to the three-story brick federal building that housed the town's post office and courtroom. Not yet fifty, the man was immaculately dressed in a single-breasted worsted suit, pressed shirt, and gleaming silk tie. His hair—blondish-silver—was expertly combed like a movie star's. The car in which he motored the four short blocks was much like the man himself: ostentatious and larger than life. It was a 1932 Duesenberg.[1] It was the car Daddy Warbucks owned and bragged about in *Annie*. It was driven only by the most elite figures in the world, many of them Hollywood celebrities, including Clark Gable, Gary Cooper, Rudolph Valentino, Greta Garbo, and Charlie Chaplin.

The man arrived at the federal building minutes later like a one-man parade. Throngs of people lined the streets and sidewalks, waiting for him. A born showman, he exited his sleek Duesenberg, waved to the crowd, and smiled for pictures. A gaggle of pressmen fired questions to the man, who was about to go on trial. The charge: passport fraud. In that charge, though, lurked the very serious contention that the man was not who he had claimed to be. Prosecutors charged that he was an imposter and asserted that they had the evidence to prove it. Hecklers gathered near the courthouse steps to bark insults amid the flashing cameras.

Reporters asked if he thought he would be found guilty. The man scanned his audience and smiled. "This is not a prosecution. It's a *persecution*," he said, adding that he would be found perfectly innocent.[2] The man glad-handed a few well-wishers as he made his way up the stone steps to the red brick courthouse and the trial that awaited him.

The man's name was Frank Bruce Robinson. He had risen out of the ashes of the Great Depression by creating—six weeks after the stock market crashed on Black Tuesday in 1929—a self-help religion he called Psychiana. The first and only mail-order, "money-back-guarantee" religion, had, by that

I'M ADVERTISING GOD

and I'm proud to be doing it. I'm telling the world of the most scintillating, dynamic, pulsing, throbbing Power which exists on this earth, which practically no one knows about. This invisible Power can do miracles for you. If you grovel in the throes of poverty, this staggering Spiritual Power can make you rich. If illness abides in your house, this amazing Power can drive it out. If you are fearful of the future, not knowing what to do or which way to turn, this miracle-working Power of God can work wonders. It can bring into your life a permanent abiding peace. You believe such a Power exists of course. But you don't know where to find it—do

you? Well, I can tell you. And believe you me, I know whereof I speak. And the beauty of it all is that it will cost you nothing to have me prove that I know what I'm talking about. Mail a post-card or write a letter to DR. FRANK B. ROBINSON, Dept. M-4, Moscow, Idaho, and so much proof of the existence of The Power of God will be sent you that it will amaze you. This is a non-commercial religious movement. I'm paying for this advertisement because I WANT YOU TO KNOW THE POWER OF GOD. I'm advertising God. So suppose you send that post-card or letter now, for the FREE evidence I'll send you. The address again . . . .

DR. FRANK B. ROBINSON
DEPT. M-4, MOSCOW, IDAHO

Typical ad written by Frank Robinson. Frank Bruce Robinson Papers, Latah County Historical Society.

morning in May 1936, swept across America and spread to some sixty-seven countries. Or so Robinson liked to claim. That Psychiana was well known at the time of his trial cannot be disputed. *Newsweek* reported that Robinson's ads reached "into between 2,000,000 and 3,000,000 homes annually" in America alone. As a result, this small-town trial had caught the attention of the nation, making headlines across the country.[3]

"Court[room] Jammed," read one newspaper headline.[4] Prosecutors summoned witnesses from Canada, New York, Washington, DC, Portland, and Seattle. Also present that day were the two federal agents whose hot and cold investigation had led them, after six long years, to this legal battleground: Stephen H. Morse, inspector of the U.S. Postal Office, and Sherwin H. Stewart, inspector of the U.S. Immigrations Bureau. Assigned to study the trial, University of Idaho law students sat at attention in their wooden seats.

While the trial was getting underway, a hive of postal workers two floors below sorted the day's mail, the majority of which was addressed to or sent from Psychiana. Upstairs, the courtroom crowd—mostly suited men and uniformed officials—waited quietly in the brightly-lit wood-paneled chamber.

When Frank and his lawyers pushed through the courtroom doors, everyone stirred, and a commotion rippled across the crowd. Two temperamentally different but equally effective attorneys spearheaded Robinson's defense team: A.L. Morgan, a bespectacled and reserved local attorney, and the stocky Ed Robertson, of Spokane, Washington. A tenacious, high-profile

Frank Robinson standing before his Duesenberg, Spokane, Washington, 1934.
Latah County Historical Society.

lawyer with a baritone southern drawl, Robertson was well-known—famous, almost—as the son of a Louisiana congressman. He never took a case he did not think he could win, and he charged handsomely for his services.[5]

With tension hanging thick in the air, Frank Robinson maintained the composure of someone who appeared to be attending the theater, rather than his own trial. He had, after all, been outstepping the law most of his life and had come to regard this succession of narrow escapes as an elaborate shell game. But his outward optimism spoke to something more than just the thrill that came from such a cat-and-mouse game. For however damaging the charges seemed that day (and indeed they were damning), Frank saw the entire spectacle as free advertising for Psychiana. Robinson's son, Alfred, later described his father as a man with "an insatiable appetite for publicity." For Robinson, even bad news was still good news. "My father needed to draw attention—either positive or negative—in whatever activities he engaged in." For Frank, "bigger was better." His impulse was "to overwhelm" the room in whatever scenario he found himself in. It was a philosophy he applied to all aspects of his life as evidenced, Alfred added, "by his [lavish] dress style, advertising methods, accumulation of goods, and sports cars." If ever he paled by comparison, Robinson fictionalized. He consistently inflated or totally invented numbers about his income, assets, insurance, the size of his workforce, the reach of his religion, or the volume of advertisements Psychiana placed. "He combined a little fantasy with real-

Psychiana clerical and bookkeeping staff in front of the Branch Mailing Department at 1st and Main Streets in downtown Moscow. University of Idaho Special Collections.

ity, but always with consequences," Alfred wrote. "Strict adherence to the 'minor details' of truth was unnecessary" in Frank's worldview. But it was this loose relationship with facts that had landed him in the defendant's chair that morning.[6]

In the courtroom, a reporter sized up Robinson, commenting on his "deep-set blue eyes, a pleasant smile, and an assured voice." Noting his distinctive traits, the reporter added how Frank wore "the mannerisms of the successful super-salesman, the easy unaffected bearing of the individual at home in any company."[7] Here was a seasoned confidence man: comfortable even as his world started to founder. Unaffected even as he looked at the judge, and pleaded "Not guilty."

What the reporters and publicity did not reveal, however, was Frank's inner turmoil and darkest fears. The previous evening, Robinson had paced the length of his home, chain-smoking and snapping at his lawyers. Serving as a makeshift trial headquarters, Robinson's living room teemed with boxes of documents and exhibits, the evidentiary trail from a lifetime of misdeeds, lies, and secrets—his history laid bare. As the clocks ticked off every aggravating minute, Frank Robinson's past was fast on his heels, threatening to catch up with him and take everything away.

———————◆———————

While the white-hot attention of the trial may or may not have been a boon for the Psychiana brand, the attendant pressures surrounding the spectacle were too much for his family to bear. Frank's wife, Pearl—the thirty-seven-year-old daughter of an Oregon judge—had long been her husband's stalwart supporter even though she did not believe in Psychiana itself. (She took their two children, Alfred and Florence, to the Presbyterian Church across town.) But Moscow, Idaho, was a small town, the kind of place where neighbors knew who made the best huckleberry pie, and whose garden produced the largest pumpkins. But they also knew the mother who kept gin in the washroom, and the father who abused his children. Like any small town, it had its secrets, and people were often given to talk. But now, to face neighbors, friends, and acquaintances in the grocery store, church, or post office in such a tightknit community was too much for her to bear.

Staying in Moscow, she and Frank came to see, would not do.

To ease matters, Robinson leased a luxurious furnished home in the posh Los Angeles suburb of Palos Verdes Estates. There, Pearl, Alfred, Florence, and their maid, Ingrid, lived amid the palm trees, renowned golf course, and elite tennis club during the federal trial. While Alf and Florence passed languorous afternoons playing in the courtyard gardens, Pearl fretted in the quiet recesses of the luxury home—cigarette in hand—while surf broke on the rocks outside.

In Moscow, the trial continued apace; in Palos Verdes, Pearl's worries deepened. "There were many anxious days [then]," Pearl recalled. "We did not know if a good husband and father would be ruthlessly snatched from us either to be put in some federal penitentiary or deported to some land—we knew not where."[8] And so Pearl paced the floors, tended her children, watched the ocean roll in and out, and waited for the phone to ring with news of her husband's fate: prison, deportation, or exoneration.

Pearl Leavitt Robinson, c. 1935.
University of Idaho Special Collections.

Part I
OUTLIER
1886–1928

CHAPTER 1

No Man Knew His History

At the peak of his notoriety, Frank Robinson was credibly accused of many improprieties, questionable business practices, and of advancing any number of dubious claims and falsehoods. He was called a charlatan, a snake-oil salesman, a cheat, and a con. But he was also worshipped, and credited for saving lives, curing illness, and even restoring sight to the blind. Given the nature and stature of his religion, Robinson was easy to label. But critics and admirers alike found that truly knowing him proved as elusive as knowing the core tenets of his unique religion. The closer they got to any clear understanding of Frank Robinson or of Psychiana, the more mysterious each became, leaving them flummoxed as to where one ended and the other began.

———————◆———————

Frank Bruce Robinson was born on Monday, July 5, 1886, in Henley-in-Arden, a grassy hamlet just eight miles north of Stratford-upon-Avon, Shakespeare's hometown.[1] The first-born of four Robinson boys, Frank was a tow-headed baby with a fair complexion and arresting blue eyes. His father—the Reverend John Henry Robinson—was then preaching in the village's Baptist church. Tall, trim, and unevenly tempered, Reverend Robinson wore wire-rimmed spectacles, had dark wavy hair, and brandished a strong, assertive jaw. His sermons sometimes carried the mettle of fire and brimstone, but were nonetheless conceived to help his parishioners, especially the poor and infirm.

Frank's mother, Hannah Rosella Coope Robinson, was the daughter of John Coope, a finance officer in the British military. Brought up among colonials, Hannah was born in Capetown, South Africa, where she spent her formative years and attended school. When she was a teen, her family moved to England and her father went to work at the War College in Camberley. Not long after their relocation, Hannah met John Henry Robinson—then a student at Spurgeon's Bible College in South Norwood Hill—and the couple married in 1885.

When Frank was two, the Robinsons left Henley-in-Arden and moved to Long Crendon, where John Henry had been called to preach. In the late nineteenth century, Long Crendon was an idyllic storybook village hemmed in by the Chiltern Hills and their fields of chequerberries, buttercups, and daisies. The village itself was poor, populated mostly by farmers, brewers, and lacemakers; the latter—all women—required bright light to spin their filigreed patterns, and so on any given day in Long Crendon, women carted their looms outside to gather light for their work.

The Baptist manse in Long Crendon was a roomy stone structure with a thatched roof and looked much like the rest of the village homes. It was an ideal setting for a young boy, and Frank often wrote that his fondest memories stemmed from those days in Long Crendon. Well-dressed, handsome, and a touch precocious, young Frank was a daydreamer. He later recalled lazy afternoons when he would lie supine on the manse's grassy yard reading, watching clouds, or stealing away into the depths of his imagination. (Decades later, Frank would tell his followers that it was on the manse lawn that he first received a "visitation" from God.) He was bookish but not in a shut-in way, and the manse's modest library—comprised primarily of theological volumes—kept Frank entertained when he was not playing outside with his brothers, Sydney, Arthur, and Leonard. He also demonstrated an aptitude for music and would play on the organ in his father's church after Sunday services.[2]

While Frank possessed precious few memories of his mother, Hannah, it is clear from his own writings that he adored her, and by all accounts she was nothing if not a doting mother. "She was the sweetest thing it has ever been my pleasure to know," he later wrote.[3]

In a hamlet of scarcely a thousand inhabitants, Frank's father figured prominently as the benevolent pastor who, according to one paper, "was most popular at Long Crendon."[4] But the reverend cast a dark shadow on Frank's otherwise happy boyhood in the English village. Frank would later describe his father as a monster who constantly issued "lacings" with his "razor strap." On one particularly violent occasion, the reverend purportedly "trounced" Frank and screamed, "'God curse the day you were born.'"[5] When it came to Frank's father, there appears to have been a radical difference between the John Henry of the pulpit, and the John Henry of fatherhood. Frank's brother, Arthur, once confided how their father was often "besides [sic] himself with rage, hatred, and passion."[6]

Reverend John Henry Robinson. Undated photograph. From *The Strange Autobiography of Frank B. Robinson.*

In the fall of 1893, John Henry was called to serve at the Lee Mount Chapel in Halifax, a gray, industrial city some two hundred miles north of the bucolic Long Crendon. Frank was seven. The English countryside was in a fury of fall color. But the scenery changed when the Robinsons' train lurched into the opulent, columned, and sand-colored Halifax Railway Station. It is easy enough to imagine. The grandeur of the depot standing in marked contrast to the sooty streets, with dingy newsies hawking their periodicals on the cobbled roads. Charcoal smoke spewing from industrial chimneys, choking the sky of its light. Here and there, coal-oil lamps winking in the murk. Draymen drawing their haulage—potatoes, cabbage, tinned fish—over the wet stones of the city. The end of the century was nigh. Beggars, businessmen, charlatans, and doomsday preachers paraded the streets of Halifax. The world was turning modern at what seemed like breakneck speed. In America, the World's Fair was underway in Chicago, where a conflation of science, technology, and even religion were on display. The Mormon Church made itself an exhibit at the World's Fair so that everyone could see, first hand, real Latter-Day Saints.[7]

Back in Halifax, the Lee Mount Baptist Chapel was a gray stone building that exuded a forlorn aura. It was the kind of chapel you can imagine bearing the million-year-old scent of wet coal and whose mill-worker congregants likely scratched out an existence on boiled scraps and little else. Halifax was, in many ways, the opposite of Long Crendon.

◆

And it was in Halifax that the Robinson family first began to falter, and then broke. In December 1896, when Hannah learned that her father John Coope had died, the inconsolable mother of four boys locked herself in her bedroom and stopped eating. Two months later, on Tuesday, February 9, 1897, Hannah Robinson, thirty-four, died of what the *Halifax Courier* called "consumption."[8]

Frank was eleven. Sydney, nine; Leonard seven; and Arthur, five.

John Henry, thirty-three, was a widower with a home filled with bereft sons. But he soon made the acquaintance of a wealthy woman by the name of Ellen Haigh, whose fiancé had also died unexpectedly. The two courted and then married on Thursday, May 4, 1899. If Haigh brought the family money (she had "a footman and a butler," Frank once noted[9]), she also brought trouble. None of the boys—save Arthur, the youngest—approved of the marriage. Their wounds were too fresh from their mother's death. At the wedding, young Frank was asked to stand behind the seated bride for the family photo. He appears visibly distressed.[10]

The emotionally strained family relocated once again, leaving the dreary city of Halifax for Huddersfield, a textile town eight miles to the south. The year 1900 brought more than the dawn of a new century for the Robinson boys. It brought a new family dynamic, and a new town. Once known as a battleground between Luddites and industrialists, Huddersfield was, by the time the Robinsons' carriage rattled into the town's stony streets, a bustling city replete with lavish Victorian architecture.

But family tensions continued to rise in their new home. Frequently absent, John Henry spent most of his free time attending to his flock, while Ellen held teas for the ladies of Huddersfield. The two younger boys, Arthur and Leonard, attended the local school and tried to make the best of a less-than-perfect situation, while Frank and his brother Sydney stewed.

Ellen's very presence made the relationship between Frank and his father all the more volatile. Once, after arriving home from his job at a carpentry shop, Frank heard what he later described as "the most terrifying screams I had ever heard in my life" coming from the kitchen. Ellen was, according to Frank, waylaying his younger brother, Arthur. "As he stood there vainly trying to defend himself, this brute of a woman of God was hammering him in the face and eyes with both fists." That is when Frank says he stepped in. "Seizing her by the black hair of her head, I threw her to the floor and gave her some of her own medicine."[11]

Later that same day in his father's study, Frank issued an ultimatum. Either Ellen had to go, or he did. According to Frank's story, the Reverend Robinson decided on the latter.

On the morning of July 5, 1901—Frank's sixteenth birthday—John Henry drove his oldest son to the Royal Navy's recruiting office in Liverpool. It was a Friday. The Reverend enlisted his son into the service for the

The Robinson brothers left to right: Arthur, Sydney, Frank (seated), and Leonard, c. 1898. From *The Strange Autobiography of Frank B. Robinson*.

standard term: twelve years. For the stern father, enlisting his son to "earn the Queen's shilling"[12] was meant to make a man of him. For Frank, however, his conscription might as well have been a prison sentence.

"I was sent to the training ship the HMS *Caledonia* near Edinburgh," Frank later wrote.[13] The *Caledonia*, which held 1000 cadets and officers, was the main training ship for British enlisted navymen, or "blue jackets," at the time. When Frank arrived on deck in July of 1901, he was issued his standard cap, dark-blue uniform, and a "ditty-box" for personal effects. He spent his days doing calisthenics, tying knots, and studying an array of subjects, from logarithms to algebraic problems and navigation.[14] According to records, his occupation in the blue jackets was "Electrician."[15]

Within the first few weeks of drawing gray mop water across the deck and "swinging the lead"—an arduous task of swinging a lead weight on a length of rope to test water depths—Frank started planning his escape. He first asked a couple of mates if getting discharged was even a possibility. "One of these chaps by the name of Pry, a Glasgow alley-cat, invited me to the upper deck one Sunday afternoon," Frank recalled. "'Now listen Robbie,' he said. 'I'll tell you how to get out of this man's navy. All you have to do is to fall overboard. Then get rheumatism. Make your knees swell up, and it will affect your heart. Then you'll get a M.C.O. which meant Morbus Corpus [sic] Organicus…organic heart disease."[16] According to Robinson, he jumped overboard—"I had quite a drop"—and then was transported to sick bay. Pry, Robinson wrote, "fixed the temperature chart" so that it showed feverish conditions. "Under the proper treatment," Frank wrote, "my knees started to swell, and I began to get quite short of breath—all under the direction of Boy Pry from Glasgow. A wise boy that Pry was." According to Robinson, he lay bedridden for a fortnight. "Then the long-coveted words M.C.O. went on my chart at the foot of my bed."[17]

Robinson's official discharge record from the British Royal Navy corroborates at least this part of his story. But it also lists his cadet rating as "bad," and under "Character," Robinson's was noted as "V.B.," for very bad. John Pry's character, by contrast, was listed as "V.G." while on the *Caledonia* (though he later served stints in the "cells" for insubordination).[18]

Frank was discharged on Friday, October 25, 1901, a little over three months after enlisting for a twelve-year commitment.[19]

———————◆———————

After his discharge, Frank returned home and began working in a Huddersfield drugstore. But according to his brother, "after serving a very short term in Needham's Drug Store, Frank was dismissed from the position for irregularities which I might state were very distressing to our father."[20] What those "distressing" "irregularities" entailed is not known.

Evidently exasperated, the reverend decided it would be best for both Frank and Sydney to leave. Permanently. Their destination: Belleville, Ontario, Canada. The location, far from arbitrary, was calculated. In 1903, the enterprise of sending British orphans and pauper children abroad was still very much in practice. A primary artery of that exploitative operation was the Home Children scheme, a child migration program established in 1869 by evangelist Annie MacPherson, that rounded up England's street children before shipping them alternately to Canada, Australia, New Zealand, or South Africa. "Well intended philanthropists in Britain," one report averred, "literally exported as many as 100,000 Home Children to Canada between 1869 and the Great Depression to serve as cheap farm labour."[21] In Frank and Sydney's case, it meant they would be sent to the Marchmont Home in Belleville, Ontario—one of the scheme's key "distribution houses"—to serve in precisely this capacity.

Reverend John Henry Robinson's motives and rationale for placing two of his sons into the Home Children scheme are both baffling and unclear. The brothers were no more orphans than they were paupers (especially after their father married the wealthy Ellen Haigh). Some of the Home Children were sent to Canada "by widowed or sick parents or by families who had fallen on hard times because there was no state social net to assist them. Some (labeled 'non-paupers' in the records) were sent over by parents who saw no hope for their offspring in Britain or simply could find no room for them at home."[22] But neither Frank nor Sydney Robinson fit neatly into any of these groups of Home Children, leaving more questions than answers as to why their father propelled them into such a service.

Nevertheless, in 1903—three weeks after Frank's seventeenth birthday—the Robinson family said their goodbyes to Frank and Sydney at Liverpool. The landing stage was crowded and noisy. Overloaded drays saddled with steamer trunks and heirloom furniture rattled along the stage planks while the throng of emigrants—encumbered with their own trunks and bags, papers in hand—stood in line for health inspections. Frank and Sydney were instructed to pack light. They were by turns eager and nervous as they hugged their brothers and shook hands with their father. Once they gave their farewells, the two boys took their places in the crowded line boarding the *Parisian*—a 5,000-ton steamship bound for North America.

(The *Parisian* was one of many ships the Home Children syndicate relied on to transport children from Liverpool to Canada. In 1903 alone, that single ship brought some 100 children from England to Quebec. In January of that year, the *Detroit Free Press* confirmed that 1,256 children had been sent from Liverpool to Ontario in 1902, further remarking how "the percentage of crime among the children of this class has greatly diminished, and this is attributed to the close inspections made at Liverpool."[23])

Four days after its launch, the *Parisian* nudged its way down the St. Lawrence River and the passengers readied for disembarkation. "Sitting astride one of the large cables in the bow of that steamer," Frank wrote, "were two young boys, one, your writer, then fourteen years of age [he was seventeen]. Sydney, too young, in fact, to be sent to a new and strange land; but here they were, all excitement as the steamer docked."[24]

Frank would never see his father, stepmother, or two younger brothers again.

Chapter 2
Vagabond

From Montreal, the Robinson brothers were whisked off to Belleville, Ontario, on the Grand Trunk Railroad, arriving at the Marchmont Home in the first week of August 1903. What Frank and Sydney may not have known was that a dark stigma was attached to Home Children (known colloquially as "home boys" and "home girls"). Largely considered the "throw-away" children of prostitutes, drunks, and criminals, the residents of Marchmont Home and other "distribution houses" in Canada were contracted out to farmers and industries for cheap and often dangerous labor.[25] Uprooted, stigmatized, and overworked, these children were often abused (although the types and severity of abuse is largely unknown).[26]

Overseeing operations at the Marchmont Home in August of 1903 was Reverend Robert Wallace,[27] a thin, bearded forty-eight-year-old Scotsman, who was married to Ellen Bilbrough, one of the child migration scheme's central advocates and proponents. In short order, Wallace

The Marchmont Home, Belleville, Ontario c. 1900. From *A Souvenir of Belleville: The Beautiful City of the Bay*, by Arthur McGinnis. Courtesy of the Toronto Public Library.

16

farmed out the Robinson boys as day laborers doing a variety of menial work: shoveling coal, driving hacks, laying concrete, cutting ice in the Bay of Quinte. None of the Home Children were paid wages for their labor. When Sydney caught pneumonia from harvesting ice with no socks and ratty shoes, Frank—fearing for his brother's life—dispatched a letter to their father, who evidently offered little in the way of help or sympathy. Hospitalized, Sydney regained his health, recovering slowly but entirely.

Soon afterwards, the brothers parted ways, striking out on their own. For Home Children, this separation was not uncommon. "Brothers and sisters lost track of each other," one paper reported decades later. "Over the years some of them managed to find friends and relatives, but many just buried the past and went on with their lives."[28]

Three years later after leaving Marchmont Home, Frank took a pharmacy job at Templeton's Drugstore in Belleville, and secured suitable accommodations, renting a bunk in a boardinghouse with a group of students from the local Ontario Business College.

At twenty, Frank stood over six feet tall, with the build of an athlete and a champion's smile. He wore the finest clothes his druggist salary could afford, later boasting that his new position—unlike his previous jobs in Belleville—was "a come-up" and a "white collar" job that paid "$5.00 a week." With his room and board costing him $3.50 a week, Frank had $1.50 left to spend on clothes, beer, and cigarettes. Young and independent, Frank was financially stable and happy.[29]

One afternoon, after buying a pack of cigarettes from the tobacconist next to his boarding house (something he did regularly), Frank's luck took an odd—and some would later argue, revelatory—turn. Mrs. Thomas, the cashier who had sold him the cigarettes, along with "an unidentified government witness," reported Frank to the police, alleging that he had "passed counterfeit money." Robinson was immediately arrested and taken into custody by the local constabulary. "The prisoner pleaded not guilty," the *Windsor Star* reported, "and said that he had received the money, a bogus Yankee dollar, from a man whom he drove out to Cannifton. He redeemed the coin when told it was spurious."[30] Lacking sufficient evidence to suggest ill-intent on Frank's part, Belleville's Judge Francis Flynn acquitted the dapper young man of "willfully and knowing, and feloniously" distributing counterfeit currency.[31]

After his skirmish with local law enforcement, Frank moved on to Toronto, where he again secured work in what was beginning to look like his calling: pharmacology. Frank's Belleville employer arranged for a job at a pharmacy under the management of John Whiting, but the job ended under mysterious circumstances. "For reasons I will not mention," Frank later wrote, "I left [Whiting's] valuable employ." Frank's brother added this unexplained detail: "The drug business was left high and dry by [Frank] with disastrous results to himself, one of them being so much so that [Whiting] had him arrested."[32]

Adrift and unemployed, Robinson spent his evenings "playing checkers with the boys" down at the Cowan Street Fire House, and attending a Baptist church on Sundays.[33] He joined the congregation's choir, attended activities and socials, and was eventually invited to deliver sermons. Frank would later tell his followers that this period marked his first concerted effort to seek out the "true God," going so far as to enter the Toronto Bible Training School.

Frank Robinson had scarcely undertaken his theological training before he started to question the very tenets of the Christian faith. He did not, for instance, believe in the Immaculate Conception, Christ's resurrection, or anything, really, about the Old Testament. He began openly questioning the legitimacy of Jesus Christ as the son of God, and even the existence of God at all. As for what he did believe, Frank was at a loss. Disillusionment turned into depression, and his depression only compounded when he dropped out of school and turned to alcohol.

Frank Robinson in Toronto. Undated photo. Back of photo reads, "Tired of Living." Latah County Historical Society.

In 1910, the wayward man made his way through frigid, snow-packed streets of Toronto to the recruiting offices of the Royal Northwest Mounted Police and signed up. He wanted a "chance to go out West and get away from everything."[34] His paperwork entailed an Oath of Allegiance wherein he signed and swore to "be faithful and bear true allegiance to His Majesty King Edward VII." He also signed an Oath of Office, and on his enlistment record, under the box that read, "Country of Birth," Frank Robinson wrote in elegant cursive, "England."[35]

✦

When Frank stepped off the train amidst the surging engine steam and the last blow of the whistle in the wan, wintry light, he met a city on the move. In early February 1910, Regina, Saskatchewan, was a snow-blown prairie city, a huddle of burgeoning brick buildings and frontier clapboard storefronts on the frozen flatlands.

His enlistment contract and Oath of Allegiance to King Edward VII committed him to five years of service in the Mounties. But his drinking began to affect his performance and he was soon kicked out, receiving his discharge papers on Wednesday, April 27, 1910.

He had lasted all of two and a half months.

✦

Later that year, Frank Robinson boarded a train in Vancouver, crossed the border into Washington state, and traveled to Portland, Oregon, seemingly without incident. Now in the United States, Robinson applied for a pharmacy license, claiming this time to have been born in New York—not England. Having evidently shed his English accent, Frank scrapped the private sector within a few months, enlisting instead in the U.S. Navy as Hospital Apprentice—First Class. It was April 1912. He was ordered to report for duty at the Puget Sound Naval Yard in Bremerton, Washington. There he would serve for a brief period aboard the USS *Philadelphia*.

The naval yard was a spectacle at the time. The Bremerton Naval Hospital, in which Robinson trained, was a new, state-of-the-art facility. A massive, two-story brick complex of neoclassical architecture, the hospital maintained some 200 beds and was situated on a hill overlooking Puget Sound, where patients could enjoy the sea breezes and fresh air.[36] The hospital, Frank wrote, was "one of the most completely equipped hospitals I have ever seen. The food was good, the doctors were good, and everything one could desire was there."³⁷ The naval yard was large and modern, and stretched out along the waterfront. Just across Puget Sound from Robinson's post, the Church of Christian Science—a metaphysical religion swelling in popularity in the early twentieth century—was busy building a new temple in bustling Seattle.

Dressed in his crisp whites, Hospital Apprentice First Class Frank Robinson drilled on an encyclopedic array of subjects, from basic bandaging to aseptic operation drills and sterilization. Robinson signed up for four years with the Navy. Then on August 8, 1912, he received an "undesirable discharge." His discharge record called Robinson a "chronic alcoholic" who was "unreliable as to his veracity." And while Robinson freely admits that he was kicked out of the Navy for being a "chronic alcoholic"³⁸ ("Uncle Sam very rightly will not stand for that sort of thing," he later wrote), he does not mention the latter charge: "unreliable as to his veracity."

Frank Robinson—the newly self-anointed American—was, in other words, a drunk and a liar.

———————————◆———————————

Broke and homeless once again, Robinson made his way to Seattle, where he took up employment in the Olympic Pharmacy, but after an all-night drunken bender, he "jumped on the first train [he] saw moving." It was a train bound for Spokane, Washington, by way of Ellensburg. Robinson had reached a new low in his life. "I was useless and just a common drunk," he reflected.³⁹

At 3:00 the following morning, when the train stopped in Ellensburg, a rail-yard worker starting pummeling the vagabonds with stones, ordering them all to "pile off." Drunk, weary, cold, and rail-rattled, Frank spotted a sawdust pile nearby. He curled up in the sawdust where he fell asleep breathing in the piney scent of the shavings. The following morning, he shook off what sawdust he could and tramped downtown, where he found a local YMCA. There he was immediately befriended.

Robinson lived in Ellensburg and worked, once again, as a pharmacist, and seemed genuinely happy. Although he described himself as barely making ends meet, photos show an immaculately dressed, almost flamboyant Frank Robinson during his Ellensburg days. But it would not last long. One night, after witnessing a traveling evangelist delivering a doomsday monologue in front of the Ellensburg Courthouse, Robinson—who by that point had decried all organized religion as "a fake" and "a sham"—

pushed into a saloon where he got "drunk as a lord," and, jumping onto another train, left Ellensburg behind.

Frank (left) and unknown friend. Undated photo. Latah County Historical Society.

For the next four years, Frank Robinson roamed the Pacific Northwest—Vancouver, Portland, Tacoma, Seattle—gaining and then quickly losing one pharmacy job after another on account of his worsening alcoholism. In 1916, Robinson was thirty years old and pacing the steep streets of San Francisco. He spent his nights in the saloons and bars on Market and Mission Streets and passing out on benches in parks near North Shore or Telegraph Hill.

One morning following an all night bar-crawl, Frank, in a drunken delirium, joined the United States Army, 31st Infantry Division. "I have never had the faintest recollection of joining the Army," he wrote. "It later turned out that I had given another name, [and] told them the wildest stories about who I was." He had said his name was Earl Meyer, and that he was from Ellensburg, Washington. Robinson shipped out to the Philippines aboard the U.S. Army Transport *Sheridan*, and was stationed at the dormant Army base in Manila.[40]

Frank Robinson—a.k.a. Earl Meyer—would not see any action during his military stint. The 31st Infantry's role in the Philippines was merely precautionary, as war mounted overseas. From the sprawling military base, Robinson would have had a clear view of the bay and the diminutive local boats—*cascos* and *bancas*—bobbing on the water. Off base, officers strolled seashell pathways amidst the pink, yellow, and teal British colonial homes and government buildings. Military brass attended services at the Manila Cathedral and ate meals at the Hotel de Oriente, dining on Bombay duck, chutneys, and fried breadfruit.

---✦---

While most officers and soldiers enjoyed an otherwise humdrum posting in Manila, Frank ran into trouble, although the exact nature of the incident remains unclear. Robinson would later spin a tale that involved a love triangle and an embittered officer who threatened to surgically remove Frank's teeth. According to the yarn, Frank refused the operation and was charged on the grounds of "willful disobedience of orders." For non-compliance, he purportedly received "eighteen months in a disciplinary barracks" in Batangas and a dishonorable discharge.[41] Whatever may have triggered the incident, Frank's actions eventually landed him in a holding cell stateside. "In 1917," one paper reported, "[Frank Robinson] was court martialed and sent to Alcatraz prison."[42]

---✦---

Six months later, Robinson was out of prison, a free man on the streets of San Francisco. In 1917, the city's streets were busy with motor cars, horse-drawn carriages, and clanging trolleys. The sites and scenes were all too familiar to the ex-con. The metallic scents of the sea and the fish markets. Women selling their fresh produce and wares on the narrow sidewalks, while boys sold the day's headlines about the war overseas. And of course there were the saloons Frank had often frequented before joining the Army. Like a tide pulled to shore, Robinson entered an old haunt and put his money on the bar. But instead of ordering a whiskey or beer, Frank asked for a glass of milk. He never took another drink again.

After working odd jobs in the Bay Area (one entailed hauling dead horses to a glue factory for five dollars a month), Frank spotted a position open with the Pelican Bay Lumber Company in Klamath Falls, Oregon. Thirty-one years old, tall, gaunt, and sober, Robinson took a train from San Francisco to Klamath Falls and set to work in the lumber industry at Rocky Point.

The timber job was a welcome change after hauling dead horses, and the money was good. Physically, Frank was in top shape after his "profitable season on the mountain."[43] But in 1919, an advertisement for a pharmacy job at the Star Drug Store in Klamath Falls lured Frank away from the toil of timber work. On hiring Robinson, the proprietor, Carl Plath, issued Frank routine employment papers to complete. For country of origin, Frank said England—not New York or Ellensburg—as his place of birth.

In late summer of that same year, Pearl Leavitt—a smart, tall, and popular daughter of a prominent Klamath Falls judge—was preparing to enter the University of Oregon as a freshman, with the eventual plan of serving a mission in the Republic of China. On a particular afternoon she later recalled as "bright and sunny," Pearl had just finished washing her hair when she heard a knock at the door. When she answered, she found her girlfriend and a young handsome man named Frank standing on the porch. They made introductions.

"Call me Robbie," the stranger said.

"It was love at first sight," she later confessed.[44]

Robbie and Pearl started courting at once. As the relationship grew more serious, however, Judge Leavitt's opinion of his daughter's suitor shifted from irked to outrage. Pearl's father was accomplished and highly educated, having earned his law degree from the University of California. The product of a prominent New Hampshire pedigree, the judge read the classics aloud to his family every Sunday evening, and everyone was expected to attend and to be on time. That his daughter was suddenly in love with a wandering druggist with a murky background was a fact that did not fly with the patriarch.[45]

For starters, Frank was nothing like the boys Pearl had been socializing with earlier that summer: the college-bound types with familiar last names who took her to ballroom dances bedecked in Oregon's school colors—yellow and green. Frank could not even compare. For one thing, he was fourteen years her senior. But it may have been his differentness, age, and mysterious background that most appealed to Pearl, who was known for her rebellious streak. "I reject authority—period!" she confided years later to her son, Alf. "I was not afraid of my father, and he didn't abuse me physically or psychologically. But both my parents ruled the family by making us feel guilty if we disobeyed them."[46]

Always the glad-hander, Frank won many friends in Klamath Falls, most of whom he met while working in the Star Drug Store, where locals often gathered to gossip and chat about the news. The general mood of the day was mixed. On the one hand, the war had ended ten months earlier, but on the other, steel workers across America were preparing to strike. Demagogues in Washington, DC, were drafting legislation calling for the prohibition of

alcohol, and the Cincinnati Reds and the Chicago White Sox were headed
to one of the most controversial World Series in baseball history. There
was a lot to talk about, both nationally and locally. Pearl's sister, Maybelle
Leavitt—the society columnist for Klamath Falls' newspaper *The Evening
Herald*—was a regular at the Star Drug Store, and made it a point to visit
with Frank in the mornings while keeping an ear open for a good story.

On September 13, 1919, three days after Woodrow Wilson signed the
Treaty of Saint-Germaine in Laye, Maybelle dropped into Star Drug, per
her morning routine. But on that day, she noticed something "off" about
Robbie. He was not his usual charming self. That is when he informed her
about a grim telegram he had just received. That night, *The Evening Herald*
reported the story: "Deep Sorrow Comes to Frank Robertson [sic]."

> Grief and intense sorrow are the lot of Frank Robertson, employee
> of the Star Drug Company, who received word this morning that his
> brother, Captain Leonard Robertson was shot on the battlefield in
> Gallipoli on August 25, and that his father, John Henry Robertson had
> died from heart failure in England…Captain Leonard Robertson was
> a physician and surgeon…The day prior to [Leonard's] death, he was
> awarded the distinguished service medal for gallantry on the battlefield.
> He has previously made an enviable record in New York, where he was
> on the staff of one of the largest hospitals in that city. [He] is survived
> by a wife and young daughter.[47]

The Evening Herald added a few somber words about the effect the story
would no doubt have on the community at large. "The many friends in
Klamath Falls of Frank Robertson will be grieved to learn of the deep
sorrow that has come into his life. He lost a mother when he was but a few
years of age. His other brother died some few years ago."

As stories go, this one was heart-wrenching, particularly because Frank
had not seen his brother in over fifteen years. But that is about the extent of
sadness Frank could have legitimately felt. What the readers of *The Evening
Herald* would not have known was that the majority of the story was a total
fabrication, invented by Frank himself. While Leonard Robinson had indeed
been killed in Gallipoli, he was not nor had he ever been a physician. He was
not married, did not have a daughter, had never been to the United States
(much less worked in a New York hospital), and he never received medals—distinguished or otherwise—for "gallantry." Moreover, Frank's "other
brother," Arthur, and father, John Henry, were alive and well in England.

Not three weeks later, in early October, Frank typed a letter to Mary Robinson, his half-sister by his father's second marriage. The letter was short, upbeat, and playful. He talked about work and how he planned to go out that night for a "little drive in the country." He then added, "If I take some pictures I will send you some."[48] There is no mention of the alleged tragedies, not a reassuring word nor inquiry into the state of affairs.

All the while, Pearl and Robbie continued to see one another, and their relationship bloomed into an engagement, much to the dismay of Pearl's parents. Despite the family's protestations, the couple married on November 26, 1919. "Popular Girl Becomes Bride," *The Evening Herald* reported. Nine months later, a different kind of family announcement appeared in the pages the Klamath Falls paper.

Three Lives in One Family are Freedom's Price.
Four of Mr. Robinson's family saw active service during the great war, and three of them made the supreme sacrifice. The father, Colonel John Henry Robinson, as surgeon with the Royal Army Medical corps, was killed by the explosion of a shell in the hospital tent in which he was rendering first aid on the battlefront. Captain Leonard Robinson, killed on the Gallipoli peninsula, won five medals including the coveted Victoria Cross, and in this connection it is worthy of note that another brother, Arthur Robinson, who lost his life in a submarine, also won the Victoria Cross, making one of the very few instances on record of two crosses in one family...Frank Robinson, to round out the story, served as U.S. laboratory assistant at Manila P.I., during the war. This constitutes a remarkable story of all-around family service to 'make the world safe for democracy.'[49]

These latest details—the death of his brother Arthur, the Victoria Crosses, along with the sudden resurrection, promotion, and *second* death of Frank's father—all stemmed, it appears, from the fertile imagination of the town's local druggist. The story is striking, too, for what it did not say: Frank's court martial and subsequent imprisonment at Alcatraz.

But within this bizarre show of fictional family stories and self-promotion, Frank may have stumbled on to the germ of an idea that would, for better or worse, serve him well for the rest of his life: the emotional power of the printed word, the power of advertising.

———————◆———————

By the time the second story was in print in 1920, Frank had moved on from the Star Drug Store to the local hospital pharmacy, where he took the position of manager. There, he further nurtured his latent talents by writing a bevy of advertisements for the pharmacy but also for himself. Each promo featured a photograph of a young and handsome "Robbie," beneath which he touted an array of conspicuous credentials.

> Bachelor of Pharmacy. Bachelor of Science. Two post-graduate courses. Four years' service with the United States Govt. both in Army and Navy as dispenser.[50]

Like the family stories of tragedy and heroism, these advertisements were more fiction than fact.

------------◆------------

In 1922, Frank took a job with the United States Veterans Bureau in Tucson, Arizona. Pearl was pregnant and poised to leave her home of Klamath Falls for the first time. The job was a step up in pay and stature, making their move seem more sure-footed. On his official employment records, Frank stated plainly that he had been born in New York and that he had no prior "government service," military or otherwise, in his background.

In Tucson, Pearl delivered their first child, Alfred Bruce Robinson, on March 1, 1923. Within four months of Alf's birth, Frank would, for unknown reasons, quit the U.S. Veterans Bureau and move on, relocating the family to Hollywood, California, to begin anew as a stockbroker.

Having established his first office in the Pacific Mutual Building on Sixth and Grand downtown, Frank ran his first cold-call advertisement on October 1, 1924.

INVESTORS

> I want a few keen, shrewd conservative investors to get in touch with me at once. I have an unusually attractive, safe, well-paying business proposition. Write for Appointment.

> Frank B. Robinson[51]

By June of the following year, Frank Robinson had moved his office about two blocks to the Financial Center Building, and changed his firm's name to "The Winn-Robinson Company." (It remains unclear who the "Winn" was in the arrangement.) Robinson's ads had changed dramatically since his first bulletin. In one of his new ads, he had created both a hook and a theme.

500 STOCK SALESMEN

If there are 500 Stock Salesmen in Los Angeles who can meet the requirements, I CAN USE THEM ALL

THE REQUIREMENTS ARE:

A CLEAN personality, and a record of CLEAN sales. This is a CLEAN issue being sold for CLEAN men by a CLEAN broker and my salesmen must be CLEAN also—making the whole deal CLEAN. Salesmen will never get anything to sell out of this office that isn't CLEAN, and consequently some nice CLEAN money is to be made and a permanent connection established. But you MUST meet the requirements.

FRANK B ROBINSON, Fiscal Agent.

THE WINN-ROBINSON COMPANY,

Commercial Experts and Advisers

(*Open Evenings This Week*)[52]

It was not long, however, before Winn-Robinson became Kent & Robinson with the brokerage moving once more, this time to Suite 207 of the Hollywood Professional Building, then home to the Academy of Motion Picture Arts and Sciences and the Screen Actors Guild.

Despite moving and changing brokerages, Frank Robinson made ends meet in Hollywood. In his biggest deal, Frank sold $10,000 in stock to Hollywood celebrity Tom Mix, a seasoned showman known later for the showy Duesenberg automobile he drove around Los Angeles. Other Hollywood deals followed. Robinson sold public issues of stock on the construction of the famous Roosevelt Hotel (home to the first-ever Academy Awards), penning snappy ads like "Opportunities Like This Are Seldom Available to the Public!"[53]

Hollywood was the land of opportunity, a veritable El Dorado for anyone with a dream and a newspaper advertisement. People were getting rich in Hollywood every day in any number of businesses, both legal and not. Beyond films, stocks, and real estate, there was always religion. At the same time Frank was trying to lure investors with his ads in the *Los Angeles Times* and his personal charm on the streets of Hollywood, a short, elfin man by the name of Ernest Holmes was trying to recruit believers to his new religious philosophy with just as many ads in the *Times*, and no less charm. Holmes had been giving lectures on Wilshire Boulevard that he called "The

Science of Mind" and "Religious Science." Holmes hobnobbed with Hollywood A-listers and was starting to travel the country on a lecture circuit. His philosophy was rooted in New Thought, a spiritual movement started in the nineteenth century, and was beginning to catch on.

Whether or not the two men crossed paths in Hollywood then is not known. Over a decade later, however, they would meet and form a fascinating alliance. But for the time, each man was but a satellite passing through the orbit of the other.

A social animal with natural charm, Frank Robinson enjoyed salesmanship, especially if the product was himself. Stocks, he found, were not always as easy to sell. With the money he made on the Tom Mix deal, Frank had secured a small home for his family of three, a new car, and some furniture. The new assets, however, burned up all of his available cash and before he knew it, Frank Robinson was broke. "Mother told me they had to walk away from everything," Alf recalled.[54] Creditors arrived at the Robinson home, repossessing the house, their sedan, and all of their furniture. Pearl, then mother to a toddler, was devastated.

Of this period, Frank's official autobiography is notably abbreviated. "I shall have to pass over the details of our few years in Los Angeles," he wrote, "for if I put them all in this book, it would be too large."[55] Defeated in the throes of the roaring twenties, Robinson sent his wife and son back to Klamath Falls, and took a train bound north for Portland, where he hoped to regain some financial footing.

Drawing on his scant business experience writing ads for the pharmacy in Klamath Falls and selling stock in Hollywood, Frank began selling door-to-door "get rich quick" books on how to advertise effectively. Successful and secure enough to rent a quaint home from John Suter, a Portland printer, Robinson wired for Pearl and Alf to rejoin him.

According to the propaganda he later disseminated to his students, Frank's time in Portland marked a critical moment in his journey toward what he would call "the God Power." He had in recent days chanced upon some books that would have a lasting impact on his life. "I had been lying under a tree in High Grant Park," he said, "studying some new works along the religious new thought [sic] line. The particular set of books, as

I recall it, was a volume called *The Secret of the Ages*, by Robert Collier…
These small books helped open the way."[56] Collier's books were runaway
bestsellers at the time, and New Thought—an amorphous system of belief
that regards God as a unifying life force—was all the rage. Many New
Thought authors like Collier advocated various methods of self-affirma-
tion and "positive thinking," long before that term itself came into vogue.
A good many authors, too, aligned their spiritual message with an overt
sense of American can-do capitalism. "The essence of this law," Collier
wrote, "is that you must think abundance; see abundance, feel abundance,
believe abundance. Let no thought of limitation enter your mind."[57] For
the wandering druggist, recovering alcoholic, husband, father, and fabulist,
Collier's words made a lasting impression certainly, although that impression may have inspired opportunism over enlightenment.

"The impulse which came to me that day," Frank would tell his followers, "was to relax absolutely, keep very still, and allow the invisible Spirit of
God to manifest itself to me."[58] In High Grant Part, Frank said, "a feeling
of absolute security and perfect assurance was mine that day. It was not
until later, though, in the Suter home that I experienced the same 'visitation' I had while a child in Long Crendon." Frank later pointed to that
"visitation" as the moment God selected him personally to start a movement. "When God decides to manifest His Power to a human being, that
man is the sanest man this side of heaven," he wrote. That experience, he
claimed, was "no doubt a direct communion with God."

> It was the thing I needed to assure me beyond doubt that God lives on
> this earth today, and can, through His Power, bring to this earth that
> Divine Power in such measure that wars[,] illness, fears, doubt, death—
> all these can once and for all be completely banished…Immortality is
> possible here and now.

According to Frank, the only reason humans had not yet discovered
the possibility of immortality was because of organized religion, which, he
claimed, had "usurp[ed] the place of God."[59]

◆

Despite his apparent communion with God in Portland, Frank was still
struggling to pay the bills and began looking for better pay, which he found
in a Yakima, Washington, drugstore, although the position was evidently
temporary. Leaving Pearl and Alfred in Portland, Frank set out for Yaki-

ma's Pioneer Drug, where he ran into old friends from Ellensburg and, according to his narrative, sharpened his salesmanship skills. "My checks there at Pioneer were always larger than anyone else's for commissions...I felt proud of my selling ability." In Yakima, Frank "worked hard," saving up as much money as he could, "and in every spare moment [he] was keeping very close to God."[60]

Frank worked the graveyard shift at Pioneer Drug in Yakima, sending money home to Pearl as it would allow. During his late night shifts, Frank struck upon a vague notion, and that notion morphed into an idea. He wanted to start a "Movement," and began plotting logistics. "I considered the 'soap-box' method of distribution," he recalled, "but ruled that out, deciding that by mail was the only feasible way...I would make a charge for it, refunding their money if not completely satisfied, and then someday, some wealthy man would endow the Movement and I could send it around the world free of all charges."[61] It was a grand idea, a wild scheme, one that would require a more permanent foundation from which to grow. Critically, he wanted a job that left his nights free to pursue the Movement. "With this in mind," he wrote, "I sent a wire to the Spokane Drug Company, asking them if they knew of a position where the drug stores closed at six o'clock. The next day came a wire that stated there was a position in Moscow, Idaho, at the Corner Drugstore, working for C.E. Bolles."[62]

After making all the arrangements, Frank rejoined Pearl and Alfred and the Robinsons made their final move.

Part II
"DEAR FRIEND & STUDENT"
1928–1934

CHAPTER 3
From the Ashes

S een from above, Moscow, Idaho, was little more than a settlement blot on an ocean of wheat fields when the Robinsons first arrived in 1928. Main Street ran through a shallow canyon of brick buildings housing local businesses such as Samm's Furniture, The Lotus confectionary and tobacco shop, Varsity Café, the Kenworthy Theater, the Palace of Sweets, and Charlie Bolles' Corner Drug Store. Quaint neighborhoods sprawled outward from the town's center, and the University of Idaho sat atop a gentle hill on the east side of the community. Beyond the town's borders lay a vast geography called the Palouse, an undulating farmland producing a patchwork of commodities including peas, lentils, rapeseed, and wheat. Aerial views showing the rolling hills of the Palouse belie the often dramatic nature of the hills around Moscow with swales deep enough to conceal a team of forty draft horses or the flight of a biplane. Deep green forests of pine and ponderosa punctuate the Palouse cropland here and there, while a network of streams and rivers course through its topography. In some ways, the landscape may have reminded Frank of his native England. (Alf later wrote that Northumberland, not too far from Halifax and where John Henry retired, was "the Idaho Palouse country of northern England.")

In Moscow, the Robinsons seemed to have settled in fairly quickly into what was available at the time: a cramped apartment in the Thatuna complex. Following a brief interval there, the Robinsons relocated into the more spacious Butterfield Apartments on the other side of town. Moscow's Presbyterian Minister, Clifford M. Drury, was first among those to greet the Robinsons on their arrival. A World War I veteran and son of an Iowa Congressman, Drury was thirty-one with dark hair, brown eyes, and gentle face. "I invited them to a church picnic," he recalled.[1] That picnic marked the beginning of an enduring friendship between the minister and Frank, and a strong affiliation between Pearl and the local church itself.

Fitted into a colonial-style house, the Butterfield Apartments boasted four massive white columns in front with a walkout porch upstairs. "Our balcony faced east," Alf remembered, "and we would sometimes sit outside when it rained."[2] They lived in the historic Fort Russell neighborhood of tree-lined streets and dappled leaf light, within walking distance of a park, elementary school, several churches, and the library.

It is reasonable to assume that Frank—an omnivorous reader—would have taken full advantage of Moscow's Carnegie library. For leisure reading, he enjoyed detective novels, but he also read widely (though not always deeply) from a dizzying array of religious texts, particularly New Thought authors in the same vein as Robert Collier. He read foundational works by Phineas Quimby, the progenitor of the New Thought movement, and Mary Baker Eddy, founder of Christian Science. But he also read writers like Charles Haanel, popular author of *The Master Key System*. Originally published in 1912, *The Master Key System* was a correspondence course of twenty-four lessons disseminated every two weeks over the course of a year, entailing readings and examination questions. Haanel's vision— driven by the capitalist's conception of success—promised power, health, and happiness.

Haanel spent his career building upon many of his 1912 concepts and in 1928, the year the Robinsons made their final move to Moscow, Idaho, he published *The New Psychology*, a book that seems to have been foremost in Frank's mind as he sketched out the design and substance of his Movement. As a phenomenon, "new psychology" stems from a critical shift in nineteenth-century thinking when practitioners like Wilhelm Wundt argued that psychology was not a philosophy but a science, a discipline of systematic inquiry built upon the scientific method and analysis. A disciple of this school, Haanel insisted that his theories were rooted in science, not philosophy. "Science," he wrote in 1928, "is not idealistic, nor spiritualistic, nor materialistic, but simply natural."[3] Guiding that science, he wrote, was a series of fundamental laws. "You have an inheritance of worth that is endless," he proclaimed. "While it is already given to you, it will only be possessed by you in so far as you make paths for it to come to you by the fulfillment of natural, mental, and Spiritual laws." The concept of "laws" provided the rhetorical and strategic foundation for much of the self-help literature of the day, including Haanel's. "'Chance,' 'Fate,' 'Luck,' and 'Destiny' seem to be blind influences at work behind every experience," he wrote. "This is not so, but every experience is governed by immutable laws, which may be controlled so as to produce the conditions that we desire." This control, he posited, was resident in what he and like-minded proponents of new psychology called "the universal mind," a veritable source of omnipotence. "The nervous system is matter," he continued. "Its energy is mind. It is therefore an instrument of the Universal Mind. It is the link between matter and spirit—between our consciousness and the Cosmic Consciousness. It is the gateway of Infinite Power."[4]

For his own part, Frank was obsessed with "immutable laws" and the concept of "the universal mind," but especially with "infinite power." The latter, it seems, is all he thought about, and it is easy to understand why. After leading a freewheeling, vagabond life of questionable employment history, reckless military service, alcoholism, imprisonment, compulsive lying, fraud, and bankruptcy, Frank—a forty-two-year-old husband and father—was middle-aged and had almost nothing to show for his life. Starting his Movement was a last ditch effort to make something of himself.

I had no money [then] and was working in a Drug Store making a fair salary and that was all. However, every moment of my life was filled with the desire to know something actual regarding the Realm of God…I made up my mind to either find Spiritual Truth or die in the attempt…I carried a little notebook in my pocket with me and as Spiritual revelations would come over me, I would jot them down in this little book. Whenever I was unpacking a box of drugs or cleaning a showcase, my mind would continually be on this God Realm.[5]

It was the late summer of 1929, and Frank's plans continued apace, even if only in outline form. "There was no name [for the Movement] at this point," Alf later noted, "but the mechanics of attracting adherents and disseminating literature were being loosely formulated." His dissemination model would look like many correspondence courses of the day, but it also looked a lot like Haanel's "Master Key" model. "My father planned to distribute his Lessons every two weeks," Alf wrote.[6]

As late summer bled into early fall, University of Idaho students were back on campus, and Moscow's downtown was bustling. Maple trees burned in a wash of fiery colors. When he was not buried in his studies, "Robbie" was making a name for himself as the new druggist in town, while Pearl became more active in the Presbyterian Church (the faith to which most prominent Moscow residents then belonged). Even as the Robinsons worked to establish themselves into the social fabric of the small town, their personal lives—at least on matters of faith—seem to have set out in different directions. If Pearl had doubts, objections, or concerns about Robbie's plans to start a religious movement, she evidently kept them to herself, opting instead to become his most stalwart supporter. That did not mean, however, she would also become his most loyal follower. It was a distinction on which she would never waver, and there is no evidence that Frank ever expected Pearl to become an adherent of his Movement.

When the name for his Movement finally came to him, it appeared, Frank would tell his followers, in a dream. In that dream, Frank was standing at the door to a room "about twelve feet square, painted black, and in the middle of it," he said, stood a "Helen Gould canvas army cot." A dead man lay on the cot "with his hands folded across his breasts." Another man stood over the cot pointing at the corpse. When Frank asked the man what he was pointing to, the man turned to him and said, "'You ought to know. This is Psychiana, the Power which will bring new life to a spiritually dead world.'" Robinson woke, he wrote, "like a flash." He jostled Pearl awake and told her he had found the name of his correspondence course. "I knew the name of this Movement would have to be a definite entity," he said, as if intuiting the power of branding. "It would have to be something entirely new."[7]

With the basic structure of his Movement sketched out, and now with a new and sciencey-sounding name, Frank needed to take his idea to the next level. "I began to look around for a typewriter," he wrote, "finally locating one, an old Corona, which was owned by Carey Smith, a clothes-presser in Moscow." At home in the Butterfield Apartments, Frank sat at a rickety desk, punching the old Corona's keys in a rising fever. While chain smoking and guzzling coffee, Frank furiously typed a set of twenty "Lessons" he culled from the leaves of his little notebook. Each Lesson averaged about twenty single-spaced pages, totaling some 200,000 words for the first course of study.[8]

Frank titled his serial tome, "PSYCHIANA: (THE NEW PSYCHO-LOGICAL RELIGION)." The note accompanying his title explained his Movement:

A NEW AND REVOLUTIONARY TEACHING FOUNDED ON THE WORDS OF THE GALILEAN CARPENTER AND DESIGNED TO SHOW ITS FOLLOWERS HOW

TO ACTUALLY FIND AND USE THE MOST POTENT, DYNAMIC POWER IN THE UNIVERSE—THE POWER OF THE LIVING GOD.[9]

The Lesson's premise that Robinson's teachings were "founded on the words" of Christ was more bait than substance and his reliance upon buzz words like "revolutionary," "dynamic," "potent," and "power" reveal his early penchant for sensationalism.

Those over-the-top tendencies dovetailed with his almost preter-natural understanding of direct mail marketing. Robinson immediately capitalized on the I/You dialogue construction, for instance, creating an intimate tone noticeably absent from much of the self-help literature of the day. Frank brought his readers into his daily life, introducing them to his family, friends, neighbors, and the small town of Moscow, Idaho, generally. This tactic turned out to be incredibly effective, as it furnished Robinson with the "everyman" credibility he needed, while simultaneously entertaining his audience in the privacy of their own homes. The bi-weekly nature of his mailings added the intangible product of anticipation, as students waited eagerly by their mailboxes.

Solemnizing that intimacy in the Introductory Lesson, Frank contin-ued on, asking readers to "be quiet and thoughtful" while reading the course materials. "Get away from everybody," he instructed. "Be alone." Only in solitude will the truths of "the Living God" be revealed, he asserted.

Even from these initial writings, it is clear that Frank's vision was grand, or at least designed to *look* grand. The overuse of ALL CAPS, for instance, and his invocation of the royal "we" point to Robinson's ambi-tion and mindset. "We presume that you are very much in earnest in your search for the actual truth as it exists," he wrote. "Otherwise you would not be reading this." Frank also used his Introductory Lesson as the proving ground for his newly formulated persona, "Dr. Robinson." How and by what means Frank had suddenly become a doctor of anything are details ghosted from the Introductory Lecture *in toto*, but this persona, revised over time, ranged in countenance from benevolent savior, religious provo-cateur, friendly neighbor, and iconoclast, to father figure, CEO, didactic headmaster, and ad man. His deftness for teeing up controversy existed from the outset, as evident in the Introductory Lecture, and was effec-tive at getting people to bite: "Some of the statements made herein may seem 'uncharitable' and somewhat 'cold blooded,'" he warned. "But let it be remembered that Dr. Robinson hews to the line—letting the chips fall where they may. The truth as it exists has been so clouded and befuddled by dogma and superstition that gloves cannot be used."[10]

This baiting strategy was both a feature and a necessity as he competed for attention in an increasingly flooded market of get-rich/get-happy schemes at the close of the American jazz age. A telling trait of Frank's vision and character concerned his propensity to borrow liberally from his competitors (if only to rebuff them).

> There is nothing strange or supernatural about this. It is simply the Law of being…[C]ause and effect are supreme in a universe governed by immutable law. —Charles Haanel[11]

> There is nothing supernatural in the entire universe. All is governed by immutable, inviolable and never-changing Law…I include in the term 'universe' every living thing, every animate and inanimate object. The same immutable law governs them all. —Frank B. Robinson[12]

> Is it not wonderful to realize that this law is no respecter of persons, that it makes no difference what your habit of thought may be, and that the way has been prepared? —Charles Haanel[13]

> This mighty Creative God-Law of the universe is no respecter of persons. Nor is the Power of that Law limited. —Frank B. Robinson[14]

> Both the cerebrospinal and the sympathetic nervous system[s] are controlled by nervous energy. —Charles Hannel[15]

> If the same thought [is] repeated a sufficient number of times a definite thought channel in the cerebrospinal system is created. —Frank B. Robinson[16]

In the Introductory Lecture, Frank calls out New Psychology specifically and criticizes what he saw as its fundamental flaw: the belief in a subconscious mind. "We have then according to the New Psychology—the 'conscious mind', the 'subconscious mind—and the 'universal mind'," Frank wrote. "BUT—WHEN PRESSED FOR A PLAIN UNDERSTANDABLE DEFINITION OF THESE 'MINDS', THE NEW PSYCHOLOGY DOES NOT AND CANNOT GIVE IT."[17] Robinson insisted that these various "minds" were all part of one thing known as the "God Law," "God Power," or "Spiritual Law," though he was never consistent on its name. Whereas in Robinson's mind, the New Psychology

"CAME WONDERFULLY CLOSE TO THE LIVING TRUTH," conventional faith only led people into darkness.[18]

For Frank, it was vital to draw an even more emphatic line between Psychiana and all iterations of contemporary theology. "I defy any man," he charged, "to glean one single solitary scientific fact about GOD from the thousands of different sects, creeds and denominations, masquerading as teachers of religion in the present day." Robinson's virulent insistence on this particular distinction may have stemmed from a deeper motive: scorn for his father, Reverend John Henry Robinson. "BLIND BELIEF," he asserted, "IS UNSCIENTIFIC AND CANNOT POSSIBLY LEAD ANYONE ANYWHERE EXCEPT PERHAPS INTO MORE DOUBT."[19]

In his Introductory Lecture, Robinson had thrown down the gauntlet. "From this point on will you please follow me closely," he implored. "If you read wisely, you may find the answer to the 'riddle of the universe.'"[20]

How to solve that riddle and access the God Power was the subject of his Lessons, which were available to anyone and everyone at $1.00 each. Frank even offered a money-back guarantee. "Every second Monday," Frank began, "there will be mailed to you one Lesson. You are to do your part in making this course of instruction as profitable to your self [sic] as the truths herein contained are profitable.

"You must read this Lesson quietly EVERY DAY. REMEMBER— you are endeavoring to contact what I call the most DYNAMIC UNSEEN POWER in the universe, so please obey my instructions TO THE LET-TER. It is absolutely necessary for you to entirely discard whatever theories or notions you may have about who and what God is."[21]

For those students who were not "earnest" in their commitments to Psychiana, the consequences were clear. "Unless you actually do the various exercises that I prescribe, chances are you will get nowhere, and only be a loser...It remains essential that you give me your undivided attention."[22]

CHAPTER 4

Ad Man

Frank now had something substantially more concrete than a man's musings in a notebook. Indeed, with a focus on recent news of the day such as the Cosmic Ray—a discovery made by Nobel laureate Robert A. Millikan (a discovery Robinson would go on to tout as proof of the God Power), he had a religious Movement with a thick set of Lessons grounded, he would argue, in *science*. He had a message, a plan, and a brand. Now all he had to do was sell it. In Frank's official narrative, though, he was adrift in uncharted waters when it came to promoting and advertising. "I knew nothing whatsoever about advertising," he later wrote. Contrary to his experience writing ads in Klamath Falls, promoting bonds in Hollywood, and selling business books in Portland, Frank assured his readers of his ignorance on the subject. "I was no promoter," he said. "I had never written an ad in my life."

> Borrowing a sheet of paper from the local newspaper, I sat down to try my hand at writing an ad. I had not the faintest idea how to go about it. Then, from nowhere, came this thought, 'Don't write an ad, tell the people what you have to offer them.' That is exactly what I did, and all I did. It was all I knew how to do.[23]

The advertisement Robinson drafted was ingenious. It was simple and deceptively modest. But it was also audacious, bordering on radical. The "product" behind the ad might as well have been air, but Frank packaged and sold it as if "talking to God" was as material and real as a box of work boots. After some drafting and polish, Frank's ad read, "I Talked with God—(Yes, I did, Actually & Literally)."

The advertisement then asked its reader: "Success or Failure—Wealth or Poverty—Happiness or Despair—Which?" In this first advertisement, one can see Robinson's deftness and savvy understanding of personal correspondence. "Dear Friend & Student," he wrote, "I would like you to imagine I am sitting opposite you in a chair talking to you, and I would like us to both be quiet."[24]

Only a few key steps remained to launch Psychiana in earnest, the first of which was securing capital.

"I did not have any money at all and furthermore, did not know where I could get any," Robinson wrote of those initial days. "The work was written through, and if my philosophy of life and of God were true," he added, "where the money would come from would be quite secondary, I reasoned."[25]

In a bold move, the Moscow newcomer set out in the winter of 1929 to borrow money from local businessmen. "I needed about $2,500.00 before I could put my new teaching before the public." He put his twenty Lesson manuscript in a briefcase, snapped it shut and set out from the Corner Drugstore. "It was snowing hard that night," he recalled, "and very cold." Outside on Moscow's Main Street, he spotted Ned Phillips, a young local merchant. Frank asked him if he could spare some time, and followed the merchant to his apartment where he showed Phillips the Lessons. "Ned gave me $500.00," Frank wrote. "Then I asked him if he knew of anyone else who had another $500.00 and might like to let me have it. He called up his brother-in-law, George Benson, a bookkeeper in Ward's hardware store."[26] According to Frank, Benson heard him out and committed to a $500 loan. Elmer Anderson, a bank employee, agreed to give an additional $750, and his brother, Oscar Anderson, along with Senator W. L. Korter, supplied the remaining money Robinson needed. "I was treading on air in those days," Frank recalled, "for I knew that the philosophy of life I was about to advance was true."[27]

It is difficult to say which is more extraordinary, the fact that these men—civic leaders—agreed to give a veritable stranger that much money based on his twenty Psychiana Lessons, or that he asked for it in the first place.

———◆———

From his start-up capital, Frank paid a printer to publish the first 1,000 sets of Lessons. He had also printed 10,000 sales letters. He then used $400 to place his advertisement—"I Talked with God (Yes, I did, Actually & Literally)"—with *Psychology Magazine*. "You can imagine," he wrote, "that I was very anxious for replies to the announcement to come in." In the winter of 1929, Frank Robinson had rolled the dice, making perhaps the biggest gamble of his life. "When the [Lessons] were paid for and when the first advertisement was paid for," he recalled, "we had exactly $16.47 left in the bank." If the venture had been a gamble for Frank Robinson, it was even a bigger gamble for his investors. "I had told these young men that if they wanted to back out of it, it was perfectly all right, but none of them felt like doing that."

So, they waited.

In the meantime, Frank Robinson continued his daily shifts at the Corner Drugstore, preserving his evenings for fine-tuning his message, movement, and business. Along with his initial investors, Frank rented a small, second-story office space for $10.00 a month. When the men finished their day jobs, they donned overalls and went to work outfitting the office for a potential flood of mailings. "We built rough shelving and rough tables in that room," Frank reported. "Here we were buying lumber and equipping an office with not a single reply in yet."[28]

That would soon change, however. "One day, a few replies were received and the next day, a few more. Finally, the number grew until we were receiving several hundred every day."[29] With the money their solitary advertisement generated, Frank was able to take out more ads in *Physical Culture* and *Pathfinder*, publications with a much wider reach and richer demographic. His strategy paid off. The replies came in such a number that Frank's small office was overrun. "At night we would all go up to our little office and fold and assemble many replies," he wrote. "After a few weeks, the work became so heavy on us at night that I engaged the services of a girl to work half a day…In a few days, we had to increase her to full time."[30]

Whether Frank knew it or not, 1929 marked the pinnacle of American advertising up to that point. Businesses doled out a record-breaking $2 billion that year on ads across the nation. Advertising as a profession really came into its own in the 1920s, and was finally considered an integral facet of enterprise and entrepreneurialism. "We grew up founding our dreams on the infinite promises of American advertising," Zelda Fitzgerald once remarked. "I still believe," she said, "that one can learn to play piano by mail and that mud will give you a perfect complexion."[31] In *Advertising the American Dream*, Roland Marchland rightly called the ad-men of the 1920s and 1930s "apostles of modernity."[32] American intellectuals took a more cynical view, seeing through the scrim and sleight-of-hand trickery in product promotion. Sinclair Lewis quipped, "Advertising is a valuable economic factor because it is the cheapest way of selling goods, particularly if the goods are worthless."[33] Stephen Leacock bandied how, "Advertising may be described as the science of arresting the human intelligence long enough to get money from it."[34]

———————————◆———————————

Robinson was forty-three, a middle-aged man reinventing himself once again. The furnace of activity that burned in his small office space was strangely at odds with the gathering darkness across U.S. financial markets, even if the full magnitude of that calamity had not yet set in. Denial was still a popular refuge, especially with those who had shackled themselves to the President's policy. "Any lack of confidence in the economic future or the basic strength of business in the United States is foolish," Hoover bellowed in December 1929.[35]

When he was not responding to requests, Robinson was busy writing his first book, *The God Nobody Knows*. Its title was a play on the 1925 bestseller, *The Man Nobody Knows*, by Bruce Barton, an American adman who yoked self-help business advice with the life of Jesus. (Barton once quipped that, "In good times, people want to advertise; in bad times, they have to."[36]) Robinson wrote in a raging fury in those days, and in all the days and weeks and years to follow. "He wrote fast and boasted that he never revised," Clifford Drury, the Presbyterian minister, remembered.[37]

The God Nobody Knows was a straight-forward attack on Christianity, and organized religion generally. "As a Psychologist," Frank announced in the "Introductory" of the book, "I would not be in the slightest degree interested if all the denominations and religions in the world swore to me on a stack of Bibles that their individual religion was the right one." Christianity, Robinson argued, came from violence. "Certainly the bloodshed which bathed the dark ages," he continued, was spread "in the name of God."[38] *The God Nobody Knows* also attacked Ussher's chronology, stipulating that the world was created in 4004 B.C. "The unmistakable evidence of the science of geology," Robinson charged, "is that this earth is many millions of years of age. There can be no mistake about the geological findings as to the age of this earth." Robinson constantly pivoted to science (and pseudo-science) when refuting conventional religion. "The science of archaeology in turn also utterly disproves any such statement as to the age of this earth." He continued:

Paleontology says and proves the very opposite [of Ussher's claim]. Comparative philology also gives us unmistakable [sic] evidence that [his] statement is false in its entirety. And by the way, these same sciences also very effectively controvert the bible story that the creation only took six days of time.[39]

For all of its bombast, *The God Nobody Knows* struck a conspicuously progressive note when it came to Robinson's conception of God. "God as He exists, if there be a God at all," he wrote, "*must be a universal God whose power may be universally drawn upon by white man and black man and yellow man alike*" [italics original].[40]

Robinson also returned to his preoccupation with New Psychology in his debut book, particularly on the grounds of the subconscious mind. Whereas in some of his original materials and lectures, Robinson denied the existence of a "subconscious mind," he now allowed room for its possibility, hedging only to suggest that it was not a "mind" at all, but evidence of the God Law at work.

"Where the 'conscious mind' ceases *its* activities," he explained, "this other 'mind' begins its activities…The theory is advanced that while this body of ours was in an embryonic state, the 'great subconscious' took charge of the building of this body." The subconscious mind, Robinson reported, gained its "knowledge" from the "universal mind." The "universal mind," he added, "gives to the 'subconscious mind' whatever of wisdom and power it possesses and therefore the 'subconscious' is all-powerful, almighty, all-wise. In fact, once a person 'contacts' this mighty 'subconscious mind' it, in turn, drawing upon the marvelous wisdom of the 'universal mind,' can and does give us 'whatsoever things we desired.'"

But accessing these "minds" was an ability limited to psychotherapists who, Robinson wrote, "are able to push the 'conscious mind' into the background *talking directly to what they call the 'subconscious,' and the results obtained from this practice are little short of miraculous*" [italics original].[41]

Not everyone, however, had access to, or could afford, a psychotherapist to yield these "miraculous" "results," and certainly not by 1930. But what if you did not need a psychotherapist to access your subconscious mind? What if you already had that power, but just did not know it? That power, Robinson claimed, could equal that of Jesus Christ. "The Galilean Carpenter said: *The things that I do shall ye do also*." Walking on water was not a miracle limited to a messiah. Nor was eternal life the sole provenance of the Son of God. In Frank's teaching, Jesus was no more or less divine than anyone else. The only difference between Jesus and the person on the street, Robinson contended, was that Jesus knew how to access the "universal mind" (i.e., the God-Law). But clergymen the nation over never preached this, Frank complained. "If this 'church,' as we have it with us today, possesses any power of any sort then where is it?" Christianity had 2,000 years to prove its results but had failed to do so, while those in psychotherapy were making great strides, Robinson contended. "When I see the Scientists and the Psychologists absolutely duplicating the very works of the Galilean Carpenter, and when I see these 'church doors' closed from one Sunday to another, then my blood begins to boil within me, for the evidence is very strong that the God of the present 'church' *is not the God of the universe.*"[42]

———◆———

Frank Robinson's life was split between his family's apartment, the Corner Drugstore, and his Psychiana office nook, which was becoming overrun with letters, envelopes, manuscript pages, and ad copy. "Soon the little office became too small and the adjoining office was rented," he wrote. "This, however, also proved to be entirely too small, so we leased a large building about forty feet by one hundred feet and moved into it. I had bought a multi-graph machine and our staff of girls had increased to six."[43]

Day by day, letters fluttered in with paid student subscriptions. But it was one letter in particular from northern Africa that would change Frank's life forever.

CHAPTER 5
"Keyed Up to a High Pitch"

Alexandria, Egypt
October 24, 1930

From his office at Peel & Co. Ltd, Geoffrey Peel Birley held a command-ing commercial footing in the heart of Britain's colonial business district in Alexandria. His office was not far from the Mediterranean Sea, but even in October the African city was still hot and the sun would send, as it always did, droves of beach-goers to the shoreline, where skiffs and schooners floated in the bay. Sandstorms could be a problem. Within minutes, a miasmic ochre-hued cloud of sand could swallow the city and shut down commerce as well as shipping, and sap the streets of life. On calm days, the air was still while the azure bay shimmered in the sun. Watery sunlight flitted through palm fronds and it was common for young men to play backgammon outside the cafes, sipping from cocktails of fruit and milk, sugarcane, and hibiscus.[44]

Birley was twenty-one with dark hair, a high forehead, dimpled chin, and a brief smile-shaped mustache. With easy brown eyes, long brows that nearly touched and vaguely feminine lips, the young bachelor cotton exporter was training to take over his family's Egyptian cotton house.

Educated in England at the Uppingham School, where he excelled at music and cricket, and later at Cambridge, Birley lived in Alexandria at the peak of British colonialism. Like the other colonials in the ancient city, Birley was an active member of the Royal Yachting Club of Egypt, Turf Club, Alexandria Sport Club, Auto Club, Equestrian Club, British Boat Club, and Hunting Club. Little is known about his father, Kenneth Peel Birley, save that he was reserved, respected, and held as many board-ap-pointed positions in the international cotton industry as Geoffrey did in club memberships. The family fortune—built upon the backs of indige-nous laborers—stemmed, in part, from Geoffrey's grandfather, Arthur Birley, and his pith-helmeted forays into India's rubber trade.[45]

Geoffrey Peel Birley. Undated photograph. From *The Strange Autobiography of Frank B. Robinson.*

Sometime in early 1930, Geoffrey Peel Birley chanced upon Frank Robinson's advertisement in the American periodical, *Psychology Magazine.* Given Psychiana's promises of "health, wealth, and happiness," Birley was an unlikely demographical target in Robinson's advertising campaign. He was young and wanted for nothing. His inherited wealth was largely insulated from the ups and downs of the American market, and his activities at the Egyptian sporting clubs ostensibly nullified any lingering questions about his health. One can only speculate on what the young cotton merchant found so captivating about Robinson's ad. He may have been unhappy, dissatisfied with his faith, predisposed to new ways of thinking, or all of the above. Whatever the appeal, the ad enticed Birley to complete the reply coupon, enclose his subscription fee, and drop an envelope in the outgoing post from Egypt to Idaho, making him Psychiana's first, and most important, international student.

◆

By October of that year, Birley had received his fourth Psychiana Lesson and was far from expressing buyer's remorse. He was as committed as he was enthralled, and felt compelled to write Robinson directly, expressing his satisfaction. When the young man sat down at his typewriter, it was on a Friday, and Alexandria was on edge. Labor disputes had led to rioting in the city just days earlier. A governmental standoff was afoot between the Dynastic King Fuad and the Wafd, a growing flank of dissidents who demanded a legitimate constitutionally based government run by parliament and not a dictator. A cotton crisis strained an already tense city. The King was trying to bend the Wafdist constitution to his favor. On the same day Birley sat at his typewriter, London's *Guardian* reported that the King's power-grab entailed "muzzling the press…interfering with the rights of free speech, and now by fundamentally altering the Constitution in such a way as to increase the powers of the King at the expense of Parliament." Where these tensions left British colonials like Birley was an open question. "The policy of the British Government in regard to these troubles in Egypt," the *Guardian* added, "has rightly been one of non-interference, except only in so far as the lives and property of foreign nationals resident there are affected by them."[46] If Birley worried about the upheaval, he did not say so in his letter. Instead, he was upbeat and engaged.

"Dr. Robinson; I received Lesson 4 yesterday & stayed up till one o'clock this morning reading it through," he wrote. "No words of mine can adequately express the glorious thrill it gave me."[47]

Lesson 4—the one Birley referenced in his letter—was titled "THE CREATION AND FALL OF MAN," and amounted to a reinterpretation of Genesis. Robinson argued that prior to the fall, Adam and Eve were not cognizant of their corporeality. Their eyes were "closed" to the reality of their own bodies.

> THE MOMENT THEY DELIBERATELY CHOSE TO OBEY THE SNAKE RATHER THAN GOD, AND THE MOMENT THEY ACTUALLY DISOBEYED GOD, THEIR EYES WERE OPENED AND THEY KNEW THEY WERE NAKED.[48]

In Lesson 4, Robinson contended that Adam and Eve's disobedience forfeited their ability to see and interact within in the "invisible" God realm. Eyes open, they then knew only the physical realm, the realm of mere mortals. Robinson wrote, "You will also begin to grasp the truth that whatsoever we have on this earth is ONLY SECONDARY TO THINGS AS THEY REALLY ARE. The REAL things are the UNSEEN things. The things which are seen are temporal—but the things which are UNSEEN—are eternal."

By enrolling in Psychiana, students would learn how to access the "unseen" realm that Adam and Eve had known before. The Lesson continues on:

> Another thing you can see is the fact that if the opening of the eyes of man to physical things closed his eyes to spiritual things, or, in other words, to THINGS AS THEY ARE, then, as long as we are physical, OUR EYES WILL STILL BE CLOSED TO THE REAL OR THE SPIRITUAL THINGS. This was a fact until the appearance of the Galilean Carpenter. Up to His manifestation it was NOT POSSIBLE FOR A SINGLE HUMAN SOUL TO PENETRATE THE VEIL OF CONSCIOUSNESS NOR TO GLEAN ONE SINGLE TRUTH FROM THE UNSEEN REALM...I shall now show you in this les-

son how to actually SPEAK TO THE LIVING GOD. The thought of being able to do this will probably take your breath away. BUT IT IS A POSITIVE FACT THAT YOU CAN DO SO.[49]

The "veil of consciousness" or "sense veil," as he called it, was the sole barrier between humans living in the "here and now" and the God realm. Once schooled in a series of meditations and affirmations, students could learn how to "penetrate" the sense veil and talk with God.

This part of Lesson 4 spoke directly to Birley. "The thought of being able to actually speak to the Living God, the Mighty Life Spirit," he wrote, "fairly took my breath away, as you said it would do. I was keyed up to a high pitch, 100% wide-awake & expectant, when I came to that passage." Typing out a few more thoughts on Lesson 4, Birley added:

> The story of the creation & fall of man, as unfolded by you, is one of the most marvellous revelations I shall ever experience. To think that this earthly life is "death" makes you long to discover something definite about our future existence. Will your later lessons give any enlightenment on this important phase of existence?…It's impossible in a letter to show you my true appreciation of your wonderful work as I cannot possibly thank you sufficiently.[50]

Back in the United States, the news was not much better than it was in Egypt. The reality of an impending depression was becoming clear to some, and many of those prescient individuals could not bear the thought of total ruination. Crime escalated, church attendance plummeted, and suicides were becoming increasingly common.

Not everyone, however, seemed worried about the economy. Convinced that good press alone would turn things around, President Hoover's cronies filled the papers with optimistic headlines. "Wave Of Business Optimism Sweeps Nation," touted one paper on the same day Birley wrote his letter. "'Turning Point' Reached, Is General Belief; Boosters See Cause for Bright Hopes Here."[51] Such hollow rhetoric was not lost on the more astute observers, however. Claude G. Bowers, who keynoted the 1928 Democratic Convention, blasted the Hoover administration. "Bowers Calls Hoover Regime Utter Failure," *The Scranton Republican* reported. Bowers charged that, "Unemployment Is Result of Republican Ineptitude and Indifference."[52]

With a newly hired staff busy sorting the Lessons, Robinson was beginning to turn a small profit. Then one day, a strange thing happened. "I was walking by the desk of the lady who opened the mail then," he wrote. "And I happened to see a photograph lying on top of a group of enrollment blanks." Robinson wrote that he recognized the man in the portrait. "It suddenly flashed upon me that this was a photograph of the man I had seen in the dream standing over the head of a corpse. Here, looking right at me, was the same man who gave me the name of this Movement in that strange dream." When Robinson asked for the student's enrollment papers, he learned that the man lived in Alexandria, Egypt, and his name was Geoffrey Peel Birley.[53]

Robinson had an idea, an audacious one at that. He called on his private secretary to take a letter. Addressed to the young cotton exporter, the letter asked Birley for $40,000 to help fully launch Psychiana. When he was satisfied with the note, Frank instructed the secretary to send it out with the rest of the day's mail.

Three weeks elapsed, and Frank had not heard anything back from Alexandria. Then one morning, while working at his desk, the phone rang. On the other line was Sam Kimbrough of the Spokane Eastern Trust Company. A check had arrived, Kimbrough said, in the amount of $20,000, with a note indicating that an additional $20,000 would be sent in two weeks.

Psychiana's sudden cash infusion—the equivalent of over a half a million dollars today—secured Robinson's future during precarious times, while Americans across the United States faced dire headlines in the morning papers. A sampling from *The Brooklyn Daily Eagle* paints the picture: "The Fight to Save Savings Accounts in Business Banks"; "Stocks Erratic"; and "Spain's Rebels Flee as 'Republic' Fails Government Claims."[54] But for Frank Robinson, the future shined bright. Moving his family out of the small Butterfield apartment, he bought a new—albeit modest—home on Howard Street along with a large adjacent lot. After a life on the move, after decades of restlessness, Frank Robinson was planting roots.

Chapter 6

Occult Appeal

With 1930 drawing to a close, America was anything but stable. On December 12, *The Guardian* announced the closing of New York's Bank of the United States (a bank independent of the federal government). With some five dozen New York branches, the banking giant "closed its doors, and was taken over by the State Bank Superintendent."[55] Still, on New Year's Eve, papers rang a bell of optimism for the coming year and new decade. "Nation Greets New Year Gaily as Hopes Rise," the *Press and Sun-Bulletin* announced. "Heads of All Industries Say Bedrock Reached, Improvement Certain."

> Father Time, when he ushers in the new year at midnight, will chase the wolf from many a door, replace pessimism with optimism and institute a period of decided improvement in business conditions, according to opinions expressed by leaders of the nation today.[56]

Just seventy-two hours after "Father Time" ushered in a new decade, a mob of five hundred broken and hungry farmers stormed a grocery store in Arkansas, demanding "food for themselves and their families."[57] Four days later, President Hoover's Emergency Committee for Unemployment released its jobless estimate, finding some four to five million Americans were unemployed.[58]

On January 13, six days after the unemployment announcement, Pearl Robinson gave birth to a daughter, Florence Joan. With seven-year-old Alfred, the Robinsons were now a family of four.

───────◆───────

With Psychiana's success came much criticism for the Movement and for Robinson himself. Bob Feeney, a Davenport, Iowa, newspaperman, penned a response to the latest issue of *Psychology Magazine* in his column, "Homade [sic] Hooch."

The man who desires health, wealth or fame and fails to acquire them, deserves little sympathy. Instead of moaning his fate he should spend 25 cents for a February copy of the *Psychology Magazine*. Spread before him in the advertisements he will find the secrets of success, and all may be procured at a very moderate cost. Most of them, in fact, can be secured on five days free trial without obligation.[59]

Feeney added how, "Not since Aladdin and the Genii held the national doubles championship has opportunity knocked as persistently as now." One such ad read, "LEADERSHIP—INDEPENDENCE—HAPPI-NESS—HEALTH. How would you like to possess the complete key to life's supreme prizes? You get all this for $5.95 in Henry Knight Miller's 14-lesson course." Another read, in part, "I'll Give You Magnetic Power in 24 hours—or No Cost!" Still another asked, "Are you a prisoner of self? Have you often felt the urge to do certain things? The longing of the heart for things you haven't? If so, a two-cent stamp will bring you a 6,000-word lecture on Christian psychology from Judge Daniel A. Simmons."

Then Feeney turned to another ad that stood out. "On the back cover," he wrote, "we find 'Psychiana—the new psychological religion.' Roll all the good effects of yeast, bran, Coca-Cola and Listerine into one, and multiply it by a thousand fold, and still you will not equal the power of Psychiana."[60]

Despite stinging attacks such as this, Robinson's religious start-up was growing every day. He bought more equipment, rented more office space, and hired a new business manager. With the leftover cash from Birley's investment Robinson bought a brand-new supercharged Cord sedan. "Dad's taste for fancy cars was probably developed in Hollywood in the 1920s," Alf wrote. While the rest of the country faced economic uncertainty, Frank Robinson was getting rich, a fact he flaunted. "In Moscow," Alf noted, "Dad would drive his brand new car and feel good about it because he was on center stage and everyone was watching." Frank had even convinced the local sheriff, Hap Moody, to bestow upon him a deputy sheriff's badge, emboldening Robinson to install a police siren in his new car. "It was exciting to me, as an eleven-year-old youngster," Alf recalled, "to streak down the highway with Dad, passing and startling other drivers with a push of the 'siren' button on the dash."[61]

Among the many people now watching Psychiana's mailing operations was Harvey F. Lovejoy, a clerk in the office of the Postmaster General in Washington, DC. At sixty, Lovejoy had reached the final rung of his career, as Acting Third Assistant Postmaster General. Bullet-headed and large-eyed, the St. Louis native lacked discernible eyebrows and was nearly bald.[62] Robinson had recently submitted to Lovejoy's office an application to have his new magazine, *Psychiana Monthly*, granted the second-class mail status reserved for church and other nonprofit bulk mailers. After reading a copy of *Psychiana Monthly*, however, Lovejoy sent up a flare. On May 14, 1931—a cool and cloudy Thursday—Lovejoy drafted a letter to the postmaster in Moscow, Idaho. "An examination of the copy of the issue for July, 1931," Lovejoy wrote, "discloses that a considerable portion of the textual matter and advertisements relate to the activities of the publishers as psychologists, lecturers and publishers. Some of the articles are of such a tenor," he continued, "as to lead the readers to seek the advice or services of the publishers in matters for which charges are made, thus tying in with advertisements of the publishers in the issue." Robinson's application, Lovejoy added, "does not meet the requirements of the law governing second-class matter but comes within the prohibition quoted ['Act of March 3, 1879, section 394, P., L, and R.'] and is not entitled to entry as second-class matter."[63]

The letter and its judgment delivered a blow to Robinson, but it did not deter him—not outwardly, anyway. However, Lovejoy's injunction did trigger a potentially more significant threat, one that Frank likely had not considered. Now the U.S. Post Office had an official case file on Psychiana and its leader.

People in Washington, DC, were beginning to pay attention.

———————◆———————

In December 1931, Robinson launched his most ambitious undertaking since the original Lessons: *Psychiana Monthly*. It featured an eye-popping yellow cover, blood-red ink, and the slogan, "supports the true, and exposes the false." The first page of the magazine announced a new campaign called the "Psychiana Brotherhood," and included an enrollment blank and teaser.

SPECIAL NOTICE TO STUDENTS OF 'PSYCHIANA'

There has been an insistent demand amongst our students for further instruction in Dr. Robinson's teachings. So to fill this demand we have brought into existence 'PSYCHIANA BROTHERHOOD.' This Brotherhood will be a banding together of students of 'PSYCHIANA' and will also embrace anyone wishing to know more of Dr. Robinson's teachings than is contained in the large course of Lessons. Every member of the Brotherhood will receive one advanced Lesson every two weeks, and will also have the privilege of taking up with Dr. Robinson direct, whatever questions may arise as long as membership is held in the Brotherhood. Each member will receive a Certificate of Membership, and will also be given a 'PSYCHIANA' badge. The membership fee is $2.50 and the monthly dues are $2.00.[64]

To help defray postage costs, Robinson began including outside advertisements in his magazine. One of the more curious of these ads appeared under an eye-catching call-out:

SPECIAL NOTICE TO ADVANCED STUDENTS
We will disclose a short cut to INITIATION to ALL those who are willing to perform THE GREAT WORK! Here is the TEST. Can you do exactly as you are told, just one simple easy thing, and KEEP SILENT FOREVER about your success? Then send your name and address with one dollar to C. F. Russell Secretary.

CHORNOZON CLUB, PO BOX 181, Chicago.

MAKE SURE YOU KNOW YOUR OWN MIND BEFORE YOU ANSWER![65]

It was Cecil Frederick Russell, an early pupil of Aleister Crowley, who placed the cryptic advertisement in *Psychiana Monthly*. Russell, who had been a member of Crowley's Ordo Templi Orientis organization, was, like Robinson, a disgraced Navy man. Russell's dishonorable discharge did not stem from "chronic alcoholism" like Frank's, but instead resulted from "injecting a huge dose of cocaine and attempting to burn a piece of glass through sheer will."[66] Russell had lived with Crowley at the mystic's infamous hilltop Abbey of Thelema in Cefalú, Italy, where the elder Crowley expected sexual favors from Russell, and the younger pupil, high on ether, complied. Not long afterwards, Crowley tired of Russell and kicked him out of the abbey. Dejected, Russell packed for the United States, and started the Choronzon Club (later called the G.B.G.) in Chicago. Convened loosely under the aegis of Crowley's teaching (e.g. *The Book of the Law*), the Choronzon Club was a sexual-magick[67] club almost exclusively for gay men, though Russell is most well-known for his baffling four-volume autobiographical work, *Znuz is Znees: Memoirs of a Magician.*[68]

Russell's ad in Robinson's magazine was neither unusual nor misplaced. The occult, séances, black magick, mystics, metaphysics, and mediums were not completely fringe fascinations in the early 1930s. Of course, some movements were more fringe than others. But groups like the American Society for Psychical Research (ASPR), for instance—an institution that is very much alive and well today—saw their engagement with the metaphysics, telepathy, and the paranormal as *scientific*, and not fantastic, pursuits. ASPR counted among its members many paragons of America's intelligentsia. Former dean of the Harvard Medical School Edward Charles Pickering, Alexander Graham Bell, and William James were among the founding members. Although not an official member, Aleister Crowley had passing contact with a host of its members, and knew well the inner workings of the society.[69] Frank Robinson was confirmed as a member of ASPR in February of 1931.

Around the same time that Robinson was planning his launch of *Psychiana Monthly*, newspapers across the country were reporting that Lady Arthur Conan Doyle had been receiving direct messages from her dead husband, and often had "smelled the peculiar ozone-like smell of ectoplasm." A *Hartford Daily Courant* headline spoke to the phenomenon: "Adrift in the Spirit World."[70] A member of the UK-based Society for Psychical Research, Sir Arthur Conan Doyle was fascinated by the occult, had attended séances and sessions on telepathy, and believed in mediums. This preoccupation was not uncommon. A year later, a full-page story, "Séance to Communicate with [Rudolph] Valentino's Spirit Described," appeared in the *San Francisco Examiner*.[71] Nor was the occult's popularity limited to the United States and England. In Italy, as Prime Minister Benito Mussolini's grip tightened, news spread of a crackdown there on the occult. Lurid, page-one exposés ran in papers around the globe: "Queer Disclosures in Italy's Crusade Against Black Magic and the Evil Eye: How Prince Christopher of Greece and Other Aristocrats Became Devotees of Weird Rites."[72]

The popularity of the occult—particularly among celebrities and intellectuals—is correlated in part to diminishing church attendance, but the fad also explains how something like Psychiana not only got traction, but flourished.

In 1930s America, the occult was good business.

———◆———

The December 1931 issue of *Psychiana Monthly* is more than a roadmap of Robinson's Movement and the issues then preoccupying his mind.[73] It

is a snapshot of what many Americans were likely thinking, but not saying. The *Monthly*'s readership was not mainstream, but it was not that far
from center, either. Feature articles—each penned by Robinson—carried
titles such as, "How the Church God Heals"; "Psychic Hocus-Pocus"; and
"Fearing God."

In his article on spiritual healing, Robinson made no grand claims. He
recalled visiting a congregation where the parishioners were speaking in
tongues. "To me," he wrote, "they appeared like a bunch of insane morons."
Criticizing "faith-healing," Robinson was clear about how his conception
of God differed from these "Holy rollers" and even Christian Science, from
whose teachings he occasionally borrowed.[74] Remembering a time when
he was deathly ill, Robinson wrote how he reached out to God for the
restoration of his health, and got it. "Let me not be misunderstood," he
cautioned. "So plain was [God's] message to me that I did exactly what
the intelligence of God told me to do...I secured the very best physician
obtainable."[75]

In the Questions & Answers section of the *Monthly*, Robinson takes
up the issue of faith healing once more in response to a student query.

Q: I am 88 years of age, and have a cancer of the lip. Can you or your
God heal that cancer?

A: My God can—I can't...I do not claim to be a 'healer' either.

Another Psychiana student asked if Robinson believed in "thought transference"—a study of mental telepathy that the ASPR took seriously. "I
most assuredly do," Robinson wrote. "There are too many authentic cases
on record for me not to." Clarifying his position, Robinson added, "I do
not believe in crystal balls...nor do I believe in clairvoyance. I think most
of that is spiritualistic bunk. Thought transference, however, is definitely an
established fact, and opens up quite a realm of thought."[76]

Harvey F. Lovejoy's second-class postage denial for *Psychiana Monthly*
forced Robinson to scale-down the publication's frequency to a quarterly
magazine, but it also spoke to the tightening purse-strings throughout the
country.

By the beginning of 1932, an exasperated Hoover asked Congress to
adopt a suite of measures he believed would stabilize a radically faltering
market. Alarmingly out of touch, Hoover shouted at Congress: "We can

and must replace the unjustifiable fear in the country by confidence."[77] Increasingly unpopular, Hoover had long (and mistakenly) seen credit as the sole arbiter of the Depression, while maintaining that goading consumer confidence was the definitive cure. "Nobody is actually starving," he often sniped to his closest advisers.[78] But hunger crept up on vulnerable families rapidly and without prejudice. One study found that in rural areas, many families were "eating weeds" and that in cities, men were prowling through "garbage cans and city dumps." A recently widowed woman in Chicago took her glasses off before eating spoiled meat so she could "avoid seeing the maggots she was eating."[79]

Benjamin Roth, a Youngstown lawyer, kept a diary throughout the Depression which corroborates much of the public record during this period.[80] Although he had no known affiliation with Psychiana, his personal writings provide a vivid context for the era in which Psychiana thrived. "The stock market continues downward and there seems to be no end to it," he observed.[81] There were strikes in Chicago and soup lines trailed around corners of untold buildings nationwide. But in Moscow, Idaho, news as it related to Robinson was bright. "Psychiana Elects Officers for 1932," one paper reported on January 15, 1932.[82] As of that point, Robinson claimed "10,000 active students in 74 countries" and stated that his business revenues had reached $250,000 annually.[83] Later that same January, Roth noted in his diary that he had just returned from a trip. "The streets are crowded with the shabby, and unemployed—vacant store rooms everywhere—signs on closed banks—bankruptcy sales and half-price sales in the stores that are open—soup kitchens." The impression was searing. "It will take a long time to forget these things."[84]

On March 31, 1932—thirty days after the kidnapping of Charles Lindbergh Jr.—Robinson bought a building on Moscow's Third Street, intended solely for storing the hundreds of boxes of envelopes and letterhead for his mail-order religion. Alf, who was then nine years old, remembered "how cold it was in there," adding how he "used to play on the cartons" of envelopes.[85] One day Clifford Drury, the Presbyterian Minister, pushed through the doorway at Psychiana's headquarters and paid "Doc" a visit. The day's mail had just arrived in dozens of large canvas bags. Ever the showman, Robinson revealed to Drury his accounting "system." Frank placed a single canvas mailbag on a scale. "He would weigh the bags," Drury said, "and then estimate how much money he would get."[86]

———————◆———————

Business mail was not the only kind of correspondence on Robinson's mind then, no matter how much poured into his office. Robinson had lately been thinking about home—England—and his family. The last time he had heard from his half-sister Mary had been when he was working at the Star Drugstore in Klamath Falls. So on Saturday, May 28, 1932, Robinson sat down at his typewriter and began clacking at the keys in a letter, breaking the long silence.[87] It was a pleasant day after nearly a week of statewide spring rains. The economy was still floundering. (Douglas National Bank in Chicago had closed its doors the previous day, and it had been just over two weeks since the body of the infant Lindberg boy had been found.[88]) After decades of a vagabond existence, Robinson now truly had something substantive to write home about. He had just returned from a trip to Toronto where he visited his brother, Sydney, whom, Robinson wrote, he "had not seen in twenty-five years."

He said to Mary: "This letter will probably come as a surprise to you and yet I am happy to write it, for I never did understand why thirteen or fourteen years ago you suddenly stopped writing to me when we were having such a nice correspondence." The bulk of the letter entails Robinson trying to clear his name. He wrote:

> I have suspected for some time that these stories about me probably led you to believe that I was guilty of every crime under the sun from petty thievery to first degree murder. I now know that this is a fact, and I was not a bit surprised to hear of it, as there are many things I know that you probably do not know and never will know.

On the visit to their brother, Robinson wrote, "Sydney told me a lot of very interesting things and I was as much amazed to hear of them as you will probably be to know that they are not true." What those exact stories entailed is unknown. He continued:

> You will probably be surprised to know that I own one of the finest homes in Moscow, have one of the largest mail businesses in the United States, and keep twelve people steadily employed to handle the executive end of this business. My writings are going all over the civilized world and I have students and followers by the thousands. So, you see, I am probably not quite as bad as certain people have tried to make you believe.

Frank told her about his family but stopped short of including any photos of Pearl, Alf, or baby Florence. Enclosed, he wrote, was "a photograph of myself seated at the console of my pipe organ which I had installed in my home last year." He then closed the letter with some pleasantries and potential travel plans.

> [One] of these days, perhaps next year, I am coming to England and I surely will look you up...This is all I am going to say this time, but I just wanted you to know that I have never forgotten little Mary and never will. I shall be very happy to hear from you any time you feel like replying and assure you that you may have no hesitancy about writing to me at all.

> With best love, Frank.[89]

Robinson's boasts to Mary were not entirely unfounded. (He was not a numbers man, but he loved throwing around inflated figures.) "Dad was not a detailed, follow-through person," Alf confided. "He was not a businessman type, interested in financial statements and such."[90] In fact, a third-party accounting firm from Spokane reported Psychiana's gross earnings for "the first three months of 1932" at $47,677.17.[91]

Meanwhile, frail and grim-faced veterans were descending upon the nation's capitol to demand the financial bonuses they had been promised by their government for their service in the World War. Tens of thousands of them poured in from all corners of the country for the Bonus Army March on Washington. Wobbling and road-spent sedans sputtered into the city on fumes. Sooty-faced men with thin children and worried wives rode in jalopies and boxcars across America to protest. Others encumbered with grimy rucksacks hitched rides along wind-swept highways. It was the summer of 1932 and these war-torn men—both black and white—were hungry, and were growing angrier by the day.

In the Anacostia neighborhood, the veterans erected a tent city that looked not unlike the combat camps they had survived in France. Smoke churned up from cook-fires and American flags waved over the encampment. Impromptu musical ensembles entertained the "Bonus Expeditionary Forces," as they called themselves. Others delivered stump speeches. Children darted throughout the tent city, reveling in the novelty of the scene. The Hoover administration regarded the protesters as mere coyotes yowling in the shadows of the U.S. Capitol building.

Then, on July 28, 1932, President Hoover ordered the evacuation of the Bonus Army protesters. When they refused to decamp, General Douglas MacArthur, Major Dwight D. Eisenhower, and Major George S. Patton mobilized a full-scale military operation backed by tanks and field artillery to force the war veterans out. They did so by force of might, intimidation, tear gas, drawn rifles, and glinting bayonets. One protester was killed. Never in their lives did these combat veterans think they would see American soldiers, under the American flag, and by order of the president of the United States, raise weapons against themselves. And yet they did. Parading on horseback, General MacArthur ordered his men to set Anacostia's tent city ablaze, where some 15,000 veterans had camped.[92]

———————◆———————

In November 1932, Democratic candidate Franklin Delano Roosevelt won the presidency by a decisive landslide. Ever the opportunist, Frank Robinson, a Republican, sent a note of congratulations to the president-elect. Back in the Northwest on Thanksgiving Day—and two days before Frank and Pearl's thirteen-year anniversary—*The Spokane Press* featured an article on Robinson's Psychiana. "Doctor With New Idea Puts Little City on Map," the headline read. "World Turns Eyes Toward Moscow." The article shows a photo of Robinson standing next to his newly purchased Super Charged Cord automobile. "Dr. Robinson's new car, which he purchased to enable him to better move about swiftly in the daily work," the caption noted.

The article further reported that, "the mail at the Moscow post office has grown to enormous portions, making it a first-class post office in the eyes of the department at Washington."[93]

Some of those eyes, however, belonged to officials like Harvey Lovejoy and the men he answered to, officials with investigatory powers.

CHAPTER 7

"The Shackles Are Off"

Hope, New Mexico
December 4, 1932

Fewer than three hundred souls called Hope, New Mexico, their home in 1932. Theirs was a village of four buildings—a church, post office, bank, and general store—and a smattering of shacks, mere hulls of domesticity strewn about one square mile of interminably flat, wind-scrubbed land. A leaden thread of macadam highway, warped and split, ran through the shantytown, and the sandy moonscape was blotted here and there with greasewood and creosote. Flashfloods were not infrequent. Rangy vultures scouted carrion on the Hope Highway. The nearest town was Artesia, twenty miles east. Despite its name, Hope huddled upon a land known more for what it lacked than what it offered. It was a hard land in a jinxed country.[94]

Hope's Methodist minister in 1932 was John Klassen. A Dutch immigrant who, at twenty three, had left his native Arnhem in 1924, Reverend Klassen was thirty years old, wore an easy smile, and had a high forehead forecasting baldness. Standing nearly five feet, eleven inches, John Klassen was of medium build with blue eyes and glasses.[95]

Klassen, his wife, Mamie, and their two children—Jessie May, aged two, and David Morris, one—had moved to Hope from El Paso, Texas, two years earlier. The Klassen home—the church's parsonage—was one of the nicer houses in Hope. It was an adobe-style ranch home with a modest yard that stood next to the mission-style church. From his front porch, Reverend Klassen could gaze across a pasture and view the backside of the general store on Main Street.[96] In the Klassen home, Mamie's days would have been busy with domestic duties and the demands of caring for her young children. She was also pregnant with their third child in December of 1932. In January 1933, they would celebrate their three-year wedding anniversary.

On the evening of December 4, the Reverend Klassen sat down at

NEW PASTOR—The Rev. John Klassen, formerly pastor of the First Methodist Church in El Paso, Tex., has been transferred to Los Alamos as pastor of the First Methodist Church. Rev. Klassen replaces the Rev. Wayne Douglas, who has been transferred to Oklahoma.

News item on John Klassen from the Santa Fe *New Mexican*, May 17, 1961.

his typewriter in his study to compose a short letter. "Dear Dr. Robinson," Klassen typed. "I AM FREE. A strange statement with which to start a letter, but the only kind of statement that will explain the exultation that has taken possession of me."[97] He felt as though he had made a breakthrough discovery, aided by Dr. Robinson's vision. "This morning as I was making last minute preparations [before] going to my pulpit," he wrote, "I realized how I was harassed and bound by the traditions of man and by the dogmas of previous times."[98] While that morning's *Albuquerque Journal* delivered grim news—"City Pay Cuts Effective Dec. 1,"—Reverend Klassen had reason to be hopeful.[99] "Your lessons have given me the very things which were dark in my mind," he wrote. He was no longer locked down by the old systems. "The shackles are off," he declared. "I was in my study when it happened. The thought came to me, with force unexplainable, that no longer would I be tied by things expected of a preacher. The results? I am willing to leave that to the Power which controls the Universe."

It is impossible to know for sure which of Frank's Lessons had moved Reverend Klassen so, or if he was moved by the entire course itself. He may have been responding to Lesson 6 when he mentioned being "harassed" by the "dogmas" of a bygone era.

In Lesson 6, Robinson wrote of the "Dark Ages" when, for one thousand years, "religious superstition" ruled the world. "In such periods," Frank wrote, "reason and science are completely buried. Nothing matters except the black pall of religious superstition covering that period."[100] He then points to those who finally forged a path out of the darkness, torchbearers with names like Bruno, Galileo, and Copernicus. These "torch-bearers of truth," Frank added,

did not believe in the religious superstition vaunting itself on the earth in those days, and masquerading as an agent of God. They saw further than that. They saw beyond the black night. They saw the cruel flames sear and destroy the bodies of those who would not believe the stories told by these superstitionists, and they used their reason—they wondered what sort of a God it could be who produced such a murdering mob of followers.[101]

The Lesson supplied other names to this list of "torch-bearers" who started an intellectual backlash against conventional religious strictures. These thinkers, Robinson wrote, "wanted nothing to do with such a 'god' and they frankly said so." Identifying the trailblazers, Robinson wrote, "Lamarck came to France, and Kant to Germany, Spinoza appeared in Holland and Locke in England. Then came Charles Darwin who gave to the world his ORIGIN of SPECIES." Referring to the Scopes Trial, Robinson added how "the religious superstitionists fought [evolution] as bitterly as they knew how to fight it. But to no avail. TRUTH TRIUMPHED. And today the fact of evolution is as firmly established as is the fact of gravitation."[102]

It may have been Robinson's apparent appeal to reason over old, homiletic systems of thought that made Psychiana attractive to so many people—even faithful people like Reverend Klassen of Hope, New Mexico. While the winter of 1932 saw the highest unemployment rate in U.S. history,[103] it also saw a continuing drop in church attendance nationwide. As early as 1930, *The Literary Digest* had sounded the alarm in an article titled, "The Dangerous Decline of the Church."[104] It was an article that Robinson liked to quote at length. In his book, *The God Nobody Knows*, Frank drew on the article's many data points. "For the first time since the Civil War," he cited, "the Methodist Episcopal Church showed a net loss of nearly 25,000 members."[105] Indeed some scholars have called this phenomenon the "religious depression," although as T.H. Watkins wrote in *The Hungry Years*, "church attendance and financial support had been declining for years, beginning in the early twenties."[106]

The size of Reverend Klassen's flock in Hope was no doubt small. With little to no opportunity in that howling desert settlement during the Depression, residents drifted away like weeds in fugitive winds. It was not always so. As early as 1910, there were 417 people who called Hope home. That number actually climbed to 430 by 1920, but when Reverend Klassen and his family arrived in 1930, there were only 275 inhabitants trying to make a go of it. Within forty years, that number would drop to a mere ninety residents.[107]

Hope was dying out.

Klassen's evident break with convention in whatever form evidently allowed a new kind of freedom, and with it some uncertainty. But Reverend Klassen was not worried. "I do not know where my new course will lead me," he confessed. "Stranger still, I do not care." Reverend Klassen still saw himself preaching, but his sermons would no longer be solely grounded in the old dogmas. Instead, they would be informed by Psychiana's God Law. "In my future preaching," he wrote, "I will, of course, speak some of the truth as you have made me to see. I can never tell you the real appreciation that I feel toward the teachings of Psychiana."[108]

The few residents of Hope who had the relative luxury of owning radios would have listened to the Albuquerque KOB's evening lineup of programs such as "Old Familiar Hymns," "Fireside Melodies," and shows like "Clarence and Lela" and the "Southwest Serenaders."[109] They would have listened, too, to the political campaigns leading up to Franklin Roosevelt's victory in the presidential election the month prior. Eight days after Reverend Klassen sent his heartfelt letter to Frank Robinson, President-Elect Roosevelt sent a note of thanks to Dr. Robinson from the Executive Mansion in Albany. "My dear Dr. Robinson," the form letter read. "Your message of good will and congratulations touched me very much. It is my earnest wish that I may always deserve the confidence which has been shown in me."[110]

Knowing or not, the small Methodist congregation in Hope, New Mexico, was receiving trace elements of Frank Robinson's teaching, folded in with Reverend Klassen's usual sermons. Pausing briefly over the broader implication of Robinson's influence on his sermons, Klassen questioned his own ethics. "Will this be fair to you? Will it be fair to the denomination that has engaged me?"

On the latter question, Klassen took comfort in what he perceived to be an elastic view within his church. "It so happens that the denomination with which I am related gives to its ministers remarkable freedom of thought."

Still, he had found himself wanting, and later, thankful. "Your Lessons have given me the very things which were dark in my own mind."[111]

Reverend Klassen's letter to Frank Robinson was driven, it seems, by an undercurrent of hopefulness unique in such an unsettling time. Christmas was coming to Hope, New Mexico, in three weeks, and in Albuquerque, children's shoes were on sale for sixty-eight cents. "Brother, Can You Spare a Dime," the most popular song that year, crackled over the radios of the fortunate, even, perhaps, in places like the Klassen home in Hope.

Chapter 8

Toil

Today brings to a close the most difficult and dismal year in my business experience," Benjamin Roth wrote in his diary.[112] It was New Year's Eve, 1932, nearly four weeks after Reverend Klassen's letter to Robinson. "The outlook for 1933 is not much better," he lamented. "Thirty thousand people in Youngstown are being supported by charity—begging and holdups and murder are frequent—bankruptcy and receiverships and foreclosures are no longer a disgrace."[113] A week later, a Hamilton, Ohio, newspaper printed a bulletin titled, "The Church Invites You," with a quotation from former Secretary of War Newton D. Baker: "A soup line is not enough; a man's spirit must be saved as well as his body...Courage, morale and wise guidance are needed today as they have seldom been in the history of our country." The bulletin then reminded its readers that "the supreme character building agency is the church. Why not accept the invitation and COME TO CHURCH NEXT SUNDAY!"[114]

People were losing faith, and bureaucrats were still alarmingly out of touch with the crushing realities nationwide.

------◆------

On March 4, 1933—just over a month after Adolph Hitler had been installed as chancellor in Germany—a polio-besieged Franklin Delano Roosevelt gripped the podium at his inauguration and told millions that fear itself was the only thing they had to fear. He promised a New Deal for the American people, and all across the nation, a beleaguered citizenry tuned in. The day before, Roosevelt had met with Democratic lawmakers on the issue of banks. He did not want to waste a single minute when it came to the economy.

Overlooking the sea of faces attending his inauguration, Roosevelt spoke with confidence and surety. "In such a spirit on my part and on yours we face our common difficulties," he said.

They concern, thank God, only material things. Values have shrunken to fantastic levels; taxes have risen; our ability to pay has fallen; government of all kinds is faced by serious curtailment of income; the means of exchange are frozen in the currents of trade; the withered leaves of industrial enterprise lie on every side; farmers find no markets for their produce; the savings of many years in thousands of families are gone.

Then, cutting to the heart of the American depression, he added how "a host of unemployed citizens face the grim problem of existence, and an equally great number toil with little return." Taking direct aim at the Depression deniers and other rank-and-file Hooverites, Roosevelt added how, "Only a foolish optimist can deny the dark realities of the moment."[115]

CHAPTER 9

"Does the LAW Work?"

Houston, Texas
April 12, 1933

It had been a tempestuous year for Leslie Beeching and his wife, Cecile. On July 1, 1932, while the Democratic National Convention bustled in Chicago, Leslie and Cecile in Houston, Texas, had lost their home on Griggs Avenue. Leslie, 42, and Cecile, 36, had lived quietly with their son, Walter, and Cecile's mother, Louisa, in their modest home on that pan-flat stretch of Texas oil land.[116] But theirs had become an all-too-familiar story across Depression-era America: the mortgage payment was too much, the wages too little. Abandoned homes haunted much of the American landscape. Shuttered windows, yawning and broken screen doors swinging in errant gusts, and boarded-up doorways were fresh reminders of an endangered American dream.

   In Houston, the Beeching family had to secure affordable housing quickly. The good news, if there was any, was that Leslie had a job. He was a telegraph operator for the railroad yards in Houston. His was a venerable trade that harkened back to the nineteenth century and was as critical then to public safety as air-traffic controllers are to today's air travel. He was a member of the Order of Railroad Telegraphers, a labor union of men and women that had long published its heralded trade magazine, *The Railroad Telegrapher*. But if he found some semblance of safety in his job, Leslie Beeching would have also had reason to be worried about the one good thing going for him. By the early 1930s, two forces threatened his occupation: the Depression itself and advancing technology. Nationwide, railroads were consolidating operations, laying off telegraph operators, and implementing new systems of communication known as Centralized Traffic Control, or CTCs. Individual telegraphers were no longer needed in the number they had been in years past.

Having lost the house, Leslie Beeching was as down as he had ever been. After all, the family had lived in the same house for a decade. Their son, Walter, had grown up there. It was their home, and now it was gone.

Not long afterwards, however, Leslie happened to spot a Psychiana advertisement in a local paper. Figuring he had nothing to lose, Leslie Beeching wrote to Frank Robinson, asking for more information. After receiving and then reviewing the free information packet from Psychiana's headquarters in Moscow, Idaho, Leslie felt inspired. He discussed the possibility of enrolling in the course of study with Cecile, and when she agreed, Leslie sent off for the first set of Lessons. They studied them faithfully together, sending money in for each successive Lesson. The Beechings were fascinated by the implications of the God Law.

It had not even been a year since the Beeching family lost their home on Griggs Avenue when Leslie sat down to report on his progress to his teacher. In his April 12 letter, he told Robinson the story of losing his home the previous July. "We were very much depressed," he wrote. "We loved the place." He then mentioned how he came across one of Psychiana's ads and how his new-found faith turned everything around. "As my wife and I progressed in your Lessons," Leslie continued, "we put them into practice." What happened afterwards was the stuff of miracles. "And believe it or not, on April 1st, 1933, just nine months after losing our home, we got it back."[117] Not only did the Beeching family get their home back, but they were able to negotiate a lucrative deal. "What I want to say is that we got it for $1000 less than we owed on it when we lost it, and also got it for $24.00 less on monthly payments." This sudden turn of fortune, Leslie argued, was the direct result of putting Psychiana's spiritual powers to work in their daily lives. "Does the LAW work?" Leslie asked. "I'll say it DOES, when properly applied. We are now studying the 17th Lesson of the Course and I want to say that I can truthfully say I have learned more from the Course of instruction regarding life and Spiritual things than I learned in all the rest of my 43 years of life."[118]

Like so many people in Depression-era America, Leslie Beeching had become disillusioned with conventional religious teaching. He was looking for something that would help him in the moment, not in some promised afterlife. And what Frank Robinson offered was precisely the brand of faith Leslie Beeching had been seeking. "I never was much of a believer in 'Church teachings,'" Leslie confessed. "But until I began studying your

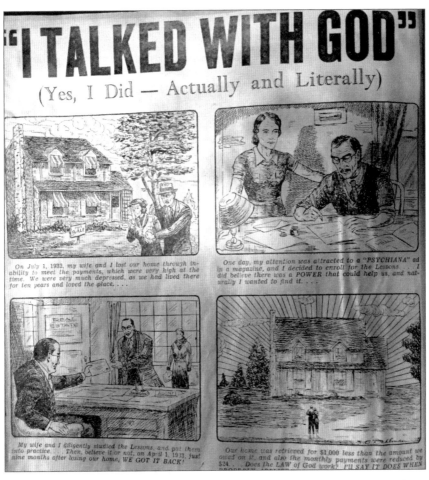

Robinson wasted no time in converting Beeching's success story into an illustrated advertisement for Psychiana. Undated. Latah County Historical Society.

Course of instructions I never could fathom what 'God' was. I know now what 'God' is, and I know that you and your teachings are RIGHT." Moreover, Leslie came to see that it was fate that he stumbled across one of Dr. Robinson's catchy ads. "I now believe that my attention was called to your advertisement thru this 'God Law' in order that I might profit by it. Well, I have." He closed his letter this way: "My wife and I both believe this to be the most wonderful teaching we have ever come in contact with."[119]

Lesson 17, the one Leslie mentioned that he and Cecile were working on as of his writing on April 12, was described by Robinson as dealing with "the most stupendous problem we have to face." That problem, he argued, was "life itself."[120] In the beginning of the lesson, he asked his students to imagine a world without life: no people, no animals, dead plant life, "and on every hand nothing but disintegration and death." He then reminded his students that what made the world so miraculous was life—the very life of his individual students. He pointed out that most people take life for granted. "The farmer on the farm," he explained, " becomes so used to sowing the grain and reaping the harvest, that he seldom ever thinks of the miracle of the transformation of one grain of wheat into several hundreds. LIFE was created where before it did not exist."[121] Before extoling platitudes such as "YOU ARE LIFE" and "LIFE is EVERYTHING THERE IS IN EXISTENCE" and "LIFE—which is God—or which is TRUTH" and "GOD IS LIFE," Robinson added, "I wish I had the money right now that has been spent by honest intelligent souls in trying to find something of the secret underlying the universe. They want to be successful. They want to be happy. They want to be healthy, and so millions of dollars have been paid by them in what to date seems to have been a somewhat fruitless search for TRUTH."[122]

How long the Beechings remained active in Psychiana is not known. But records indicate that the Beechings' hardest days were by and large behind them. Some two decades after enrolling in Psychiana and reclaiming his home, Leslie Beeching hit a high point in his professional life when *Railroad Magazine* featured a story on him and the critical post he worked in the Houston rail-yards.

In the first third of the magazine's February 1952 edition, there appeared a photo-essay titled, "T. & N.O. JCT" by Philip R. Hastings.[123] Wanting to write about Houston's busiest railroad junction, Hastings was told he ought to spend time out at Tower 81 of the Texas and New Orleans Junction where a mind-boggling number of freighters and passenger trains from Galveston, Sante Fe, Missouri, and Fort Worth crisscrossed incessantly. After hopping a commuter car out to Tower 81, Hastings arrived at dawn, climbing the stairs to the tower's control room. "The operator," Hastings wrote, "turned out to be a conscientious railroader and challenged my trespass of his lofty domain, but quickly became friendly when I showed him my letter of authority from T&NO Railroad."[124]

For twenty-six years, Beeching had worked as the operator in Tower 81, Hastings wrote. On average, Beeching oversaw "83 train movements each day, of which two-thirds are through, and the remainder switching moves in connection with the yard." For each move, Beeching had to maneuver the "chest-high switch levers," with each of these eighty-three moves requiring 10 lever switches each." Not only was the work physically taxing, accounting for Beeching's "excellent muscular development," as Hastings put it, but it was mentally demanding in the extreme. Beeching had to meticulously document every single lever movement, and report those movements up the chain of command, for one lapse of judgment could be disastrous.[125]

Not only had Beeching held on to his job in the midst of the Depression and through the ongoing threats of evolving technology, but he became a ranking operator of one of the most significant rail junctions in the country. The degree to which he credited Psychiana for his professional good fortune over the years remains unclear, but in April 1933 when he wrote to Frank, his mind was clear, and his resolve unwavering. "I agreed to report all benefits derived from the study of your Course of instruction," he had said. "I am happier, healthier, and enjoy life."[126]

For Leslie Beeching, Psychiana delivered precisely on its promises.

Leslie Beeching working in the railyard. From *Railroad Magazine*, February 1952.

CHAPTER 10

"At the Hour You Took Command"

San Francisco, CA
April 16, 1933

On Easter Sunday, four days after Leslie Beeching reported the miraculous story of his family's recovery, Ethel Cone sent a letter to Frank Robinson from her apartment at 303 Church Street in San Francisco.[127] Over a hundred miles south in Monterey, a cast of itinerant workers heeded the screech of Cannery Row's morning whistles amid the metallic, marine stench of sardines, but up north in San Francisco, the city's cannery was bustling with a workforce canning not fish but peaches in the Del Monte fruit packing plant. Seven miles west, the chattering of construction could be heard in any direction as workers pushed forward on the new and ambitious Golden Gate Bridge project. "Industries, Labor, Farmers, Join in Cry for Inflation; Congress Session Prolonged," read one headline in the day's *Oakland Tribune*. "Drastic Action Urged to Check Tide of Unemployment; Threats Heard."[128] Down on Howard Street, a thirty-seven-year-old photographer with a polio-induced limp was shooting pictures of broken men and the breadlines they stood in. The photographer was Dorothea Lange.[129] Great kits of pigeons flew from rooftop to rooftop, and the recent bombings in Seattle had been attributed to labor disputes. Against this backdrop, Ethel Cone was feeling profound relief. A San Francisco transplant, she was a lifetime away from her native Tennessee where she had grown up in a family of twelve, as the second child of Catherine Rhuemma (Emma) and Wiley Tucker, a sharecropper and veteran of the Confederacy.

Ethel was petite, almost child-sized, standing scarcely five feet tall, and weighing an anemic eighty pounds. At sixty and with gray hair, Ethel wore glasses through which her blue eyes peered.[130]

Over the past five days, Ethel and her husband, Percy, had been in constant communication with their spiritual leader, Frank Robinson, as

Ethel's life had depended on it. Percy Cone was even farther away from his native land than Ethel. Percival Claude Cone was a forty-six-year-old Australian-born merchant marine who, some two decades earlier, had abandoned his first wife, Sarah Anne, and two children in Sydney. The legal judgment against him stipulated that he had "willfully deserted her, and without any such cause or excuse left her continuously so deserted during three years and upwards." His first child, Daphne, died in infancy, and his son, Albert Percy, died in a bicycle race at the age of twenty-one. Cone, who had immigrated to the United States in 1906, had traveled the world aboard massive cargo ships like the SS *Flying Dragon*, SS *Vanguard*, and the *Coastal Nomad*, shipping raw goods and materials from Calcutta, Guam, and the Philippines. Like his older brothers who had served in World War I, Percy had a compact physique, standing five feet, seven inches, sporting tattoos on both arms. With a shock of dark hair and blue eyes, Percy Cone was a true believer in Psychiana.[131]

Frank had met Ethel Cone in 1932. "I remember that I had talked with this lady," he wrote in his Advanced Course #2, "on a tour of the Pacific Coast cities."[132] He added that Ethel "was a wonderful little lady" and that "her husband sails the seas and is not at home all the time."

But on April 11, 1933, Percy was home in San Francisco when Ethel's health took an alarming turn for the worse. Desperate, Percy sent a cable to Robinson.

SKSNM -- SAN FRANCISCO
DR. FRANK B. ROBINSON
PSYCHIANA MOSCOW IDAHO.

MISS ETHEL CONE IS DANGEROULSY ILL   PHYSICIAN HAS GIVEN HER OPIATES   SHE IS CALLING FOR YOU TO HELP HER URGENT.

The following day, Frank sent his reply: "AM REMEMBERING ETHEL CONE LOOK FOR IMMEDIATE IMPROVEMENT." Still her condition worsened, prompting Percy to phone Robinson at home.

"I received a telephone call," Robinson recalled,

at about 2:30 in the morning to be exact, and the telephone call was from San Francisco. Naturally it was a case of life and death or this family would not have called me at that hour. However, I care not what the hour may be, if it is a serious matter, my students are welcome to call me and I shall be more than willing to respond.[133]

Over the phone, Robinson assured the Cones of Ethel's full recovery. On his words alone, Percy and Ethel held fast. That night passed, and then a few days ensued before Ethel could write again. "Four days ago you were called upon for help," she began, "and it was impossible for me to express just how serious my case was at the hour you heard from us over the phone," she wrote. "And you said you would certainly do all that you could do." The situation, she added, had grown grim. "The Physician was here, and waiting to take me to a hospital for an immediate operation, and HE SAID I COULD NOT LIVE. He informed us that I was DYING THEN, with my bowels in a strangulated condition, which condition came on very suddenly." Ethel was likely suffering from a strangulated hernia, which in 1933, as now, was a potentially fatal condition. "I asked if he could not wait until I could get in touch with you. He told me that I could not live anyhow but I said I would live for MY LIFE WAS GOD." Her early morning phone call to Robinson, she testified, was all that she needed. "IN ONE HOUR AFTER YOU SPOKE OVER THE PHONE I WAS RESTING SO EASILY THAT I COULD RELAX AND BREATE EASILY, AND NO ONE IN THE HOUSE WITH ME CAN UNDERSTAND HOW I AM STILL ALIVE AND ABLE TO BE UP." Ethel Cone's apparent recovery was proof positive that the God Law worked. "This demonstration," she wrote, "has brought to one physician at least what it means to know the Power of God, as the God you have so patiently been trying to teach me and others of. The physician's name was Dr. W.H. Banks and he said he was amazed." Cone then offered her recovery story to Robinson as a kind of advertisement for the powers of Psychiana, an offer he took at once.

"The time was ripe," she added,

> for me to show my faith in what I had learned and I knew I was part of the Living God, and if you have anyone who is afraid to trust in the God you are teaching, will you kindly refer them to me[?] For I can PROVE, by a responsible physician and other witnesses, responsible eye-witnesses, that every word is the plain truth, only I am not telling you HOW LOW MY LIFE WAS AT THE HOUR YOU TOOK COMMAND…If you had not been a channel for the Living God Spirit who was working through you, I would not be here to write this letter

of thankfulness and gratefulness to you. For God alone, through you as His channel, raised me from my bed and again I express my gratitude.

I remain gratefully yours,

Ethel Cone[134]

CHAPTER 11
Faith Factory

Incorporating a Psychiana medical service was an idea that preoccupied Robinson in the spring and summer of 1933, prompting him to establish an exclusive hospital for Psychiana students. "I am happy to inform my students," Robinson announced in the June 1933 *Psychiana Quarterly*, "that there now exists in Moscow a beautiful Clinic where the best medical and surgical advice of which we are capable may be obtained by our students." Though in its infancy, the Clinic and its operations, Robinson boasted, would soon "be known the entire world over, for here the scientific and ethical practice of medicine and surgery will be combined with the healing power of the Living God."[135]

Heading up the Psychiana medical services was Dr. Charles F. Magee, a graduate of McGill University in Toronto. At the announcement of Frank's clinic and its chief doctor, critics might have rightly asked, what kind of doctor would align himself with Psychiana so publicly and in such a small town?

A Canada native, Magee had served in World War I as a medic, once writing home about how a visit to the Canterbury Cathedral had resonated with him. "It's the finest, grandest, most impressive sight I have ever seen," the young medic reported. "When we used to read about the Archbishop of Canterbury," he added, "I did not realize how it would feel to be on the spot."[136] In 1914, two years before his enlistment, however, Magee had been charged "with performing an illegal operation upon Madame Phila Martin" in Vancouver. The jury deliberated for two hours but could not reach a verdict. Magee was released on "two sureties of $5000 each and his own personal bond of $10,000."[137] After the war, Magee ran into more trouble. In September 1919, then in Ottawa, he had been "charged with issuing too many prescriptions for liquor in one person." In this case, he simply failed to appear in court.[138] Six years later, Magee was living in Moscow, Idaho, and again practicing medicine. But in February 1925, he

"PSYCHIANA" CLINIC

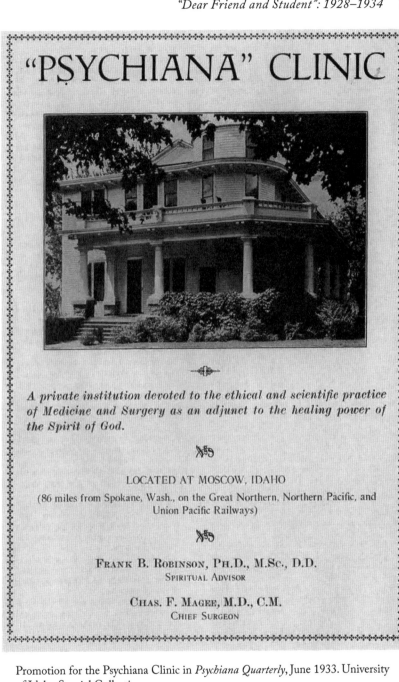

A private institution devoted to the ethical and scientific practice of Medicine and Surgery as an adjunct to the healing power of the Spirit of God.

LOCATED AT MOSCOW, IDAHO

(86 miles from Spokane, Wash., on the Great Northern, Northern Pacific, and Union Pacific Railways)

FRANK B. ROBINSON, PH.D., M.Sc., D.D.
SPIRITUAL ADVISOR

CHAS. F. MAGEE, M.D., C.M.
CHIEF SURGEON

Promotion for the Psychiana Clinic in *Psychiana Quarterly*, June 1933. University of Idaho Special Collections.

faced a malpractice suit in the death of local resident Willie Mary Sprouse. Alex Sprouse, the deceased's husband, sued Magee, and the case climbed to the state Supreme Court. Ultimately, Dr. Magee escaped prosecution and continued to practice privately.[139] It was sometime after this trial when he was approached by Frank Robinson, who was then scouting for a doctor willing to endorse Psychiana and sign on as its chief physician.

It is likely that Robinson identified with Magee, for the two of them were not entirely dissimilar. Ambitious men with Canadian ties and military service in the medical ranks, each had been trying to outrun embattled and controversial personal histories before landing in Moscow, Idaho.

In the early 1930s, Magee, his wife, Dawn, brother in-law John, nurse Hazel Norton, and cook Rika Enneking lived and worked in a derelict mansion two blocks north of Psychiana's world headquarters.[140] "Dr. Magee," Robinson wrote, "is known throughout the Inland Empire as perhaps the cleverest physician and surgeon we have. He is a man of deep religious convictions and more than that, he has an abiding faith in God, and when you find a physician who recognizes the fact that the Spirit of God is behind all healings, you are fortunate."[141]

Treatment costs at the Psychiana Clinic, Robinson advertised, would be low. "We are making charges at the Clinic as reasonable as we possibly can. I have no surplus money and therefore this Clinic must be on a self-supporting basis. I am not interested in making money out of it." Nevertheless, running even a rudimentary clinic was still an expensive endeavor. All "physio-therapy or X-ray or other treatments" would be billed at "the regular rates set by the American Medical Association," Robinson added. "Whatever medicines may be necessary will be provided and charged for extra." Of course it was the pharmaceutical department that stood to make Robinson money. "I own a drug store in Moscow and will see that the charges of these medicines are as low as is consistent with good business."[142]

The June 1933 *Psychiana Quarterly* also included the Clinic's mission statement: "The Psychiana Clinic is an institution for the scientific, medical and surgical treatment of the human body and mind under the supervision of the most competent physicians and surgeons we can find. It is conducted according to the highest standards of medical ethics and scrupulous care is given to see that these standards are observed." Single rooms in the Clinic with meals included cost students $5.00 per day. "Ward beds,"

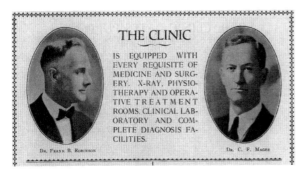

THE CLINIC

IS EQUIPPED WITH
EVERY REQUISITE OF
MEDICINE AND SURG-
ERY. X-RAY, PHYSIO-
THERAPY AND OPERA-
TIVE TREATMENT
ROOMS. CLINICAL LAB-
ORATORY AND COM-
PLETE DIAGNOSIS FA-
CILITIES.

Dr. Frank B. Robinson   Dr. C. F. Magee

Frank Robinson and Charles Magee as presented in the Psychiana Clinic article in *Psychiana Quarterly*, June 1933. University of Idaho Special Collections.

also with meals included, cost $3.00 per day. A private nurse was available for an additional $5.00 per day. For those students who were unable to travel to the clinic in Moscow, Robinson had devised what he called a Mail Consultation Department. Students were encouraged to complete a form detailing their symptoms, and mail it in. Dr. Magee and Robinson would then offer a diagnosis and advice for $5.00, and return their consultation via post.[143]

While launching the Clinic in the summer of 1933, Robinson also began rethinking his entire printing operation, which, next to payroll, was his single greatest expense. From the earliest days of Psychiana's operations, Robinson had outsourced his heavy print loads to George Lamphere, the publisher of Moscow's only newspaper, *The Daily Star-Mirror*. Robinson reportedly doled out over $2,000 a month to Lamphere, making Psychiana Lamphere's most lucrative customer.

"Two thousand dollars a month was a lot of money to pay for printing," Robinson later wrote. "Yet I did not know how to get around it, as this sum was in addition to our two multigraph machines." Three crews each worked an eight-hour shift so that their printing operations could run around the clock. Still, it was not enough. "We could not keep abreast of the demand for the Teaching." Robinson was at an impasse financially and technologically. If he wanted to expand his operations (and he did), he had to figure out how to radically reduce his printing costs. For whatever anxiety this bind brought Robinson, it also thrust him to the fore of a critical juncture in his thinking, for few people understood the power of the written word quite like Robinson did in 1933.[144]

Robinson's promotional savvy seldom squared with the more conservative tenor of his adopted hometown, however, often galling Moscow's more prominent residents. A telling moment in this ongoing standoff can be traced to the large signboards Robinson had erected on the highways leading into town. "MOSCOW, IDAHO," the welcome signs read, "Known the World Over as the Home of Psychiana—the New Psychological Religion."[145]

In the late spring of 1933, when the lilacs still hung heavy on the branches in Moscow, Frank Robinson stood at the intersection of American commercial power. Ink on paper was the prevailing form of media; the printing press was the best technology; the postal service provided the premier delivery system; and advertising had become the corporate doctrine. Lacking control over the most critical aspects of his operation, Robinson began looking beyond Lamphere for his printing needs.

Serendipitously, Frank had heard that William Marineau, a former senator and then-publisher of the *Elk River News*—a nearby small-town daily—was selling his printing press. By integrating a press into his business, Frank could cut Lamphere (and all other middlemen) out of the picture, and retain total control over his media enterprise.

It was late spring when Robinson purchased the press and had it moved by tractor-trailer forty-five miles west to Moscow. Having established a fully operational printing plant, Robinson was now free to print what he wanted when he wanted, and funnel the savings back into expanding his operations, including his newly established clinic.

But for Robinson, merely owning the printing press was not enough. His ambitions only grew. He had the money, equipment, facilities, and personnel to do nearly anything he could dream up. That is when he chanced on another audacious idea. On June 8, 1933, *The Spokesman Review* covered the new development in the otherwise quiet college town. "Moscow to Have New Newspaper," read the headline.[146]

A town of scarcely 5,000 residents, Moscow now had a second daily paper, *The News Review*. Marineau would serve as editor, leaving Frank with the title of publisher. Thirty days after Frank bought the printing press, *The News Review* was rolling out on a regular basis, threatening the very existence of the *Star-Mirror*, the erstwhile hometown paper. The sudden development leveled a devastating double-blow to publisher George Lamphere. Not only had he lost his biggest printing customer—Psychiana—but now his newspaper was fighting for its life.

Robinson's two-pronged offensive sparked an intense local rivalry, the reverberations from which were felt throughout the community. Alf recalled the reaction to his father's launch of the newspaper. Its genesis, he wrote, immediately "split the townspeople into two warring factions."[147] And those factions broke along political lines. Robinson was—when it was expedient—a Republican, and Lamphere, a Democrat. But the divisions skewed in other ways, too. Many of the town's legacy families viewed Frank as a showboat and charlatan. After all, he was still an outsider whose murky background raised questions about his trustworthiness. Lamphere, on the other hand, was a local through-and-through, a household name, and bona fide Moscowite. The more charitably minded townspeople saw Frank and his business as credits to the community, and viewed Lamphere's protestations as general grouchiness.

For the paper's inaugural issue, titled simply, "Our Introduction," Frank addressed the community's tensions head on.

> We are here to fight no one. Our editorial policy will be peculiarly our own. We shall defend what we believe to be right and shall denounce what we believe to be wrong. We shall respect the opinions of others, at the same time having opinions ourselves. In other words, while this paper will enter into no controversy with anyone, it will have a backbone of its own, and will not hesitate to fearlessly stand up for the right.[148]

More salvo than salutation, Frank's introduction seemed to have codified rather than curtailed the simmering tensions.

That same summer, Mildred Hensley, twenty, logged her shifts in the Psychiana advertising and mailing building. She did not believe in Psychiana. None of the employees did. But Mildred needed a little extra money because she was "between teaching positions," as she put it, and office work appealed to her. "My experience in the Psychiana 'factory'," she recalled, "consisted of addressing envelopes, using a magnifying glass and finding names in alphabetical order from the Los Angeles, New York, St. Louis telephone directories." She had seen Frank Robinson around the offices, shuffling through papers, sorting mail, and attending to the printing equipment. But she did not really know him. "I did not know Mr. Robinson well enough to carry on a conversation with him," she said. Her immediate interactions were limited to her co-workers and supervisor. "There were several young girls working in the office," she remarked, "and I remember his 'hard-nosed' woman office manager who really rode herd on our output of mailings."[149] That manager was Juanita Tisdall, a twenty-three-year-old veteran of the Psychiana workforce.[150] Like Robinson's personal secretary,

Juanita had worked for Frank since the early days of Psychiana. The daughter of a local businessman, Juanita demanded constant output. For the first two weeks in the "factory," Mildred recalled, she had to "type 200 envelopes an hour, 50 every 15 minutes, all day, for two weeks."[151]

Frank was running two campaigns that summer. One was advertising for the course material, and the other was to offer shares of Psychiana to investors. "At the time," Mildred remembered, "we were circularizing prospective purchasers of Psychiana literature and stock to bring in revenue." For the remaining two weeks that Mildred toiled away in the Psychiana mailing factory, her job had switched. "The next two weeks, we stuffed the envelopes. It was not the most inspiring work," she added. Mildred was impressed, she said, by the amount of mail that came in and how it "brought money from people in all parts of the country." But as impressed as Mildred was at the magnitude and diversity of mailings, she was also dubious. "I remember wondering what kinds of people these were, and being turned off when I ventured to ask for details on Mr. Robinson's background, and professional degrees."[152]

Beulah Herrmann also worked in the Psychiana factory, and had a somewhat different take on Robinson and his business. "All of us that worked there definitely felt Robinson was very nice." Like Mildred, however, Beulah found the work to be "monotonous"; however, she was quick to point out, "but then again, it was a job." And like Mildred, Beulah also remembered the supervisors cracking down on the girls to churn out mailers. "We mailed thousands and thousands of letters a day," she added. "We had to sort them, just like they do in the post office." The supervisors, she said, "expected us to do an awful lot. If we put out 35,000 mailers a day, they thought we should put out 40 or 50,000 in a day."[153]

One of the more peculiar rules, or "regulations" of working for Psychiana, Beulah recalled, concerned the Psychiana literature itself. The workers were not allowed to read any of the materials. "And of course if one of the supervisors seen it [caught a worker reading the literature], why, she would always come over and bawl 'em out."

Further, if anyone from Moscow, Idaho, or nearby Pullman, Washington, requested Lessons from Psychiana, those requests were to be ignored. "If there was any from Moscow, we threw them out," she recalled. "Moscow and Pullman and towns around close, we threw them out. That was regulation." The rationale? According to Beulah, it was because Robinson knew that "people of Moscow didn't go along with him or his beliefs."[154] Robinson claimed that he did not want to sap the local congregations of their membership. More likely, he did not want the local citizenry to really know what he was selling, or to somehow use his teachings against him or his family.

Psychiana Lessons were produced in a separate Psychiana building, while the mailers and advertising were produced in yet another building, the one in which Mildred and Beulah worked. The building's interior was split in half. "In the back of our building," Beulah remembered, "was where all the printing machines was, where they done all the printing and folding." It was Goldie Campbell who ran the printing and copying department. The size of the operation required a dedicated manager. Campbell, a Moscow native, wore a no-nonsense bob, a mannered gaze, smart clothing, and the look of someone always moving at a high-clip. Daily she oversaw the monstrous output of Psychiana's state-of-the-art machine: a brand-new Set O-Type multigraph machine.[155]

Once the materials rolled out from the network of printing presses and the multigraph, workers wheeled the mailers into the front half of the building where Beulah's crew set to work on them. "Most of the time we had four or five different folding things that we put in an envelope, and then they were put in these envelopes that were already addressed." The pressure to mass-produce came, in part, from logistics. The mailers had to be assembled, sorted, and stamped. "It had to be done and delivered to the post office each day so they could be sent out." At peak times, Beulah recalled, the workload was staggering. "Lots of times I know that we mailed as high as 65 and 70,000 a day."

Frank poured a substantial portion of Psychiana revenues into buying lists of names from advertising clearing houses. "A lot of people yet today wonder how they get an advertisement in the mail," Beulah said. "Well, it's very easy for me to know, because that was one of my jobs." The lists came in heavy boxes, she remembered. "I opened up the boxes by the hundreds and hundreds." The names came from all across America and points beyond. St. Louis. Baltimore. Fargo. Tampa. Little Rock. Tucson. Beulah and her coworkers sent the mailers to "everyplace in the United States," she said, "and around the world." She remembered too that they mailed them "to different places in Europe and different islands."[156]

Frank pumped even more advertising money into pulp westerns, detective, and science-fiction magazines. Frank regularly advertised in *Western*

Psychiana employees assembling Lesson packets on a revolving table. Undated photo. University of Idaho Special Collections.

Aces, Western Trails, 10 Story Detective, All Star Detective, Western Short Stories, Spicy Mysteries, Phantom Detective, G-Men, and *Skyfighters.* These same magazines also happened to feature the short stories of an up-and-coming pulp and science-fiction writer named L. Ron Hubbard.[157]

Psychiana employees were given a one-hour lunch, Beulah said, and one fifteen-minute break per day. "We could either take it in the morning or we could take it in the afternoon and only two of us went out together and that was it." The money, however, was good relative to the times. "When I started," she said, "I was getting sixty some dollars a month but that was pretty good pay at the time." Robinson ensured that his employees got raises, too. He also understood that his employees lived on strict budgets and they needed a steady income. "If we were out a few days sick, he never docked our pay." If they called in ill, Beulah said, "we still got paid." Sixty dollars a month was in fact a respectable wage in the Great Depression, when the national annual average wage for women workers was around $500 and twice that for men. Beulah made over $700 annually by comparison, and she was not even one of the higher-paid employees. "The girls that did the typing, they got more pay, and of course the supervisors got more pay," she added. "That was during hard times, but that was pretty good pay for us."[158]

CHAPTER 12

"The Magic Wand"

London, England
July 16, 1933

In his apartment in the six-story sandy-hued stone building on 20 Jermyn Street, Geoffrey Peel Birley put pen to paper. It was a Sunday and Birley was on holiday in England, visiting with friends and relatives. The London papers had been abuzz with conspicuous, if not alarming, changes in the German government. "Hitler's Latest Edict," was one headline that stuck out in the *Western Morning News.*[159] "Last night the fiat was sent forth in Germany, on the authority of Herr Hitler, that the Fascist greeting alone is in future to be the official greeting between civil servants. The handshake thus passes out as a form of greeting, and instead of extending a hand, the true German will now extend his arm upwards." The reports coming out of Berlin did not seem top of mind for Birley, who seemed rather upbeat on a warm day when Wimbledon was in full swing.

My dear Dr. Robinson—

I haven't written to you for sometime but I think of you nevertheless every minute of the day. I have before me your letters of the 26th of June & July 1st. I was simply astounded with your printing press & the paper & the lightning activity with which you managed to dismantel [sic] the plant, move it from Elk River, over the mountains, reassemble it in Moscow & print the paper, & all this in 30 days.

You mentioned that Mr. Marineau was a hustler & by jove he is a hustler. I hope you will both accept my profound congratulations over this piece of work. It's the finest piece of business I've ever heard of.

The building of the new newspaper & printing plant is magnificent. Many thanks for the photo & copy of the newspaper. I was tremendously impressed with that modern building. It's far nicer than anything I'd ever imagined it would be, & as for the paper, well it is a knock out & no doubt about it.

'Boost for Moscow!' Eh? Well that's the sort of talk I like. It's a real wizard. Everyone seems to have made a rush for that paper, especially the advertisers, Ford, General Mills, etc. etc.[160]

Birley's letter sheds light not only on Frank's growing operation, but also on their ongoing financial arrangement. "Will you please let me know how much of the Psychiana stock is still outstanding because if you are short of funds I may be able to help you buy some of it in October or November." He then made a note of Frank's savvy advertising campaigns.

I also am exceedingly happy that I saw your advertisement in the *Physical Culture* magazine. I was bound to come across one of your ads sooner or later but I'm glad I did it early on. In fact I must have been one of the first of your foreign students. I'm exceedingly glad of our agreement & I assure you [that] you won't be dissapointed [sic] in the funds I shall remit."

Addressing the economic instability in America, Birley added, "This fall in the dollar has somewhat favored the conversion, as I shall have to sell sterling & remit you dollars. I shall have @ least £10,000, which say @ exchange 4.60 to the £. Means $46,000—it may be more, I cannot say yet."[161]

All told, Birley seemed genuinely pleased with their arrangement. However, the same letter suggests that the relationship had not always been on a solid footing. "I am all the more happy over our agreement," Birley confessed, "when I look back & think of what I call the 'black period' which was the time when I received 2 damaging & utterly unfair reports about you. I cannot tell you how these reports shook me & how unhappy I was over them. But one of the luckiest things I ever did was to tear up these documents & throw them in the wastepaper basket & trust in my own intuition, which proved to be the right guide." Birley then closed the letter on a bright note citing his pleasure in knowing that "the Roosevelt administration is so popular." It is impossible to know exactly what those two "damaging" documents contained, or, for that matter, who sent them to Birley's attention. But it seems clear that the contents were severe enough to cast Psychiana's venture capitalist into a "black period."[162]

In a postscript, Birley made mention of positive changes in his life since Psychiana found its way into his world. "There is just one other item

I wish to mention & that is that ever since I got in touch with you, things have gone well. It was as if you brought a magic wand into my life & I'm not forgetting it."

CHAPTER 13

Under the Banner of Advertising

On August 3, 1933, Moscow's Presbyterian minister, Clifford M. Drury, published an article about Psychiana and its founder for his church's circular, *The Presbyterian Banner*. He wrote the article in part because he had been watching the growth of Psychiana over the course of nearly four years, and in part because of his personal connection to Robinson. "I met him and his family soon after he came [to Moscow]," he wrote, "and have known him intimately these intervening years."[163] Unlike other ministers who disparaged Robinson and his Movement, Drury took a wider if occasionally naïve view. Of Psychiana's uncanny success in such lean times, Drury's message was clear and fair. "Such a movement...deserves to be known and studied by Church people, and especially by ministers," he wrote. "It cannot be lightly dismissed with a sarcastic remark."[164] For Drury, the rise of Psychiana and other alternative religious movements was less a cultural fluke than a symptom of modernity, something warranting examination.

Drury deserves credit for taking Robinson's Movement seriously when it was widely dismissed by the ministry at large, but his article was unwittingly flawed only because he was a trusting man (part of his job) and took Robinson at his word. A graduate of the San Francisco Theological Seminary and one-time pastor of the American Church in Shanghai, Moscow's Presbyterian minister had no reason not to believe Frank Robinson, particularly when it came to biographical details.

"Frank B. Robinson was born in New York City 48 years ago," Drury wrote. "In his teens, he put himself through a school of pharmacy in Toronto." His religious convictions, Drury noted, led him to enroll at McMaster University. "He was ordained to the Baptist ministry, and for some six months was engaged in evangelistic work. However, due to doubts he had regarding many facts of the Christian religion, Robinson gave up the active work of the ministry."[165] Those doubts, however, did not prevent Robinson from finishing his studies at McMaster, at least according to this account. "Dr. William James, the famous psychologist of Harvard, had been invited to give the graduation address to the class of McMaster University to which Robinson belonged," Drury added. "This contact led to a friendship which lasted many years. It prompted Robinson to study psychology."[166]

Robinson's formal education evidently did not stop there. "For three years, 1915–1918," Drury added, "he attended the College of Divine Metaphysics, from which institution he received the degree of doctor of divinity and, recently, the honorary degree of master of science…He has traveled abroad, during which travels he has visited Palestine."[167]

The *Presbyterian Banner* article on Psychiana is at its best when Drury relies on his own perceptions. In this, some of his insights are spot on. Frank Robinson, he observed "is both greatly hated and greatly loved," "he is a man of unusual vitality and endurance," and he "is a born advertiser" who understood the power of branding his product. "So far he is jealously guarding the use of the name Psychiana and is forbidding any unauthorized person to go out on a lecture platform under this advertised name."[168]

Robinson knew the power of advertising more than most and was willing to pay handsomely for it. He was also shrewd enough to understand that advertising the amount of money he paid for advertising was, itself, a potent form of advertising. "During the past 30 days," Drury continued, "the advertising bill of Psychiana, Inc., has been in the neighborhood of $10,000."[169]

Broadcasting the often exorbitant amounts of money that passed in and out of Psychiana was—in Robinson's mind—not only evidence of Psychiana's efficacy in tenuous times, but was as important as advertising the Movement's core messaging. Stripped down to the basics, money was the message.

As for Robinson's personal salary, Pastor Drury informed The *Presbyterian Banner* readership that the Psychiana "corporation is now paying him $500 a month." A $6,000 annual salary in 1933 was six times the national average for men, and twelve times that of women. "It is interesting to note that the original stockholders have received to date 115 per cent return on their investment, besides the compensation which the Dr. himself has received."[170]

Robinson's personal importance was also central to the article. "One of the unexpected developments of his teachings was the call for his assistance in faith healing Telegrams and long distance telephone calls coming in by the score," Drury wrote. "So many visitors came to Moscow to see him that he had to advertise for them not to come, as they interfered with his work."[171] If the article is to be believed, droves of Psychiana students were flocking to Moscow, their mecca, even before the Clinic had been conceived. Like so many of Robinson's claims, the pilgrimage anecdote carried the peculiar distinction of being brilliant ad copy because it was almost impossible to verify.

Robinson was in such high demand, the article pointed out, that he was obliged to crisscross the map. "Frequently he takes long trips to see some particular patient whose case has excited his sympathy. He now drives a fine Auburn twin-six car."[172]

━━━━━━━━◆━━━━━━━━

Despite Frank Robinson's indulgences and the controversial nature of his Movement, Clifford Drury gave Psychiana, its leader, and—most importantly—the students the benefit of the doubt. "Surely here is a movement," he wrote, "of which we in the Church should take cognizance. Some of his criticisms of the Church are justified. Even though many disagree with

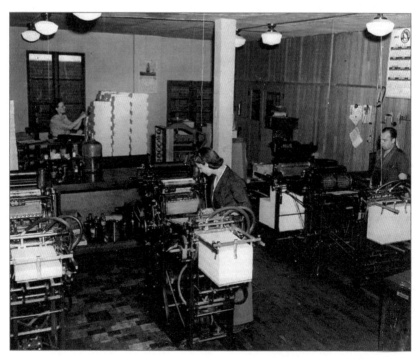

Psychiana printing plant, circa 1933. University of Idaho Special Collections.

him frankly and emphatically on many points, still we must recognize that he is giving to thousands just what they want."[173]

To what degree Robinson himself urged Drury to write an article for the *Presbyterian Banner* is not known, but it is almost certain that Robinson would have viewed the piece as free advertising. Surely he sensed, too, that the best way to sell his official biography—especially the fictionalized parts—was to have someone else sell it for him; better still if that person was a credible man of faith.

———————◆———————

Outside of Moscow and its environs, times were still hard. Two days prior to the publication of Clifford Drury's article in *The Presbyterian Banner*, President Roosevelt enacted the National Recovery Act, a bold piece of legislation that would forever change the landscape of American labor. An increase in wages and reduction in working hours were central tenets of the legislation. Consumers were encouraged to engage in business only with those proprietors whose companies bore the blue eagle stamp of the National Recovery Act. Tycoons and mid-level businessmen who had ridden the high tide of American extravagance in the 1920s were now loath to conduct business under Roosevelt's stringent rules. The cleverest of proprietors found ways around the mandates, however, earning them the name of "chiselers." Just two days after the NRA became law, and on the same day Clifford Drury's article ran in *The Presbyterian Banner*, Benjamin Roth took once more to his diary. "A good many 'chiselers' are doing business under the N.R.A. sign," he complained, on August 3. "One restaurant in town boosted wages of waitresses from $8 per week (plus meals) to $14 per week and then charged back $1 per day for meals. The government promises to prosecute such violations."[174]

Always adapting to a changing political landscape, Robinson joined up with the National Recovery Act, ensuring that all Psychiana materials bore the ubiquitous blue eagle stamp. "Recognizing world conditions," Robinson wrote in the December issue of *Psychiana Quarterly*, "the President has gathered round him men of vision and experience, and these men, though but human, are trying hard and effectively to put into operation a code known as the N.R.A. This code is designed to bring this country back to a semblance of normalcy, which semblance of normalcy we have had in years gone by."[175]

————————◆————————

Concurrent with stamping the NRA insignia on all Psychiana materials, Robinson launched the first of many campaigns to put the squeeze on delinquent students. In his inaugural tactic, Robinson sent a loop of string to each student in arrears. He then instructed the pupil to tie the string around his or her finger as a reminder to pay their bill. A second campaign included a straight pin. "Dear friend and Fellow-Student: Here is a pin, a magic pin…I am sending you this pin so that you can use it to pin your check for what you owe me to a letter…I must have these payments. I must have yours. You promised, through the mail, to make certain payments every month. On the strength of that promise, I have sent you my Lessons—merchandise, if you will."[176]

Robinson added further that, "it is not fair to take my Lessons, and cause me to spend money to help you, and you not live up to your contract you sent through the mail." Other letters struck a more intimidating tone. "[O]ur records show that you have no inclination to liquidate this indebtedness. That you may be fully cognizant of the law, may I suggest that obtaining goods with an intent to defraud constitutes a criminal act, and, if fraud is proved, the person committing it is liable to imprisonment… Don't force me to turn your account over to our legal department. We have one."[177]

For Psychiana students trying to eke out a living, Robinson's threats alongside the promises on how to become healthy, wealthy, and happy, would have been jarring and dissonant. But the more astute students—delinquent or not—should have expected nothing less from a psychological religion that regularly advertised itself so frankly as a machine of capitalism.

CHAPTER 14

No Narrow Creed

Those early years shaped Frank Robinson into a creature of exacting habits. He woke at 5:30 every morning, had breakfast with Pearl, and was at work by 7:00 a.m.[178] Robinson's office then was handsomely appointed with large windows that allowed sunlight to fill the room, lighting up the new linoleum flooring. The office featured two desks facing each other: his and that of his secretary, Marjorie Reynolds. This place was his command center, ground zero for Psychiana. A heavy black phone waited on his desk alongside a telegraph machine. Pens, notebooks, newspapers, and an ashtray were all within reach. A radio stood against the wall between his desk and Marjorie's.[179] Across the hall, Head Cashier Hazel Plasket and her assistant would wheel a cart containing the previous week's earnings into a room that housed Psychiana's large cannonball safe.

Every day, for two hours straight, Robinson would lock his office door to meditate. He burned incense and listened to the gramophone. "I'm a natural-born thinker," he liked to say when talking about his meditations. When the workday was finished, he was home by 6:00 sharp, where he "stripped down to his shirtsleeves," as one reporter noted.[180] After dinner, Robinson sat down at 9:00 to his massive, newly installed pipe organ (whose pipes occupied two entire rooms in the home's basement) and played his favorite songs. (Johann Strauss II's "Tales from the Vienna Woods" was a favorite.) At 10:00 p.m., he listened to the news on the radio, after which he got ready for bed by drinking a large glass of cold coffee. In his free time (of which there was little), Frank liked to take Alf on drives around the rolling hills of the Palouse, or go fishing. When he was not reading something work-related, he preferred pulp detective novels. He seldom went out in the evenings, save Monday nights, when he attended Moscow's weekly Rotary Club meetings downtown.[181]

Robinson deserved to be called many things, perhaps, but lazy was not one of them. His immense output of writings—books, Lessons, ads, brochures, newsletters, weeklies, monthlies, and quarterlies—bears this out. And the typos peppered throughout his oeuvre speak to a man driven by the bigger picture, and not its particulars. He was impatient, frequently hot-headed, and, according to Alf, gave "poor attention to detail," often lacking "good judgment."[182]

That he was a constant one-man show is without question. Robinson's hunger for self-promotion bordered on megalomania. On Monday, March 12, 1934, Robinson opened the doors of Psychiana's operations for his first-ever "Open House." It was unseasonably warm, and for weeks Robinson had been distributing around Moscow a twenty-two page booklet titled, "PSYCHIANA: Visitors Week." A classic Robinson publication, it opened to a full-page portrait of himself bedecked in a luxurious fur coat, posh homburg hat, and a smoking pipe. "FRANK B. ROBINSON," the caption read, "Ph.D., M.Sc., D.D."[183] The second page was a photostatic copy of a letter to Robinson from Eleanor Roosevelt. Dated January 3, and printed on White House stationery, the letter read,

> My dear Dr. Robinson:
>
> Thank you so much for the lovely basket of flowers. It was indeed very thoughtful of you and we are deeply appreciative. With all good wishes that this New Year will bring you happiness and prosperity, I am very sincerely yours, Eleanor Roosevelt[184]

Although no doubt penned by a staffer, the form letter was all the evidence Robinson needed to prove his celebrity status and national standing. "Dr. Robinson has correspondence with many world leaders," the caption read. "The above letter is one of several received from the White House."[185]

The open house booklet would not have been a true Psychiana product without a show of financial figures, purporting to represent revenues and costs. Included, too, were the photographs and job descriptions of everyone who worked for him either in Psychiana's operations, at the *The News Review*, or in his two pharmacies. Taken as a whole, the booklet read like a business prospectus and slim yearbook of office workers all in service to one man.

Two weeks after the Psychiana open house, Frank Robinson was back on the lecture circuit, taking the stage in massive auditoriums such as Spokane's Masonic Temple. There, on Easter Sunday 1934, Robinson was prepared to present his most recent Psychiana lecture, a bulwark against a country spinning out of control. Just one day earlier, the notorious gangster John Dillinger—armed with a submachine gun—blazed his way out of an apartment building in St. Paul, Minnesota. He would be dead inside three months.[186] That same day, in Bremerton, Washington—across the state from where Robinson stood—six people had been bound, gagged, robbed of their jewels, and shot to death.[187] And Idaho's *Post–Register* was reporting that a "Half Million U.S. Workers Promised Increase in Wage."[188] If anything, uncertainty was a sign of the times, which is why President Roosevelt had started calling for a New Deal.

Uncertainty, curiosity, and a desire for something new may have explained the large crowd at Spokane's grand and columned Masonic Temple. Still, the crowd was unusually large, given that it was Easter Sunday. The high-ceilinged auditorium was packed as Robinson stared out over the immense gathering from his center-stage lectern. On stage, he was flanked by two Psychiana secretaries, poised for transcription. Behind and above him hung a dazzling sign, ablaze in electric lights, that read, "Psychiana, The Religion of Power." The lecture was broadcast over several radio networks. Standing at the temple's doors, well-dressed Psychiana workers handed out postage-paid postcards to everyone who entered, inviting them to request information on membership in Psychiana. The postcards also functioned as clever data-gathering tools for advertising and marketing.

By every outward measure, Frank Robinson epitomized the successful American businessman, a sure stand-out in Depression-era America. He was tall, confident, fatherly, wealthy; he wore an easy smile, and spoke freely in a calming, often erudite voice. Standing at the lectern beneath the bright auditorium lights, Robinson waited for the crowd to quiet down before he started his lecture. While attendees settled into their seats, Frank made a couple of introductory remarks, including a call for donations to be given to the "Kiwanas Health Center for undernourished children."

> I have trodden on the toes of some orthodox people who choose to still believe that the earth was made in six days. That same type of person also believes that a deep sleep was caused to come over one person and a rib was taken from him and another person made. In the first place, it

isn't true. I think that sort of religion and the picture as it exists today, ladies and gentlemen, isn't true. We are living in a changing age. We are living in an age of new deals. Practically over night new deals are given to us. We have a new deal in our social structure. We have a new deal in our economic structure and yet, in the realm of religion, we are supposed to stand perfectly still and believe what the old philosophers taught five thousand years ago, originating and told by some old sheep herder or other. Let me say this to you, if the Realm of religion does not progress and does not grow it will fall by the weight of its own error.[189]

Inherent in that "error" Robinson argued, was conventional religion's disavowal of science. For Robinson—an ardent Darwinian—science, and not antiquated myths, was the surest way to the True God. As for the anti-science crowd who saw the discipline as a threat to their religious institutions and way of life, Frank Robinson had an answer for them.

Science has taken nothing she hasn't returned a hundred fold. She has taken away the cosmogony of Genesis and has given us astronomy and geology. She has taken away the creation of man and has given us his evolution. She has taken away the story of Babel and has given us Philology. She has taken away miracles and has given us natural law and order. She has taken away superstition and ignorance and has given us law, order and scientific truth.[190]

As Robinson grew bolder and bolder in his lecture, cutting broadly across sacred texts and beliefs, the audience shifted in the auditorium. The lecturer on stage was just getting warmed up. "But the work of science is not yet finished," he said, his voice carrying easily to the back wall of the temple.

The dogmatic walls of the old faith must be torn down, for they cumber the ground where the edifice of a greater religion is being built. Already the foundations are laid, and on those, the spiritual architects are building better and grander than the world has ever known, a temple of universal religion. No narrow creed shall bar the sacred portals of that temple, but her doors shall ever stand open to all who seek the truth. Within her sacred walls the devotees of every faith may worship in security. No cup of hemlock there shall still the philosophic tongue. No crown of thorns shall there adorn the brow of innocents. No burning fagots shall there await the doubting mind. No voice shall there command except the still, small voice of reason. On the sacred altar of this temple will rest the Bible, and every other book that has inspired the heavy heart of man.[191]

The primary question Frank posed to his audience that night—"Did Jesus Christ rise from the dead?"—stemmed from Lesson 8, enumerating all previous religious saviors who had themselves been crucified, and was meant to shock and provoke.

It was a lot to lay on a largely conservative audience in Spokane, Washington, on Easter Sunday. But something about Robinson and his voice, his measured cadence, his blonde hair and blue eyes, his charm, his elegant suit, those Psychiana lights winking wildly above him—something about the spectacle of it all held the crowd spellbound. That is when Robinson took his lecture to another level.

> Now if we accept the resurrection of Jesus Christ as being true, then we are bound also to accept the resurrections of these other crucified Gods as being true, for there is no more evidence that the resurrection of Jesus Christ was a fact than there is that the resurrection of these other crucified saviors was a fact…And mind you, the corner stone of Christianity is based on the resurrection of Jesus Christ. If Christ did not rise from the dead, then Christianity cannot be. If it is possible to prove that Christ did not rise from the dead, then automatically you prove that Christianity is but a superstition—a superstition born of ignorance and credulity, of piety and fraud, of weakness and cunning of priestcraft and persecution and the entire structure will crumble at your feet.[192]

Some of the more conservative audience members became agitated. Some waved their hats dismissively. Some heckled from the balconies. Others walked out.

Robinson kept his resolve. He had struck a nerve, which was exactly what he had intended. As the few spectators filed out of the temple, Robinson addressed them briefly. "I rather expected this," he said. "I don't know if there are any more here, but if there should be those here who can't stand scientific truth, right now is a good time to get out. The rest of us will have a grand time."[193]

Whether out of tacit courtesy or genuine interest, the majority of the large crowd remained seated, waiting to hear what Robinson had to say next. "Christ did not rise from the dead on that fabled Easter morning," Robinson concluded. "Nor has anyone risen before for the simple reason that it is a law of God that a dead man has the universal habit of staying dead…The promise of the future welcomes the steps of those who want to see the Light," he added. Gripping the podium, Robinson gazed over the remaining crowd and continued on.

> Now, ladies and gentlemen, all over the world, the Light—Spiritual Light—is breaking and it is not breaking through any religious organizations of any kind. It is breaking because men and women are getting tired of these old superstitions and are getting rid of all that bologna. Let's find out some natural truths about God.

The crowd broke into applause.[194]

> I do not say this under any consideration to be sacrilegious at all, but I am out to try and preach a logical, sane religion and not one dependent upon hearsay evidence of that kind for its proof. If we take a common sense view of the thing…then we will find what Spiritual Truth there is to be found.[195]

Robinson's closing remarks landed squarely on his belief that he was the target of persecution advanced by the clergy, and that his teachings were putting his life in danger. "At the present time," he confided to his audience, "there are three different movements to try to upset Psychiana. You know, I have to go around with a loaded thirty-eight under my arm and I have a state permit to carry it. That is what they think of me in the church organization."[196]

The evening lecture at the Masonic Temple ended with a standing ovation, white hot camera flashes, glad-handing. Psychiana staffers working the doors ensured that no one left the temple without his or her Psychiana postcard and the chance to enroll as a student.

CHAPTER 15

Passport to Trouble

Not long after the Easter Sunday lecture, two suited men entered the
Psychiana offices on Sixth Street and Main on a spring day, and
asked to meet with Dr. Robinson. They were inspectors James J. Doran
and Stephen Howard Morse from the United States Postal Service. At
forty-seven, Doran was a matter-of-fact, scowl-faced man who had been
promoted to Chief Postal Inspector over New York City just a year earlier.[197] For sixteen years, tracking down mail fraud had been his mission,
and his reputation would prompt one paper to describe him as a "grizzled
crime-tracker of many famous cases."[198] Doran would go on to serve as
the country's top chief inspector of the postal service in Washington, DC.

Twelve years Doran's senior, S.H. Morse had more than thirty years of
experience as a United States Postal Inspector. Morse was well groomed,
white-haired with an expertly trimmed mustache, and he spoke with a Massachusetts accent. The equivalent of a cybercrimes detective today, the legendary
investigator had worked in Philadelphia, New York, and San Francisco before
landing in Eugene, Oregon, where he first learned of Psychiana and its leader.

Bearing the distinctive look of G-men, the inspectors informed Robinson that Psychiana was being investigated for possible mail fraud. Over the
following weeks, they spent eight-hour days in the Psychiana Headquarters, combing through towers of paperwork with, one can imagine, their
shirtsleeves rolled to the elbow, cigarettes smoldering in trays on desks.
Their mere presence would have made for tense days, while the employees
processed thousands of Psychiana mailers under the already-rigid direction
of their supervisors against the thunderous clacking of typewriters and
bells. Finally, after two weeks of investigation, the inspectors snapped their
briefcases shut and announced their departure. Doran would be handing
the case over to Morse's regional team, though they would stay in regular
contact. Morse, a postal inspector veteran of some three decades, assured
Robinson he would be in touch.[199]

Two months later, on June 18, Frank Robinson walked into the bright and airy Moscow post office to submit his application for a passport. After exchanging pleasantries with the postal workers commenting, perhaps, on the amount of their work that was devoted to his Movement, he entered the office of Harry Thatcher, who, at seventy, still enjoyed working.

Robinson asked for a signature on the application, making it official.

"Are you going away?" Thatcher asked.

"I am taking a little trip abroad."[200]

Making good on his promise to his half-sister Mary, Robinson was planning an extended trip to England where, among other things, he would look up his father. A visit to Geoffrey Peel Birley in Alexandria, Egypt, was also in order.

The application was standard issue and straightforward. For place of birth, Frank Robinson wrote New York City, adding that his parents had lived in New York between 1883 and 1887. Not only did he stipulate that his mother was deceased, but he claimed his father was dead as well.

Strangely, Robinson further stated that he and Pearl had married on September 30, 1921, and not on November 26, 1919, their actual wedding date. When the application asked if the applicant had ever been out of the United States, Robinson gave an unequivocal "no."[201]

Having no reason to question the veracity of the application's contents or its submitter, Thatcher reached for his seal but could not find it. It was upstairs, he said. Thatcher dismissed himself to retrieve the seal with Frank trailing behind. Then upstairs, the application was signed, sealed, and witnessed before Judge Hodge. Frank shook hands with the gentlemen, and that was that. He was officially cleared to leave the country.[202]

Alfred later wrote that his father's seemingly benign passport application "triggered repercussions in our lives for the next seven years."[203]

With his passport application submitted, Robinson went back to work, making arrangements for a vacation that conspicuously did not include his family. Among the arrangements was a brief announcement to his students about his forthcoming trip. A holiday had been previously out of the question for Psychiana's leader. "I have been too interested in my students," he wrote in a mailer, "and have been too interested in the message I have to proclaim to the world." But it was time, he told them. "Now that the

Movement is well under way and now that the mechanical end of it is in very good hands here, and feeling the need of a little change, I have decided to take a vacation of one or two months." Prevaricating, he added, "I don't know where I shall go. I may take the car and start out, having no destination in mind, or I may take an ocean voyage to England." He then made clear his reasoning for the special letter. "I feel that every student should know of this vacation," he added, "and this letter to you will explain why any letters you write to me, personally, cannot be answered until after September first."[204]

For Robinson, announcing a vacation was more than just a housekeeping item. It was a veiled boast at a time when most people did not even have jobs from which they had the fortune of taking a vacation. And like all of Robinson's brags, his vacation was further evidence that the God Power was working.

———◆———

It was an unsettling time to be visiting Europe. On June 17—one day prior to Robinson's passport application—Franz Von Papen, Vice Chancellor under the newly installed Chancellor Adolf Hitler, broke ranks and delivered a prescient and incendiary speech to Marburg University students, warning them of the Nazi party's "unbridled control of the Reich," as one paper put it.[205] Hitler immediately instigated a complete media ban of the speech. Three days previously, a casually dressed Hitler had met with a perfectly uniformed Mussolini in Venice. The meeting was profound in its failure, and yet both dictators were careful to spin the meeting as victorious. "Premier Mussolini was so impressed with the results of his personal meeting with Chancellor Hitler," one paper reported, "that he intends to repay the call."[206] Back at home, President Roosevelt was celebrating the one-year anniversary of the National Recovery Act, while steel workers were striking across the nation. In the months leading up to that morning when Frank filled out his passport application, diarist Benjamin Roth observed how, "The country is now threatened by huge national strikes in the auto and railroad industries." Other diary entries reflected a similar outlook. "The stock market remains stagnant," he wrote. A month later, he observed how "investigations and indictments of men high in finance are still the order of the day."[207]

———————◆———————

On July 1, 1934, Frank Robinson stood at the landing station in New York waiting to board the American Line's SS *Hamburg*, a fast and formidable steamer bound for Southampton. It was a Sunday, the skies were gray, and a light rain fell on the docks.[208] Despite the gloomy weather, throngs of well-wishers looked on as the passengers made their way to the canopied gangplank marked "HAMBURG AMERICAN LINE" in large white letters. As always, Frank's attire was fit for the opera, with overcoat and stylish fedora. On the *Hamburg*'s passenger list, Frank identified his occupation as simply "writer."[209] The night before, in Nazi Germany, Hitler had activated "Operation Hummingbird," the brutal and bloody coup that, over the next twenty-four hours, would lay waste to his detractors, real and perceived. A late city edition of *The New York Times* reported on the gruesome events out of Berlin under the headline, "Hitler Crushes Revolt by Nazi Radicals." But as of that first day in July, it was still too early to know the extent of the atrocity, later referred to as the "Night of the Long Knives."[210]

While deckhands steered carts teeming with luggage, vessel horns bellowed in the harbor and the sea-brine air hung sharp in the weak, gray light. On this Atlantic crossing, Frank Robinson would not be eating cakes of flour and water down in the rancid squalor of steerage. This time he had a stateroom and dined on an array of first-class offerings, ranging from deviled sardines on toast, boiled salmon with béarnaise sauce, Long Island duckling with oranges, and prime rib of beef. This time Robinson would drink coffee in the opulent 300-seat dining room, read in the stylishly appointed library, and visit with other gentlemen in the walnut smoking room.[211]

News over the wires during Robinson's four-day voyage included Germany's overnight transformation into a "military dictatorship," violent labor strikes on San Francisco's waterfront, and a prominent minister's call for "safeguarding" America's "soul" with "genuine religion."[212] Reverend Dr. Hugh K. Walker of the Presbyterian Church told his congregants that, "There are so many schemes, such a multitude of novel prescriptions, such an army of practitioners seeking to heal the hearts of the people, that some persons have voiced the opinion that the nation is taking the place of God." There was the tenor of alarm in the minister's speech. "If we forget God," he said, "and put any one, anything, or any system in His place, we shall surely perish."[213]

———————◆———————

When the SS *Hamburg* reached the littorals of Southampton, it was Thursday, July 5, 1934, Frank's forty-eighth birthday. It was the first time he had been on English soil since he had boarded the *Parisian* thirty-one years earlier. His first goal was to reconnect with his father, whom he had listed as dead on his passport not even two weeks earlier. But the elder evidently refused to see his estranged son. Frank also tried—and evidently failed—to get in touch with his half-sister, Mary, with whom he had been writing. Something there, too, had gone awry. Frank's youngest brother, Arthur—an officer in the British Navy—later wrote, rather obliquely, "It is not for me to pass any comment on Fathers [sic] action. But it is to be regretted that you did not get in direct touch, either with Mary, or at my home address…This much I must say, neither Mary, Mrs. J.H. Robinson nor myself agree with [Father's] attitude and had I been in England every effort on my part would have been exerted to avoid what is bound to be great regrets."[214]

Reverend Robinson's refusal to see Frank undoubtedly leveled a deep blow to the otherwise unflappable Psychiana guru. From that point forward, John Henry Robinson—alive and well in England—would be utterly dead to Frank.

Departing the English countryside, Frank boarded a train bound for Italy. He wanted to see Pompeii. He loved the Italian culture and its history in particular. From Pompeii, he traveled again by train to the port city of Genoa. After nearly a week of sightseeing and touring, Frank Robinson booked passage to Alexandria, Egypt, on the SS *Esperia*, the most luxurious steamship then plying that route.

———————◆———————

When Robinson stepped off the ocean liner at Alexandria's Western Harbor—the largest in the Mediterranean—he was greeted by twenty-four-year-old Geoffrey Birley. The temperature would have been in the upper seventies, the landing stage crowded. Egypt in the summer of 1934 was in its roaring heyday of British colonial indulgence. During the days, the frolicking crowd of cotton barons, artists, diplomats, writers, and bohemians would gather on the beach near the Corniche to sunbathe, drink cocktails and tea, and listen to jazz on hand-crank gramophones. During the evenings the young colonials threw arabesque parties and impromptu piano concerts in their villas, where they would drink champagne beneath pluming palm fronds in their lush courtyard gardens. Costume parties were common, as were sporting excursions. Socialites like Birley were members of the exclusive Royal Yachting Club, and actively engaged in tennis, cricket, and sailing.

Robinson checked into the six-story Hotel Cecil—the most regal hotel in the city. A cacophony of motor cars, donkey carts, and clattering electric trams sounded in the streets of Alexandria while Frank settled in and washed up in his room. From his balcony, Psychiana's leader could see the water of the Mediterranean Sea, the palm-lined city squares, and the rooftops of several city mosques. Frank was to dine with the Birley family that evening at their home on 4 Rue Carver, in Bulkeley, an upscale suburb in Ramleh where many of Alexandria's British colonials resided.

Not unlike their peers, the Birleys would have maintained house-keepers, cooks, waiters, and chauffeurs, most of whom would have been Bedouins. Few details exist regarding Robinson's first encounter with Birley and his parents, Kenneth and Rachel.

Kenneth Peel Birley, at sixty-six, was more reserved than his nephew and business partner, Sir Edward Peel, the flamboyant sportsman and colonel. Some seven years after Robinson's visit, Peel and his wife would host author Roald Dahl for an extended visit at their villa on Rue Ptole-mees, while he recovered from an accident. Dahl, who had had an affluent upbringing, was astonished by the wealth of the Peels, whom he considered "probably the nicest and richest people" in Alexandria. Dahl, who slept on "silk and linen sheets" at the Peel villa and "listened to Beethoven, Bra-hams, and Elgar on the gramophone," noted their "five cars, large motor yacht, and twin-engined aeroplane" as conspicuous markers of wealth.[215]

Kenneth Peel Birley, on the other hand, was not as hip, as one expa-triate party-goer once noted in his social diary: "Afterwards to Kenneth Birley's Ball at San Stefano. A big affair, birthday party for his daughter, but left an impression of the commonplace. He didn't spare expense, but there was no style or chic."[216] The party-goer attributed Birley's lack of style or chic to his being rather conservative and too, well, British.

There is evidence to suggest that the Birley's dinner with Frank Rob-inson in Alexandria was strained and awkward. His own flamboyance and showmanship were likely at odds with Kenneth Birley's more moderated temperament. And then there was the obvious difference: everything about Robinson screamed American nouveau-riche. He lacked the ped-igree, formal education, and nearly innate savvy to read the deeply coded social cues that comprised the currency of the British ruling class. He was seen as brash and loud. And worst of all, the Birleys saw him as untrustworthy and greedy. But their good manners did not seem to betray their true judgments of this unusual guest. It is easy to imagine Frank Robinson—eighteen years Kenneth's junior—misreading their pretended niceties for sincerity. Making matters worse, Frank Robinson needed more capital from Geoffrey. Even as the Birleys, Peels, and Robinson enjoyed a leisurely day at the Royal Yacht Club, Geoffrey knew the difficult news he inevitably had to deliver to his teacher. Everyone in the party knew. The only one who did not know was Frank.

In all, Frank Robinson spent nearly a month abroad. Toward the end of July 1934, Robinson said his farewell to the Birley family and made his way back to Southampton, England. On Sunday, July 29, 1934, Frank Robinson boarded the sleek SS *Bremen* for passage to New York. Four days later, as the crew of the *Bremen* prepared for arrival in New York, German President Paul Von Hindenburg died at home in Neudeck, East Prussia, after a prolonged bladder ailment. Gaunt and smoky-eyed with a burly white mustache, Germany's "Grand Old Man" had died at age eighty-seven. By the time Robinson inched his way down the gangplank to New York's landing station, wiry paperboys were yelling, "Extra! Extra!" over the mass of voyagers. The August 2 front-page headline from *The New York Times* read "Hitler Takes Presidency." Another paper added this portentous detail: "It was announced from Berlin, immediately afterwards, that a law had been adopted by the German Cabinet that in future the offices of Chancellor and President shall be together, and Herr Hitler has taken over both."[217]

Back in Moscow, Idaho, Frank Robinson rolled up his shirtsleeves and got to work. The first order of the day was to issue a press release to his daily paper, *The News Review*. The subject of the press release was his trip to Europe. "Palouse Welcome View to Traveler," the resulting headline read. "In 18,000 miles of travel [Robinson] found nothing that compared to the Palouse district for prosperity and peace, Dr. Frank B. Robinson declared Monday upon his return from a seven-week tour of Europe and the Mediterranean." (In typical Robinson fashion, he embellished his four-week trip, making it seven.) Other falsehoods followed. "Visiting relatives in England and Scotland for several days, he made a brief swing through Paris. Dr. Robinson said he was in Berlin the night of Hitler's 'purge' of the nazi [sic] party," the article continued, "and on advice of the American consul left immediately." The article portrayed Robinson as a global elite. "In London he talked for half an hour with the Prince of Wales." His trip, the report noted, was cut short on account of his sick daughter, Florence.

The article, like his passport, was riddled with untruths, part of a great and roving fiction of the self-made man in a self-destructing America.[218]

Chapter 16

"There Will Be No Peace in Our Household"

The Manor Farm
Bledington, Kingham, England
September 22, 1934

It was on a Saturday at the Birleys' rural farm in Kingham, Oxfordshire, when Geoffrey resolved to write a letter he had no doubt been dreading. It had been nearly two months since he had seen Robinson in Egypt, and he was presently enjoying the English countryside. The Birley home was a stylish brick villa set in an idyllic countryside some eighty miles west of London. A bucolic village, Kingham was a still, quiet place, almost portrait-like, interrupted only when the sharp blue feathers of a kingfisher darted here or there.

In the Birley villa, however, things were not nearly as tranquil as the greater English landscape. Relations between Frank Robinson and the young cotton merchant had been strained ever since Robinson's visit. According to that morning's *Manchester Guardian*, business was likely the reason for Birley's stay in England. "A general meeting of all firms in the Egyptian [cotton] section has been called for next Tuesday at the headquarters of the Federation of Master Cotton Spinners in Manchester."[219] Although Egyptian cotton markets had stabilized in recent days, the American cotton market was still precarious, having emerged from labor strikes and nettlesome negotiations under the new rules of the National Recovery Act.

In short, finances weighed heavily on Birley's mind. "My dear Frank," he wrote. "I have received your letter of the 20th August, together with the written note saying I have no responsibility in the business, etc., for which many thanks. As usual, in that last letter you show yourself the true friend that you are." Birley then got right to the heart of their tension. "With regard

107

to my father," he confessed, "things are not going to be so easy. He wants me to break away from Psychiana just as soon as possible, because, in spite of your last note, he still considers I shall be held responsible if things go wrong." Hinting at some interaction Robinson may have had with Kenneth Birley, Geoffrey remarked that his father "is a very difficult man to argue with, as perhaps you discovered." The young cotton baron continued to wring his hands, caught between two fathers. "I told him it will not be easy to find another buyer who could take my place, especially during the present times and on this he agreed but he is still extremely worried over the whole affair, though there is absolutely no reason for him to be so at all."[220]

Trying to lift the mood the best he could, Geoffrey suggested that his parents were not exactly a united front on the matter. "I think my mother realizes this," he added, "because she was very impressed with you." After conveying that one small ray of promise, however, Geoffrey leveled with Robinson.

> I really do not know what to do in this matter, but I think the best thing would be for me to try to arrange a journey to the States sometime next summer. It would be a pity not to go and I think I should go. As it will be extremely difficult to find another person to take over my holding in Psychiana, it might be a good thing to try to sell my share in either one or two of the drug stores. Would you yourself take them both over or else find another partner for one or both? If I could sell my share in these drug stores it will show my father that I am gradually retiring from Psychiana.[221]

The pressure on Geoffrey would have been severe and constant. "I know there will be no peace in our household until I finally retire altogether," Birley confided. "It seems amazing that he can be so anxious over the whole question, but he is." Evidently, Frank had suggested that Geoffrey encourage his father to read one of Robinson's most recent books as a way of bringing him around. "I think it a very nice suggestion of sending my father a copy of the latest book you have just written. Whether it will induce him to alter his views or not I do not know, but think not."

The more Geoffrey thought about his role in the Psychiana empire, the more he started to share his father's worries, though he tried to keep his feelings somewhat veiled. "You mentioned in your last letter something about getting everything registered in your wife's name," he wrote to Robinson. "What advantage does this give you in the business, and why have you got Psychiana registered in your wife's name and not your own? Again, what would my position be if something were to happen to you?" Tempering his alarm, Birley continued: "There is not a likelihood of anything happening of course, but what would my position be in this event?" Birley's letter then took on a kind of circling movement, coming back to his departure from Frank and the Movement. "As the chances appear so slim of my working with you in the States, I think it would be advisable for me to gradually sell out my holdings in Psychiana, starting first of all with one of the drug stores. What possibilities would there be in this respect?"

Not wanting to end the letter on a sour note, Geoffrey wished his teacher well. "I shall never forget your sporting journey to Alexandria and the short stay you had there. Sincerely yours, Geoffrey Birley."[222]

Part III
MESSIAH ON TRIAL
1934–1937

CHAPTER 17

American Spectacle

There can be little doubt that Robinson viewed Birley's letter as anything but undesirable news. Where the Birleys were panicked by Geoffrey's large holdings in Psychiana during America's Great Depression, Robinson could not have been more upbeat. After all, Psychiana's year-end revenue for 1934 totaled $422,000, or nearly $8 million in today's dollars. "Our family was living affluently in 1934," Alf Robinson later recalled, "enjoying the luxury of a handyman to take care of janitorial duties at the newspaper, pharmacies, Psychiana buildings, and to perform the maintenance and yard work at home." In an otherwise stagnant economy, the Robinsons wanted for nothing. "Mother had a live-in maid," Alf continued, "and our family was able to travel and enjoy luxuries."[1] It was at the end of 1934 when Frank Robinson purchased his Duesenberg for $7,000, though he bragged it cost him $10,000. "The Duesenberg was an immediate attraction in the area," Alf wrote. "Dad would always lend his special car for commercial displays where it always drew large crowds." Robinson loved large, adulatory crowds.[2]

———————◆———————

On Sunday, January 6, 1935, Frank Robinson stepped into the opulent lobby of the famed Biltmore Hotel in Los Angeles with a troop of suited bellhops trailing behind him. The weather glass reported fair conditions with a high of 61 degrees. Los Angeles residents welcomed the moderate weather after the winds and flooding in the previous days. In Los Angeles's theater district, Zane Grey's *The Last Roundup* was showing that night, along with Bing Crosby's *Here is My Heart*, while Katherine Hepburn starred in J.M. Barrie's *The Little Minister*.[3]

After Robinson checked in, he made himself comfortable in his room. His lecture was scheduled for that evening. The suite's complimentary copy of the *Los Angeles Times* reported on a number of news items that would have roused Robinson's interest. There had been a development in the Charles Lindburgh Jr. abduction case. Defense attorney for Bruno Richard Hauptmann—the German immigrant accused of the "Crime of the Century"—claimed that he had the names of "four persons" who were the "actual kidnappers."[4] Everyone in America was following the case.

Other news entailed peace talks between Italy and France, Cornelius Vanderbilt's third marriage, and anti-trust suits against a majority of Hollywood film companies. In recent days, nearly 2,000 pounds of meat had vanished from one of Chicago's Relief Supply warehouses. The American Federation of Labor was in Washington, DC, negotiating a shorter workweek, and on the same page of the *Times*—situated above ads for "T.D.'s Antiseptic Mouthwash," "Hershey's Breakfast Cocoa," and "Enders' SPEED razor blades"—an ad read, "Dr. Frank B. Robinson—Founder of 'PSYCHIANA'—Brings to Los Angeles a 'NEW VISION OF GOD.'" He was speaking at Trinity Auditorium. "Doors Open at 7 P.M.," the ad declared. Admission was $1.10—about $20.00 today—and the lecture started at "8 Sharp." The ad was bold and featured the portrait of Psychiana's founder smiling at the camera.[5]

That night, however, when Robinson entered the expansive Trinity Auditorium on West 9th and Grand Avenue, he was greeted by sparsely occupied seats. He checked the time. It was still early. Robinson paced the floor, glad-handed the few people who had paid the price of admission to hear about the "new vision of God" he had advertised. Some in the audience were already Psychiana students and were thrilled to see their prophet in the flesh.

As the eight o'clock hour struck, Robinson took the stage, disappointed by the small crowd. Still he smiled, summoned his inner salesman, and endeavored to spin the crowd size into something potentially positive. "I am happy to be with you in Los Angeles this evening," he began. He rested his hands on the podium and continued. "But I am sorry that my stay cannot be longer. I would like to see the house filled and am sorry I did not have the opportunity to give more publicity…A lot of my students have asked me if it will be possible to see me," Robinson said. "I am at the Biltmore Hotel and you can call me sometime Wednesday." Business aside, Robinson got right down to the central thesis of his lecture.

The question we are to consider is the all-important question of God, and if your experience was anything like mine, it was the old orthodox boyhood story, which I respect, of the God far removed from the human race, in the sky, manifesting himself on earth some two thousand years ago in the form of a crucified savior. As a child I accepted that story; there was nothing else I could do.[6]

Robinson said that he had challenged his professors in divinity school to provide him proof of the Christian god. They told him he lacked faith. "We have in this country nearly four hundred different operating religions," he told his crowd. "I heard a minister say this morning, 'I welcome you to join this church. All that you have to do to join is to believe in Jesus Christ.'" Robinson let his words sink for a split moment before carrying on.

If that is the requirement for membership, then how about the millions that have an entirely different philosophy for God's plan of salvation? If it only fits those who believe certain creeds and denominations, it is the wrong impression of God. The picture of God as he exists in the world hasn't come yet and there is a great tendency to make mistakes.[7]

Central to so much of what Robinson was writing about and lecturing on in the early to mid-1930s was debunking the Bible. It was tricky business. On the one hand, Robinson was a provocateur; on the other hand, he was a salesman. "My little boy Alfred goes to Sunday School," he said, "that is, he goes if he wishes to but is not compelled to and he usually goes because his friends go and he has a good time there." Subtly reassuring his audience, perhaps, that he was not an outright heretic, Robinson then turned to the Book of Matthew. "The other Sunday [Alfred's class] was told the story about the multitude being fed by a couple of little sardines and five loaves of bread. Alfred asked his teacher, 'Do you really mean to tell me that actually happened?' His teacher replied, 'Why of course.' Then [Alf] asked, 'Then you don't have any objections to my sending it in to Ripley, do you?'" Some in the crowd chuckled, others stirred uncomfortably. "Here is what I am getting at," he said. "When a Bible miracle appears to an eleven-year-old child to be funny, I am telling you there is none of the truth of God behind it, for when you know the God law as it exists you will find it the simplest power that has ever come into your life."[8]

As usual, Robinson closed his lecture with what was becoming a trio of themes: money, crowd sizes, and his persecution. "I am coming back in about three or four weeks and I have the Shrine Auditorium," he said, "and I am not going to charge for that. I put in considerable money last year and have given much of it away." Straying from the truth, Robinson boasted to his crowd, "Students write in and I simply send them literature whether they can afford to pay for it or not...I am going to fill the Auditorium three or four weeks from now," he promised. "That place will be packed to the doors. I am going to ask you people...to think of me and that Shrine Auditorium meeting and I am saying to you that we will make some of the churches in Los Angeles sit up and take notice by the power we will bring to this city."[9] Just then, Robinson changed tack, and made a rather strange accusation. "I am going to tell you a secret tonight," he confided. The crowd quieted down. Robinson waited a moment before speaking out over his podium. "The receipts of this auditorium were [gathered] five minutes before the lecture started. There is a sheriff sitting over there. He is going to take [the money] all away with him. My attorney is also in the building and he will have it back before tomorrow night." Then, shifting into third person, he added how the money was taken "purely to block the efforts of Dr. Robinson in this town and that is just the way to make Dr. Robinson fight."[10]

Given the high cost of his upcoming lecture at the Shrine Auditorium, the fact that he did not plan to charge admission, and the alleged confiscation of his entrance fees that night, Robinson clearly needed money to continue. "I want to get that auditorium and get it for about a week," he asserted. "It costs me $350.00 a night and I figure we can take up an offer for enough to cover that." Robinson wanted to be clear, however, that he was not out to make a profit, that his was no scheme or scam. "I don't want any money from anybody," he averred. "I want enough to get by on. I have no interest in Psychiana. The money that is taken in tonight is not mine and if I told you what they paid me it would surprise you. I am not interested in money."

As a couple of Psychiana workers passed collection plates around the Trinity Auditorium, Frank took in the sight beneath the house lights and drew his lecture to a close. "I will advertise in the papers and in between now and then please remember that Shrine Auditorium meeting and just keep quiet and let your thoughts flow directly to me and that Shrine Auditorium and let's see if we can't show Los Angeles what we know and what we are talking about."[11]

A smattering of applause came from the small crowd.

It was somewhat strange for Robinson—the roving "super salesman—

to face a diminished crowd when Psychiana in many ways was peaking in American culture. One explanation could be as simple as competition, for Robinson was not the only one working the religious/self-help circuit in 1935. That same night of January 6, not even four miles up the road at the massive Angelus Temple in Echo Park, megastar Aimee Semple McPherson—founder of the Foursquare Church—was keynoting the twenty-fifth anniversary of her mega-religion.[12] Like Robinson, McPherson was charismatic, attractive, and knew how to best harness the media to advance her cause. And like Robinson, she was not without her own controversies. Rumors of infidelities clouded her several marriages. Squabbles between McPherson and her mother made headlines. Finances were a constant problem, and when she was allegedly kidnapped in 1928, many suspected the supposed abduction was an elaborate publicity stunt. Still, thousands attended the celebration that night across town, and the event may have siphoned more than a few people who might otherwise have attended the Psychiana lecture.

Back at his hotel, Robinson sat down with a reporter from a local paper for an interview. Despite the low turnout, Robinson was in good spirits. He was, the reporter wrote, "relaxed in luxurious quarters."[13] Robinson recapped how his Movement had started, its rapid growth, and his future plans. The article related that "Robinson has come to Los Angeles to establish a world headquarters for the Psychiana Movement, a school of new religious thought." The reporter added that, "Robinson will build a $100,000 temple here. Architects already are at work on the plans. He will employ a large corps of assistants, he said, many of whom will come here from Moscow, where he has carried on the development of the cult."[14] *The Los Angeles Times* also picked up the story, adding that "Dr. Robinson said plans are being completed to transfer the headquarters of 'Psychiana' from Moscow to this city." The Psychiana Temple, or "Cathedral," as Frank called it, not only would serve as the center of the Movement's global operations, but also would function as a university campus for Psychiana students who wanted—and who could afford—to advance up in the ranks of Robinson's "dynamic" teachings.[15]

Robinson had already developed a more complex, pay-as-you-go system of teaching that had broadened in scope and risen in price to nearly $30 for a single set of lessons. Completing the first three Advanced Courses would cost Psychiana students over $1,500 in today's currency.

What is more, Robinson initiated a system of ordination, granting Doctor of Divinity degrees to applicants who completed all undergraduate and graduate Psychiana Lessons and paid all associated fees. Ordination candidates were additionally obliged to sign a lengthy oath of allegiance to the Movement, include the names and contact information for two references, and have their application publically notarized. (Four years later, Robinson added a financial disclosure schedule to the ordination application.)

Robinson's plan to build a cathedral in the heart of Los Angeles was a significant departure from a business model that was not only unique to Psychiana, but was also prescient in how it dispensed with "bricks and mortar" operations, relying instead on media and technology for distribution, sales, and membership.

———————◆———————

True to his word, Robinson scheduled five more nights of lectures—not at the Shrine Auditorium, however, but back at the Trinity Auditorium. And true to his word, he packed the venue nightly. (It helped that on this visit he was not competing with Aimee Semple McPherson, and more so that he was not charging admission.) Indeed, California was fertile ground for Robinson. Days after the Trinity Auditorium lectures, Frank broadcast his first-ever Psychiana radio show titled "Flashes of Truth," on KNX-Hollywood. The fifteen-minute program aired on Sunday evenings at 7:30 p.m. and was heard between numbers such as "Emil Baffa's Concert Orchestra" and "Judge Rutherford."[16] Listeners up and down the California coast heard the lilting, unassuming voice of the program host beginning the show. "Ladies and gentlemen," the host announced,

> in just a moment you are going to hear the voice of a man who will tell you some tremendously important facts—some AMAZING facts. The voice of the man who has made a discovery that is revolutionizing human thought, changing human lives—bringing happiness and success where discontent and failure were before.

The radio program was set up as a "dialogue" between what the script calls the "GUIDE" and Robinson.

> GUIDE: I'm going to be just a bit skeptical now—HOW does [Psychiana] enable a person to turn failure into success?

DR: Let me answer that by asking YOU a question. Do you know anything about a radio set?

GUIDE: Well, I know how to twist a dial.

DR: But you've seen the various devices that go INTO a radio set, haven't you?

GUIDE: Yes.

DR: Now, if I give you all the things you need—tubes, amplifiers and so on—could you put them together so that sitting here...you could hear an orchestra playing in New York?

GUIDE: No, I'm afraid not.

DR: Why?

GUIDE: Well, because I don't know the principle upon which a radio set operates.

DR: That's the answer to your question.[17]

————————◆————————

Robinson left California on such a high note that when he returned to Moscow, he convinced Pearl that they all needed a vacation to the coast. In June, they rented a summer home at Monterey Bay's Pebble Beach.

Like the Biltmore Hotel, Pebble Beach was a haven for celebrities, Hollywood movie-stars, and the super-wealthy. It was a groomed resort peopled with golfers in starchy whites amid the views of the famous Cypress Point. America's elite enjoyed poolside cocktails, swimming, and tennis. Children were enlisted in Pebble Beach's summer camps where they paddled canoes, learned archery, performed plays, and hiked trails.

A month earlier, on May 11, President Roosevelt launched the Works Progress Administration, putting millions of jobless down-and-outers back to work. That same month, just thirty miles from the Robinsons' vacation home, Dorothea Lange was stamping through crop fields photographing Filipino workers with long sleeves, brimmed hats and gloves, hunched in the sun, lopping lettuce heads from the brown earth. Beyond the green vegetable rows, Lange saw the destitute on the margins. "A trek of bums, tramps, single transients, and undesirable indigents out of Los Angeles," she wrote, were wandering ghosted highways in the Salinas and Monterey valleys.[18] Broken, dream-starved men tramped the forlorn byways of America's so-called El Dorado. Every few miles one could spot ramshackle camps of itinerant workers and their road-sick families. The images were haunting. Shanties and tents sprouting rusted stovepipes. Heirloom dressers parked on the sun-cracked earth. Dining room tables stood outside in the field grass and weeds while the rancid smoke of cook-fires hung in the stillness. Women slaved over washtubs of greasy water. Sickly children with dirty feet stared into nothingness. The god-fearing migrant workers who had not yet turned their backs on the Lord tacked signs onto shacks that read, in at least one case, "PENTACOSTAL CHURCH OF GOD."[19] They prayed at night, on bended knees beside their ratty cots and lumpy bedrolls, but the next morning everything was the same and nothing was different.

———————◆———————

At Pebble Beach, Frank Robinson caught up on his reading, took phone calls, wrote letters, dined on fresh seafood, and worked on new lectures. For Psychiana's leader, nothing could go wrong.

CHAPTER 18

"That We Should Enter Again into Our Partnership"

Seven Trees
44 Lubbock Road
Chislehurst, Kent
England
July 9, 1935

On the afternoon of July 9, Geoffrey Birley was staying with friends at Seven Trees, a sprawling four-story red-brick mansion tucked away in the idyllic greenery of Chislehurst, a village that, as its name suggests, seems to have been carved entirely from stone.[20] He decided to write Robinson. "My dearest, Frank," he began, "I received your letter from Pebble Beach this morning saying you will probably be back in Moscow soon," Birley wrote. "So I am writing to Psychiana direct."

As was his custom, Birley allowed for the usual pleasantries in his letter. "Many thanks indeed for…those excellent photos," he continued. "They are a real treat and help to show what a really remarkable development has taken place." The photographs Birley mentioned would likely have been of the Clinic or the new Robinson Professional Building that was underway in downtown Moscow. The tone and tenor of Birley's letter marked a conspicuous shift over the past year.

> I liked all those photos very much indeed and was greatly interested in them. I think the best one of the lot though was the picture of you in your car outside your house. It's a splendid photo and I like it immensely and if it had been autographed I should have liked it even better still. But all the photographs were excellent and I do appreciate them a whole lot. I am hoping you enjoyed Pebble Beach and had a good rest for a holiday.[21]

121

Birley then made a passing comment on a mutual friend. "I shall remember you to Tommy when I see him again," Birley wrote. "He is somewhere in Cardiff, in Wales, at the moment and I think I have his address." Birley was likely referring to former Heavyweight Champion of the World and Psychiana devotee Tommy Burns. Retired from the ring, the pugilist was living in England and had been following Psychiana for some time.

As for Birley, his own commitment to Robinson's teachings had far from faltered. In fact, his devotion seemed to have been rekindled. "I have taken the full Psychiana course over to England with me and have it here now," he continued. "I read the Lessons every evening." There in the Seven Trees mansion at Chislehurst, Birley read his Lessons in the library, perhaps, or in the privacy of his own room. "I still think that No. 4 is about the best of them all and that is the one I read most," he added.

But the God Law was not the only thing on Birley's mind that day. Word out of Germany was growing darker by the day, and Mussolini—a man Frank Robinson claimed to have spent personal time with on his European tour—was sharpening his sabers. "Have you noticed how your friend Mussolini is determined to start a campaign in Abyssinia?"[22] Birley asked. The young cotton merchant was right on point, for in that morning's edition of *The Guardian*, there appeared the headline, "Germany and the Abyssinian Dispute."[23] At stake, the paper noted, was the resolve of the League of Nations. "Signor Mussolini's determination to wage war upon Abyssinia means in the German view the end of the collective system of security," they announced. "Italy is determined at all costs to carry out her venture at the cost of a fifty years friendship with Britain, the heavy sacrifices of a colonial war, the danger of the disruption of the League, and the burial of collective ideas."

It was a story that had been on Birley's mind for a while. "Some months ago I had interesting talk with a man in the Sudan Civil Service and he thought war was bound to come unless a miracle happened." Birley's view was typical of British colonials.

Unfortunately thousands of Italians have to be sent home, suffering from malaria and new regiments take their places. Both Eritrea and Italian Somalia appear to be foul places. Hot, damp, fever ridden, no proper water supply. The Italians are getting their water from Port Sudan and shipping it to Massawa, a distance of 300 miles and are paying £. 8 a ton for it!

Birley was correct, however, that Mussolini's invasion justification, at least in part, stemmed from the crushing defeat Italy suffered from Ethiopia in the Adowa War of 1896. "In all the Italian speeches," Birley wrote, "reference is made to Adowa." *The Guardian* echoed Birley's sentiment. "Italy, it would be said here, is out for military prestige and determined to obliterate her earlier Abyssinian defeat." Then offering his views on the latest developments as something potentially useful to Robinson, Birley added, "This is the latest news from the Sudan and might interest Mr. Marineau." Mr. Marineau, of course, was the editor of Robinson's daily paper, *The News Review*.

If the political situation in Europe was unstable, so too was the economic outlook in America. Four days before Birley sat down at Seven Trees to pen his letter to Robinson, President Roosevelt signed the Wagner Act into law, thereby instituting the single most important piece of labor legislation in the history of the country. (Frank Robinson was staunchly anti-labor, later writing how "business enterprises are forced to deal with labor groups even though such dealings saps the very life out of the Constitution.") From that day forward, workers had collective bargaining rights, making labor unions more accessible to workers than ever before. While ambitious in scope, the Wagner Act (and the president's previous bills, for that matter) was still a gamble in the government's efforts to pull America back from the brink of economic collapse.

As for Birley's own financial situation, he seemed less panicked than he had been a year earlier. Indeed, he and Robinson were far from breaking off ties. In fact, they had been renegotiating Geoffrey's stake and role in Psychiana's operations. "I note with thanks that you have accepted my suggestion made sometime back, that if I join up with you in Psychiana as my intention is to do so, that we enter again into our partnership agreement." Birley underscored their financial arrangements going forward. "I refund you the $500 I am now receiving monthly," he wrote, "less $300 (received before as salary and interest on money invested) making in all $200 a month from the time the capital repayment began."

Closing up his midsummer letter at Seven Trees, Birley complimented Frank on a new publication Robinson was planning. "I see that you are producing a new illustrated booklet in which all the photos you sent me will be reproduced. It should be a great success. Best wishes, Geoffrey."

Robinson would likely have had Birley's letter in mind when he was writing an article for a forthcoming Christmas edition of *Psychiana Quarterly.* In "God and the World Mess," Robinson took aim at "civilization" writing in part that, "there is very little real civilization left. There is a thin shell or veneer, which we can call civilization for want of a better word, but as far as actual civilization goes, there isn't any. As I write this, there are riots and revolts in Egypt against British rule, and that certainly adds to the confusion of world conditions in Europe which already are charged with dynamite."[24] Robinson's British sympathies were in reference to the student riots in Cairo and Alexandria and the protests against British colonialism. Meanwhile, the British government was fuming at Italy's growing military presence in Ethiopia. "Great Britain's attitude on the Italo-Ethiopian dispute became clearer today as a result of the Anti-British riots in Egypt," a United Press cable read.[25]

As for Robinson, he only claimed friendship with Mussolini when it was politically expedient.

> The world knows what the "Mad Man of Italy" is attempting to do, and as I stand on the side-lines and watch history being made, I am of the opinion that praying will have mighty little effect on those conditions. This lunatic, who in my opinion is absolutely insane or drunk with military power, cares nothing whatsoever about human life. He defies the world, and so little is his regard for human life that he sends dynamite bombs, machine guns, tanks, and hundreds of thousands of soldiers equipped with high-powered rifles into another man's land, and ruthlessly slaughters uneducated savages who are totally unequipped to meet an opposing army equipped with modern methods of warfare. These modern methods of warfare I suppose are called civilized methods.[26]

Robinson then made something of a dour prediction in his article. "I don't believe the European question will ever be settled," he remarked, "until there has been a major catastrophe, which will involve practically every nation on the face of the earth." Exasperated, he added, "This is civilization. This is after two thousand years of prayer."[27]

CHAPTER 19
"The Suffering of Humanity"

St. Louis, Missouri
January 8, 1936

Edgar Giles Baity (or "E.G. Baity," as he signed his formal correspondence) was sixty-two, father of five grown children, married, and lived by all accounts a happy life—first at 4114 East Prairie Street in St. Louis, and then two blocks north at 4361 De Soto Avenue. On De Soto Avenue, Edgar and his wife, Marjorie Jeanette—"Nettie" to her friends—settled into a small, blockish, two-story, no-frills red brick apartment building.[28]

Six days a week, Edgar donned his official uniform: white dress shirt, snappy tie, slacks, brass-buttoned jacket, and his embossed, peaked cap with its insignia. Tall, trim, with blue eyes and dark hair, Edgar was a "motorman" for St. Louis's Public Service Company, the central nervous system of the city's streetcars.[29] He enjoyed his job and was paid well, too. "I make about $25.00 per week," he wrote to Frank Robinson. "So you see I'm not lousy with money—just getting by very nicely."[30] Edgar arrived daily at the "street-car barns" at Delmar and DeBaliviere, the Public Service hub of operations, ready to work. He was a company man through and through, having worked as a conductor for over twenty years, beginning with the United Railway Company before it was taken over by the Public Service Company.

St. Louis streetcars in 1936 were boxy creatures with ten side windows, cast-in doors, a monitor roof rowed with low-profile frosted panes, and a cyclops headlight. From his conductor's chair amid the clink and clatter of the street car, and the clanging of its bell, Edgar had a front-row seat to all the beautiful and broken sites St. Louis had to offer in Depression-era America. The grand hotels, whose Jazz Age luster seemed dulled by 1936, towered over the main drags. The Statler on Washington Avenue. The Chase on Kingshighway. The opulent Coronado on Lindell.

Edgar would have known the city by heart, its map burned indelibly in his mind. He would have known the daily hum and thrum of the Wellston Loop, the city's busiest transfer station. He would have known how passengers would pack the lines on North Grand Avenue before and after a Cardinals game at Sportsman's Park. In fact, when the Cardinals won the 1926 World Series in Game Seven, after Babe Ruth was tagged out while trying to steal second base, North Grand Avenue exploded into such a fury that Edgar had been inspired to write a short story for *The Motorman and Conductor* magazine. Titled "The Sadder and Madder Man," Edgar's piece was a faux-eulogy of "Bill Bailey," a motorman who had to flee the madness of St. Louis after the World Series. "And it came to pass," he wrote, "when Motorman Bill Bailey, by reason of avoirdupois, escapeth injury by the mob when the Cardinals winneth the world's championship, he sayeth unto himself, 'Verily, the people are demented! I will take a three days' and most of three nights' journey into the wilderness and waste my substance in riotous living! Selah!' So he gathereth all his possessions together in one place, loadeth them on a spring-wagon, hitcheth it to a Ford, and, with a loud noise, hitteth trail 61 in the night." From there, Edgar's tale traces the folly of his character's decision to abandon his career as a motorman.[31]

On warm and pleasant days, Edgar's car would fill with sunlight while passengers crowded on, armed with the day's papers. In the winter, banks of dense fog, mist, and sooty clouds of industrial and domestic coal smoke could make day look like night, forcing motormen like Edgar to fire up the cyclops lamp during the lunch hour.

Edgar Baity also bore witness to the darker parts of St. Louis in the midst of the Depression. He would have seen the endless lines of unemployed men outside the Volunteer for America building on 1604 Market Street, where they waited for food or work. They packed the sidewalks, too, at 2027 Washington Avenue at the Citizens' Committee on Public Relief. Failing those options, the rest of the jobless and forlorn crowd gathered outside the Civil Works Administration Office at 7805 Forsyth Boulevard. Beginning that January in 1936, thousands upon thousands in St. Louis feared being pulled off of the Relief Rolls.

Through it all, the streetcars lurched and clattered, their bells clanging out the cadence of the city itself. From point to point, and from transfer station to transfer station, the trolleys rolled along, sporting ads for cigarettes and sugar, movies and radio programs, soap and laundry powder.

After work, Edgar would have likely drunk coffee with the other Public Service motormen who frequented the diner across the street from the barns. It is a scene from a bygone era. All of them lined up at the counter with their peaked caps stylishly tilted on their heads, chatting about this and that, about the latest rumors of the Cardinals moving to another city, say, or about Ripper Collins's historic past season. If the diner had a radio, the motormen could have caught Eddie Randle's Orchestra on KWK, an episode of Popeye the Sailor on KSD, or Fred Astaire's "Top Hat, White Tie, and Tails" on any of the popular stations.

The service industry suited Edgar. He maintained an upbeat, can-do demeanor, and prided himself on his willingness to help someone in need. He was an optimist of the first order, all of his jars filled half-full. One of Edgar's claims to fame was his first-hand report on a meteor shower he had witnessed in 1930. After seeing the heavenly phenomenon, he dashed off a letter to Professor Edwin Brant Frost at Chicago's famed Yerkes Observatory. Professor Frost—the well-known bespectacled astronomer—forwarded Baity's keen observations to the University of Iowa, where researchers were compiling data on recent meteoric events. From that day forward, E.G. Baity's notes on the cosmic occurrence of June 12, 1930, would be permanently recorded in the annals of science. His observations were recorded, too, in the local papers, which would have been a point of pride for the motorman.[32]

Edgar saw himself as a helper. He had, in fact, helped at least two people make what he saw as miraculous recoveries by "open[ing] up a channel" to the "God Power." On that drizzly gray day in St. Louis, when the forecast called for a high of 35 degrees and more rain, Edgar had finished his route, gone home, and sat down to type a letter to his teacher in Moscow, Idaho.

"Enclosed you will find reports of two outstanding experiences with the GOD LAW," Baity wrote. "I am mighty proud of what little I do know about this wonderful Law, God, Father or whatever you wish to call it," he continued, "and am doing all in my power to find out more about it." Edgar could hardly contain his enthusiasm for Psychiana's teaching. It was as if he felt on the brink of a great discovery. "Dr. Robinson," he confided, "I know mighty little about [the God Law] but I sure get lots of happiness with that little." For Baity, money was not his first aim. "It seems my desire is more for healing," he reflected. "I have many successes in minor cases, and some failures. But I have enough success to make me want to go on and on until I become a perfect operator." Compelled to share his successes in faith healing, Edgar noted that, "In an emergency as in the cases reported, it has never failed." Edgar's desire was as genuine as it was selfless. He genuinely wanted to help those who were struggling and desperate for help. "Please do what you can to help me carry on and relieve the suffering of humanity," he wrote. "You are at liberty to use these reports in any way you see fit. I am pulling for you Dr. Robinson and may God bless you."[33]

The first report concerned an incident that Edgar encountered six months earlier. "Last July," he wrote, "a man came to me and said, 'They have taken my son-in-law to the insane asylum where he will undergo treatment for softening of the brain. Will you do what you can?'" Edgar told the man that he would do everything within his power to help. "Then he asked, 'Do you realize that you are undertaking a mighty big job? The specialists say they will do all they can but that they can offer us no encouragement what ever. That about one in ten thousand respond to the treatment.'"

Edgar allowed that he understood the magnitude of the situation and the odds, but he was also a true believer in Psychiana. "I answered, 'Brother do you realize the possibilities of the God-Power are unlimited? Jesus said that if you have faith the size of a mustard seed, you can move a mountain. Well, it shouldn't require near so much to heal a sick man,'" he told him. Baity wanted to make clear, however, that he was no faith-healer himself. "Understand brother," he said, "that I am not doing the healing. If I were, you know me well enough to know that the young man would be healed right now. All I can do is to open up a channel through which the Power can operate and let God do the healing." Once Edgar established his role in the healing process, he told his friend what to expect. "You and your family can help wonderfully to open the channel by expecting good results. When we have succeeded in clearing the channel, well, he'll just have to get well, that's all." Edgar then relayed the status. "Well, Dr. Robinson, the young man was pronounced cured, released from the asylum, has a good job, and is getting along better than ever."

The cured man released from the asylum was not Edgar's only instance wherein he invoked the God Law to an apparent successful end. A second case offered further proof of Psychiana's power. "Arriving at the street-car barns where I am employed as conductor," he wrote, "about three o'clock P.M., I heard that the wife of one of our motormen was in the hospital and that the family had just been notified to come at once as the lady was dying." Edgar had been married to Nettie for forty-two years, and he may very well have put himself in his coworker's shoes. "Dr. Robinson," he continued, "I have known this man for many years, even before his marriage, although I have never met his wife. I knew he was a poor man with several small children, I was deeply touched."

Even though he was about to begin his shift, Edgar readied himself. "I said nothing to any one but went to work on my car—concentrating," he reported. "The lady was unconscious, I had told no one I was trying to direct the mighty God-Power to her." Edgar wanted to make clear to Robinson that he acted alone in the matter. "No one knew it but myself. Yet about 4:30 P.M. I made contact—I got the assurance—Blessed assurance," he wrote. From 4:30 to the end of his shift, Edgar felt confident he had aided his friend's wife. "Next day I saw the husband's brother," he wrote. "I said to him, 'Your brother's wife is better isn't she?'" Edgar's question was almost rhetorical.

"'Yes,' he replied. 'But the doctors say it is only a question of a few hours at most—that there is no possible chance for her. You see, she had blood poisoning in her hand, it healed up and they thought it was well. Now they say that it was still in her system and has settled in her kidneys. She is also expecting to become a mother again.'" Edgar then asked the man if she had not started feeling better at about 4:30 the previous day. "'Well,' he replied, 'that's about the time they came out and told us she was rallying. But how do you know?'" Edgar told him with frank confidence. "'I made contact about that time and I felt like she was going to pull through. I'm pulling for her and that's the way I feel about it." Another day passed. Edgar saw the brother once more. The situation had not improved. She could die, he had said, within a couple of days. When Edgar finally met up with the woman's husband forty-eight hours later, however, everything had changed.

"I saw [the husband] the next day," Edgar wrote. "He said, 'I went over [to the hospital] last night, I saw her. She was conscious and was in no pain. But what do you think they told me the next morning? They called me up by phone and told me that after I left she gave birth to a baby boy. That both were just fine. She was running no temperature whatever. The doctors can't understand it.'"

"'No,' I replied, "they can't understand it.'" Edgar wrapped up his report to Robinson of the miraculous outcome. "Well," he wrote, "the lady is at home now fine and dandy."

Acting on Edgar's suggestion to use his reports any way he saw fit, Robinson featured Baity's two reports prominently in the following issue of *Psychiana Quarterly* under the simple title, "ONCE MORE—GOD."[34]

CHAPTER 20
Prosecution

Just a few days before Edgar Baity wrote his letter to Robinson in January 1936, Frank made plans to travel east. He was scheduled to give a lecture in New York and then travel on to Washington, DC. Frank had recently purchased sixty acres of land west of his adopted hometown of Moscow, and then donated the parcel to the county for a recreation area. "Robinson Park,"[35] as it would be called, would also feature a dam and reservoir for boating, swimming, and fishing. Because the project required workers from the Army Corps of Engineers as well as Roosevelt's Civilian Conservation Corps, Robinson claimed to have scheduled a meeting with the president to discuss the details.

Before Frank departed, he left a memo at the Psychiana Offices: "INSTRUCTIONS FOR ELMER AND JENNIE AFTER I'M GONE EAST," it read. The memo was all business, and reflected the workplace attitudes of the day. "After the column envelopes have been stuffed and mailed," he instructed, "the fat woman (Nelson) and the Gossett girl can go. Also the Jones girl, if another one better has taken her place. Do not keep any more help than is necessary." Frank then issued a swift directive to the nerve-center of the Psychiana operation: the mailing department. "There must be no talking in the mailing dept.," he wrote. "The mail must go out…If any girl insists on jabbering, call her to one side and tell her she'll have to go to church if she wants to gossip—not here."[36]

In New York, Robinson settled into his luxurious suite at the New Yorker Hotel. The next morning, the hotel patched through an urgent phone call for Dr. Robinson. It was Friday, January 10. Outside, the day was piercingly cold. Icy winds knifed through 8th Avenue and West 34th Street. Smoke moved in the frigid air like itinerant thunderheads. The sun was a mere cocoon of light in the frosted smog. The phone call was from the secretary of New Jersey's governor, Harold G. Hoffman.

The governor, the secretary said, is "exceedingly anxious" to obtain all written correspondence from a specific Psychiana student.

That student was Bruno Richard Hauptmann, the man who had been arrested for the abduction and killing of Charles Lindberg's baby.

━━━━━━━━━◆━━━━━━━━━

Emphatically maintaining his innocence, Hauptmann had been incarcerated in the Flemington, New Jersey jail from mid-October 1934 until his trial in January 1935, one year earlier. Because the Lindbergh kidnapper had written fourteen ransom notes, handwriting analysis was central to the case. Federal investigators needed to match the handwriting on the ransom notes to Hauptmann's own hand to prove his culpability.

Governor Hoffman was one of the only public officials involved in the case to question Hauptmann's ultimate role in the Lindbergh kidnapping. Although he thought Hauptmann was guilty, Governor Hoffman doubted he had worked alone.

━━━━━━━━━◆━━━━━━━━━

Robinson told the governor's secretary that he would wire his business manager at Psychiana at once, ensuring the correspondence from Hauptmann would be sent via airmail directly to Governor Hoffman's office. Robinson hung up the phone and prepared a wire to Moscow with urgent instructions. Standing in his hotel room on that frigid January morning, Robinson would have realized two things. First, the magnitude of the situation, and the seriousness of the charges at hand. But, because he was both a newspaper publisher and a deft adman, he knew that tying Psychiana (regardless of the insinuation) to one of the greatest news stories in modern America was a golden opportunity.

━━━━━━━━━◆━━━━━━━━━

Bruno Richard Hauptmann's brush with Psychiana came just one month after his conviction. While incarcerated, the German immigrant with limited English had been looking for any ray of hope that might spare his life when he had chanced upon a Psychiana advertisement in a periodical. From his jail cell, Hauptmann wrote a brisk note to Robinson in the deliberate, stick-like penmanship of a child: "Dr. please send me the great truth of God. Obriciat [appreciate?], by Richard Hauptmann." The request for Lessons turned out to be the only known correspondence between Psychiana and Hauptmann, but it was nonetheless furnished to authorities.

"I don't know whether the card will help Hauptmann or hinder him," Robinson told the United Press. But, he added, he was "glad to furnish it" to Hoffman and the board of pardons.[37]

It is easy, perhaps, to lose track of the dark irony in Hauptmann's case. Here was a man who vehemently maintained his innocence (indeed, he may have been; the investigation remains controversial), and who, in his most desperate hours, sought the help of Psychiana, only to have his eleventh-hour religious correspondence used against him in a court of law.

It may be the only time that self-help became self-incrimination.

◆

Robinson wrapped up his business in the city, checked out of the New Yorker, and boarded a train for Washington, DC. "The next day I had a conference with the President," Robinson later wrote in his autobiography. In the alleged meeting, Roosevelt had, according to Frank, asked him if he was familiar with the works of Phillip Brooks—the Episcopalian clergyman from Boston, and lyricist of the song "Little Town of Bethlehem."

Frank with hat, pipe, and coat, c. 1935. University of Idaho Special Collections.

"He asked me how progress was being made on Robinson Park," Frank wrote. "The government had offered to build a large dam, thereby creating a beautiful artificial lake if someone would buy the land and donate it to the city or the county. I bought the land. When I left the President shook hands cordially and asked me never to come to Washington without calling on him."[38]

Afterwards, Robinson met with his friend, Idaho Senator William Borah, and the two enjoyed a pleasant lunch in the nation's capital. Among other topics, they discussed the amount of attention Robinson's Movement was attracting. According to Robinson, Borah knew Frank and Psychiana were being scrutinized by an array of agencies, and advised him to "lie low," advice Frank seemed utterly incapable of heeding.[39]

After lunch, Frank boarded an afternoon train heading to the Twin Cities, where he had a speaking engagement. In Minneapolis, Frank pushed into the lobby of the massive and elegant Nicollet Hotel like the showman he was, bedecked in his fur coat and homburg, and followed by the usual hustle of bellboys and the small caravan of trunks and leather bags. But when he reached the front desk, he found a wire awaiting him with sobering news. The wire was from a man named Robert C. Bannerman, Chief Special Agent of the State Department. The wire read, "Would like to see you regarding statements made in passport application signed by you in 1934. When will you be in Washington?"[40]

Special agents like Bannerman were a relatively new addition to the State Department, as anxiousness about potential espionage settled like a fog over Washington. Such agents were charged to build "upon existing security measures [that] enabled the Department to undertake several new security initiatives such as passport fraud investigations."[41]

After he checked into his room upstairs, Robinson wired Bannerman back, stating he had just left DC, suggesting that another time might be better. After he sent the wire, Robinson removed to the dining room for dinner, coffee, and a cigarette. Then he received a return cable from Bannerman. The agent insisted that Robinson report to his office the following Monday.

"Leaving Minneapolis on the *Hiawatha* that night," Robinson recalled, "I doubled back to Washington."[42]

———————————◆———————————

The country was still struggling to recover financially in early January 1936. The previous August, President Roosevelt had signed into law the Social Security Act. Part of the name spoke to that which the country yearned for: security and help. But the other part, "Social," sparked controversy. Conservatives saw it as the death knell to the "rugged individualism" that had shaped American character as typified by Teddy Roosevelt. But it was now the era of the New Deal, and even that broad program was, like the Act itself, contentious.

When the orange and silver *Hiawatha* engine lurched into Union Station, Robinson was exhausted, both physically and emotionally. Despite the confident face he posed to the public, reporters, his employees, students, and, most importantly, his family, there can be little doubt that he was starting to panic. He had gone on for years skating on charm and chance, embellishing his origin story to fit the given moment. But two things that Robinson had always had going for him were absent now: in the past he had never attracted much, if any, public scrutiny; and he never stayed in any one place or occupation long enough to face inevitable questions. But now, things were different. Now he was in the limelight. He was easily traceable. His name was out there for all to see and track down.

The next day, Robinson hailed a cab to the State Department where he was to meet with Special Agent Bannerman.

At sixty-two, clean-shaven, and raven-eyed, Special Agent Bannerman was twelve years Robinson's senior, and a legend in government work. A former postal inspector, he had started his career as Chief Special Agent in 1920, essentially inventing what we know today as "security detail" for high-profile government officials. His specialty included passport fraud and immigration cases, and his pioneering groundwork and tactics on those issues are still practiced today. Bannerman was a dyed-in-the-wool serviceman whose son and grandson would also go on to serve in the State Department. Later called the "King's Protector," Bannerman served as the personal security agent for King George VI during his 1939 visit to the United States. But it was his background as a postal inspector coupled with his training in passport fraud that made him a formidable opponent to someone like Frank Robinson.[43]

At their brisk meeting, the two men exchanged idle pleasantries, and then Bannerman got down to business. Robinson listened but said little. "All I did," Robinson wrote, "was ask when the indictment would be returned."[44] Bannerman replied that it would be soon, but that was not all. There was yet another indictment coming down on Dr. Robinson.

Beleaguered and besieged, Robinson left Bannerman's office and bought a ticket for a final train home.

———————✦———————

By the end of January, Psychiana's frontman was back in Moscow engaged in daily operations at his office. Across the country, World War I veterans were waiting to see if Congress would override Roosevelt's veto of the Bonus Army bill, the long and embattled cause they had marched for some four years earlier. On the one hand, they were due the monies that had been promised, and politicians knew as much. On the other, if paid out, the billions of dollars the U.S. government owed its veterans could seriously threaten any sense of economic stability the precarious nation had acquired.

Nearly three weeks after his meeting with Special Agent Bannerman, Frank Robinson was indicted. It was Thursday, February 13, the day before Valentine's Day. Notice had come from the state capitol in Boise. The following day, papers hummed with the news. "U.S. JURY LANDS ON MOSCOW MAN," *The Spokesman Review* reported. "Federal District Attorney John A. Carver said tonight that the federal grand jury had returned a secret indictment against Frank B. Robinson, Moscow, charging falsification of information used in obtaining a passport. Judge C.C. Cavanaugh fixed Robinson's bond at $1250." D.A. Carver, a dark-haired, hazel-eyed Mormon, said, "Specifically, Robinson was charged with stating that his place of birth was America, whereas in reality it was in England."[45]

When veteran Postal Inspector Stephen Howard Morse received word that Psychiana's Frank Robinson had been indicted, he knew it was an important development in a case he had been monitoring since he and Inspector James J. Doran had visited Robinson two years prior.

Morse's rich and unusual experience made him distinctly qualified to investigate the likes of Robinson and his Movement. The inspector had built a career out of taking down complex mail-fraud operations, organized gangs, corrupt postal employees, false advertising scams, bogus businesses, and anyone who used the U.S. mails illegally.[46] As early as July 26, 1902, Morse made the front pages of newspapers under the headline, "A 'GREEN GOODS' PLOT UNEARTHED BY GOVERNMENT." According to the *Harrisburg Telegraph*, the "green goods game" (i.e., counterfeiting ring) was brought to a speedy and dramatic end "as the result of a shrewd plot laid by Postoffice [sic] Inspector, S.H. Morse." Other headlines involving Morse's investigations through the years were no less dramatic: "Murders Banker for Five Dollars: Shocking Crime that Drove Blackmailing Gang from Philadelphia"; "Gigantic Land Swindle May Reach Millions"; and "Marriage Sharks: Postal Authorities Prepared to Drive them Out of Business."

Morse was also much admired by his peers. "He solved many difficult problems and brought to a successful conclusion the investigation of numerous and complicated cases," fellow inspector F. L. Armitage recalled.[47] Morse spent nearly seven years deep in the Yucatan, investigating one of America's largest fraud rings operating out of Campeche, Mexico. His testimony led to the 1912 convictions of five robber barons who had defrauded stockholders of some six million dollars in bogus companies. Morse brought down bribery schemes and elaborate networks of blackmailers.

◆

On learning of Robinson's indictment, Inspector Morse wasted no time. In a letter dispatched on the day the headline broke in *The Spokesman Review*, he wrote to the United States District Court in Boise: "Dear Sir—Will you kindly furnish me with the following information: Date of indictment returned against Frank B. Robinson, Moscow, Idaho, if that action was taken when the case was presented February 11, 1936; Docket number, if indictment returned; [and] If indictment was placed on secret file, please so advise." Morse then added one more request. "In the event Mr. Robinson shall be arrested, will you kindly furnish information requested on the enclosed yellow form?"[48]

◆

It was mid-February in northern Idaho. The winter days were short, the light a metal gray. Despite Robinson's winning smile, "flashy clothes," and the relentless overtures he made to the press and his family, the façade of the man and his Movement had been compromised. Pearl, his steadfast supporter, grew uneasy. She likely cringed at the thought of facing her church friends, Bridge Club, and acquaintances on Main Street in the small college town. The rumors and negative attention would have been a lot for anyone to withstand. Any reasonable person in her situation might have looked for an exit. But leaving would have been complicated for Pearl, a wife and mother devoted to keeping the family together. After some discussion, Frank and Pearl decided to rent a furnished home in Palos Verdes

Estates, outside of Los Angeles, where she and the children could get on comfortably in relative anonymity. Before the end of February, the plans were finalized; Pearl, Alf, Florence, and their maid, Ingrid, settled into a plush ocean-front home.[49]

———————◆———————

Back in Moscow, a trial date had been set for May, which meant that Robinson had to assemble the greatest legal team money could buy. But it also meant that the prosecution had ample time to amass the evidence they needed for a conviction. Robinson, now alone in his spacious home, placed calls to his allies, both political and professional. After donating untold amounts of money to politicians on both sides of the aisle, Robinson was now poised to call in some favors.

Certainly Idaho's Senator Borah was in Frank's corner.

For his defense team, Robinson hired local attorney A.L. Morgan and Ed Robertson of Spokane, Washington. Born into a family of lawyers, Ed Robertson was forty-eight and took his looks from his paternal grandfather and namesake, Edward White Robertson, a former Louisiana congressman. He had a square-set, prominent nose, and the physique of a leisurely sportsman. He also had his grandfather's high forehead, thick eyebrows, and sooty eyes. A 1911 graduate of Louisiana State University and valedictorian of his class, Ed Robertson—a southerner of long lineage—entered the University of Washington Law School in Seattle and graduated in 1912. He served as a captain in World War I before returning to Washington state to practice law, where he was known for southern charm and acrobatic oratory.[50]

Albert Loren Morgan was fourteen years Robertson's senior, and although he lacked the pedigree and natural charisma of his colleague (he had grown up in rural Kansas, the son of a farmer, and had had only one year of college), he possessed a zealot's determination whenever he got behind a case. His doggedness would pave the way to his becoming president of the Idaho Bar Association in July 1937. Thin-lipped and business-minded, Morgan wore wire-rimmed spectacles and had a nest of wild white hair.[51]

While Ed Robertson and A.L. Morgan reviewed the case and set to work on a defense strategy, Frank attended to his movement. Spinning his indictment into a positive narrative was the first order of business. The government was attacking him because of his criticisms of Christianity, he reasoned. "This is not a prosecution, but a *persecution*," he said frequently enough that it sounded more like a campaign slogan than a defense. His opponents, he maintained, were spreading fake news, misinformation, and gossip. He appealed to his students first, to set the record straight (lest they waiver in their faith), and second, to solicit money. The stakes could not be higher, he suggested. Their health, wealth, and happiness hung in the balance. After all, this was a war between good and evil. Between truth and lies. Between the freedom of religion and an "Anti-Americanism."

As the May trial date neared, Robinson's legal meetings became more frequent and urgent, and thus more expensive. Already costing him thousands, his legal expenses accrued on top of the money he was spending on the Palos Verdes Estates home.

Rallying his followers was now financially paramount.

In the March 1936 issue of *Psychiana Quarterly*—the one featuring Edgar Baity's reports of helping friends—Robinson appealed to his students, addressing the indictment head-on. "At last," he wrote, "what I have expected to happen has happened. It came in the form of a Federal Grand Jury Indictment." Restating what had already been printed in the papers, Robinson only offered his readers the briefest of context: "The Indictment charges that I made a false statement, knowingly, in regard to my passport application filed by me when I went to Europe in 1934. I don't need to tell my students and friends that no false statement of any kind was knowingly made by me on a passport application, or anywhere else."[52] Robinson continued, "The question concerns my birth and at the proper time I will show how little there is to this accusation." As for any clear exculpatory claims, Robinson intended to keep his powder dry. "I shall have nothing to say regarding my evidence, however, until the trial."[53] Evidence notwithstanding, Robinson dispensed sweeping claims of innocence. "My friends and students throughout the United States and the rest of the world have faith enough in me; and they know that my whole life and intentions are good enough not to want to defraud or knowingly make any kind of false statement with regard to a passport or anything else."[54]

Robinson assured his readership that the indictment was phony, little more than a witch-hunt. The people behind the judgment, Frank wrote, "would love to see Psychiana and Dr. Frank B. Robinson wiped entirely off the map." The passport charge, in other words, was the government's justification to shut down the real threat: his teaching. "Two thousand years ago, I should have been burned alive as a 'male-witch.'" The whole episode, he averred, was "the outgrowth of one of the most vicious attacks made on any man in this country." Never one to back down, Robinson predicted that the ordeal "will leave 'Psychiana' and its founder completely vindicated and on a higher pinnacle of success than ever before."[55]

The March issue of *Psychiana Quarterly* reflected a flash point not only in Robinson's legal troubles, but also in the fringe thinking of the day. "Eight years ago," Frank wrote, "I released and published...a very revolutionary statement, but the followers of orthodox theology immediately began to cry 'faker,' 'quack' and all the rest of that sort of thing. They insinuated that I did not know of what I was speaking. Now let's see whether I did or not. The statement made was to the effect that when Spiritual Law is known as it exists, physical death will not be necessary."[56]

Robinson was about to turn fifty, and that fact alone may have led him to the subject of immortality for *Psychiana Quarterly*.

"It is interesting to note," he wrote, "how science, while a few years ago was so materialistic, is now endorsing the theory that death is not necessary in the eternal scheme of things."[57] Robinson pointed to the latest work of Nobel Laureate Dr. Alexis Carrel of the Rockefeller Institute. The previous December, the media was touting Carrel's experiments in prolonging life. "Visions Man Keeping Alive for Centuries," *The Des Moines Register* announced.[58] Carrel—whose countenance was made peculiar by having one blue eye and one brown—had succeeded in keeping a chicken heart alive in "cold storage." Adding to the hype was the role of Charles Lindbergh in the experiment. "Last summer," the *Register* added, "Col. Charles A. Lindbergh perfected an artificial heart which keeps whole organs alive outside the body."[59] Lindbergh's role in Carrel's work was, some speculated, a matter of publicity rather than substance. On the other hand, Lindbergh, like Carrel, was a eugenicist, and was more than sympathetic to Hitler's vision of an Aryan race.

In many ways, Carrel and Robinson seemed cut from the same root. Each was eccentric. Each craved publicity. And like Robinson, Carrel saw himself as a kind of messiah. "[Carrel] has investigated the experience of mediums receiving messages they think come from the dead," Robinson continued. "He said the importance of the facts cannot be denied. But in his own investigations he finds positive reason to think the messages are explained by clairvoyance or telepathy, rather than as communications from the dead. Clairvoyance and telepathy he holds as proven facts."[60]

CHAPTER 21

On Trial

In the weeks leading up to the trial date, there appeared this headline in the local newspaper *The Latah Journal*:

FEDERAL OFFICIALS GATHERING EVIDENCE AGAINST
DR. ROBINSON
CLAIM TO HAVE MUCH THAT IS DAMAGING.[61]

In a direct response to Frank's carefully constructed persecution narrative, a "government official" is quoted in the opening of the article. "'The government never persecutes any one, but it does prosecute those who are believed to be guilty of violation of federal laws, but prosecutions against these are never started until it is believed sufficient evidence to convict has been obtained and then it prosecutes most vigorously.'"[62]

The federal prosecution was led by Erle Hoyt Casterlin, a Michigan-born, Columbia-educated prosecutor who had spent two years teaching history in Puerto Rico before becoming a high school superintendent in the small town of Salmon, Idaho. In short order, however, Casterlin left academics and rose quickly in the ranks of law. By the time he came to lead the federal prosecution against Frank B. Robinson, Casterlin was widely regarded as a formidable legal expert, with the legal record to show for it. He was two weeks away from turning fifty-two, but looked older than he was. He appeared pale and turtle-like, with loose swags of fresh beneath his chin. His hair was white, neatly shaved on the sides and his high forehead suggested baldness. His preference for old-school flared bowties made him look dowdy. Behind the lenses of his wire-framed glasses, however, Casterlin's eyes were steely and knowing.[63]

While Casterlin could not compete with Ed Robertson's good looks, grooming, or southern charm, he had enough evidence to give Frank and his legal team plenty to worry about. He and his troop of prosecutors had done their homework. They had documentation, including Klamath Falls' *The*

Evening Herald story from 1919 about Robinson's father dying of heart failure—an article they argued was fabricated. They had insurance applications on which Robinson variously cited New York City and Toronto as his places of birth. They had Frank's signed discharge record from the Royal Northwest Mounted Police, clearly stating that he had been born in England. They had his Canadian Oath of Allegiance. And, of course, they had the passport application itself. Casterlin's team had subpoenaed nearly twenty witnesses from New York, Washington, DC, and Canada, including Robinson's own sister-in-law, Maybelle Barnhisel, who had written *The Evening Herald* story about the supposed death of Frank's father and brothers.

Meanwhile, attorneys Morgan and Robertson argued that Robinson simply believed he had been born in New York City. Any documents suggesting otherwise, they contended, were matters of clerical errors or memory lapses. In pre-trial prep, the lawyers coached their client repeatedly to keep quiet and say as little as possible, directions that ran counter to Robinson's outspokenness and impulses to fight back.

———————◆———————

Following jury selection and other formalities, the trial got underway in earnest on May 16, 1936. It was a Saturday, which may have explained the large crowd of onlookers swarming Moscow's three-story federal building. Mixed into the crowd was a fedora-clad throng of pressmen scribbling in their notebooks. Camera bulbs popped as the procession of witnesses, jurors, University of Idaho law students, and legal teams filed into the courtroom. When Frank Robinson arrived in his Duesenberg, all eyes were on the immaculately dressed religious leader. Robinson took a moment to restate his position: this was a persecution of the worst sort. He was guilty of nothing. His trial was another case of the orthodox Christian leaders using the government to rid the world of Psychiana once and for all. Robinson then entered the building and headed for his seat at the trial that awaited him.

With a rap of the gavel by the robed Judge Charles C. Cavanaugh, the trial began. It was 10:00 sharp. Sunlight flooded the courtroom. Federal prosecutors made their opening remarks, stating unequivocally that in the case of the United States of America vs. Frank B. Robinson on three counts of passport fraud, the accused was guilty, and they would show the jury the evidence to prove their case.

Frank's own recollection, on the other hand, painted the federal prosecutors in a weak light. According to Robinson, Frank Griffin—an assistant D.A.—

opened with a few measured concessions. "'Of course the government has not the funds with which to engage the noted counsel the defendant has here. Over there sits the Honorable A. L. Morgan, President of the Idaho Bar Association, while over here, internationally known, sits Edward W. Robertson—the Mark Anthony [sic] of the American Bar.'"[64] In his second memoir, *The Strange Autobiography of Frank B. Robinson*, Frank recreated the scene that followed.

> When [Ed Robertson] arose to make his opening statement, a smile stole all over his handsome face. 'Gennelmen of the joowy—ah've been in the practice of criminal law a long time now, and during that time, ah've been called most everything a lawyer can be called. But this is the first time I have ever been called Mark Anthony [sic]. If I remember mah history correctly, Mark Anthony [sic] is the gennelman who knocked at Cleopatra's boudoir and when she opened the door, he told her he had not come there to talk.' Naturally, this speech brought down the house.[65]

When the time came, Ed Robertson called Frank to the witness stand where he was sworn in.

The courtroom was quiet save the occasional shuffling of spectators in the seats. Robertson approached the witness stand. "Your name is Frank Bruce Robinson?"[66]

"Yes, sir."

"You are the defendant in this case."

"Yes, sir."

Robertson then turned straightaway to the story Frank's sister in-law, Maybelle, had written for the Klamath Falls newspaper *The Evening Herald*. "With reference to the telegram which your sister-in-law has testified to or about, I will ask you if you received such a telegram?"

"Yes, sir."

"I will ask you if you have such a telegram now?"

"No."

"What became of it?"

"I don't know."

"Have you made a search for it?"

"Yes, sir."

"Are you able to find it?"

"No."

"That is all." Robertson regarded his client and the jury and removed to his seat.

Erle Casterlin stood and approached the witness stand, picking up where Robertson had left off. "Where did you search?" he asked.[67]

"I have about fifteen or twenty thousand telegrams in the office," he said, "which were carefully gone through."

"Do you know of any other telegram that was not kept by you, Doctor?"

"Well, I receive a great many and it may be—"

"But the only place that you searched was in your own office and your own private effects?"

"I would not personally have any other place to search."

Casterlin paced the floor, acknowledging the jury and onlookers now and again. "The telegram which you have reference to," he said, turning to Robinson, "was received from whom, from what company?"

"The cablegram," Frank said, "which was delivered to me by the Western Union Company at Klamath Falls came from London, England."

"It was delivered by the Western Union Company?"

"Yes, sir.

"What date?"

"Well," he essayed, "sometime that month, probably a few days before that article appeared."

"Objection," Robertson called out.

Some argument ensued and both Robertson and Casterlin approached the bench. After a few minutes, Robertson cross-examined Frank. Addressing the embattled religious leader, Robertson turned to his client. "Please state your name."

"Frank Bruce Robinson."[68]

"Where do you live, Doctor Robinson?"

"Moscow, Idaho."

"How long have you lived in Moscow, Idaho?"

"Eight years, about eight years."

"Are you a married man?"

"Yes, sir."

"Of whom does your family consist?"

"Mrs. Robinson, and Alfred age fourteen, and Florence aged five years."

"What is your business?"

"I am an author, publisher and druggist."

"Doctor Robinson," Ed Robertson said, "going directly to the point in the issue here, I will ask you as to whether or not you ever had any conversations with your father or mother relative to your place of birth."

Robinson did not waver. This was part of the defense he had prepared for. "Yes, I did."

"By the way," Robertson interjected. "What was your father's occupation?"

Staying with the past tense, Robinson answered easily. "He was a preacher."

"A preacher?"

"Yes."

"What was his name?"

"John Henry Robinson."

Robertson paced the floor. Onlookers fanned themselves in the warm courtroom. "What was the occasion of this conversation," he said, "and how old were you at the time it occurred?"

"There were several occasions on which that was mentioned," Frank said. "The first one that I go back to was either on my fifth or sixth birthday, at which time my aunt who was visiting with us called me a little Yankee."[69]

The defense attorney continued his line of questioning. "What was the occasion of that which made it remain in your memory?"

"It was my birthday," Frank said. "And they bought me a new sailor suit of clothes, and I remember I had a cord and whistle and I used to lisp. I couldn't say the letter S, couldn't pronounce it, and they stood me in the middle of the table and called me 'brath buttonths' and I was for years trying to say brass buttons, and they would call me 'brath buttonths' for years afterward on account of the lisping."

"And what brought up the conversation as to your place of birth?"

"After that aunt had called me a little Yankee, she said, 'How's my little Yankee'—"

"Now, Doctor Robinson, what was said by anyone, and by whom was it said, after that?"

"I asked Father why she was calling me a little Yankee, and he said because you were—."

"Objection," Casterlin shouted. Addressing Judge Cavanah, Casterlin stood. "We object to the testimony now, of this witness with respect to any statement of his father's on the grounds that it would be the declaration of an ancestor without the proper foundation being laid; that the ancestor is now dead."[70]

"We don't have the ability to bring witnesses from England to testify," the defense retorted.

Eyeing Ed Robertson, Judge Cavanah intervened. "I think I will overrule the objection," he said.

Murmurs sounded throughout the courtroom.

Casterlin countered: "In this case there was a law requiring the registration of births in England," he said.

Weighing the prosecution's reasoning, Cavanaugh addressed the prosecutor. "You are asking for information that this man got from someone, that is as I understand the question—."

Frank began where he had been cut off—"that I was born in New York City."

Ed Robertson disregarded the disruption and pressed forward with his direct examination. He turned to his client in the witness stand. "I will ask you what, if anything, your mother said on that occasion?"

Frank regained his composure. "She told me that she and my father lived in New York several years before I was born and that I was taken to England as a very small child."

"What other occasions, as you remember them, was the subject of your birth or birth-place brought up?"

"It was brought up again when—one or two nights before my mother died—when I was about ten, the aunt had been called up or telegraphed by my father on account of the impending death of Mother and she came to the house. While she was there, she again alluded to me as the little Yankee, and at that time the statement was again made that I was born in New York and taken to England as a baby."[71]

The defense allowed the jury to absorb Frank's recollections before taking a slightly different tack. "Dr. Robinson, I will ask you to state what the treatment and relationship was by and between your father and yourself?"

Seeing the emotional tactic for what it was, Casterlin pounced. "Objected to as incompetent, irrelevant and immaterial on the grounds that it doesn't tend to prove or disprove any issues." Casterlin was zeroing in on the seemingly untenable case of what Frank believed or did not believe. "The point counsel is reaching is whether or not this witness believed his father was dead," he said, adding, "the fact that he didn't hear from him is one thing, and the reason is entirely another. We think that the reason why he didn't hear from his father is too remote to be received here as material evidence."

Beginning to look somewhat sympathetic to Frank's case, Judge Cavanaugh disagreed. "Some circumstances might show why he did not correspond. We are going now to the question of whether he believed his father was deceased," he said. "Overruled." Cavanaugh looked at Frank Robinson. "Go ahead."

The jurors eyes swept to the witness stand.

Frank continued. "He was cruel and harsh, on one occasion—"

"Move to strike the answer as a conclusion of this witness," Casterlin said.

"It may be stricken," the Judge said. "Just state what occurred."

Regaining his line of questioning, Robertson addressed his client. "What did he do to you?"

"Well," Frank said, "he threw a ruler at me one night and hit me on the head and knocked me unconscious."

"What age were you when that occurred?"[72]

"That was shortly after my mother's death. I cannot state the exact year of that occurrence."

"Do you still have the scar as a result of that blow?"

Casterlin objected. "Incompetent, irrelevant and immaterial, the fact that his father hit him on the head."

"I have ruled that he may show their relation, what was their relationship where you have made an issue here, in this, that he stated that his father was deceased, now he may show as to what occurred between he and his father. If there was a such a relationship," the Judge added, "he may show it. Overruled."

"Yes, sir."

Ed Robertson then invited his client down to the courtroom floor. "Just step down and show the scar to the jury."

"We object," Casterlin said, "to his showing any scar to the jury here."

"Overruled."

"Just over the left eye," Ed Robertson said, posing his client to the jury. "Do you see it?"

"Your honor," Casterlin interjected, "we object to the statement of the witness."

Cavanaugh ignored the objection.

"Were there any other occasions on which your father administered corporal punishment to you," the defense asked.

"Plenty," Robinson said.[73]

"How old were you when your Father died—I mean your mother died?"

"Ten."

"How long after your mother's death was it that your father married another woman?"

At this question, the court adjourned for a recess. Both prosecution and defense teams regrouped, assessed their respective strategies, consulted their notes, and charted their next steps forward.

After the crowd filed back into the courtroom and the jurors took their seats, Judge Cavanaugh reconvened the trial. Frank Robinson sat in the witness stand, poised for the questioning his lawyers had prepared him for.

The defense picked up where they had left off. "Doctor Robinson, how long after your mother's death was it that your father married another woman?" Ed Robertson asked.

"Approximately one year."

Robertson shifted gears, angling toward his client's early education. "At what age did you begin school?'

"Three."

"What schools did you attend?"

"I attended Board school at Halifax, and another higher in Huddersfield."

"Did you ever attend school in York?"

"No sir."

"Did you ever live in York?"

"No sir."

"At about the age of thirteen what, if anything, did your father do to you?"

"Took me to the British Navy recruiting office and forced me to join the British Navy."[74]

Casterlin perked up. "We move to strike the words 'forced me to join the British Navy.'"

"It may be stricken," the judge said.

"Made me join the British Navy," Robinson essayed.

"We move to strike the answer, 'made me join the British Navy,'" Casterlin echoed.

"Yes," the judge said. "It may be stricken; he can state what was said and done."

Seeing another opportunity to portray his client as an abused child, the defense attorney leveraged the moment. "What did your father say to you before taking you to the British recruiting office?"

"That he wished I had never been born, and that he wanted to get rid of me."

"Who went to the British recruiting office with you?"

"Just Father."

"Then what happened?"

"I was admitted as a boy apprentice and sent to a training ship."

"And how long were you in the British Navy as an apprentice boy?"

Without missing a beat, Frank answered: "Either two or three years."

"On your return from that apprenticeship in the British Navy, what did you do?"

Robinson's memory came quickly. "I walked up to my father's place one Sunday morning with a discharge and rang the bell."

All eyes were fixed on Frank in the witness stand.[75]

"Father came down and asked 'What are you doing here?' And I told him I had been discharged. He said, 'Well, you can't stick around here. You'll have to get out.' Then he turned me away from the house."

"At the age of seventeen," the defense counselor continued, "what if anything occurred with respect to yourself and your father?"

"He had a box built for me and a put a few clothes in there," Frank said, "and handed me ten shillings and told me to get out. He said, 'I bought you a passage to America.'"

"Who else did he send along with you?"

"My brother, two years younger than I."

"Where did you come to then?"

"Montreal."

"And from there to what place did you go?"

"Belleville, Ontario, Canada," Frank said.

"When you arrived in Belleville, what was the condition of yourself and brother, financially?"

"We had no money when we got there, and I had no ticket to Belleville, so we stood outside of the Notre Dame Cathedral with some cakes in my hand and a policeman came along. He made arrangements for us to go there."[76]

"You worked in various drugstores in Canada?"

"Yes sir."

"What year was it that you came to the United States, Doctor Robinson?"

"1910."

"Where did you go?"

"Portland, Oregon."

"During that time state whether or not you became acquainted with James Palmer, the executive secretary of the YMCA at Portland."

"Yes sir."

Hoping to establish some groundwork and preempt the thornier aspects of the case, defense counsel Robertson steered the questioning into a different direction. "In Klamath Falls," he said, "did you meet a lady—the lady who is now Mrs. Barnhisel and your sister-in-law?"

"Yes sir."

"In what way did you meet her?"[77]

"I was working for the Star Drug store and every morning she would come around to gather the news. She was working on *The Evening Herald.*"

"Did you at the time know your wife?"

"No sir."

"On or about September 13, 1919, did you or did you not receive a telegram or cablegram with reference to your father?"

"Yes sir," Robinson said.

"You have testified that you made a search for that?"

As if responding to a cue, Frank departed from his otherwise terse responses with a more robust answer, one likely devised in a prep session. "I would like to state," he began, "that after this indictment I went to Klamath Falls and went into the Western Union office and asked if they had copies of telegrams and cablegrams from that month and year. They told me they kept them for two years before destroying them, and so I went to this Western Union office and asked here—."

"—You don't need to state anything about this office," Robertson interjected. "Just state to the jury what was in that telegram."

Fully aware that the defense was relying on a non-existent telegram (i.e., that Robinson could have invented it whole cloth) with no way of proving or disproving its contents, Casterlin interceded: "The same objection as to the contents of the telegram on the grounds that no proper foundation has been laid."

"Overruled."

Frank continued apace. "It was rather a long telegram and it was stated that my brother had been killed in action and that my father had died of heart failure and there was some other statements. I didn't know the outfit that sent this telegram. It came from London and I don't recall the signature. I don't recall the name, but I think it was some firm of barristers in London."[78]

"Did you believe the contents of the telegram?"

"I had no reason not to."

"I will ask you," the defense added, "whether you told the person you were working with; did you tell him?"

"I went home."

"The question is, whether you told the person you were working with, did you tell him?"

"It is quite likely that I did."

"I will ask you whether or not you later communicated with Mrs. Barnhisel—whether you had any communications with her, the lady who wrote the story?"

"I met her the next day, this boarding house where I lived, she called up and later came out and I showed her the wire."

"What year and day were you married and where?"

"Thanksgiving day 1919, in Klamath Falls. Her father was Judge—"

"—At the time of giving that story to Mrs. Barnhisel, had you met your present wife?"

"No sir."[79]

"Did you know who she was or anything about her?"

"No sir."

"When did you come to Moscow, Idaho?"

"About eight years ago."

Wanting to sidestep one of the D.A.'s central lines of attack, Ed Robertson then picked up a sheet of paper from his table and turned to Robinson. "I hand you defendant's exhibit 18 what purports to be an application for life insurance," he said, his Louisianan accent thick in the warmed courtroom. The insurance application, he said, was signed by Frank "in Moscow, Idaho on the 4th day of May 1931."

Frank regarded the paper.

"I will ask you whether or not the signature Frank Bruce Robinson appearing thereon is or is not your signature?"

"It is."

The insurance application Frank signed lists New York City as his place of birth, and also stated that both of his parents were deceased. Ed Robertson produced another insurance application with the same information, signed by Frank.

Robertson turned to Frank and said, "I will ask you whether or not you believed at that time that you were born in New York City?"

"I would not have put it down if I hadn't."

"I will ask you whether or not you believed at the time you signed this application that you believed that your father was deceased?"

"Yes, sir."

Staying on this line of questioning, the defense attorney proceeded to introduce more copies of insurance policies Frank had applied for. "I hand you defendant's exhibit 22 purporting to be an application for insurance in the Northwest National Insurance Company made by Frank Bruce Robinson April 17, 1934 and I will ask you whether or not the signature therein contained is your own signature?"[80]

"Yes sir."

Addressing the judge, Casterlin interjected. "May I ask a question?"

"Yes, you may do so."

Rising from his seat, Casterlin approached Robinson. "I notice this date, April 17, 1934, when had you first conceived the idea or entertained the desire to travel to England that year?"

"Sometime in May."

"Was this application made in anticipation of a foreign trip?"

"I don't think so."

"You didn't take it out for additional protection while traveling abroad?"

"That, I can't answer, Mr. Casterlin," Robinson said flatly.

"Wasn't that the real reason for your taking out additional insurance at that time?"

"I don't think so."

Casterlin then regarded the bench. "We object to exhibit 22 on the ground that it is—it contains a statement or statements that are self-serving. The proximity of the application's date is so close to the date of the passport's application that it becomes a part of the transaction in the application."[81]

"Overruled. We are going to suspend at this time, until Monday morning at ten o'clock."

------------◆------------

After spending Sunday preparing his testimony, Robinson was back in the courtroom at 10:00 Monday morning.

Defense attorney Ed Robertson began: "I ask at this time permission to read exhibits 8 and 9."

"Very well," Judge Cavanaugh said.

Exhibits 8 and 9 were sworn statements by people who had known Robinson when he was a druggist in Portland, Oregon.

"To which we object," Casterlin said, "on the ground that the contents of the exhibits are hearsay."[82]

"Overruled."

Taking the exhibits from the defense table, Robertson addressed the court, reading the testimonies aloud. "'My knowledge and belief of [Frank Robinson's] place and date of birth appearing above are based upon the following facts: [He] always referred to New York City as birth place. Signed, E.E. Estes, President, Powers & Estes Retail Drugs, Portland, Oregon.'" The exhibit, Robertson told the court, had been notarized by Bess K. Gordon, making it a legal document.

In the second exhibit, the defense attorney read from another similar statement. "'The person whose name appears above is now residing in Moscow, Idaho, and was born in New York City, New York, on or about July 1886. My knowledge and belief of place and date of birth appearing above are based upon the following facts: have many times heard Frank B. Robinson speak of New York City as his birth place. Signed, Wynn S. Ward, Owner, Irvington Pharmacy, Portland, Oregon.'" This exhibit, Robertson noted, was notarized by W.E. Whiteside.[83]

Robertson shifted focus once more, moving into more preemptive territory and approached his client on the witness stand. "About when did you decide definitely to take a trip away from America?"

Frank thought for a moment. "Well, sometime in July."[84]

"That is when you made your definite decision?"

"Yes sir."

"Had you been thinking about it some time before?"

In answering, Robinson tried to have it both ways. "No, not too long," he said. "I may have, but I think I made up my mind almost instantly to go, although it may have been in my mind for a little while."

"Although you had prior to the time of sailing, procured application for passport?"

"Yes sir," Frank said."

"What was the occasion of your trip?"

The question landed squarely in Frank's comfort zone. "Well, I work pretty long hours," he said. "Up about six in the morning and working until about ten o'clock at night. I have about seventy-five people dependent upon me and I was very tired and I thought it was due both myself and the rest of my connections to take a trip over to Europe to broaden my view and to rest. I had gone for six years without a vacation of any kind."

"Calling your attention, Dr. Robinson, to a statement appearing on plaintiff's exhibit 1 [passport application]—'never outside of the United States'—I will ask you to state why that particular statement appears in that blank in the first place?"

Jumping in, Casterlin objected. "This is an endeavor to impeach the contents of a written instrument, which was signed and sworn to by this witness," he said. "It is not necessary to explain an expression in the instrument, which might be the case if the statement was cloudy or unintelligible, uncertain or indefinite. This is clearly an attempt by the witness to impeach the statement made in a public record over his oath."[85]

In what was seeming like a rare move, the judge agreed with the prosecutor. "Sustained."

Robertson continued. "As to what period of time did you have reference when you wrote the statement 'never outside of the United States'?"

"Objection—on the same ground, the word 'never' is not indefinite, uncertain or unintelligible."

"Yes," the judge said. "The word 'never' means all time. Sustained."

"Exception," Robertson stipulated. After a brief volley of semantics and parsing between the bench and defense, Robertson said, "I offer to prove by this witness that at the time he filled out the application, with the words 'never was outside of the United States' that he understood the inquiry to be directed, and his answer was intended to cover the period of time from 1910 to June 18, 1934. And that by this statement he, in good faith, meant and believed that it was only necessary for him to show any period of residence outside of the country after his entry in 1910."[86]

Circling back to his previous contention, Casterlin countered. "To which we object on the ground that the applicant does state that he was born in New York City and therefore fixes the time to include from the date of his birth to the date of the application."

Casterlin's point was an important one. The prosecution knew that if they could prove Robinson willfully lied about this part of his application, then it would unravel the veracity of all his other answers. In Casterlin's view, Robinson was trapped in his own lies. Either he was born in New York City as he claimed and raised in England (which means he had been outside of the United States, and therefore was guilty of lying on the application), or he was born in England and was not a U.S. citizen. It had to be one or the other.

As for the defense, lead counsel Robertson contended that Frank meant that he had not been out of the United States since the day he crossed the

U.S./Canada border in 1910. But this argument either knowingly or unwittingly disregards Frank's time spent in the Philippines from 1916 to 1917, a period in which Frank was very much out of the United States.

Nor did the District Attorney's team seem wise to this bit of information, though it remains unclear as to why it never came up. Presumably, Frank withheld the secret first from his application, and second from his own defense team in the hopes that his enlistment under the false identity of "Earl Meyer"—and subsequent incarceration at Alcatraz under the same name—would not surface in any background checks. Either revelation would have delivered an unequivocally fatal blow to an already shaky defense.

The judge weighed in on Casterlin's objection: "Sustained."

Robertson wrapped up his questioning, yielding the floor to the D.A.'s team for cross-examination. Casterlin rose from his table and approached the witness stand. "Doctor, will you please state the date when you were born, as you believe it to be?"[87]

"July 5, 1886."

"And do you know where your Father and Mother resided on the 31st day of July 1886, of your knowledge?"

"No."

"That would be hearsay?"

"Only on information passed to me by my mother that at the time of my birth they resided in New York City."

"You have stated that in your early years you can recall back to the age of three, is that correct?"

"Yes sir."

"What do you recall at the age of three that made such a lasting impression on your mind?"[88]

"I started school. I remember the first day, at three."

"That is rather unusual," Casterlin pressed, "is it not?"

"I don't know. I can't answer for others."[89]

"You have a degree of Doctor of Philosophy?"

"Yes sir."

"You also have a degree of Doctor of Divinity?"

"Yes sir."

"Doctor of Literature?"

"Yes sir."

"And also Doctor of Psychology."

"Yes sir."

Jurors hung on every word in the wood-paneled courtroom.

"When you entered the English Navy, Doctor."[90]

"Yes."

"You say you were thirteen?"

"Yes, sir."

"Did you sign any papers when you enrolled?

"Yes, sir."

"How long were you in the navy?"

"I don't recall what the term of enlistment was, I imagine it was two or three years."

"Did you stay during the entire enlistment?"

"Yes, that is as I recall it."

"What grade of seamanship did you have when you left?"

"I can't answer that question. That is a long time ago, and I can't recall."

"You don't recall that?"[91]

"I remember in a general way the trials they put us through," Robinson said. "We studied the different knots and splices."

"Was it a gunship you were on?

"It was a training ship off the—"

"Doctor," Casterlin pressed. "Did it have guns?"

"We had gunner's instructions, and perhaps—"

The prosecutor zeroed in. "Doctor, do you know was it one of the requirements for enlistment in the Navy that you had to be of English descent?"

All eyes were fixed on Frank Robinson.

"I don't know."

"And that you had to be a subject of England?"

"I don't know."

"Did you take an oath of allegiance to the King of England?"

Onlookers shifted in their wooden seats.

"I don't know."

"Was that ever discussed among the boys there?"

"I don't know that."

"You don't know the requirements with respect to that?"

"No, sir."

"Do you recall the year that your Mother died?"

"I was ten years of age. I am fifty now."

"You were ten years of age when your Mother died?"[92]

"Yes sir."

"At seventeen years of age you took a ship to America."

"Yes sir."

"Who went with you to the dock?"

"My stepmother and father."

"Just prior to the time that you went to the dock, isn't it a fact, Doctor Robinson, that you and your stepmother had some difficulty?"[93]

"Yes sir. It is a fact."

"That difficulty arose from an attempt of your stepmother to chastise one of your brothers?"

"Yes sir."

"Which brother was that?"

"The youngest, Arthur."

"Isn't it a fact that at that time you stepped in and—"

"Interfered?" Robinson said.

"Yes. And interfered."

"Yes sir."

"You took hold of your stepmother," Casterlin said.

"Yes sir."

"And entered into a tussle?"

"Yes sir."

"That is the reason, Doctor, that you left home."

"No sir."

"That is one of the contributing reasons."

"No sir. I don't think so," Robinson countered. "Because before that my father had shipped me to the Navy."

"Is it a dishonor to belong to the English Navy?"

"I don't think so. It is a dishonor, though, for a parent to send his boy to the English Navy at that age."

Casterlin shot a glance at the judge. "I move to strike that portion of the answer that it is a dishonor for a parent to send his boy to the English Navy at that age, as not responsive."

"I think it may stand," Judge Cavanaugh said.[94]

"Isn't it the custom for parents to enlist their children in the British Navy?" Casterlin said.

"I don't know that it is the custom to enlist their children in the British Navy."

Robinson's defense team followed along, jotting notes and sifting papers. "Object to what the custom is, that would be immaterial here."

"Sustained."

Casterlin redirected his line of questioning. "When you went to ship to Canada, who actually went through the mechanics of purchasing the tickets?"

"I presume my father."

"Were you there?"

"No."

"When was the ticket or the transportation given to you?"

"At Liverpool prior to getting on the boat."

"Did you have any conversation with your father at that time there?"

"I recall no conversation any more than my stepmother asked, 'How much money are you giving them?' And my father said, 'I think a half-pound is enough.' And I recall him telling us not to spend too much on the boat."[95]

"Did you know where you were destined?"

"Yes," Robinson stated. "We knew that we were coming to Montreal."

"Where else?"

"Montreal was the only destination of the ship, that I do recall."

Casterlin retrieved a document from the prosecution's table and handed it to Robinson. "I hand you plaintiff's exhibit 13, and I will ask you to read that with reference to the port of entry and also in reference to the destination for the purpose of refreshing your memory."

Robinson held the document, regarding its contents. "Port of arrival," he said. "Quebec. Then I stand corrected, if that document is correct, it was Quebec."

"So the port of entry was Quebec."

"Yes sir."

"And the destination was what?"

"Belleville, Ontario," Robinson said. "But the boat doesn't run up there."

"Isn't it correct that you were destined to Belleville for the purpose of entering school there?"[96]

"No sir. Absolutely not."

"It is not correct?"

"No sir."

"Do you recall Piedmont Boarding School?"[97]

"I don't know."

"Isn't it a fact that it was this Piedmont School that you were destined when you left England?"

"It is nothing of the kind," Robinson said. "If it is, it has completely left my mind, it is completely out of my mind."

Casterlin continued to press Robinson on details of his time in Canada, his work in pharmacology, and his relationship with his brothers and his father in a wider effort to show the web of inconsistencies in Frank Robinson's biography. Slowly and methodically, the prosecution punched small holes in a great and roving story. Whether or not those holes—taken in their totality—would be enough to convince the jury that Robinson had for years willfully lied about his true identity, was another matter all together.

In the natural light of the courtroom's east-facing windows, Casterlin turned to the question of Robinson's brother. "When you came to the United States, was your brother Sydney alive?"[98]

"He came with me."

"He came with you here to the United States?"

Robinson corrected himself. "Not to the United States, no. I lost track of that fellow for many years, I don't know how many."

"When was it that you lost track of Sydney?"[99]

"Objected to as immaterial," Ed Robertson said.

"We will connect this up later," Casterlin said. "It is for the purpose of testing the memory of this witness as to matters which he has testified to."

"He may answer," Cavanaugh declared.

The jury returned their gaze to Frank Robinson.

"I cannot tell you the year I lost track of him," Frank said.

"Objected to on the same ground that it goes to collateral matters."

"Overruled."

"Well," Frank said. "I don't know. We were together in Belleville and it was through those years that I lost track of him."

"Was it prior to 1910 that you lost track of him?"

"Way back of that," Frank said. "But not for all the time. There were times that I was in touch with him."

"Speaking of 1910," Casterlin said, "subsequent to that year, did you have any communications with your brother Sydney?"

"Objected to on the same ground."

"Overruled."

"I can't recall that," Frank said. "Whether I did or not."

"Did you have any letters or information from any third party concerning your brother, Sydney? Subsequent to 1910?"[100]

"I recall no such correspondence."

For his own part, Frank must not have suspected that the prosecution had obtained copies of the letters sent between him and his half-sister

Mary during 1932 when he discussed traveling to Canada to visit Sydney, and his own future plans to travel to England.

———————◆———————

The prosecution then changed tack, circling back to Klamath Falls and the purported cablegram Frank had received regarding his father and brothers in England. In particular, Casterlin pressed Frank on the details of that cablegram, specifically relating to the more sensational aspects of Robinson's family as they appeared in the local paper. Details pertaining to the alleged multiple Victoria Crosses his family had earned. Details regarding his brother's work as a physician in New York, and the deaths of his brother and father. "Did you have any conversation with Mrs. Barnhisel respecting any other matters concerning your family?"[101]

"I don't recall whether we did or not."

"Had you been out of the United States just prior to the receipt of this cablegram?" Casterlin asked.

"Not for many years," Frank said. "A number of years."

"Doctor Robinson, do you know when the World War ended?"

"1917, wasn't it?"

Defense attorney Ed Robertson waded in. "I don't think we should go back there."

"Where is this material?" Judge Cavanaugh said. "Unless you want to connect that up, in view of this *Evening Herald* article, I think perhaps the question is proper."

"I will stipulate it was in November 1918, that the war ended," Casterlin added. "Was your brother Leonard killed during the world war?"

"I have discovered since that he was."

"When did you discover that?"

"Since I came back to Moscow after this trip, from this other brother."

"When did you discover that your brother had been decorated for bravery on the battlefield?"

"I don't know anything about that statement," Robinson said flatly.

"When did you first discover that your father had died of heart failure?"

"That telegram."[102]

"How many brothers did you lose in the war, Doctor Robinson?"

Ed Robertson weighed in once again. "I object to that as going to collateral matters."

"He may answer," the judge conceded.

"Did you lose any other brothers in the world war?"

"Not to my knowledge, no."

"Doctor, do you recall what year you went to Klamath Falls?"[103]

"No sir. I was in Klamath Falls twice, the first time perhaps—well, I can't give years," he said. "The last time I went was about 1917, or 1918, 1916 perhaps."[104]

"When did you first become acquainted with Mrs. Barnhisel's sister, who I understand is now your wife?"

"It was a few weeks before we were married."

"I believe you said you were married Thanksgiving 1919?"

"I guess the day before Thanksgiving," Robinson said.

"You were not acquainted with your wife at the time you had this interview with Mrs. Barnhisel, the reporter from *The Evening Herald?*"[105]

"No sir. I had never seen her."

"I think you stated on direct examination that her father was a district judge?"

"Circuit judge."

"That would be a state judge."

"I think at the time he was a city judge or police judge or something. He was elected to the circuit bench after that."

Always shifting gears, Casterlin came at Robinson from another direction. "I think you said that you made up your mind instantly to go to England?"

"Yes."[106]

"Didn't you have your mind made up to go to England when you made application for this passport?"

"I had in mind a trip but I didn't know what boat I was to take," Frank said, deviating slightly, though tellingly, from his previous statements.

"You had in mind a trip out of the country?"

"Yes."

"The application you made out was taken by you yourself—personally—to Harry H. Thatcher?"

"Yes sir. I took it to the court house."

"You took it to the court house for the purpose of swearing to it, did you?"

"No."

"Then why did you take it there?"

"There had to be a signature of the clerk."

"Now why did you understand that it was necessary?"

"It says so on the face of it," Robinson said.

"On the face of what?"

"The application."

"Did you read the application before you took it to Mr. Thatcher?"

"Yes sir. I read it."

"So before you took it to him you were familiar with its contents?"

Frank was growing uncomfortable as Casterlin drew nearer to the heart of the trial. "Well," he said, "I will tell you: I could answer that yes or no."

"Were you familiar with the contents of the application before you took it to Mr. Thatcher?"[107]

"I can't say that I was familiar with every one of the contents for the reason that I didn't pay attention. I don't know whether I had decided—at that time I didn't know whether I would go or not, and I didn't consider it important, but so far as reading it, I think I read it."

"Now, Doctor Robinson, you have been asked about the occasion of the trip, was the occasion of your trip entirely for the purpose of your health?"[108]

"It wasn't for my health at all," Robinson said. "It was a general business trip. I would say that I went to rest, but I also went to get a larger view of things. I write for several magazines."

"There was nothing the matter with your health that required a trip abroad?"

"I wasn't suffering from any disease or ailment but I was very tired."

"Are you acquainted with a man by the name of Geoffrey Peel Birley?"[109]

"Yes sir."

"Wasn't it for the purpose of conferring with him that you took this trip?"

"No," Frank said. "He didn't know I was coming."

"You did confer with him, didn't you?"

"Yes sir."

"Where did that conference take place?"

Defense attorney Robertson called out from his table. "Objected to as going into collateral matters."

"Overruled."

"Where did you contact Mr. Birley?" Casterlin asked.

"I sent him a telegram to Alexandria."

"Where did you meet him?"

"Egypt."

"When you arrived at England you stated that you sent a telegram to your father. What address did you send it to?"

"Morpeth," Frank said. "Northumberland."

"You found out his address?"

"I found it out when I visited this little village—"

"He received the telegram at Northumberland?"

"I presume so."

"Now, at the time you made out this application for passport, you stated that you had exhibit 10, the instructions which you now hold."[110]

"It came with the application."

The defense interjected. "He doesn't refer to this exhibit."[111]

"I don't think the instruction sheet which came with that application was anything like this," Frank said. "It was another form. It seems to me it was a double faced proposition."

"Then do I understand that the instruction sheet which you had to fill out for the application was not the one you hold?"

Frank began to squirm while all eyes from the jury box fixed upon him and his words. "I am not saying," he began, "I don't know whether it was or not. It seems that it was a different shape. It seems to be in the back of my head that it was a different shape."

"Then you do not identify that as the instruction sheet that you had when you completed the application?"

"I can't say."

"Would you say that the contents of the sheet of instructions that you had at the time you filled out the application were the same as the contents of this exhibit 10 which you hold in your hand?"

"No, I wouldn't say that."

"So, you don't know whether you had—at the time you filled out the application—these instructions which you hold as exhibit 10 or not?"

"I can't swear they were identical. I have an idea that they were different, a different type, but I am not clear on it, and it was two years ago and it is a long time, a thing like this, I didn't pay much attention to it."

"When you said that you followed the instructions on this exhibit 10, when you made out the application, you might be in error?"[112]

"Not at all, if I said I followed the instructions."

"Those instructions," Casterlin asked nodding toward the document in Frank's hand.

"If this is the exhibit."

"You will not state that this is the exhibit."

"I might state that there is something in my mind that this blank was different, but that was two years ago."

From his table, Casterlin grabbed another document for the witness. "Doctor, I hand to you defendant's exhibit 18, dated May 4, and is headed application to the New York Life Insurance Company. Do you recall the time when you made that application?"

"No. But it was in Moscow, in 1931."

Casterlin's line of questioning began to zero in on how Frank had misrepresented facts about taking medical exams and about his parents in order to secure more insurance prior to his travels abroad, raising the specter of possible insurance fraud.

"Do you remember if as part of the application you were required to answer any questions respecting your father, mother, brothers, and sister?"

"No, I don't remember specific incidents."

"You have taken out at least five applications for life insurance, have you not?"

"There are several."

"On each occasion you have had a medical examination?"

"No, I think I have some that didn't require that."

"With that New York Life Insurance Company, on each of those two applications you took a medical examination?"

"Yes sir."

"And on each of those occasions you were asked questions respecting your father and mother?"

"I presume so."

"You know that to be a fact."

"No, I don't know what was in the application. It was a long time ago, and I don't know what was in each application."[113]

"Did you or did you not make any statement to the New York Life Insurance Company agent respecting your father and mother as part of the application?"

"I can't tell you any statement that I made in 1931 on an insurance application."

"Did you make any statement respecting your father and mother at the time, whether or not at that time they were alive or dead?"

"I can't answer that."

"I hand you defendant's exhibit 19, application to the New York Life Insurance Company dated July 22, 1930. At that time when you made application, did you or did you not take a medical examination?"[114]

"If a policy was issued, I did."

"Was the policy issued on the application, exhibit 19?

"I wouldn't know until I checked and found out."

"You could look at the application," Casterlin asserted.

"I have a $10,000 policy in the New York Life Insurance Company."

"On that application?" Casterlin said, indicating the paper in Robinson's hands. "Exhibit 19?"

"How would I know?"

"I am asking you."

"I have a policy," Robinson said testily. "I don't have the record, but I have a policy in the New York Life, but I can't say from 1930 to 1936 whether this application is the application or not. There is a lot of water gone over the dam since that date."

"Is that the application upon which the $10,000 policy was issued?"

"I am not prepared to answer."

For several minutes, Casterlin continued to pepper Frank with a volley of questions.

For each question posed to him, Frank returned his own volley of one-note responses. "I am not prepared to answer"; "I will not say"; "I don't recall"; "I am not able to say"; "I can't tell you"; and "I can't remember."

Departing briefly from his dogged line of questioning, Casterlin redirected Frank's attention. "Doctor Robinson, did you or did you not at the time you had the interview with Mr. Bannerman in [Washington, DC] make the statement that you left England because of difficulties with your stepmother?" Casterlin reminded Frank that Bannerman—the Chief Special Agent for the State Department—had already testified about their meeting.

"No sir," Frank said.

Ed Robertson rose from the defense table. "We didn't get into this conversation with Mr. Bannerman—"[115]

"Overruled."

"I have answered the question," Frank said.

"At the same time and place did you or did you not state to Mr. Bannerman that the trouble which your stepmother had with your brother was the last straw, and that is why you left?"

"I don't think so."

"Did you or did you not?" Casterlin said.

Flummoxed and tired, Robinson shot back: "I can't recall or recount every word of the conversation. Not every word."

"Did you or did you not make that statement?"

"I cannot answer it because I don't know."

"With respect to the letter of introduction to the Reverend Henry Wallace at Belleville, Ontario, from whom did you get that letter?"

"I don't remember that letter, from whom it came."

"Did you or did you not at an interview you had with Mr. Bannerman state to him that you had a letter from your father to Reverend Wallace at Marchmont Home, Belleville?"

"I don't recall that," Frank said. "Bannerman had a stack of papers with him, and he would read them and say, 'is this true' and 'is that true', and this other thing true. As to any statement of that kind, I am not saying that I made it at all."

"That is all," Casterlin said, returning to his seat.[116]

Ed Robertson stood, plucked a document from his table, and approached the witness stand. Sunlight poured in from the two large windows. The crowd tracked the defense attorney's movement. "Doctor Robinson," the defense lawyer began, his accent heavy in the courtroom air. "I hand you defendant's exhibit 23 containing certain statements with respect to your being born in Toronto, Canada."

Frank held the document, looking it over.

"Did you state to anyone that you were born in Toronto, Canada?"

"I did not."

"Move to strike the answer for the purpose of objection," Casterlin called out.

"It may be stricken."

"Objected to on the ground that it is calling for impeachment of a written document which is signed by this defendant, the contents of which are not uncertain, unintelligible, or ambiguous, and require no explanation—"

Judge Cavanaugh stepped in. "Does the exhibit state that he made the statement?"

"Is any part of that application in your own hand writing other than your signature?"

"No sir."

"Did you fill in any blanks contained in that application?"

"I sure didn't."

"Did you at any time observe that the person had put in your birthplace as Toronto?"[117]

"I didn't read this at any time. I never saw it."

"Did you observe in that application before your signature was added on it, that it contained the statement that your brother was killed in the war, and that your father was killed in the war."

"No I certainly didn't."

"Doctor, do you remember taking out this $3,000 policy, how you happened to apply for that?"

"No."

"Is the policy in force now?"

"No," Robinson said. "I made one payment and then dropped it."

"Who was the insurance agent?"

"George Ulrich."

"Do you remember him trying to get you to take out an insurance policy?"

"Objected to," Casterlin declared, "as incompetent, irrelevant and immaterial, and for calling for a conclusion of this witness."

Judge Cavanaugh looked at Defense Attorney Robertson. "Relating to this policy?"[118]

"Yes, this policy," he said and turned back to the witness for response.

"Yes sir, I do," Frank said.

"How many times had he seen you in reference to getting a policy?"

"I imagine about 150 times. He wouldn't let me alone. Well, not that many times, but he was running me ragged."

"Move to strike that as a conclusion," Casterlin said.

"It may be stricken."

Robertson turned back to his witness. "Did you read the application when he finally got you to take insurance?"

"No," Frank said. "He filled it all out and I just signed it."

"Objection, your honor," Casterlin said. "It doesn't make any difference whether he read it or not."

"Sustained."

"With reference to the Oregon State Board of Pharmacy, plaintiff's exhibit 24, I will ask was that prepared by you?"

"Objected to as incompetent, irrelevant and immaterial."

Judge Cavanaugh let the proceedings move along.

Examining the exhibit, Robinson looked at his lawyer. "This was not filled out by me."

"Then by whom was it filled out, Doctor?"

"John Mills, the registered pharmacist working for me. I wasn't in Klamath Falls when it was filled out. I was in San Francisco."[119]

"Did you read it before you signed it?"

"No."

"Did you know what it contained?"

"Just a moment," Judge Cavanaugh said, and looked at Robinson. "At the time you signed the application, you could not read?"

"I could."

Cavanaugh continued: "Then you are able to understand what is in that application if you could read and didn't read it."

"I could and didn't."

Ed Robertson regained the floor. "What was the occasion that prevented you from reading?"

"Objected to as calling for a conclusion on the part of the witness and is a self serving declaration in the part of the witness—"

"Doctor," Robertson said over the momentary din, "were you born in Toronto, Canada?"

"No."

"Did anybody tell you that you were born in Toronto?"

"Never."

"Did you ever tell anybody that you were born in Toronto, Canada?"

"I never told anyone that."

Satisfied, Ed Robertson regarded the judge and the room. "That is all."

———————◆———————

The trial lasted four days. The D.A.'s lawyers questioned a dozen witnesses. (Records of these testimonies have been lost.). As for the jury, they convened at 4:30 on the afternoon of May 19 and deliberated until half past midnight.[120] Then on Wednesday, May 20, 1936, the court was back in session. Dust storms had ravaged large swaths of Idaho and several other western states that day. Winds battered the large windowpanes of the courtroom. Judge Cavanaugh turned to the jury and asked them if they had reached a verdict.

Willie Turner, foreman for the jury, rose from his seat. "We have, your honor."

"We, the jury in the above entitled case," he said, "find the defendant, Frank Bruce Robinson, Not Guilty."[121]

Gasps and commotion stirred through the courtroom. Judge Cavanaugh rapped his gavel demanding order. Although it had been proven Frank was born in England, the jury bought his defense that he simply *believed* he had been born in New York. No doubt feeling relieved, Robinson basked in the joy of his victory while his lawyers clapped him on the back and shook his hand. Several supporters shoved through the crowds to congratulate Frank, while the prosecutors quietly gathered their papers and snapped their briefcases shut. Newsmen scribbled furiously into their notebooks while cameras flashed bolts of light, capturing the scene. Frank Robinson was jubilant and stood with a broad and confident smile, glad-handing all his well-wishers and reveling in the frenetic heat of his divine vindication.

One man in the crowd rose quietly from his seat, made his way through the spectators, down the ornate wooden staircase to the ground floor of the federal building, and stepped outside. His name was Sherwin H. Stewart, known as Shirl. A U.S. immigration inspector who had been on Robinson's trail for sometime, Stewart had to make a telephone call.

His work was just beginning.

———————◆———————

Meanwhile, local media reported out Robinson's exoneration. "In Passport Case," noted one paper, "Jurors Acquit." "Sealed Verdict Returned," read another, "Court Room Crowded When Report Read." "Founder of Psycho-Religious Movement Freed of Charge of Falsification."

> In a tense and crowded courtroom a federal jury here this morning brought in a "not guilty" verdict for Dr. Frank B. Robinson...The defendant sat with his head bowed until the court clerk unhurriedly came to the words "not guilty."[122]

Frank's first order of business was to call Pearl and tell her of the good news. He put in an appearance at his office, too, to make the news official. After all, his employees—fortunate to have work in such dark times—had been harboring their own fears. Last, he had to dispatch word to his students. His acquittal was the greatest proof to date that Psychiana worked, and that it was the God Law that had ushered him out of the howling wilderness of persecution and into the light of righteousness.

CHAPTER 22
"Psychiana is With Me"

At the end of June 1936, a Mrs. Pfeffer jotted down a quick note on the back of a glossy postcard, thanking her spiritual teacher. The front of the card featured a photo of the lavish restaurant inside Copenhagen's National Scala overlooking the Tivoli River. The flipside of the card was adorned with a pink stamp of Germany's President Hindenburg that read "Deutsches Riech." Mrs. Pfeffer wrote, "Dear Dr. Robinson—It will please you to hear that I am well enough to have come from California via Panama on this journey: Psychiana is with me." Very little is known about Mrs. Pfeffer other than that, after her visit to Copenhagen, she traveled with her "young and charming" niece to Berlin where she was currently staying. "We are here for the Olympics," she added. If she had sensed any uneasiness about vacationing in the center of Nazi Germany in 1936, her sentiments surely did not make their way into her brief note. Of course, the Nazi Party had essentially scrubbed the city of its anti-Jewish propaganda in advance of the global event. Far from apprehensive, Mrs. Pfeffer continued on, telling Robinson of their plans to "go to the Bayreuth Wagner Festival." There, at the famous music celebration, she would witness Adolf Hitler stepping out onto a balcony in a tuxedo and white tie, where he delivered his Nazi salute to an adoring crowd shouting "Heil Hitler." Crowding the bottom edge of her postcard, Mrs. Pfeffer closed with a simple line of gratitude: "Am grateful to you."[123]

CHAPTER 23

The Marksmen

On July 19, 1936, U.S. immigration officer Frank S. Nooney was working under the press of summer heat outside the Masonic Temple in Spokane, Washington. It was a Sunday but Nooney—a first-rate officer—was nonetheless on the clock. Born in Chester, Massachusetts—a storybook hamlet hemmed into the eastern band of the Berkshires—Nooney grew up in an upper-middle-class family. (His father, George, was a lawyer.) Following in his father's footsteps of law enforcement, Frank Nooney transferred to Portal, North Dakota, and later to International Falls, Minnesota, where he oversaw the port of entry between the United States and Ontario, Canada.[124] In 1934, he made his final career move, taking a posting in Spokane.

A thirty-nine-year-old husband and father of two, Nooney was a tall and lean WWI Navy veteran known around Spokane as a crack-shot rifleman who regularly won ultra-competitive shooting contests.[125] He had an ashen face, a high forehead, and suspecting eyes fitted behind unassuming glasses.[126] Nooney's experience along the Canadian border, and loyalty to his office, all came to bear when his superior—Sherwin H. Stewart—dropped Frank Robinson's file on his desk. Nooney was one of a select number of U.S. government officials who were aware of Robinson's legal troubles and had been following the passport fraud case closely.

Despite the heat, Nooney would have found plenty of shade behind any one of the Masonic Temple's eighteen Corinthian columns. Located downtown along the edge of the Spokane River, the sprawling neoclassical building was a point of pride for the city, and, as of that Sunday, Nooney's current stakeout. Immigration and border agents were nothing if not patient, and Nooney—the expert marksman—was no exception.

The summer of 1936 was a hot and fraught time by any measure. The geopolitical sphere was electrified, almost crackling with tensions. The United States was still mired deep in the Great Depression with no foreseeable exit. Homicide and suicide rates were up. Dust storms haunted the plains. Oswald Mosely, the British fascist, was sowing discord in the streets of London. Spain was in crisis, and Hitler's Nazi party was preparing for the Olympics in Berlin.

Frank Robinson, on the other hand, having just escaped his own fraught circumstances, dove headlong back into his work without a care in the world. He felt beyond vindicated. He felt empowered. Overcoming the fierce legal battle, onerous trial, incessant press coverage, and personal stress was precisely the boost he needed. His victory became the cornerstone of his latest Psychiana campaign. His was a David and Goliath story of the modern age, and it featured prominently into all of his marketing, advertising, and lecture materials. He was already drafting a new article, which would run in September's *Psychiana Quarterly*, titled simply, "Persecution." He was hard at work writing an entirely new set of twenty advanced Lessons. Instead of following the form of previous Lessons—"Psychiana: the New Psychological Religion"—the new Lessons' pink coversheets promoted a subtle but important rebranding: "The Church of Psychiana." Now more than ever, Robinson started printing individual testimonials in broadside form, the contents of which were gleaned from the thousands upon thousands of letters he received. The letters that mentioned the injustice of his persecution were given top priority as potential marketing material. One letter received that hot summer came from Emma Markley in Seattle. "My heart goes out to you in love and gratitude in this hour of testing," she wrote. "For I know that after the crucifixion comes the ascension, which is always cause for rejoicing. We know that divinity cannot be crucified." In closing, Markley added, "PSYCHIANA, the Oversoul, CANNOT FAIL. Never doubt it. I, your student, DO believe in the Power of the LIVING GOD."[127]

Frank had scarcely wrapped up his trial when he began a robust lecturing tour. The showman in him hungered for the energy of a live audience, and the stage is where he felt at his best. It helped, too, that lectures tended to be lucrative, and for the first time since starting Psychiana, Robinson's cash flow was radically attenuated on account of his legal fees. Some of his more ambitious projects, like his Los Angeles temple, had to be put on hold until he could remedy his delinquent accounts. Knowing that he could always count on a large and curious audience in nearby Spokane, Frank booked the Masonic Temple's great hall for Sunday, July 19.

On July 12, 1936, exactly one week before his scheduled lecture, 150 postal inspectors and affiliates of the U.S. Postal Service gathered for a two-day conference at the expansive brick Osburn Hotel in Eugene, Oregon. Attended by a veritable who's who of the country's information highway, the event addressed the field's most pressing issues: systemic change, shrinking budgets, available technology, and crime detection. (Mail fraud trended upward in hard times.) Chief organizer of the convention was Stephen Howard Morse, the seasoned Oregon-based postal inspector who had first ordered an inquiry into Frank Robinson's mail-order religion. Indicative of his broad knowledge of the postal system, Morse—the longest-serving postal inspector in U.S. history—also chaired the convention's "question box and open forum" session. (A couple of months later, *The Coos Bay Times* featured a profile of the inspector: "Meet S.H. Morse," they wrote, "Who Can Tell Ripsnorting Tales About Early Days Running U.S. Mail Into Frontier Land.") There is little doubt that Frank Robinson's case would have been a topic of conversation at the postal conference amongst those in Morse's professional orbit (if only privately), given its notoriety and (to some) notable acquittal.[128]

It was Stephen H. Morse who had reached out to Sherwin Stewart at the U.S. Immigration Office in Spokane, suggesting they open up a file on Robinson. On reviewing the brief and the evidence, Stewart looped Frank Nooney into the case. The trial may have concluded back in May, but it still left Stewart—and Morse for that matter—with significant and unanswered questions. Keeping Morse apprised of developments in what was now an immigration issue (related to, but substantively different from, passport fraud), Stewart and his team laid their plans in advance of Robinson's Spokane lecture, taking place one week after the postmasters' convention.

Inside the Masonic Temple's Commandery Auditorium, a large Psychiana sign hung prominently over the stage, backdropping the lectern. Two of his secretaries—seated at desks on either end of the stage—awaited their usual transcription duties. Volunteers staffed the doors where they handed out leaflets, took donations, and enrolled the more willing attendees into the first series of Lessons. Robinson looked like a movie star, smartly dressed to highlight his blondish-silver hair and cool blue eyes.

The lecture covered familiar ground: the God Power, student testimonials, swipes at conventional faith, nods toward popular scientific breakthroughs, and his recent "persecution." Robinson placed a heavy emphasis on his legal and financial woes before wrapping up. By all accounts the lecture was a success. After the talk, Frank spoke with well-wishers and hangers-on while his volunteers and secretaries gathered up the unused leaflets and counted the day's take. When it was all wrapped up and the last stragglers had cleared out, Frank stepped outside into the summer air, briefcase in hand.

At that moment, two men in fedoras closed in. "Frank Robinson?" The tall, lean one said, flashing his government badge.

Robinson turned, nonplussed.

"Inspector Nooney. U.S. Immigration Service. I have a warrant for your arrest," he said. "For violating United States immigration laws."[129]

Robinson was stunned and angry. The ink had no sooner dried on his acquittal papers than he was once again the target of the law. The two men cuffed Robinson, folded him into the back seat of their car, and took him to the Spokane County jail. There on a hot July Sunday evening, Frank B. Robinson was, in his own words, "fingerprinted and 'mugged' just as a criminal would have been."[130] It was a situation, Frank wrote, that "went hard," calling it a "persecution of the worst sort." He called his lawyer, Ed Robertson, and they posted the $2,000 bond for his release. Sherwin "Shirl" Stewart informed Robinson that he would be in touch regarding a date for a hearing. Frank was then released from custody, a bit tussled and a little worse for the wear.[131]

The U.S. Immigration Service's lead man, Shirl H. Stewart, cut his teeth working border-jumping cases along the Canada/Montana line during the heyday of Prohibition.[132] The Minnewaukan, North Dakota, native was one of eleven children reared in an Irish farm family. Stewart worked as a grain salesman before leaving for Havre, Montana, to patrol the border. Dark-haired and stylishly dressed, Stewart had natural good looks with a dimpled chin, resembling a young Cary Grant.[133] In his free time, Stewart enjoyed his membership in the Elks Club where, on at least one occasion, he performed in blackface at a minstrel show.[134]

Professionally, Stewart had made a name for himself as a tenacious and formidable border agent on Montana's "High Line," rounding up illegal immigrants, vagabonds, fugitives, charlatans, and smugglers alike. Anyone attempting to cross from Canada into the United States illegally was an active target to Shirl Stewart. He prosecuted one woman crossing illegally with expensive furs, and another for using several false identities. He pursued bootleggers and criminal enterprises.[135] By the late 1920s, however, Stewart had taken a promotion and transferred to Spokane, where he worked out of a nice office in the Columbia Building downtown. He and his wife, Dorothy, bought a modest brick home with a large yard in a quiet neighborhood.

In July 1936, Stewart was busy behind the scenes working the complex, multi-layered Robinson matter in addition to his regular caseload. He was nothing if not shrewd, and when he decided to train his focus on Frank Robinson, he went all in. The case became almost personal to Stewart, especially as Robinson had somehow managed to slip across the same stretch of border Stewart had been working as an immigration agent. The Robinson case also may have stuck in Stewart's craw because Frank represented the very type of person Stewart spent years pursuing and prosecuting.

Following Robinson's arrest, Stewart drafted memos, filed paperwork, held meetings, and made phone calls to ensure that everyone who needed to know his next steps was apprised. From his Spokane office, he phoned Frank Griffin, Assistant U.S. District Attorney in Boise, as a matter of courtesy. "He posted his bond," Stewart told Griffin. "Now he'll come up for a hearing either here in Spokane or in Moscow, within a few days." Griffin made a note of the call and thanked Stewart for the heads-up, later telling reporters that his office would "have nothing to do with the immigration hearing."[136]

Sherwin "Shirl" Horace Stewart (S.H. Stewart). Image provided by Edith Adkins via Ancestry.com.

Because Stewart's work sat squarely within the purview of the Department of Labor, he reported all significant cases to his chief superior, Labor Secretary Frances Perkins. His initial investigation into Frank's duplicitous background led him to believe he was now dealing with a solid deportation case, which would require clearance from the top levels of the U.S. government. In Stewart's eyes, Frank B. Robinson was more than just a religious huckster: he was an illegal alien, a squatter who had gamed the system for far too long.

On August 8, Stewart told reporters only what he had to: "Robinson," he said, "has been ordered to appear before me in a private hearing on August 13 on the charge of violating the United States immigration laws." Stewart went on to further clarify: "The July 19 arrest has no connection with Dr. Robinson's recent trial at Moscow."[137] Specifically, Stewart seems to have unearthed documents showing that Frank had crossed into Canada through Eastport, Idaho, presumably to visit his brother, Sydney. (He had alluded to such a trip to his half-sister, Mary, in his 1932 letter to her.)

Some in the media were as baffled by the development as Robinson himself, who was trying to sidestep the reporters staked out near his home and offices. It was a rare turn for Robinson, a man who hungered for press—good, bad, or otherwise. Pivoting from his usual flamboyant self, Frank merely raised a sober hand to anyone asking. "I have nothing to say."[138]

It is possible that his earlier acquittal was starting to feel like a cruel joke, a flash of false hope. It is possible, too, that Frank suspected the current charge—and the threat of deportation—was more worrisome. Indeed, it is possible that Frank Robinson felt he was reaching the end of his long con, and the jig was finally up. Nevertheless, he dug in. Despite his anemic cash-flow situation, Frank once again had to lawyer-up.

Two days later—August 10—the Psychiana guru broke his silence only to say, "I was born in the United States and have lived here continuously for 32 years. I have been nowhere near Eastport for years." Summoning his inner public relations and advertising sense, Frank then issued his standard and repeated defense: "This constitutes a persecution of the worst sort."[139]

In Spokane, Stewart stayed the course with the tenacity of a bloodhound. Fielding another volley of questions, the immigration inspector made only vague statements to the press. "The full record in this case will be sent to immigration service headquarters in Washington, DC," he noted. "And any information on disposition of the case—or the charges—will be released there."[140]

◆

Shirl Stewart confined the hearing to the parties involved, and held it in his suite of offices in the Columbia Building. He anticipated the hearing to take about two days, "possibly longer." He had placed the onus on the defense to "show cause" as to why, legally, Robinson should not be deported as an illegal alien.[141]

On behalf of his client, Ed Robertson went to work, whittling their defense down to four key points:

1. The government did not overcome the burden of proving alienage.
2. There was no competent proof of the conviction of a crime involving moral turpitude prior to entry.
3. Robinson's domicile here permitted him to visit Canada and return without an immigration visa.
4. There is no proof that Robinson entered without inspection and he should not be deported even if he did.[142]

Fleshing out the skeleton of their defense strategy and making the case that Frank B. Robinson was a model citizen, Ed Robertson had stockpiled an arsenal of his client's good deeds, real or perceived. "Dr. Robinson," the attorney stated for the record, "has lived at Moscow, Idaho, for the past eight years. His wife was born in Oregon and has never been outside the United States. He has two children, a son thirteen years of age, and a daughter five years of age, both of whom were born in America. There is nothing in this record against him and nothing is referred to unfavorably in the summary of the examining inspector subsequent to November 23, 1921."[143] The only possible blemish on Robinson's record after that date, the attorney continued, was Frank's passport application, the matter that had already been decided in Frank's favor by a federal jury. The critical date for them to keep in mind was Frank and Pearl's wedding date. The defense had to keep the hearing's focus on Robinson's life *after*, and not *before*, November 26, 1919. Everything afterwards was explainable, but Frank's life prior to that date remained a mystery, even to his closest advisors.

Inspector Stewart, however, was interested in Robinson's past and key events leading up to and beyond that date. For instance, Stewart had information showing that Robinson had gone to Canada in 1932 to see his brother, thereby negating his previous testimony, under oath, that he had never been out of the United States. Relying on his many years' experience as a border agent, Stewart zeroed in on each of Robinson's border crossings, beginning with his first in 1910.

"Were you inspected by a U.S. Immigrant Inspector at that time?" Stewart asked during the closed-door hearing.

"On the train, if there was one," Robinson said. "Although I don't recall it. I didn't make any attempt to evade it."

"You don't remember whether an inspector talked to you or not?"

"I was sleeping in an upper berth and a customs man came around but I don't think any immigration man was there."[144]

Frank's defense counsel posited legal precedents that showed entry into the United States from "favorable countries" like Canada did not require a visa, and even if one had been required, the burden of Robinson's entry—legal or not—fell on the failure of the immigration agents and not on Frank.

Stewart then turned to another trip Robinson had made to Canada in September 1935, a year before this trial. "Tell me about seeing the U.S. Immigration Inspector on the train," Stewart said. "What took place?"

"When I got on the train, the conductor knocked at the door and said that the immigration man would be around before I went to sleep. He said that they would have to disturb us for that and that is all," Frank said. "The immigrant inspector knocked at the door. I had my coat off and was washing in my compartment. I turned around and he said, 'U.S. Immigration Service.' I said, 'Come in.'"

What Robinson then disclosed is as strange as it is telling. "[The immigration official] immediately spotted my sheriff's badge and he said, 'Oh, you're a cop.' He came over and looked at the badge and he said, 'Going home?' and I said, 'Yes.'"

Stewart made a note of his response and pressed forward. "Did he ask you your name?"

"It is on the badge," Frank said.

"Did he ask where you were born?"

"It was a very short thing," Frank said. "As soon as he saw that badge, he said, 'Oh, you're a cop?' and made his visit short and got out."

"And asked no further questions?"

"I don't think so."[145]

The so-called sheriff's badge Robinson was referring to was the "honorary badge" local Moscow Sheriff Hap Moody had given him years earlier. Why, exactly, Robinson was traveling with it in the first place was a question Stewart neither asked nor pursued.

"Robinson's testimony," the defense argued, "must be believed because it is without contradiction, and it bears the stamp of truthfulness and appears to be what would naturally have occurred under the circumstances."[146] Summarizing their case before Stewart's panel, the defense took an offensive posture, especially when it came to Shirl Stewart himself. "The examining inspector who conducted these proceedings appeared throughout to have a preconceived prejudice against Robinson," they wrote. "We think this can be demonstrated by a perusal of the record in which questions were asked Robinson which served no useful purpose except to embarrass the witness with relation to things occurring many years ago."[147] Frank's lawyers were referring to his expulsions from the Royal Northwest Mounted Police and the U.S. Navy. "Clearly," they continued, "the examining inspector seems to derive satisfaction from the discharge of Robinson from the force 'as useless,' more than twenty years ago."[148]

Tearing down Stewart was one of two prongs of the defensive strategy. The second was the building-up of Robinson's character. Frank B. Robinson had, after all, just donated 60 acres of land to the city of Moscow for a recreational park. Here was a man, they argued, who was the single largest private employer in Moscow. He owned one of the two major newspapers in that town. He was a member of the Democratic National Finance Committee. He had joined Senators William Borah and James Pope in Washington, DC, when they lobbied the Agricultural Adjustment Administration to reopen wheat allotments to farmers in Idaho. Here was a man who, when he heard a child was lost on Moscow Mountain, had hired a private plane to scout for and rescue the boy. In short, this man was more good than bad, a credit to his town, state, and nation, and that he should remain in the country.

On the final day of the deportation hearing, Robinson entered his own statement for the record, stating in part, "Because I have a wife and family, a beautiful home, several hundred thousand dollars worth of property and about a half-million people depending on me for spiritual help and advice. Because I can show you many thousands of letters from responsible people all over the United States telling me in no uncertain terms what I mean to them, and I have a payroll which runs from $50,000 to $100,000 a year. I support many families in Moscow. I have put student after student through the university. I have fed destitute families every Christmas. I have chartered airplanes to find lost children. My name heads the subscription on every public charity drive that has been conducted in Latah County...I admit foolishness and drinking from the age of seventeen or eighteen years up until about twenty years ago, but I can't see why—when a man's record is as clean as mine since my marriage, or shortly after; and when the man is an outstanding citizen of the community and when he is helping hundreds of thousands of people; I don't see what is to be gained by separating that man from his business and family. It would just simply mean that a wife and children would be separated from their means of support. It would probably mean that—well, I can't find one uplifting thing which would be accomplished by any deportation of me."[149]

————————◆————————

After four days of closed-door testimony, the hearing ended on an uncertain note. "Government Ends Robinson Hearing without Decision," the *Boise Statesman* announced.[150] An impatient man by nature, Robinson was growing more and more incensed by his legal forecast. Ed Robertson laid out all scenarios for his client, knowing that no matter which course they took, the fight would be protracted. It was, one paper noted, "a long, drawn-out affair."[151]

Addressing reporters, Stewart simply stated that he had sealed all of the Robinson case files in an envelope and forwarded it to Frances Perkins, Secretary of Labor in Washington, DC, for a final decision.[152]

Everything hung in the balance.

CHAPTER 24

"A Pack of Bloody Hounds"

Manor Farm
Bledington, England
September 23, 1936

As Frank's legal battles spilled over into late summer, external and internal pressures continued to mount on the fifty-year-old. Once flush with cash, Frank was now spread impossibly thin, with most of his available revenue pouring daily into his lawyers' pockets. The entire back page of the September issue of *Psychiana Quarterly* had but one message:

$300,000 is a lot of money.

Yet this is the approximate amount due me now from students with whom I have been lenient in the payment of their accounts. I have been more interested in my students finding the Power of God than I have been in their money.

NOW I NEED HELP.

Will You Give It To Me?[153]

Beyond delinquent accounts, Frank had a heavy payroll at Psychiana's many office buildings, his drugstores, and his newspaper. He had to cover his family's expenses at their luxurious estate in Los Angeles, and he was in debt to one of his most prominent students—Geoffrey Peel Birley.

———————✦———————

On Wednesday, September 23, 1936, Birley began drafting an earnest, albeit strained, letter to Frank. He was visiting his parents at their farm in Bledington, England. "I have read about the trial," he wrote, "and it appears to me an extremely foolish and wasteful business altogether...I imagined the federal authorities would have had a bit more sense. It shows though what a pack of bloody hounds you have on your trail." Birley then dispensed with his sympathies and got right to business. "You mentioned," he continued, "that you would start on the payments as soon as possible and catch up on the back ones too, but to date nothing has been forthcoming." Birley mentions some of Frank's letters, but the young cotton exporter wanted to meet with Frank in person. "I greatly desire to come over to the States about the middle of October," he wrote, "and see you personally to discuss several problems with you."

Aside from the financial concerns Birley had about his stake in Psychiana, it remains unclear what other problems he deemed so pressing that they necessitated transcontinental travel and an in-person meeting. But Birley's urgency became suddenly clear in a subsequent letter to Frank just three days later. "I have booked passage on the *Queen Mary*," he announced, "leaving Southampton on 14th October and arriving New York on the 19th…I hope to stay in New York either one or two days, at the New Yorker, and then go straight off to Moscow." Birley again returned—if only cryptically—to the underlining issues motivating his trip. "There are many matters I want to discuss with you relating to Psychiana and the other affairs, etc. and this is best done verbally rather than by writing numerous letters."[154]

News of Birley's visit and the import of their meeting could not have come at a worse time for Psychiana's leader. Of their relationship, Alf later wrote, "I vaguely recall my father expressing his wish that he and Birley be at arm's length."[155] On October 5, Frank received a Western Union cable from Birley.

ARRIVING NEW YORK NINETEENTH OCTOBER

IMPORTANT KNOW WHEN PAYMENTS RESUME WIRE GROSVENOR HOTEL

GEOFFREY[156]

If his travels, trials, and travails had taught him anything in the past year, it was that he could no longer be everything to all people, all the time. It was as if he had aged five years in twenty-four months. He needed help. Specifically, he needed another front-man, a second face at Psychiana, someone else with the credentials and gravitas to help answer the ceaseless stream of letters pouring in daily and who could tend the shop in his absence.

Fortuitously, there happened to be a local minister looking for work. Charles Wesley Tenney, or Dr. C.W. Tenney as he was known, had been the director of the Institute of Christian Education at the University of

Idaho before budget cuts forced the program to close. Frank and Tenney had been acquainted for a number of years, and after some brief interviews and negotiations, the two men shook hands, finalizing the deal to bring Tenney on board the Psychiana operation. Each man profited from the arrangement. Tenney could remain in Moscow and earn a livable wage. Robinson could unburden himself of many of the day-to-day operations Psychiana demanded. Making it official, Robinson forwarded a press release to his editor Bill Marineau at *The News Review*. Marineau ran the story three days before Frank received Birley's latest cable.

Charles Wesley Tenney, Psychiana's second in command, c. 1939. University of Idaho Special Collections.

"Dr. Tenney was for 16 years president of Wesleyan College [Montana] and 14 years president of Gooding college [southern Idaho]," Marineau wrote.[157] Tenney was sixty-three when he took the job at Psychiana. Thirteen years older than his new boss, Tenney was tall, charismatic, clean-shaven with a prominent receding hairline. Although he lacked the flash Robinson possessed, he maintained a reserve of confidence behind his hawkish gaze. And now, the former two-time college president and one-time postmaster would be the second man in charge of Psychiana, the strange local religion whose prophet seemed to have become perpetually ensnared in legal or financial trouble.

◆

On Wednesday, October 14, Geoffrey Peel Birley boarded the elegant and nearly new *Queen Mary*. (Her maiden voyage had occurred just five months earlier.) Birley was twenty-six when he settled into his first-class cabin aboard the regal ship. Also among the first-class passengers were noted British playwright Frederick Lonsdale, American actress Claire Luce, a delegation of Spanish diplomats, and Lady Astor's husband, Viscount Waldorf Astor.[158] After pushing through a 60-mph gale and waves injuring a dozen passengers, the *Queen Mary* arrived in New York five days later, on October 19. The young cotton exporter stepped off the stately ship, hailed a cab to the New Yorker Hotel, and made the necessary travel arrangements for Moscow, Idaho, in the coming days.

CHAPTER 25

"Out in these By-Ways and Hedges"

St. Louis, Missouri
October 19, 1936

On the same day that Geoffrey Birley arrived in New York, Edgar Giles Baity, the St. Louis motorcar conductor, sat down at his typewriter on De Soto Avenue and wrote once again to Frank Robinson. This time, however, Baity's can-do attitude was tempered by an unexpected letter from Psychiana's headquarters. "Dear Dr. Robinson," he wrote, "I have just received a letter from Dr. C. W. Tenney in answer to my last letter to you, and he seems to think that probably I am violating the Federal law on copyright, and advises me to write you personally and explain exactly what I am doing."[159] Baity had previously disclosed how he had been sharing his Lessons with the less fortunate. "There are among my friends and acquaintances many poor people who need this teaching," he added, "but are absolutely unable to pay the subscription price. These poor people need this teaching more than anyone else, and I am simply trying as best I can to help those who desire to be helped." For Edgar, it was not enough to explain the God Law to his friends in need. They needed to read the Lessons for themselves. "When someone asks me to tell them about this wonderful Power in which you and I trust, how am I going to teach them unless I let them read your Lessons? You cannot tell it to them—they must study it—they must have it before them where they can study and concentrate." Baity explained to Robinson his methods for helping those who desired, like him, to know the Living God. "I would give one person Lesson 1," he wrote, and "tell them to keep it for two weeks and return it. When he returned it, I gave him Lesson 2. I copied the Lessons in case one should get [lost] I would have a duplicate." But Baity also wanted to make clear that he was not profiting in any way from his distribution of his Lessons. "I never received one penny for this. I have money offered me for healing but I would not accept it." Conveying the results of his efforts, he added, "One man who suffered an attack of sick-headache once a month was healed. He read the Lessons and saw the light. He has frequent vibrations and sees various colors. Now he is healing others." For Edgar G. Baity it was paramount that the most destitute people read the Psychiana Lessons. "I am out in the by-ways and hedges and am reaching people who otherwise would not be reached," he entreated. "Out in these by-ways and hedges you will find lots of friendship, lots of sympathy, lots of mutual assistance, lots of love; you'll find God there but you will NOT find money."[160]

The "by-ways and hedges" Edgar spoke of likely entailed the sprawling "Hoovervilles" of St. Louis. An all too common and forlorn site in America during the Depression, these improvised enclaves housed the country's growing homeless population. The St. Louis Hooverville stretched along the muddy Mississippi riverfront, a haphazard assembly of ramshackle scrap-wood shacks—many teetering on makeshift stilts—etching out a foreshortened skyline of rusty stovepipes and charcoal plumes of despair. The debris-choked ground was totally denuded of vegetation save the brambles of dead roots reaching for an unfound river.

Those living in the St. Louis Hooverville turned to the Welcome Inn, a fully operational soup kitchen founded by charitable locals. Raising money for the homeless, the Welcome Inn threw dance parties and hosted events, inviting celebrities like Helen Kane (the inspiration behind Betty Boop) to boost awareness and resources. The spirit of help and community was very much present in St. Louis, as Edgar Baity had asserted.[161] Just as the Welcome Inn provided hot meals for the physically needy, Edgar wanted to bring Psychiana to the people who were hurting the most. Yes, Tenney's official rebuke and threat had alarmed Edgar, but he hoped, too, that this latest letter would clarify his intentions. "Hoping this will clear things up and awaiting your advise [sic]," he wrote, "I remain Yours for 'PSYCHI-ANA.'"[162]

—————◆—————

By the time Geoffrey Birley made his way to Moscow, Idaho, on Wednesday, October 21, 1936, an embattled Frank Robinson was finishing up the last-minute details for a series of upcoming lectures he had planned to give in California. Birley's visit was therefore less than ideal, but if Frank had thought that his lecture circuit would keep Birley at bay, he was disappointed. Having traveled so far, Birley was not leaving without significant face-time with Frank, and so he insisted on joining his teacher on the road to California. Before leaving, however, Frank took a few days to show Birley around Moscow, the distant U.S. farm town Geoffrey had read so much about. They toured the Palouse with its own byways and hedges, and visited Psychiana's many buildings. They stopped in at Robinson's drugstores, strolled across the university campus, and chatted with locals downtown.

Meanwhile, Frank's lawyers were busy working with Idaho Senator William Borah, asking that he use his clout to ward off any deportation proceedings. And C.W. Tenney was drafting yet another letter to Edgar Baity. Addressed to "E.G. Bairy [sic]," Tenney's letter began with a platitude. "Thanks for your good letter, and we were happy to hear from you," he wrote. "In your answer to my letter, you overlooked the one point I tried to make clear, and that is—may we count on you not to copy and distribute these copyrighted Lessons until and unless the trustees of 'PSYCHIANA' give you written permission to do so?" Tenney then offers something of a carrot to induce Baity's compliance. "Would you, as a faithful and loyal Student, want your own statement—"He has frequent vibrations and sees various colors. Now he is healing others"—to go out to thousands and thousands of students as an example of what Psychiana teaches?" Tenney then changed tack and tone. "However," he wrote, "I raise only the point of 'illegality.' So we would appreciate it if you will have your answer this [question] reach me before Dr. Robinson returns November 5th. May the Spirit of Eternal Peace abide with you forever."[163]

After their busy days in Moscow, Geoffrey and Frank loaded up his car, bound for California, stopping at various points along the way. Robinson's first lecture was slated for Sunday, the 25th, at Trinity Auditorium in Los Angeles. Frank had advertised in Los Angeles papers, calling Psychiana "a philosophy of the soul."[164] He packed the halls for the rest of the week. Thousands showed up to hear about Psychiana's God Power and how they could apply it to their own lives. While the lectures themselves were free, Frank was quick to market his brand, selling enrollment subscriptions, Lessons and Advanced Lessons, membership pins, Lifetime Membership certificates, and copies of *Psychiana Quarterly* and *Psychiana Weekly*, in addition to copies of the eight books Robinson had authored up to that point. The specifics of Geoffrey and Frank's meeting are unknown, but the primary topic was Frank's debts to Geoffrey, and the lectures were a quick and sure way to create a lucrative revenue stream. The mere size of the crowds alone would have been enough to impress Birley.

After a week of lectures, Birley and Robinson made their return trip, driving through northern California and into southern Oregon where they visited Klamath Falls and nearby Crater Lake before angling east for Idaho. On November 2, the day before the presidential election wherein Alf Landon was challenging Franklin Roosevelt, Geoffrey thanked Frank for allowing him to travel along.

Robinson drove the young cotton merchant to Spokane to lodge at the historic Davenport Hotel before flying out to New York.[165] That night, Birley gave his own lecture at the stylish hotel. His topic: Roosevelt's handling of the cotton industry in America. Birley called the American president a "prophet of prosperity—for Egypt and other cotton-producing countries of the world—but not for America." Birley further added that "business is booming in Egypt, thanks to your president. Our people could hardly believe their eyes when the dispatches said Mr. Roosevelt had ordered American farmers to plow under every third row of cotton." Birley then commented on the market potential with America's vast geography.

> While air travel is common in Egypt, your American airways have the advantage of vast expanses without international borders to traverse. Although I will fly from London to Alexandria upon my return, the trip will take three days, including many stops at border control fields.[166]

The next day, Birley flew from Spokane to New York, where his outbound ship to London awaited him.

It was the last time Robinson and Birley would see each other.

CHAPTER 26

"Redeemed from the Jaws of Doubts and Agnosticism"

Binalbagan
Occidental Negros
Philippines
December 11, 1936

It had been a week since the deadly typhoon in the north islands. The rains had been incessant and catastrophic. The islanders had never seen anything like it. Officials were calling it "the greatest disaster the Philippines has experienced." Overrun with heavy rainfall, the great Cagayan River decimated entire barrios, sweeping thousands to their deaths. Rickshaws and straw huts floated out to sea like flotillas of matchsticks. The devastation was unspeakable. "Entire families were caught by the unexpected torrents," one paper reported, "and carried, screaming, toward the sea."[167]

But First Lieutenant Nicolas Boadilla Dalao and his family had been spared. They lived far enough south in Binalbagan that they avoided a direct hit. Nicolas was forty-three, with a sharp jawline, stylish hair, and a piercing gaze.[168] He had earned his bachelor's degree in civil engineering from Highland Park College in Des Moines after studying at the University of California in Berkeley, where he had served as associate editor of the *Filipino Student*. Dalao's early interests in literature are evident not by his editorship alone, but by his literary contributions to the journal as well.[169]

While a student in Iowa in 1916—the same year Frank Robinson, as Earl Meyer, was stationed in the Philippines—Nicolas and a fellow Filipino student gave a concert and "illustrated lecture" at the Christian Church in Marble Rock, Iowa, on Philippine independence. With Nicolas playing mandolin, the duo performed traditional Philippine songs for the community group. "The lecture was both instructive and entertaining," the

Marble Rock Journal reported. "The speaker, Mr. Dalao, said that his countrymen are very eager for independence to be granted them by the United States."[170] Philippine autonomy was a hot topic at the time, and a number of lawmakers were working to grant independence. Speaking on behalf of his country, Dalao "averred that they are now qualified in every way to administer their political affairs. [Dalao] further stated that they had no fear of Japanese encroachment after independence is granted them." By all accounts, Dalao excelled in school and his academic excellence would later secure him a commission in the U.S. Philippine Scouts.

In 1920, after receiving his degree from Highland Park College, Nicolas worked for a brief time in St. Louis, where he lived at 3511 Franklin Street, just two miles from Edgar Giles Baity, the city motorman and Psychiana advocate. By the early 1930s, Dalao was back in the Philippines, working as an engineer in the Scouts, and doing his best to provide for his wife and family.

Nicolas Boadilla Dalao passport photo, 1920. From U.S. Passport Applications, 1795-1925, on Ancestry.com.

It was a Friday when Nicolas sat down at his typewriter and rolled in a sheet of his custom letterhead: "N. B. DALAO: SURVEYOR AND CIVIL ENGINEER." Outside, mango orchards, coffee fields, rice paddies, and forests thick with bamboo and molave trees burned green in the damp air. Vines and ferns studded with epiphytes grew alongside wild orchids, and massive insects like tiger beetles, Magellan birdwing butterflies, and Atlas moths were common in the palm groves. Nicolas was upbeat that day when he decided to write to Frank Robinson in Moscow, Idaho. "Your autographed picture was received yesterday," he wrote. "Kindly accept my sincere gratitude for this token of generous thoughtfulness which, coming from a great teacher, I will treasure among my few precious possessions of life."

Nicolas was moved to relate his latest triumphs and how he credited Psychiana for changing his life for the better. "Also, permit me to use this occasion to tell you of the positive uplift your teaching is giving me," he wrote. Nicolas and his family had been through some dark times. "For if anyone has been in the lowest depth of despair and all but completely consumed by the spectre of fear, doubt and defeat, I think I have been that one." The Dalao family had suffered the unimaginable. He explained:

> I think I reached the bottom of the pit of hopelessness when I lost a dear child 3 years ago. It's impossible for me to convey to you even an approximate picture of the heartache I was in before your teaching came to me. The picture is now completely changed, however; I know and feel intensely that a new triumphant life is emerging for me; and I am convinced (I never was before Psychiana came to my rescue) that you are treading the spiritual track—the only right track—and here I am following you with the earnestness of one redeemed from the jaws of doubts and agnosticism during the last 24 years.

Nicolas added a postscript to his note with an attachment. "A year after the death of the child referred to above, I wrote my own conception on immortality," he wrote, "a copy of which is herewith attached as my personal gift to you." That Nicolas—a skilled writer—still felt immense pain for the loss of his daughter, Raquel, is apparent in the distant way he wrote of her as "the child referred to above," rather than writing "my daughter." The pain was still all too keenly felt.

Nicolas wanted to offer his thoughts, but was careful to note that he did not want to tax his busy teacher. "If you have the time," he added, "kindly make a comment, not on its merit as a literary composition, for frankly I am not a poet nor ever studied to become one, but on the truth or falsity of the idea expressed therein."

> On the Approach of All Saints Day, 1934
> (Raquel Remembered)
> Humbly dedicated to Dr. Frank B. Robinson.

> Gone is the form laid underneath this sod,
> Forever sealed her well remembered voice,
> Not even an echo comes out of the deep,
> To still the heartaches of a baffler's quest.

> Immortal soul, if any, what is it?
> Is it one that can hear, but can't be heard;
> and spoken to, yet won't speak; nor felt,
> tho' feeling; seeing yet cannot be seen?

Is it a thing with personality,
With all the attributes of man and more,
Or just a point with an identity
Yet no dimension, nor a place in space?

If in the hereafter, this life's continuity
Consists but just in that and nothing more,
Without the gift of personality
Then it isn't worth its pain, its prayers, its tears.

Then immortality can't mean, but this:
Not as he was, but in number infinite,
As many as the non-reducible
Immortal elements of which he's made;
Thus living, yet as one that was, he's dead.

Dalao's benediction is both haunting and elegiac, and explains, perhaps, his need to reach out to Psychiana in the first place. That Psychiana was packaged as a "scientific religion" would have been especially attractive to the civil engineer. Dalao's interests in music, culture, and literature were second only to his keen interest in science.

Like his fellow Psychianan Edgar Baity, who had dispatched a letter to Professor Frost at the Yerkes Observatory regarding cosmic phenomena, Dalao would dispatch his own letter to a renowned scientist along a similar vein almost two years after writing Robinson. Dated December 5, 1938, the letter was addressed to "Professor Albert Einstein, California Institute of Technology, Pasadena, California."

> Dear Professor Einstein:
>
> No doubt you will be surprised to receive [a letter] from so unknown a person, though a great admirer of yours, as the undersigned. Rest equally assured that it has taken me a long time of self-examination as to whether or not to forward you this letter...I have been following you through the press since the announcement after the World War, of your theory on RELATIVITY. I have made a collection of your published works on the matter, including the collection of competing essays on the subject in which Eddington of England obtained the first prize.

Dalao's chief goal in contacting Einstein stemmed, at least in part, from some of the Psychiana Lessons he had been taking, especially those discussing the Cosmic Ray.

> I am trying to glean from your work, that of Dr. Millikan on Cosmic Ray, and that of Prof. Rutherford on Neutrons something of greater import perhaps than what the ordinary lay mind at present can imply. It appears to me there is something spiritual in such works, and this idea seems to be gathering momentum with me as I study the works, also, of Sir James Jeans' *The Mysterious Universe*, Dr. Carrel's *Man the Unknown*, etc.

Following reference to these specific thinkers, Dalao then makes what appears to be an oblique connection to his studies in Frank Robinson's Psychiana. "I am convinced more than ever," he continued, "that you are, whether you admit it or not, on the threshold of discovering the greatest law of all, the only LAW of the universe because it is the SPIRITUAL LAW—God, if you so want to call it, but a LAW just the same."[171]

Whether Dalao knew it or not, the entire world was on the threshold of a major discovery, one that Einstein knew all too well and had that year apprised President Roosevelt of so that he might defend his nation against a nuclear Berlin. For it was in 1938 that the atom had been split.

Dalao would not have known that the entire world stood on the precipice of the next great war, one which would radically and violently alter his own Philippine homeland. Indeed, his speech in Iowa two decades earlier about not fearing a Japanese "encroachment" on his native soil is all the more haunting, given how history would unfold. When Japan did invade the Philippines in 1942, initiating the Bataan Death March, it appears that First Lieutenant Nicolas Dalao of the Philippine Scouts was captured. Although his name appears on several U.S. military prisoner rolls during that precise period, it is unclear if his death in 1944 at the age of 52 was caused by, or related to, his capture by the Japanese.

For the time, however, Dalao would have been content, no doubt, to know that his letter had reached Frank Robinson's attention far away in Moscow, Idaho, sometime before Christmas 1936.

CHAPTER 27

"Criminal Action"

It was two days after Christmas 1936, and Frank had to attend to some pressing business.

The weather was clear: Moscow's streets were bedecked in winking lights and the lampposts were wreathed in garland.

In his office, Frank dictated a letter. Addressed to "E.G. Bairy [sic]" of St. Louis, Missouri, the letter was anything but convivial. "I have just returned from California," Frank wrote, "and a copy of the correspondence between yourself and Dr. Tenney has been shown to me. Any reproduction of any manner of any part of this Teaching is a violation of the Federal Copyright law and subject to criminal procedure." Robinson was swift and clear. "Furthermore, if I ever find anyone reproducing my Lessons or any part of the literature after having fair warning, I shall not hesitate to start criminal action against anyone so doing. So kindly govern yourself accordingly and let there be no more copying of anything I have written."[172] Satisfied, he ordered the letter to be dispatched to St. Louis immediately, and turned to other matters.

CHAPTER 28

"The Child is the Father of Man"

Vancouver, B.C.
March 29, 1937

It is not clear how long Noah Brusso had been following Frank Robinson's Movement, but he had been a student of Psychiana for at least two years when he decided to write his teacher on that late March day in 1937.

"My dear Dr. Robinson," he began:

> Received your beautiful letter this morning and will always be happy to hear from you. I have been in business all over the world, but I have never received as much happiness as I am receiving today through your Teachings.

> This mighty God Power of the Universe is working wonders for me. I never realized that we were praying to a God that does not exist until I received your Teachings.

The twelfth of fourteen children, Noah Brusso was born in 1881 into an impoverished family in Ontario, Canada. Mercilessly beaten by his father and taunted by children at school, Brusso was constantly finding himself entangled in fistfights.

In 1900, three years before Robinson would arrive in Ontario, Brusso was a baby-faced nineteen-year-old, sure-eyed and athletically compact. Standing a scant five feet, seven inches and weighing 130 pounds, one-time lacrosse champ Noah Brusso crossed the Canadian border that year from his native Ontario into Detroit, and reinvented himself in a thriving America.

At the Detroit Athletic Club, Brusso met the once famous pugilist Sam Biddle, and started training to become a prizefighter in the backroom of Biddle's saloon. Not wanting to embarrass his mother with the stain of professional fighting, Noah Brusso changed his name to Tommy Burns. Early on, Burns became known—and publicly reviled—for being the first white boxer to openly fight across the "color line." American newspapers started calling Tommy Burns "the nigger lover."[173] Burns responded flatly, "I draw no colour line."[174]

Within six years after he started sparring and training in Sam Biddle's saloon, Tommy Burns had become the heavyweight champion of the world—the first Canadian to claim the title, and one he defended a stunning fourteen times over the next two years.

In that time, legendary African American boxer Jack Johnson had been taunting and cajoling Burns to fight him for the belt. Burns finally agreed. The pugilists met in Sydney, Australia, on Boxing Day 1908. Before a crowd of 20,000, the fighters—one black, one white—circled, jabbed, ducked, and fought through fourteen rounds before police had to intervene to stop the fight. In the end, Jack Johnson outpointed Tommy Burns, giving him the belt and the championship. Although Johnson would become the first black man to hold the title, the color of his skin preempted any kind of equitable cash award.

For his victory, Johnson took home $5,000. Burns took home a whopping $30,000, the largest purse in the history of the sport—for losing. The American papers were outraged that a white man had lost to a black fighter. Poet Henry Lawson wrote, "It was not Burns that was beaten—for a nigger has smacked your face."[175] Following the fight, a *New York Times* editorial lamented that there was a "need to do something about it at once." Jack London, the most famous novelist in America at that time, covered the fight for *The New York Herald*, and cried for a "Great White Hope" to rectify the racial "massacre."[176] Nevertheless, Burns kept fighting and earned a place in the esteemed International Boxing Hall of Fame.

On January 20, 1914, Tommy Burns was, according to *The Chicago Day Book*, worth "$500,000" (nearly $12 million by today's standards). Burns, the paper noted, was "probably the richest man the sport ever produced."[177] His first of four wives, Irene Pepper, was a "light-skinned mulatto" who "passed" as white.[178] Burns maintained homes in London, Scotland, New York, and Los Angeles. He wore the finest clothes and dined with celebrities and Hollywood actors. His nephew, Larry Keating—who became a Hollywood A-lister in the 1950s and 60s, appearing in the television series *The George Burns and Gracie Allen Show* and *Mr. Ed*—convinced Tommy to invest the majority of his wealth in the stock market. In 1929, he lost nearly everything, with the final blow coming one year later, as the *New York Times* reported:

RAIDERS SEIZE TEN, LIQUOR AND [WATER] CRAFT.
TOMMY BURNS ARRESTED
Former Heavyweight Champion is Linked to Alleged Speakeasy

Federal agents raided an elaborately furnished apartment on the second floor of a 53 West and Seventy-second street…and arrested three men. Tommy Burns, former heavyweight champion of the world, was one of them.[179]

The raid signaled a dramatic end to the luxurious life Burns had been living. Following the stock market crash and his subsequent arrest, Tommy Burns—like so many in America—was utterly ruined. Too old to fight, Burns turned to odd jobs including a stint selling insurance and working as a security guard. During this period of doubt and depression, Burns saw an advertisement for Psychiana. He sent in for the Lessons and immediately became one of its most loyal adherents. He maintained a close relationship with Frank Robinson, and credited Psychiana for rescuing him from despair. But Psychiana also taught him to love his fellow man regardless of their race or color. "Those who say the Negro is inferior to the white man do not know the power of love," he said to a black Baptist congregation in San Francisco. "Jack Johnson taught me the coloured man is as brave, as clever and as strong as anyone."[180]

Tommy Burns at 27. Signed photo mailed to Frank Robinson. University of Idaho Special Collections.

For Burns, the two most important achievements in his life were his World Champion title and his affiliation with Psychiana. "To me 'Psychiana' is my bible," Burns later wrote, "the divine word of Truth."

It's wonderful! Few people realize that God has existed from the beginning of time within the bosom of man; if they had there would not be so much crime and corruption in the world; but since the man was weaned on a lie, what can we expect? For generations people have taught their children to believe in a God that doesn't exist; therefore, as the poet put it, 'the child is father of the man:' hence, these children grow up into manhood or womanhood never questioning the authenticity of the bible. They read the bible through the eyes of a preacher or some other spell-binder. It is strange, isn't it? We all have at times marveled at the perspicacity of men along certain lines, but put a preacher in front of them or a bible and you will witness a sequaciousness that would make Mary's little lamb green with envy. Tradition has forced them to use their 15th century intelligence as their reasoning powers are soluble in the menstruum of their fears and atavistic superstition. Science has proved beyond a doubt that it is impossible for any person to live up in the ether; should we believe in proved facts? Should we utilize a little common sense? Or should we religiously believe that there is a man up in the skies taking down manifold notes on the deeds of men and issuing passports to Heaven and Hell—my early training agrees with the latter; but my common sense and reason are of sterner stuff, they can withstand the blinding shafts of Truth. It is much easier to believe that I can dethrone Joe Louis next week than to believe in such a fallacy. Heaven is right here on Earth, for when a man's thoughts are in tune with intelligence and his heart is in tune with the God within him, he need not kneel down to anyone, he has no peer; but when a man is angry. Worried or stewing all the time and bemoaning his existence, that is the Hell. I realized, after reading Dr. Robinson's 'Psychiana' and 'Lessons in Truth' by H. Emile Cady, that the teachings and living of Jesus Christ have been bootlegged to such an extent that the world does not know what it is all about.[181]

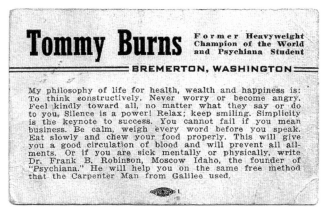

Tommy Burns' Psychiana Card. Author's private collection.

As of that March day, however, when he wrote to Frank, he was using Psychiana not for his own benefit, but for the furtherance of others. "I have two boys that I am training," he added. "I hope to have a world's champion boxer in time. I'll have the Power of the Universe behind them. We are all very happy in our work and we will see you some time in the future. Your friend, Tommy Burns.[182]

CHAPTER 29

The Lion of Idaho

The demands of Frank Robinson's businesses commanded his attention as the 1937 New Year sprung into full swing (his 1936 campaign had been called "A Million Students by 1937!"), even though legal troubles continued to dog him. At fifty years old, his hair had whitened seemingly overnight. He was paunchy and ruddy-faced. His fingernails shone yellow with nicotine. It was a period Alf later called "a time of crisis."[183] Pearl concurred, while her faith in her husband's resiliency was being put to the test. "I have seen Doctor Robinson so hemmed in," she said, "that escape seemed impossible." The last thing Frank wanted was for Pearl or the children to worry. "Let me do the worrying," he would say.[184]

But Pearl was worried and tired of their remote living arrangements (and no doubt concerned about how much their Palos Verdes Estates home was costing them). Alf was by this point in high school, having started "at Redondo Beach, bussing from the plaza at Palos Verdes five miles north to school," he wrote. "But because Mother was a candidate for election to the office of Worthy Matron, Order of the Eastern Star,[185] in Moscow, the decision was made to return." Her standing in the O.E.S. may have been one factor in the overall calculus of moving back, but it is more likely that other factors precipitated the move in the spring of 1937, such as cost and worry.[186]

◆

As it happens, there was good reason to worry. In late April of 1937, Idaho Senator William Borah was meeting with judicial leaders—both state and national—on a prickly question that had fallen in his lap recently: whether or not Frank B. Robinson, an Idaho resident, and contributor to Senator Borah's many coffers, should be deported.

Frank's legal team—headed up by Ed Robertson—had reached out to Borah for the favor. An astute politician who was widely respected,

Borah moved quietly and carefully on the issue. It was not the kind of thing he wanted reported in the press, because showing outward support of Robinson was politically questionable. On the other hand, Borah was an advocate for individual rights, especially those of his own constituency.

As feared, not everyone was pleased with Borah's involvement in the Robinson deportation case. In the first week of May, Borah received an incendiary telegram from Judge Roland Hodgins in Moscow, Idaho, telling Borah he had no right to interfere in such matters, and to stay out of it. A Canadian-born but U.S.-naturalized citizen (he was originally from Lucan, Ontario, a township a few hours southwest of Belleville), Hodgins was a well-respected local judge and merchant whose drugstore competed with Robinson's.

William Borah, on the other hand, had not earned the sobriquet "the Lion of Idaho" by acquiescing to every admonition handed down to him. He was a fighter by nature. Having metabolized the meat of the judge's telegram, Borah drafted a May 8 letter in response.

"My dear Judge Hodgins," he wrote, "I am in receipt of your telegram earnestly protesting against my appearing for Doctor Robinson in the matter of the effort to deport him. I deeply regret to have done anything to offend you."[187] Explaining his advocacy, Borah continued on: "I went through the records. I came to the conclusion he was not entitled to be deported." He further made clear that Robinson's status had no bearing on his inclination to intervene. "If he had been a convict, say, or the most disreputable citizen in my state, or the poorest, or the most worthless citizen in my state, I could not have refused to appear under those circumstances. No person in my State coming before these departments to have his cause passed upon will ever be denied my services when asked, for when I think he is being unjustly dealt with."[188] (This statement was not mere political puffery either. That same year, Borah had fought to have an Idaho woman whom the papers called a "negress" freed from prison, after being convicted of shooting her husband in self defense.)[189] As for Frank Robinson, however, his alleged crimes were not the issue for Borah. "Now, you indicate in your telegram that Robinson ought to be imprisoned. Well, that may be so," he wrote. "I do not know. But I do not feel he ought to be in Canada."[190]

CHAPTER 30

Letter from Bledington

Manor Farm
Bledington
Kingham, Oxfordshire
ENGLAND
June 4, 1937

Back on his family's farm in the English countryside, Geoffrey Birley took a moment to write a letter to Frank Robinson. It is the briefest known letter from the young cotton exporter to Robinson. "My dear Frank" he wrote. "I acknowledge receipt of Psychiana cheque for $600, date 10 May 1937, for which I thank you."[191] The letter is convivial, but reserved. "I hope the work is going on well," he added, "and I should be very pleased to hear from you sometime and know how you and your family are keeping, etc. I saw an excellent film of Crater Lake the other day in London & thought of the visit we made to it last October. It certainly is a glorious place. Sincerely, Geoffrey Birley."

Chapter 31
Loyalty

It had been only two months since Post Office Inspector Stephen Howard Morse had bid farewell to his Oregon colleagues at the Osburn Hotel in Eugene, where he was honored at an elegant dinner for his eight years of service. The sixty-four-year-old was not retiring. He was being promoted to the Seattle office, where he would oversee one of the most critical postal operations in the country.[192] The promotion was a crowning achievement after a long and robust career. One of the files he ensured moved with him as a top priority was the Frank Robinson case. An inveterate man of detail, Morse had been keeping his well-trained eye on the many moving parts of the Psychiana story.

By the middle week of June, when he and his wife, Geneva, had scarcely settled into their comfortable and stylish apartment at 421 West Roy Street—just three blocks from Elliot Bay[193]—Morse had already triggered a letter campaign targeting every confirmed Psychiana student he could track down in the United States. It is not known how many students his office reached, but the number likely reached into the thousands, possibly more.

In creating his letter campaign, Morse drew on his decades of experience in hunting down charlatans who relied on the U.S. mail system for their conduit of illegal enterprise. Because mail fraud was widely reported, postal inspectors used a preliminary form letter to gather data, helping them determine the efficacy and prevalence of suspected cases. A vast majority of mail fraud scams at the time were small, often limited to just victims within one city, county, or state. Successful mail fraud operations had to be nimble and fast. The longer they remained visible, the more vulnerable they became. The same risk held true for circulation. The bigger the broadcast, the likelier it became that the perpetrators would draw untoward attention. What made Psychiana unique was its global reach and its nearly decade long duration. In the minds of experienced investigators like Frank Nooney, Shirl Stewart, Robert C. Bannerman, and Stephen Howard

Morse, a guy like Frank Robinson was breaking the law in broad daylight, almost daring anyone to stop him.

As an instrument of investigative inquiry, the inspector's mail fraud form letter addressed the most general parameters of potential fraudulent behavior, and in this way was little more than chum in a fishing expedition.

My Dear Sir/Madam,

Will you please inform me whether your business transactions with **Psychiana, Dr. Frank B. Robinson, Moscow, Idaho,** have been satisfactory and, if not, advise me fully concerning the particulars thereof; also forward all correspondence received from them, accompanied with the envelopes in which it was transmitted through the mails, having first written your name on each piece so inclosed [sic], for proper identification.

If you have paid the person or firm any money, advise me when and in what amounts, and state:

(a) Whether paid by money order, personal check, etc.

(b) What representations were made which induced you to invest your money.

(c) Were such representations made by mail; if not, in what manner?

This letter should not be regarded as reflecting upon the character or reliability of the person or concern mentioned, and should be treated as confidential.

An official envelope, which does not require the payment of postage, is inclosed [sic] for use in transmitting the information and papers desired. If the papers are too bulky to inclose [sic] in the envelope, wrap them in a package and attach the envelope thereto.

A prompt reply, with return of this letter, will be appreciated.

Respectfully yours, S.H. Morse, Inspector[194]

Postal inspectors like Morse used this form letter in part because it was efficient, but also in part because it was effective. After all, most people want to know if they've been conned or scammed, particularly if money was involved. But Morse would soon find out that Psychiana was no ordinary mail-based scheme, and its students were not "most people."

In July 1937, Joseph P. Guajardo of Los Angeles sent his reply to Inspector Morse. "In reply to yours of June 22," he typed, "I beg to say that my transaction with Psychiana, Dr. Frank B. Robinson, Moscow, Idaho have been very satisfactory and whatever money I have sent them, I have done it out of my own free will."[195]

Another student—F.R. Moore of Detroit—also returned the questionnaire. "I have found Dr. Robinson to be a fine, honest man. He MUST be, for no man could be a seeker and FINDER of Spiritual Truths of God unless he were…In my honest opinion, Dr. Robinson is in NO WAY attempting to defraud anyone through the mails, or any other way. My personal sentiment is: GOD BLESS HIM—and I'm sure HE does."[196]

Addie Perkins of Cleveland, Ohio, struck a similar tone in her response to the Inspector. "I wish to say emphatically that Dr. Frank Robinson has always been perfectly fair and honorable with me. It has got to be a pretty pass if a person cannot worship God as they think he should be worshipped. If these people who are persecuting [Robinson] were Christians, they would not be engaged in this diabolical, devilish work."[197]

Writing from Arborfield, Saskatchewan, Mrs. W.A. Pettis mustered all the ire she could while still retaining a modicum of civility. "The persecution of Dr. Frank B. Robinson of Moscow, Idaho (the originator of Psychiana) has come to my notice," she wrote. "The investigation as I understand it is an attempt on the part of someone to make out that Psychiana's teaching is mail fraud. Such a statement will never be given out by me, for I know better! I hope to read everything Dr. Frank B. Robinson has ever given to the world, for he has written more truth than I ever discovered in the Bible."[198]

A police judge from Clay, Kentucky, also wrote to Inspector Morse in defense of Frank's Movement, countering any notion of impropriety. "Mr. Morris [sic]," Shirley G. Ramsey wrote, "instead of being in any way dissatisfied with the treatment received, I wish to advise that PSYCHIANA is one of if not the greatest movements in the world to-day." Ramsey continued on: "Please let me state that I had been a professor of Christianity thirty years when I had taken a course with Dr. Robinson, and under his instruction I learned more of the truth's [sic] of God in one lesson than I ever knew before."[199]

At some point early on in Morse's campaign Frank Robinson was alerted to the investigation underway. The news came right on the heels of the deportation hearing, enraging Robinson. In response, he lost no time in countering Morse's implications with his own form-letter campaign. It was imperative that he get on top of the narrative. Just from a public relations standpoint, another investigation in the early summer of 1937 was the last thing Robinson needed.

In what amounted to an emergency press release inserted into all Psychiana mailers, Frank hit the issue head-on. Titled "VERY IMPORT-ANT NOTICE TO ALL STUDENTS," the release read:

> I have in my possession a form letter being sent out to my Students by Postal Inspector Morse of Seattle. This form letter asks if my Student dealings have been satisfactory in every way, and asks them to notify the Postal Inspector, giving details, if they have not been satisfactory, etc. If I were to hazard a guess as to the reason for this letter going out, I should say that Mr. Morse was trying to find some dissatisfied Student who is willing to swear to a complaint which can be used as a basis for a mail fraud-charge.
>
> Inspector Morse made a personal investigation of Psychiana about two years ago, and he knows as well as I know that there is not the slightest taint of fraud connected with this Movement. If there had been, the two Postal investigations prior to this latest one would have uncovered it…I think what I have been made to go through during the past three years is perhaps the most vicious, foul, un-American persecution ever to be directed at a religious leader in 400 years.
>
> However, knowing that there is no fraud connected with this Movement, I am asking my Students to cooperate with Inspector Morse to the best of their ability. If there should be a Student anywhere (which I very much doubt) who thinks he has just cause to believe he or she has been defrauded out of money through the mail, I am asking such Student to write Inspector Morse stating fully and completely just how and when he considers he was defrauded through the mails. All I ask is that in the spirit of American fairness to me, he also send me a copy of the letter of complaint.[200]

Students who had not yet received Morse's form letter still felt—out of solidarity—compelled to respond to Frank's press release. A.W. Sweet, a brakeman for the Pennsylvania Railroad, took a few minutes to type a letter from his home in Penns Grove, New Jersey. "Morse's letter has not as yet been received," he wrote, "and should I receive one, you may rest assured Mr. Morse will hear from me, as I feel your teachings should be in every home."[201] Sweet then related some of his daily experiences with the efficacy of Psychiana and its broader appeal. "As a passenger brakeman, I come into contact with men in New York, Washington, DC, Harrisburg, Penna., Philadelphia, Penna., throughout southern New Jersey, Salem County. Each time I find a group of men together I spread your teachings."

If Inspector Morse was expecting incriminating tips or grievances from the untold number of students he polled, he was sorely disappointed. What Inspector Morse had not counted on, perhaps, was the power of belief, particularly in hard times. Instead of wavering in their faith when faced with Morse's written interrogations, the Psychiana students doubled down in their devotion and loyalty to a man so many others considered to be a pathological liar and con artist.

CHAPTER 32

Havana

While the summer of 1937 pressed on, and with temperatures climb-ing, Frank Robinson felt more cornered, threatened, vulnerable, and angered than ever. Attacks on his character and Movement seemed to be mounting by the minute, and coming from all directions. On July 14, for instance, Judge Joseph Rutherford—the once well-known Jehovah's Witness personality and leader of The Watch Tower Society—published a scathing editorial in *The Golden Age* magazine, denouncing Robinson's teachings, and insisting that Frank had been "demonized."

> When shallow minds find that there are invisible powers that may be drawn upon, they think they have found something new and valuable. Nothing of the kind. They have found only the same old evil powers that were in existence in the earth before the Flood…A Western man is flooding the mails with offers to teach anybody for $20 how to know God and obtain health, wealth and happiness.[202]

Making clear that *The Golden Age* had "purposefully avoided mentioning" Robinson, Judge Rutherford then warned his readers of the dangers surround-ing Psychiana. "This is a request to readers of *The Golden Age* not to send in for any more 'Psychiana' literature; for such is demonism, pure and simple; nobody who loves either the God of the Bible or Jesus the Ransomer and Savior of men, would have anything to do with it if he knew the origin."[203]

Some attacks—like those coming from Washington—were not so benign. Leaving nothing to chance in the most pressing entanglement of deportation, Robinson's team reached out to his congressman, Compton White of Idaho's First District, and an array of influential constituents, who, in turn, contacted their own representatives. Congressman White then met with Senator Borah on the matter, after having spoken with Labor Secretary Frances Perkins himself. In a letter to one of his concerned constituents, White wrote assuredly how he had "discussed in detail" with

Secretary Perkins his friendship with Frank "and his part in up-building the business of his community."[204] White added further that, "The Secretary was very sympathetic and took considerable interest in the matter, promising to look into the case [and] assuring me of her desire to assist."[205]

The further Robinson's file advanced up the rungs of state and judicial bureaucracy, the more politically and legally entangled his case became, even for experienced operators like Senator Borah. After weeks of reviewing the files and meeting with everyone who seemed to have a touch on the case, the venerable senator came to realize there was no easy way forward for Frank Robinson.

Following a string of complex negotiations, Ed Robertson told Frank there was good news and bad news, and to brace for the initial fallout. In the end, Borah knew there was no getting around the ultimate deportation of Frank B. Robinson. Secretary Perkins may have been "very sympathetic," as Congressman White said, but in the end, she was unmoved by any mitigating claims of character when it came to Robinson. For her, the law was clear: Frank Robinson was a subject of England, and had been living in the United States as an illegal immigrant. If she blinked on his case, her decision could set a slippery precedent for countless subsequent cases. Her decision was firm: Frank Bruce Robinson was to be deported posthaste.[206]

But *how* he was to be deported and the particulars of that deportation were far more malleable, as she and Senator Borah both knew. Perkins conceded that Frank could go to any country of his choosing. Once there, he could quietly apply for a visa, and then re-enter the United States legally. The whole affair could be settled and put to rest with relative speed. Hardliners would be happy that she deported him, and the sympathizers would be happy that he could return to his normal life in small town Idaho.

It was important to Frank that he place blame on the party or parties allegedly responsible for everything leading up to and beyond the trial itself, including the present deportation proceedings. The recipients of his blame and ire happened to be both specific and nebulous: the specific recipient was his old Moscow nemesis, George Lamphere, who had originally printed Psychiana's Lessons before Robinson bought his own press and launched *The News Review*, rivaling Lamphere's daily paper. Lamphere, Robinson claimed, tipped off federal authorities about the passport as retaliation. Frank later wrote that when Lamphere learned of his acquittal for passport fraud, George was "fighting mad," and that "all the joy" he had had over

Frank's initial indictment had been sapped by the ruling.[207] (When asked decades later about Lamphere, investigators Shirl Stewart, Frank Nooney, and Stephen Morse all said they had never even heard of the man, much less relied upon him in the investigation.[208]) In addition to Lamphere, there was the more nebulous party Frank blamed, namely a conspiratorial league of religious leaders who were "working so quietly, yet so viciously" against him. Stopping short of naming any such church outright, Robinson stated only that, "It is not an American system of religion."[209]

———————◆———————

Local media reported out the more sensational aspect of the deal: "Labor Bureau Demands Frank Robinson Leave This Country."[210] The proverbial clock was ticking. The obvious countries into which he could be deported were Canada and Mexico. But for reasons that are not clear, neither country approved Robinson's entry, creating more legal hurdles and further compounding the entire process. Borah went back to the drawing board, finally brokering a deal with the government of Cuba. Once the plans had been solidified, Frank made the necessary arrangements, traveling first by rail from Spokane to Chicago, where he checked into the Stevens Hotel. "While resting at the hotel," Frank later wrote in *The Strange Autobiography*,

> I received a long-distance call from Senator Borah. 'The enemy is getting very vicious,' he said. He also told me to keep him advised every hour of the day where I would be. Then he informed me that he had talked with the Cuban Ambassador to the United States, and I had been made a diplomatic Representative of the Republic of Cuba, and this would insure my re-admission to the United States again. My papers would be given to me in Havana.[211]

Traveling on to Miami, Frank boarded the palatial SS *Florida*, bound for Havana, putting his adopted country behind him for the time being.

When he arrived in the island country, he was met by a small group of emissaries from the American Consulate, who took him through the vibrant and pastel-colored streets to the Hotel Nacional, where he would wait for all the paperwork on his past, present, and future to be reconciled. It was August 1, 1937. Frank was fifty-one years old, on the run once again, and tired. In the hotel lobby, he signed the registration book, checked into room 734, sat down on his bed, and waited for further instructions from Washington.[212]

CHAPTER 33

"It is Terrible Discouraging Here"

Liberal, Kansas
Monday, August 2, 1937

They were the unforgiving days of windblown failure. It had been just over two years since that Sunday afternoon when the sky turned black with sand and roared over the plains, a hell-driven cloud of doom that choked out cropland, ravaged bony livestock, and broke already frail and sun-haunted farmers. The small town of Liberal, Kansas, took a direct hit. But by the grace of God, Nettie Long, her husband, John, and their nine children survived. But that is all they had been doing in those past two years: surviving. They toiled in a landscape dotted with skeletal sand-wracked farmsteads; defunct windmills creaking in phantom winds. Rusted harrows lay buried in sand, the ruined iron teeth that once symbolized the yeoman dream. Miles of wayward fence posts perforated an otherwise forlorn American wasteland.[213]

And still—as of that afternoon on August 2, 1937, the day after Frank Robinson checked into his Havana hotel room—the Long family had won no reprieve. Nettie—forty-two and in ill health—had just endured another succession of misfortunes nearly biblical in their issuance and consequence. Dogged by grief, she put pencil to several ruled sheets of paper and reached out to Frank Robinson.

> Dear Friend and Teacher, I'm studing my Lesson with all my Might as I realy wont to no all of them as it is terrible discouraging here. I wont change to come…We farmed 5 quarter land here and this year 6 quarter.[214]

Five months earlier, on March 24, another sandstorm swept across those forsaken flatlands, robbing them of their wheat seed. In nearby Fowler, Kansas, a farmer's wife noted the storm in her diary: "48 mile wind worst wind in 37 yr. Worst dirt storm for any single day we ever had fear all our wheat is gone."[215]

210

Nettie also wrote of the mood in those days. "Ower naber are all leaving," she observed, "an what isn't is so discouraged, it Look Bad."[216]
Then, as those previous summer months burned on, the Longs faced even more disaster. But this time it was not a decimating vortex of wind, and it was not a massive thunderhead of storm-sand. "I tell you we Planted and rePlanted," she wrote, "an the Hopper took ower crop 3 times this year." A ravenous cloud of grasshoppers had descended upon Liberal and the outlying scablands. It was a plague so ruinous and bewitching that the National Guard was called in to kill them. The Longs were not alone. "Not just us But ower naber all so."[217]

"The last good crop," Nettie added, "was 1928." That had been a heady year, in which a roaring America was riding out a soon-dead dream. Wheat prices had risen to an historic peak in April of that year.[218] Since then, however, it had been nearly a decade of insurmountable misery, with each year pressing harder and harder on the backs of the most vulnerable, people like the Longs in Liberal, Kansas. "The children are gitting to beleave we not make it," she confessed. "I shore hope we can save ower Land an home an I can right tell you how happie [Psychiana] making us. I'm try lurn all I can out this Lesson an I wont to apply it to ower very nead."[219]

------◆------

After the third wheat crop had been destroyed by the plague of grasshoppers, the Longs applied for yet another loan. (They had mortgaged their house years before.) Downtrodden, they were looking for someone to give them "help or a lone for seed wheat." But there was no loan, and no help. And none came. All the banks and public works administrators turned them down. "But they say no it Margen land we worked it an worked it to keep from lusing what we [own]." As the end of summer approached, Nettie despaired: "But it look as tho we got Nother Bad year to face."[220]

Psychiana, she thought, could change their luck if she could fully grasp the teachings and then utilize them in their lives. "But I hope I can soon Lurne how to use the Power of God Law or the Spiritual force or what ever Power God Law is." She was sincere in her efforts. "I'm not fooling," she wrote, "as I am 42 an Husband is 52 now an it Ben hard Battle to raize family 9 children keep going."[221]

As if the sandstorms and wind and hoppers were not enough, the Longs and neighboring wheat farmers were facing even more bad news. On that same day in August 1937, *The Emporia Daily Gazette* reported this grim headline: "Wheat Futures Sag."

It was as if God had turned against them.

Still, Nettie tried to hold on. "I allway tryed say I not give up an I hant yet." Word in town was there was brick laying work at the Buster Plant. "If Husband cood get the job up Buster Plant he cood make $1.25 [an] ower and then we cood By the seed so you see how it is here with us."[222]

Profound discouragement infected the scorched-earth towns like an epidemic. Residents had difficulty breathing, and a troop of Red Cross workers in gas masks were deployed to Liberal.[223] People like Nettie Long were suffering from what was called the "Dust Blues." She would spend hours every day scooping dust from her house only to turn around and see it settling again. Ceiling collapses were common, as few people thought to check their attics and clear out the sand accumulating in the hidden crawl spaces. Crashing ceilings felt like cruel omens or morose metaphors in those desperate days. On the rare afternoon when the air was still for a spell, Nettie could hang out her wash. But more often than not, dust hung in the air, an ever-present enemy in the red burn of a menacing sun. Discouragement and dismay colored the days and nights on that cracked and reddened pan-land. The farm lady who recorded the dust storm in her diary wrote, "Did not go to S[unday] S[chool] today. I'm so discouraged today, have cleaned dirt about all day & the wind is blowing so bad it won't do any good only for a few minutes. Clarence is right my pretended religion is about gone."[224]

At night, Nettie would sit in bed with her Psychiana Lessons and conduct her breathing exercises just as Dr. Robinson instructed. She read and re-read his Lessons on the "God Law," the powerful "Creative Life Force" that would bring his students "health, wealth, and happiness." By murky lamplight she read his words.

"I say [the God Law] WILL awaken you," the Lesson read, "to your vast possibilities and will begin doing that in the moment you WANT TO BE AWAKENED. So in these Lessons, my friend, be sure that you are in earnest. Be sure that you mean business."[225]

She wrote back: "I only ame for you to no I'm in earnest an not one ho give up so easie."[226]

The breathing exercises also required a series of affirmations. Students like Nettie were told to repeat, "I BELIEVE IN THE POWER OF THE LIVING GOD,"[227] over and over again at the top of every waking hour, and right before bed.

"I do hope God Law or Power will change ower luck."[228]

It had become a cloudless, rainless world. All sun and sand and sorrow. Grown men like John Long, once muscular and hopeful, and who, in days long gone, had thrown their brawn behind the ploughs that cut through the rich earth, now had to drill new eyelets into their greasy leather belts before cinching sagging pants up above their bladed hipbones. Hungry children—gaunt and vacant-eyed, wearing hobnailed shoes filled with sand—watched their fathers, mere silhouettes of the men they used to be, stand on the horizon and eye the immense futility of a vacuous world.

Nettie struggled to see the small "white spot" or "white light" Dr. Robinson spoke of in his Lessons. The white light was evidence of the God-Law.[229] "Now about the white spot," she wrote, "I can git it siting up But at night it seams harde for me to find it or is it easier to see it in day Light."[230] Nettie adhered to her Lessons fiercely, even though she could scarcely afford them. For Nettie Long, Psychiana was the shining beacon in an unraveling world. "My first Lisson," she wrote, "I cood feel the Dynimetic Power as I reached my hand up repeated I do Beleave in Power of the Living God."[231]

Outside her farmstead, cyclonic dust devils yawed through barren fields and across the hot asphalt highways. Jalopies encumbered with trunks and luggage sputtered into the burnt horizon toward a rumor called California. A mass exodus of broken tenant farmers and sharecroppers driven west by the sword of misfortune. In the Long farmyard, bony cattle bellowed in the sandy heat.

"But there not even Leave[s] on sage brush out here only where chicken run as hopper has eaten it all up But stems," Nettie wrote. "It only russhion thissel that the cattle have to eat so you can see how bad it realy is the Leave are all off the tree except at hous where the chicken keep the hopper catched out."[232]

Still, Nettie Long held fast, wrapped up in her Lessons. "Well I like to Lurne an hope I do [succeed] in Lurning as I wont save ower hard earning an ower home an I wont to use Power an God Law." But to access the God Law, she would need to buy more Lessons. "If we had a real harvest I send you all my payment at once But as it is I half to pay it in Payment till I can git money enuf to pay it all But I'm fateful an in earnest."[233]

A month earlier, Nettie had received a strange letter in the mail. At the top, the letter read, "POST OFFICE DEPARTMENT: Office of the

Inspector." The letter appeared to be a questionnaire of some kind. The missive was signed by S.H. Morse. Nettie drafted two copies by hand of her response to the inquiry. One for Inspector Morse, and one for Frank Robinson.

> Mr. Morse, I am righting you in regard to Psychiana teaching I am satsfied with it. I've had the hay fever it don't Bother me now it gon and those gallstones they don't hurt me an sor on my [leg] is about gon it was 6 inches long an 5 inches wide Praze Spiritual Power of God for heeling me and I hope god good worke continues threw Mr. Frank Roberson.[234]

With the threat of more wind and sand just beyond her kitchen window, Nettie Long—the true believer—signed her letter to Frank Robinson and folded the note along with the copy of the letter to Inspector Morse into an envelope bound for Psychiana's mailing department in Moscow, Idaho. That night she would again try to see the white spot of the God Law and pray to it with all her might.

Five days later, Frank's secretary, Marjorie Reynolds, replied to Nettie.

> My dear Mrs. Long, Dr. Robinson is out of town, so allow me to thank you for your good letter and your fine spirit of cooperation. Kindly remember that this Power of the Realm of God is absolutely limitless as far as accomplishing things in human lives goes. With this thought in mind, transmit your desires into this Realm and then remain steadfast in your faith that these things are being accomplished. Be very sure that you remain ever steadfast in your faith, because the Realm of God never failed anyone yet when proper faith was manifested. Now, begin to apply these Spiritual Truths to your own affairs and let us know soon of the things that are being accomplished in your own life since you have learned how to apply the great God-Law.[235]

CHAPTER 34

Return

In all, Frank Robinson spent nearly a month in Havana. The details of his exile are unknown. "There is much I could say here," he wrote about his time in Cuba, "but I shall leave it out of the picture."[236] While the particulars of his deportation agreement were known to those involved, they were less clear to those on the outside. Speculation ran amok in the small town of Moscow. "Dr. Robinson has been missing from Moscow for a considerable time," *The Latah Journal* wrote in an incendiary op-ed:[237]

And the question—'Where is Dr. Robinson?'—has been asked, but not answered, many, many times. Then rumors began to fly. One rumor said he had gone to Canada. Another that he had gone to Mexico. Another that he had gone to Cuba, and still another, evidently a silly, unfounded rumor, that he had gone to New York to take a post-graduate course in selling tickets to heaven from Father Divine, the Negro 'god' of Harlem...The *Journal* representative asked a Moscow attorney who had assisted in gathering evidence for the federal government in investigations of Dr. Robinson about these rumors. This attorney said '[Robinson] positively has been refused entry into Canada and Mexico. This is positive. It is reported he has gone to Cuba.' A few of the 'faithful' in Moscow received postal cards from Robinson last Saturday. These had been mailed in Cuba, solving the mystery of the missing psychic.

Now people are wondering and asking, 'Will he come back? Can he come back? Does deportation by our government merely mean that a man ordered deported can get to a country where he had never previously been, and return to the United States, 'cleansed of his sins' and become a citizen of the United States? Should the 'resurrection' of this modern Messiah occur and he come back to Moscow, we may expect some pretty loud crowing over how he 'put it over' and Uncle Sam will probably be branded as another 'sucker.'[238]

Demurring on the question of what he did in Cuba all that time, and indeed all questions relating to his deportation, Robinson merely said, when asked, "I shall just say that three weeks later I received the visa and came back to Moscow, Idaho."[239]

CHAPTER 35

"Through the Bright Spot, Out Into Somewhere"

September 6, 1937
Cranesville, Pennsylvania

"It is with doubt that I address you because I haven't the slightest idea that you ever see my letters," Mildred Gage wrote to Frank Robinson.[240] It was Monday, the temperature hot, and a few clouds lingered over the five hundred or so residents of Cranesville, a small village some fourteen miles from the shores of Lake Erie. As Mildred sat at her typewriter, she wrestled with an array of conflicting feelings, fears, and frustrations. "Certainly you never answer [my letters]," she continued, "but I promised to report any benefits received through Psychiana, and I'm giving full credit for the following benefit to your teaching."[241]

Mildred was a thirty-eight-year-old bookkeeper, independent and bright with a no-nonsense attitude. She was lithe, beautiful, with daring eyes and a quick, brunette bob. By that point in her life she had been married and divorced three times, with the latter two marriages occurring each within a month of their respective divorces. Her only son, Boyd, was seventeen, the offspring of her first husband, Carlton McIntosh Gage. Born into an average farming family in Findley, New York, Mildred came of age during the Jazz age and seemed restless, never settling down in one place with any one person for too long.

Her older half-sister, Augusta Mosier or "Gussie," lived ten miles farther inland in nearby Cussewago, and was something of a foil to Mildred: she had married only once, had four children (though their first, Nessie, died young), and for the most part had stayed put.

It had been three years since the sisters' father, George Thomas, had died at the age of eighty of a cerebral brain hemorrhage at Gussie's home, where he had been living for a short while.

It was now election season in Erie County, and the local papers were running candidate photos alongside sports scores, advertisements (gasoline was going for $0.12 per gallon), and cartoon strips like "Reg'lar Fellers." Other popular features in regional papers like *The Conneautville Courier* included the "Sunday School Lesson," "Looking Back" columns, eye-catching promos for Doan's Pills, and advertisements featuring Ford V-8s for $575, as well as local gossip columns in which Mildred's sister appeared infrequently.

Mildred continued on:

> I wrote you a short time ago telling you that two different doctors had called a lump in my left breast a tumor, and urged an immediate operation to avoid a cancer. In my letter I asked you for help, to which your secretary replied suggesting that I visit another doctor. To say that I was disappointed is mild. If you had just said, 'I'm making no promises, but I'll do what I can,' even though you had done nothing, it would have bolstered up my faith a thousand times. But you didn't, and I strongly suspect that I didn't get any help from Moscow, regardless of the many times you speak in your lessons of helping people.
>
> I went to another doctor; in fact, two of them. The verdict was the same: immediate removal of the entire breast. I decided right then if you would not help me, I'd at least take a fling at helping myself before I went to the hospital. I had a week's time, and decided to make the most of it.[242]

Drawing on her Psychiana Lessons—particularly the ones discussing the "white spot" or "bright spot" you can "see" when your eyes are closed—Mildred went to work.

> Straight through the bright spot, out into somewhere, I forced a mental picture of that lump. I did this from three to five times daily. I did not repeat any affirmation about being made whole by the Living God, because that only drew my attention to the trouble. I tried in every way to forget it. When it was brought forcibly to my mind by questioning, I stated that the lump was getting smaller, and I would not go to the hospital until I was sure that it would not disappear, which I firmly believed it would do. To say I was the object of much censure is but a smattering of the truth. It got around to my family doctor that I was not going to the hospital for awhile and expected the lump to disappear.[243]

Her doctor, a WWI veteran who had served as a medic in France, was, Mildred said, "very rough spoken" and when he learned of her plan, she conveyed how, "he gave me all the highlights of his vocabulary."[244] She was not deterred by his protest, however. "I stuck it out," she wrote. Mildred initially thought she could shrink the size of the tumor through the power of Psychiana. "But the fact is," she confessed, "it was not getting smaller. It was growing larger and at an alarming rate. By the latter part of the week it had grown to the size of a large's hen's egg, and ached and pained so that I was in bed the better part of two days."[245] That is when she decided to undergo the surgery after all. "I expressed my opinion of Psychiana to myself," she wrote, "not out loud, because Grandmother was here, and if she had known I was doing anything like trying to have God make the lump disappear, she would have called the interne of the Insane Asylum instantly."[246]

Despite her pain and fear, Mildred elected to remain positive. "The night after the second day of intense pain," she added,

> I lay in bed, almost asleep. Even though I had decided that I would not be helped, I still continued the relaxation exercises, forcing the picture of that lump through the bright spot. I couldn't seem to stop. On this particular night, I had finished the exercises and was nearly asleep, thinking, 'Well, I'll have to go to the hospital, and I might as well make up my mind to it.' All of a sudden, I heard my Mother's voice. Mother has been dead two years, but her voice was as plain as if she had been in the room. It broke into my thoughts of going to the hospital, and all she said was, 'Mildred! Mildred!' in just that same reproving tone she used when living if I was doing or saying something of which she did not approve.
>
> Indeed, I was panicky. I took the entire wrong attitude, and was thoroughly frightened. I thought I had meddled with something in my exercises which I had no right to meddle with—superstition, of course— and I felt that voice was calling me. I'm not afraid to die, that was not it, but I do have a son who needs me very much for the next four years. If I dreaded an operation before, I dreaded it doubly now. I dreaded taking ether, because I felt that when I went to sleep Mother would call me right to her, just as she always called me when she was living, Then I didn't dare go to the hospital. What was I to do?
>
> In a couple of days more the swelling went down and the pain disappeared. Understand I was still doing the exercises. I couldn't seem to stop, even though I was afraid to do it. I did it anyway. Pretty soon, Dr. Robinson, that lump was smaller, and it continued to get smaller. Today it is practically gone, just a little lump about the size of a pea, and it is going. There is no question about that.

Then the meaning of everything came to me. Mother was not reproving me, fool that I was. She was warning me not to go to the hospital. She was reproving me for my disbelief. No one can ever tell me otherwise, because if ever I heard my mother's voice, I heard it that night, and I wasn't even thinking of her, neither had I been during the day, In a couple of days more when every last trace of that lump has gone, I'm going back over to my doctor and listen to him rave. He will probably swear I swallowed it, but I know where it went.

There are lots of things in the Lessons I don't understand, and if they are not cleared up in the next two or three Lessons, I'm going to write and ask you about it. Somebody up there can surely explain so that I will understand, and there is no point in studying them if they are not entirely clear. I thank you, Sincerely, Mildred Gage.[247]

In a handwritten post-script, Mildred added the following lines on a blank sheet of paper: "I wrote this letter two days ago. Today that lump can scarcely be felt at all. What more can anybody ask to prove that Psychiana is right?"

For years, it seemed, Mildred had been trying to find her own bright spot, out into somewhere, anywhere.

Within the year, Mildred met Joseph Wallace Edwards, a lumber mill operator from Elk Township, a wooded village some ninety miles from Cranesville. What he lacked in formal education (he left school after the sixth grade), he must have made up for in charm because in early 1938, Mildred married Joseph, leaving Cranesville behind.

On September 16, 1939—two years and ten days after writing to Frank Robinson reporting on the success Psychiana brought in reducing the size of the tumor in her left breast— Mildred was home alone in Elk Township. Joseph had gone out for the evening with their neighbor friends, the Merrills, but Mildred insisted they go without her. She wanted to "prepare for visitors" they were having the following day, she had said. Sometime after Joseph and the Merrills had gone

Mildred Gage, c. 1927. From Ancestry.com.

out, Mildred loaded a .22 revolver, and walked out into their yard under the hot summer night sky where only a comma of a moon shone bright in a field of stars.[248] After gazing into the pin-lit sky, out into somewhere, perhaps, Mildred drew the muzzle of the pistol against her left breast, and fired.

She was forty years old.

Joseph and the Merrills discovered Mildred's body when they pulled into the drive late that evening. "According to the husband," the *Warren Times Mirror* reported, "Mrs. Edwards had been despondent for some time."[249] Ed Lowrey, the coroner, confirmed the cause of death: "a bullet wound in the left breast was self inflicted by a .22 caliber revolver." The same paper added that Mildred "had recently been undergoing treatment for a mental ailment." Her death certificate noted that a contributing factor to her suicide was "despondency due to illness."

CHAPTER 36
"My Road is Pretty Rocky"

Reading, Pennsylvania
October 16, 1937

It was a Saturday when Anna Jane Ernst, a seamstress, decided to write another letter to her teacher, Frank Robinson, asking for help. Divorced for over twenty years from a man who, according to court filings, had deserted her, she lived alone, every day a quiet, nearly anonymous struggle.[250] She sat in her cramped, row-house apartment on South 11th Street in Reading with her pen and paper. The small apartments were so crowded together and overrun with poor families that tenants like Anna could hear the cries of children, warring marriages, laughter, radio programs like the Fred Allen Show, and the brassy hits of Guy Lombardo, Count Basie, and Benny Goodman.

Outside her window, children shot marbles, groomed dolls, played hopscotch, and kicked cans along the warped blacktop, making a tinny racket. Women hung laundry out of their windows and swept their stoops. Sinewy men—some unemployed, others elderly—stood in their doorframes staring into mild oblivion. The weather was fair that day, but there had been an unusual cold snap in the preceding week, and with winter coming, Anna was worried. A month and a half earlier, her stove stopped working. "I had to save every penny I could scrape together for at *least* six weeks," she wrote to Robinson.[251] The gas range she finally bought set her back "$5.00." But it was a necessary purchase. Without it, she added, "I would go hungry or [live] on cold meals." Money was extremely tight for Anna, and paying her bills was a constant worry. "Now I have to save for coal." She bought her coal directly from the local mines, whose distributors, she reported, "want cash." On top of that, there were other bills. "I have 1 electric bill to pay and a gas bill coming due." Anna—who had grown up in a Christian family—earned a mere $3.40 per week at a local hosiery mill where her father, Erasmus, had served as a watchman. Anna's annual income was an anemic $176.80, while the average woman in 1937 made

$525 annually, and men averaged nearly double that at $1,027 per year. "So you see my road is pretty rocky," she wrote.[252]

In eleven days, Anna would turn fifty-one, though she did not mention this to her teacher. The truth was that she had not been feeling well in those early autumn days—she suffered from "ailments"—and turning a year older with no hope in sight was likely an event she did not care to think of, much less celebrate or mention in her letter. If she had the money she might go to a movie (a precious pastime) for her birthday (*Snow White* and Cary Grant's *When You're in Love* were hits that year), but as it stood, that indulgence seemed unlikely. "I have been to only two shows thus far for 1937, and I have been to 1 in 1936." The gray autumn days no doubt carried a sustained mood of uncertainty and resignation on South 11th Street for Anna.

The headlines in *The Reading Times* that morning hinted at even worse things to come. "Britain Warns Italy Patience is Near an End," which was followed by, "Japanese Bomb Coastal Cities in North China." Closer to home there were other grim hints—"Meat Prices Up to Stay." Subtle, but still worrying to people like Anna Ernst.

Economically, the market appeared to be fairly stable. But four days after Anna sat down to write her letter to Psychiana's founder, the market crashed again. Benjamin Roth, the Youngstown, Ohio lawyer and diarist, made an entry on October 20, 1937, one week before Anna's birthday. His observations—always keen and sure-footed—were not promising. "The stock break which has continued since early in September resulted in the worst break since 1929—on Monday and Tuesday…It is generally believed that business will be slow this winter. There is fear and pessimism in the air. Nobody seems to be able to explain why it happened."[253]

They were fragile days and nights rife with fear and worry. From Wall Street to South 11th Street in Reading, Pennsylvania, disquietude worked its way into the hearts of the people without discrimination. No one, it seemed, could get a break.

Writing to Frank Robinson likely made Anna Ernst feel less alone even as she sat amid the daily din of the neighborhood. But sometimes she felt even more lonely, especially when Frank failed to write back. "I have written to you at least 4 letters pleading with you and begging you to help me but I never receive an answer." The occasional letters she did find in her mailbox from Psychiana were form letters. "I know by the letters that come back to me," she complained, "that you don't even read my letters." Anna made this last point by way of example. "The questions I ask never get answered and the letters which are returned to me do not show evidence that they reached the individual it was intended for."[254]

Ernst's legitimate complaint went beyond the generic responses she received from Psychiana, pointing to some of the more fundamental problems with pay-to-pray religions. Not only did she have to pay her Psychiana dues and spend money on her individual Lessons, but she also had to buy the paper, envelopes, and stamps. "Do I have to send a you a telegram if I need help like the other students do?" For Anna, telegrams were out of the question. "Isn't a letter sufficient? I can't afford telegrams," she added. "They are expensive."[255]

The standardized and indifferent letters that spooled out of Psychiana's assembly line irked Anna because she actually put thought and time into her letters, and, more than that, she was revealing private aspects of her life. Her health. Her finances. Her worries, fears, and vulnerabilities. "I always mark my letters private or personal and I don't see why [they] should be read by anyone but that person." Addressing Robinson directly, she added, "You even promised me that such letters would not be read by anyone but you."[256]

As of that day in October when Anna penned her letter, as sooty plumes of coal smoke hung over the neighborhood on South 11th Street, she had completed Lesson 10 in Psychiana's ADVANCED COURSE: Number One. Even still, she had not seen much change in her circumstances. In Lesson 10, Robinson proffers an analogy for how the "God Law" works. It has to do, he stated, with circumstances and compliance. His analogy is that if you plant "barley seeds" in a barrel filled with metal shavings, the seeds will not sprout. But if the seeds are sowed in soil, they will grow. "So it is in your own life," Robinson wrote. "Whenever the conditions governing the GOD-LAW are complied with, THE RESULTS ARE VERY SURE. When they are NOT complied with, nothing but failure and disaster can ever manifest. Either that, or a very mediocre existence is lived."[257]

Cultivating and improving your personal conditions through meditation, daily breathing exercises, affirmations, and Lesson study, were essential in accessing the GOD-LAW. In Psychiana, not complying with the conditions of the God Law was tantamount to "violating" the God Law.[258]

"And in regards to not living the God Law as it should be as…in the 10th Lesson," Anna continued, "I don't think that I am guilty of violating the God Law for I don't swear and I never wish anything to anybody but good luck, and I never go anywhere except after my business such as paying bills and doing shopping, or to a show once in a while."[259]

Still, she adhered to the edicts of Psychiana, her only faith. (Her neighborhood had four churches within walking distance from her apartment.) "I don't bother with church or Sunday School," she wrote. "I have not seen the inside of [a church] for at least 7 years which would be a terrible crime to all my Relatives."[260] One of Anna's pressing concerns was that she was not putting enough time into her Lessons. If she had more time to devote to her Psychiana studies, then perhaps the God Law would make itself known and her conditions would improve. But between the demands of work and keeping her house in order, there was little time left over for her coursework. "I read my Lessons every night and twice on Sunday," she added. "I'm folling [sic] everything you hand me and I can't help if things go slow for me for I am doing the best I can do under the circumstances I am in."[261]

But it was not all bad. There were, she noted, a few signs that the God Law was working for her. At night and after supper, Anna would relax and smoke a cigarette before cleaning up. That previous Tuesday evening, on October 12, she was feeling "very miserable" and had felt that way "off and on for a few weeks." "I made supper and after meals I usually smoke a Kool, which is a mentholated cigarette." (Here she wanted to make clear to her teacher that her smoking was not a habit. "It is a habit now-a-days with women to smoke but not with me. They keep my nose and throat clear, so that is why I do smoke.") But on that night, as she was smoking her Kool, Anna noticed something change. "So I sat there very quiet for say a half or perhaps three quarters of an hour and I had only one thought in my mind and when I got up to clear the table and wash the dishes I felt much better and after my work was done I sat again for the rest of the evening and all the ill feelings of that day left me."[262]

She had also recently come by a bit of luck that she attributed to the God Law. "One day," she recalled, "I was out shopping and while walking I picked up 14- 20¢ stamps which if I can cash them in somewhere will give me $2.80." As encouraged as she was by her find, her enthusiasm waned a bit upon reflection. "I wish those things would happen more often."

Her talk of money and the God Law circled back, inevitably, to Psychiana and, specifically, her standing in the faith. "I am a little in arrears in my payments to you and I am very sorry, I am trying to do the best I can all around and I can only give you a dollar this time, and I will try to send more as soon as I can." Her payment of one dollar equaled one-third of her weekly income. Still, Anna Ernst sent it in.

CHAPTER 37

Be Quiet

OCTOBER 25, 1937
Psychiana Headquarters
Moscow, ID
Letter to: Anna J. Ernst, Reading, Pennsylvania

My dear Friend and Student: Thanks for your remittance of $1.00 and we appreciate this cooperation. I am happy to know that you are really demonstrating a little bit of what you have learned to date. I have a little suggestion to make to you, and that is that you spend a little time being quiet and trying to actually contact the Power of the great God-Realm...

Sincerely your friend and teacher,

C.W. Tenney, Assistant to Dr. Robinson.[263]

CHAPTER 38

Fallout

One of the more disheartening consequences of Frank's trials and legal problems concerned Pearl herself. As soon as the government determined conclusively that Frank B. Robinson was not a legal resident of the United States, and was in fact a British subject, their decision automatically triggered the legal revocation of Pearl Robinson's citizenship. After all, she had unwittingly married an illegal alien, which under law, rendered her own citizenship invalid.[264]

The action must have seemed like an utterly cruel punishment to a woman whose only crime was love and the loyalty that accompanies it. However she took the news, though, remains a mystery, overshadowed—like much of her life—by her husband's own story. Now an alien in her own country, the Oregon-born daughter of a judge had to begin the long process of applying for citizenship. Just like her husband.

Part IV
THROUGH WAR TO GOD
1938–1945

CHAPTER 39

Radio Psychiana

By January 1938, Frank had emerged from his legal battles a little worse for the wear, but cautiously sure-footed. His finances had taken an extraordinary hit, and so too had his health. Photos of Frank from that period show a white-haired man with sunken, watery eyes. Nevertheless, he pushed forward, constantly seeking new ways to promote, advertise, and boost Psychiana's message and increase student numbers. For Robinson, that meant investing what he could into sweeping radio campaigns, spots, and advertisements, teasing listeners across the country with promises of the God Law. Building on his pilot radio program in Hollywood, Frank was aggressive in his radio campaign. The spots were thirty seconds long and ran throughout the country, all across the airwaves. Typically, they opened with a pseudo-diagnostic question or series of questions.

What's the matter? Has life got you down?
Are you tired, discouraged, reaching vainly for
success, peace and happiness? Then listen! Here's
wonderful news for you. A transcribed message of
HOPE! And ENCOURGEMENT! Dr. Frank B. Robinson, noted
psychologist and founder of Psychiana, the new scientific
Teaching, is willing to HELP YOU SOLVE YOUR PROBLEMS! ...
Listen for the actual voice of Frank B. Robinson, when he broadcasts
over this station.[1]

Set to orchestral music with the intimate and consoling voice of a man talking directly to his listener, each radio spot was geared to the vulnerable individual at home. Unlike many of Robinson's letter campaigns or magazine ads, which relied heavily upon bandwagon appeals, reprinting testimonials and student letters, Psychiana radio ads were cutting edge for their time. Moreover, Psychiana radio ads signaled a crucial inflection point for Robinson: Psychiana was now mainstream.

231

Why are you lonely? . . . . Tired of it all? Have you
Lost your courage. Does DISCONTENT trouble and torture
you…has it plunged you into a turbulent black
chasm of blindness and brooding despair? Then listen! YOU
CAN DO AND BECOME WHAT YOU WILL! Write to Dr. Frank
B. Robinson at Moscow, Idaho. In return you will receive a revolutionary
6,000 word treatise absolutely free, along with a picture of Dr. Robinson,
the humble drug clerk who made himself a focus of dynamic power.[2]

Other spots followed, playing on similar themes and using the direct
diagnostic address. "Has it been a hard day? Do you feel let down? Are you
weary of struggle, of fighting against the desolating forces of envy, bitterness,
jealousy and fear! [sic]"[3] "Why be blue? Is the way so confused? Surely life
holds more than just disappointment for you? It isn't all meaningless."[4]

Given Robinson's spate of recent troubles, years of legal turmoil, forced
family estrangement, crippling finances, and personal defamation, it is easy
perhaps to see these radio spots as more than just advertisements aimed at
potential students. Indeed, they could be just as easily read as projections of
what Frank B. Robinson was feeling about himself at the beginning of 1938.

Still, if he had any doubts or lingering fears, his spirits would be lifted
by the one thing he craved most: publicity. *Time* magazine sent a reporter
to Idaho to do a story on Psychiana and its infamous, embattled leader.
Titled, "The Money-Back Religion," the article featured a photograph
of a smiling Frank Robinson seated at his office desk behind a towering
stack of student letters, with a Dictaphone microphone in his hand. In the
photo, Robinson wears a white dress shirt, vest, and tie. Beneath the photo,
the caption reads, "Frank Bruce Robinson. He vomited hellfire."[5]

The article is heavy on biography, subtle on snark, and overly reliant on
statistics furnished by Frank himself, but it does capture the tenor and gist
of Psychiana, as one of the most turbulent decades in American history
drew to a close.

Ten years ago in Moscow, Idaho, a tall, husky, smooth-talking drug
clerk borrowed $500 from a friend, and spent $400 of it to buy some
advertising space in a psychology magazine…As a mail order gospel
propagated by advertising (in 400 newspapers, 50 magazines), Psychiana
passed a milestone last week when Founder Robinson motored from
Moscow to Portland, Ore., ordered 5,000,000 envelopes—a year's

supply—and announced a new policy which will make Psychiana more like a church. Half a million letters will shortly go out to Psychiana students throughout the world informing them how to organize their study groups (resembling religious congregations) in their cities.[6]

On his background, the article noted, "Where Frank Bruce Robinson was born, he does not know." As a young man, Robinson, the article continued, "came to disbelieve Christianity. 'My parents pumped hellfire and damnation into me until I was sick. I just vomited it up.'" *Time* also added how Robinson blamed Christian organizations for all his legal and business troubles: his deportation saga, Postal Inspector's investigation, and even the latest "attempts to have his transcribed radio programs (from 18 stations) put off the air."[7]

And just like his Hollywood radio program, these also entailed the voice of a "Guide" taking the reader into the northern stretches of Idaho to listen to Psychiana's founder at a time when middle-class families still gathered around their Zenith radios after supper to listen to their favorite programs like the "Fannie Rhinehart Hour," "King Cowboy," "Café Cabana," and "Interesting Neighbors." They began with intro music and the Guide's voice.

> The road to [the God Law] is tranquil. It leads to Moscow, Idaho to the home of Dr. Frank B. Robinson, noted psychologist and founder of Psychiana. This home you will visit today stands as a symbol of strength and courage…(MUSIC SWELLS; MUSIC COMES TO AN END).[8]

The entire scripted program was written by Frank, and followed in broad strokes many of his individual Lessons in enough detail to pique interest and hopefully entice new inquiries and subscriptions.

GUIDE: How does this God Law operate?

DOCTOR: With remarkable precision for all. You can understand what I mean when I tell you tell you that IF the realm of God DID NOT OPERATE as LAW, then this entire universe would hang on chance, and that I cannot admit. Nor can you…

GUIDE: And accessing the God Power means—

DOCTOR: That man can now talk with God!

GUIDE: And being able to talk with God—

DOCTOR: Means that they are able to bring to themselves everything they need for their complete happiness—HERE AND NOW.

GUIDE: And any obstacles can be overcome. You yourself have proved that.

DOCTOR: Yes, and sometimes the obstacles seem almost unsurmountable [sic]. And when that happens, I like to sit at my pipe organ and play over the old melodies. That's when the peace of the God Realm steals over me (MUSIC IN). When I'm like this—trials of the day forgotten. In their place comes a hallowed peace.

GUIDE: A hallowed peace.

DOCTOR: Sometimes the tears fall as I recognize the stupendous magnitude of the task before me. I'm often misunderstood. Often maligned, and blasphemed. But I must, to the very best of my ability, carry the message that was given to me on to others.[9]

———————◆———————

As Frank Robinson was busy carrying his message over the airwaves nationwide to his scattershot flock and potential students, William E. Dodd, former ambassador to Germany, was delivering a series of grim speeches in New York and Washington, warning of Adolf Hitler's regime. "Mankind is in grave danger," he warned his dinner guests one night in New York.[10] "But the democratic governments seem not to know what to do." He then added, "Another world war would almost certainly wreck the governments and people of our time."

At that very time—those early months of 1938—Hitler was planning a full-blown invasion of Austria. Astute Americans, recalling the precipitating signs that had led the country into the Great War a little over two decades earlier, tracked the news closely, even more so on the radio. It was in 1938, the year Psychiana hit the airwaves, when radio began rendering the newspaper "extra" editions all but useless. "People didn't run out into the street for the news; they tuned their dials, and they listened," observed one historian.[11] They listened to stay informed and to be entertained. And they listened to get solace and help.

CHAPTER 40

"You Are God's Moses to Me"

February 4, 1938
Lock Box 59
Phone: dial 354
Franklin, Virginia

Reverend Charles Sidney Burke—Psychiana student number 7-2093—
could not sleep. It was 12:43 a.m. when he eased himself into the seat
of his study, keeping quiet so as not to wake his wife, Annie. Thirty-nine
years old, Reverend Burke had recently been assigned to a small all-black
Baptist congregation in the one-fuel-pump town of Franklin, Virginia. It
was a sleepy community in 1938, flanked by the tannin-stained Blackwater
River, heavily wooded, and fiercely segregated. Some of Reverend Burke's
congregants fished for shad in the Blackwater, and cooled their feet on
hot days. While the young minister would have preferred preaching at
a larger church, he and his wife had settled down in Franklin, making it
their home. But the early months of 1938 had been extraordinarily trying
for Charles, so he turned to his teacher at Psychiana. "First of all I want to
say 'may God bless you,'" he wrote. "I have read your teaching in 1, 2 & 3
lessons and I am now to start my fourth one that I received today."[12] The
reverend was sick with worry. "May I say I have done my best thus far," he
wrote:

> I am a Baptist Minister pastoring here in the city, a small church of
> course, but I am frank to say to you your teachings have confirmed
> more solidly my former beliefs, with a field of new matter and reality of
> things I never dreamed of. You are wonderful and God shall continue
> to bless you, [and] that he may bless thousands through you and your
> teachings. Please believe me when I say to you that I do regret I was
> so long in contacting you.[13]

Reverend Burke then touched on his tardiness in his Psychiana payments. "Now, Doctor," he wrote, "on the 13th Inst. when I get my salary I shall send you at least $3.00. Please bear with me." Turning to the chief matter he wanted to write Robinson about, the Reverend opened up. "I have had it so hard," he confessed. "My wife was operated on. Her left breast was taken off. They treated her before the operation, also since." Their doctors were located in Norfolk, some fifty miles away. "Yesterday," he continued, "I took her back to Norfolk. The doctor that gave the radium treatments, also the doctor that performed the operation, told me she would hardly live another year! I don't know what to do. I am almost crazy, seemingly."

Beset with fear and grief, he felt helpless. But when he turned to his Psychiana Lessons, something changed. "This afternoon," he added, "she came into my room, I told her, as I finished reading 12 pages of my 4th lesson, that I had a new feeling altogether, and that I believed in the Power of the Living God and in you, and that I would write you about her condition." His wife, he noted, "smiled and said she believed too." Reverend Burke was desperate. "Doctor," he pleaded, "she is worthy of being saved." His love for his wife was full, true, and complete. "She is the person I prayed for. God gave her to me." Now she might be taken away. "Do please by the Power of the God Law help her. She is a saintly loyal wife, and very loyal to me."[14]

By all appearances, she looked "the picture of health." But the prognosis was not good. "The doctors are keeping her doped," he wrote, "so that she may not suffer, waiting for the end." It was the finality of it all that seemed to hurt the reverend most. He needed some sort of assurance. "But as I can almost feel the very presence of some power now, I believe you are going to pray and the God Law shall cure her as it has others." The God Law alone, he explained, "is the only thing that can save my wife." Since her surgery, there came more bad news, however. "Other small cancers or tumors," he wrote, had appeared "on the left shoulder near her neck." Another one, "the size of one's hand," was on the "left side" of her torso. "Also the place where the breast was taken off is worrying her. She failed to sleep until they gave her anti-pain capsules yesterday."[15] Reverend Burke then turned to his abiding faith in Psychiana.

Will you please let me hear from you? I feel better now since I have written her condition tonight. Now I find I have more ease of mind in my church work since studying your lessons, than I have for the past 4 or 5 years, during which time I lost my fine city work and am now in a small town with only a 3rd or 4th class church, but by the <u>God Law</u>, I mean to over come, after my dear wife recovers. I believe she will, by the power of the GOD LAW. Doctor, I am trusting absolutely nothing but the GOD LAW and YOU. Please don't fail me. I shall never betray my trust. Even though I am all in debt, my creditors are very nice to me. On the 15th Inst. I send you at least $3.00 to catch up. I might ask that my name not be published <u>just now</u>.

I beg to remain your student, Charles S. Burke

Reverend Burke had aimed to end the letter there, but then added a final thought.

P.S. I send you my photo as per request in my next letter. The longing within my soul has never been satisfide [sic]. I continued in the darkness alone until "Psychiana"—through you—came to me. I can even preach with a better understanding of what God is for I am abundantly satisfide [sic] with myself. You are God's Moses to me, for you brought me out of Egypt.[16]

◆

Ten days later, on February 14, Frank Robinson did something he had not done in a long time, and certainly not since hiring C.W. Tenney, his assistant and second in command. He sat at his desk in the main Psychiana office building in downtown Moscow, Idaho, and wrote a personal response to Reverend Burke. It was a Monday, and in addition to it being Valentine's Day, it was also the four-year anniversary of his indictment for passport fraud, which had triggered a staggering series of costly events for Frank. He had been working full-bore ever since. He had just returned from Boise where he attended the Lincoln Day Banquet, the state's primary Republican fundraising event. Photos from the event show an aged Frank Robinson (who attended merely as a "newspaper publisher") with snowy white hair, and beneath the photos there was the caption reading, "A Gatherin' of the Clan."[17]

But on that day, having read Reverend Burke's letter, Frank was moved to write a real response, dispensing with the form letter system all together. Because Reverend Burke had sent in his photograph, Frank Robinson would have known he was African American, but Burke's color did not seem to phase Robinson. In a world split between black churches and white churches, Psychiana obliterated such distinctions, crossed borders via the postal system, and cut across boundaries through the airwaves. Psychiana was a truly color-blind religion.

Frank wrote to Reverend Burke:

Regarding your wife, you will recall in the Bible, although I very seldom read it, you will recall the man having the wither [sic] hand. He walked up [to the] Master, and Christ looked at him and said, "What do you want?" Or, in other words, "What wilt thou have me to do?" The man told him that he wanted his withered arm restored. Note then the remarkableness of the statement of Christ. He just simply asked that man to stretch forth his hand. In other words, he asked him to do something which he had never been able to do before, or he thought he had never been able to do before, and with the attempt to obey came the cure. The same thing is abundantly possible with your wife, my friend.

I sit here at my desk all day long, week in and week out, month in and month out, and we have thousands and tens of thousands of cases who write to me and tell me what the power of the Great God realm has done in every conceivable type of disease from cancer on down. It isn't a case of whether the realm of God can do it, it is a case of whether we will believe that it can or not.

Somewhere in the Bible is a statement that reads something like this: "When the son of man cometh, shall he find faith on the earth?" I question very much whether he will. Certainly he couldn't have found it until this Movement started, and it so happens that this Movement, believe it or not, is the one religious Movement to the face of the earth which actually believes God and which is actually able to manifest the Power of God on this earth.

If you can grasp what I am saying to you now, you can place your hand on the head of that good wife and through the Power of the Living God can order whatever disease there is there to leave, and the Power of the Living God will see that it does, simply because the disease cannot exist where the life-giving power of God is thrown against it.

No, I shall not pray. I never pray. Instead of praying, I keep absolutely quiet and let the Power of the Realm of the Spirit of God manifest itself to me. I am too little a man to ever attempt to insult God by asking him for any single thing. That isn't prayer. That isn't the way God operates. He knows what is necessary better than we do and already he's provided the answer. Now, it is up to us poor unbelieving creatures down here to manifest faith even as a grain of mustard seed. Although I don't know you, I just trust that you are man enough to do that.

When the little boat was storm-tossed on the lake, they woke the great Christ of Nazareth and told him that the ship was going to sink and that they were all going to perish, and then note his reply: "Where is YOUR faith?" In other words, he told them that their faith could still the tempest just as well as his could.

The only thing I am sorry [about] is that it will be three or four days before the stenographers get around to transcribing this letter. You will understand that I get in my study early in the morning and work all day and sometimes half the night answering hundreds and hundreds of letters, and at the present time the machines are absolutely loaded and have several thousand letters ahead of them. But I think the girls will get to it inside of three or four days, and then you will get the answer, and I will instruct them to send the answer off airmail.

I will not publish your name in the magazine. May the Spirit of Infinite Peace and Power abide with you forever.

Sincerely, your friend and teacher,

Frank B. Robinson.[18]

CHAPTER 41

"On the Ether Waves & the Cosmic Rays"

Windsor, Ontario, Canada
March 31, 1938

Alfred John Carter, who went by A.J. and Jack variously, took some time out of his day to write a letter to Frank Robinson. At fifty-four, A.J. was nearly three years older than his teacher. In 1938, he lived on Josephine Avenue, a neat and narrow street lined with lookalike bungalows. His home was a modest two-story brick dwelling with a nice porch, three white columns, a small patch of grass in the front, and it stood close enough to its neighbors on either side that you could open a window and touch either house with a broom handle. He lived about a half-mile from the Detroit River, and if he stood in the middle of Josephine Avenue and gazed south, A.J. could see the Motor City skyline. (Within a couple of years, the Carters would move to a roomier, three-story brick home on Rankin Avenue.) The weather that day was fair, but cool. News of an impending auto-strike in Detroit grabbed the headlines in that morning's edition of the *Windsor Star*.

A.J. was born in the scenic Great Lakes town of Point Edward, Ontario, about seventy miles north of Windsor. Later settling in nearby Sarnia, A.J., a skilled carpenter, married Margaret May Corcoran on December 25, 1906. A local paper called A.J. and Margaret May, "a popular young couple of the town."[19]

At the time, Sarnia was a bustling harbor town whose wharves were a constant show of sailboats and steamers. Cable car bells sounded on the streets amid the massive brick hotels, churches, schools, and storefronts. The Carters made their first home in a humble cottage on Cobden Street, and set about building a comfortable life and family.

As A.J. began his hand-written letter to Frank Robinson on the last day of March, he would have no doubt been reflecting on the preceding

240

weeks, which had been tempestuous. His sixteen-year-old son, David, was in the hospital fighting a serious infection. A week earlier, A.J. had written to Frank that on one occasion he had visited the hospital "between 7 PM and 8 PM." His son "was an awful looking sight all his head bandaged, lips easily three times their normal size, and all discolored."[20] His son's suffering distressed the Windsor-area carpenter. "Even his fingers and toenails were black," he wrote. The infection's worsening symptoms alarmed A.J. "I made very definite inquiries from different doctors & nurses as to his condition."Their responses were not encouraging. "Some said 'very dangerous,' others said 'very little hope.'" When he returned home from the hospital, A.J. picked up the phone and called another doctor, one he knew he could trust. "I knew [him] very well, having served with him for about 4 ½ years overseas during the Great War." A.J. had enlisted in the Canadian Expeditionary Forces on August 27, 1915.

Standing a scant five feet, four inches tall, and weighing 120 pounds, A.J. was built more like a jockey than a soldier. Compact and muscular, A.J. had dark skin, brown hair, brown eyes, and tattoos coloring both arms. As part of the 70th Overseas Battalion of the CEF, A.J. Carter was fortunate not to have sustained any serious injuries during the war. But his records show three recurring ailments not uncommon for soldiers: headaches, grippe, and depression.[21] Over a four-year period, Carter—who had been promoted to sergeant before he left the service—was frequently admitted into Bear Wood, a Canadian convalescent hospital in Workingham, England. Carter would have gotten to know the massive mansion-cum-hospital very well, along with its rolling grounds and YMCA hut (complete with a library and commissary).[22]

During and following the war, A.J. wrote verse to help make sense of his experiences on the front. From the war's outset, he had penned a sheaf of poems with titles like, "Wondrous Dead," "Somewhere in France," "His Last Parade," and "Carry On." One poem, published in the *Windsor Star*, honored a recent royal visit to Canada, and was titled, "Who'll Live Should England Die?"

From the shores of dear old England,

Out across Atlantic's main.

To the shores of our dominion

Far across its vast domain

Up the great St. Lawrence River

To Quebec of ancient fame,

Came our loved and honored Sovereign
And our Queen, God bless her name.
Through our cities, towns and hamlets
To our prairies stretching wide
All with one accord we welcome
With fond love and deepest pride
Our grand and noble sailor King.
His bonnie Scottish bride:
Our princess Beth and Margaret Rose
Across the ocean wide.
Almighty God, be pleased to spare
Their rule for many years.
Heaven bless and keep them safe
Through sunshine, clouds and tears.
He has his joys and sorrows,
Like ourselves sometimes a care
And a Queen to less the burden—
"None but the brave deserve the fair."
And should I live to see the day
That I could shake her hand,
Just like any King. I know I'd be
The proudest in the land.
So on across the Rockies High
Unto Vancouver's Isle,
They leave behind a wake of love
Growing dearer every mile.
And when they sail for England
Far across the bounding main,
I know that every heart will sing:
"Will ye no come back again?"
"From burning hands" the torch was
thrown.

"A charge to keep have I."
The unanswerable query I must ask:
Who'll live should England die?
A.J. Carter
Sergeant 70th O.S.
Battalion, C.E.F.
545 Josephine Ave, Windsor[23]

From his poems, it seems clear that A.J. was a man who preferred to convey his most pressing thoughts in the form of writing, be it verse or correspondence. Distraught, A.J. impressed upon Frank that he was seeking solid answers about his son's condition, which is why he turned to his medic friend with whom he had served in the war (and why he reached out to Frank as well).

"I knew he would tell me the truth, if he really knew it," A.J. wrote to Psychiana's founder. After A.J. had described David's symptoms, the war medic leveled with him: "Jack," he said, "I wouldn't like to say."

Instead of sleeping that night, A.J. turned to Psychiana. "All through the night I was calling silently to this great God Law." The next morning, he wrote another letter to Frank. He took the letter "to the nearest postboy," he said. "And the moment that letter left my hand I knew that [my] desire was being fully manifest."

Later, A.J. and his oldest daughter paid a visit to David in the hospital. To their surprise, David had nearly made a full recovery. "Bandages gone," A.J. confirmed to Frank. "Lips about normal size, temperature normal, fingers normal, sitting up in bed and had eaten his breakfast." A.J. made it clear to Frank that it was the power of the God Law that healed David. "It was a pleasure and a great joy," he testified, "to know that here on this earth there dwells a power which I [k]now is actually working through the realm of thought diverted on the ether waves and the cosmic rays to the Great God Law."

David Carter did make a full recovery and was fit enough that in May 1942—a year after his older brother Jack had been killed in a violent car crash—he was recruited into the Royal Canadian Air Force. Following in his father's footsteps, David shipped out to fight in a great war as a pilot. But in 1944, word reached A.J. that his son, David, was missing. Then it was confirmed: his son, David, for whom he prayed so fervently six years previously to Frank Robinson, had been killed in action.

CHAPTER 42

"I Used to Go to the Hills and Pray to that God in the Sky"

Fort Peck Indian Reservation
Wolf Point, Montana
August 28, 1938

In Wolf Point, Montana, the sweeping prairie land is so vast—stretching into Canada to the north, and east into North Dakota—that it feels like one can see the curvature of the earth while standing in any fixed position. The sky overwhelms the land, even more so when charcoal thunderheads roil overhead, making a person feel small and insect-like. The patient eye will catch sight of a rare buffalo herd charging here, grazing there.

Wolf Point sits on the southwestern border of the Fort Peck Indian Reservation in the northeastern part of the state. Home to the Assiniboine and Sioux people, the reservation is large and its boundary lines make it look like a miniature Montana within the state itself, like a thumbnail or microcosm. Dominating the geography as much as the sky, Fort Peck Lake and the Missouri River are lifelines for the people and their land.

Chief Moses White Horse, fifty-two, came from a long line of Assiniboine leaders, sages, and tribal diplomats. Like most of the Assiniboine people, Moses had been shaped by a successive chain of tragedies large and small. And like most Assiniboine people, he had learned to live in two worlds: the Assiniboine world, and the white man's world. Since childhood he had been walking this cultural high-wire, sometimes by choice, but more often by force. By August 1938, the month of the *capasapsaba* moon, Moses White Horse had grown tired and torn. "Dr. Frank B. Robinson," he wrote:

> My dear friend and teacher—I, Moses White Horse Jr., a full blood Assiniboine Indian of the Fort Peck Indian Reservation, Montana, do hereby make this testimony. My father told me my mother died when

I was a small baby, and he left me from this world when I was six years old. I left my people at an early age immediately after my father's death. I went to an Indian school at Carlisle, Pennsylvania in June 1892.[24]

The brainchild of Richard Henry Pratt, the Carlisle Indian School embodied the worst outcomes of Manifest Destiny (removal, subjugation, assimilation). In 1879, Pratt—a former U.S. military officer who had led a unit of "Buffalo Soldiers"—secured a defunct military base in Carlisle and established what would become the paragon of Indian schools nationwide. In a now infamous lecture he delivered at a convention in 1892 (the same year Moses White Horse arrived at Carlisle), Pratt famously espoused his "kill the Indian, save the man" ideology of anglo-Christian indoctrination. The Carlisle School, he bragged, "has always planted treason to the tribe and loyalty to the nation at large."[25]

Rare newspaper photo of Moses White Horse, in the *Great Falls (MT) Tribune*, May 20, 1928.

I stayed 9 years and had forgotten my Indian language. While in school, I was taught that super-natural religion but never knew that I was being lead [sic] in a wrong direction.[26]

White Horse was eager to go home after spending nearly a decade wearing impossible clothes, his long hair lopped off, in what amounted to parochial captivity.

Back in Montana, he began reconnecting with the tribal world from which he had been taken. One winter, while hunting on Wolf Creek, Moses shot and wounded an eagle. When he tried to pick it up, however, the eagle struck back. "The wounded bird grabbed his wrist," *The Great Falls Tribune* reported, "and it required all the strength of White Horse's other hand and arm to loosen the bird's hold. The eagle proved to be of unusual size."[27]

White Horse had been briefly married twice before marrying Emma St. Germaine in July 1927. A year later, Moses was named secretary of the Indian Protective Association of America, and became an outspoken advocate for his people. Another *Great Falls Tribune* article titled, "White Horse Fights for Indian Rights," shows a photo of Moses in tribal dress. "Moses White Horse is an Indian with a chip on his shoulder," the paper reported. "This chip is the question of Indian rights and anyone with the temerity to knock it off will have a fight on his hands for White Horse is a fighter." The story continued on:

> He is now engaged in fighting the Indian bureau, a governmental agency from which the arrows of many an educated Indian have glanced off harmlessly in past decades. But White Horse is Secretary of the Indian Protective Association of America and he hopes to sometime drive a shaft through the armor of the Indian bureau that will reach a vital spot. His particular aversion of this governmental department is over the government's refusal to recognize the treaty of 1886, negotiated with the Indians at Fort Union where this treaty was signed by his paternal grandfather, Redstone, Chief of the Assiniboine.[28]

The Indian bureau, which White Horse dubbed the "American czar to the Indians," was nothing short of complicit in the modern atrocities carried out by the white settlers, he contended. "In the winter of 1883–1884," he added, "he [i.e., the bureau] let several hundred of his people die of starvation right before his eyes. And the Indian commissioner says the Treaty of 1866 was never ratified. There are just a few of us who are fighting for our rights but the time is now at hand when we will be free from slavery and free from the [bureau]." White Horse added, "I am not fighting with bows and arrows but I am fighting the bureau with its own weapons."[29]

But it had been ten years since he had begun the struggle, and Moses White Horse felt more like turning to faith than fighting. Faith, however, was complicated for the fifty-two-year-old. In addition to his traditional beliefs, White Horse practiced the Christianity he had been taught at Carlisle. "I kept on this religion of a God in heaven up to a year ago," he wrote, "and when I saw an advertisement in a magazine, I got in touch with you." His life at home had steadily grown unstable, particularly with his wife. "I told her of things which she must look out for as [they] will surely come to pass if she did not listen to me. How I came to warn her is something I do not know to this day." For reasons that are not clear, White Horse's wife, Emma, left him and their four children, and never came back.

Here is the part where I now believe that there is no such a thing as a God in the sky. After she left, my small baby boy—he cries in the evening and the rest of them would join their brother, and I would break down myself. I used to go to the hills with them and pray to that God in the sky. Way in the night I would ask for relief and comfort and early before sun rise I kept it up for several months but no response.[30]

Then in January 1938, he wrote to Frank Robinson for help. That is when he started receiving the Lessons. "Today, I am glad to say that the Creative Intelligence has witness[ed] my thoughts which I am now putting in writing. Since I have had these Lessons I have had visions showing my future, and I have experienced considerable change since I tried to forget this super-natural religion." White Horse seems to have been searching for a belief system residing somewhere between his ancestral beliefs and Christianity, and he apparently found that system in Psychiana.

I have been doing my part when circumstances permit to talk to others about the Great Life Spirit and I am glad to say that there are some of my Indian people beginning to see the Light in a material way. I hope the day will come when my Indian people all over the United States will know the real God and which I have found with my own efforts earnestly, sincerely and faithfully since I have studied the Lessons. Just as I have said in my former letter that everything is working against me but I realize that I will overcome all these things.[31]

After nearly a lifetime of living by a conventional Christian doctrine, White Horse had redirected his faith to Frank Robinson's vision of the God Law and the God Power. "I am letting the Spirit lead me right now," he added, "as I know the God Law will lead in the right direction. I shall never regret that I accepted this message." In closing his letter, White Horse attended to some housekeeping items. "I will not be able to be at the Convention as I am not financially able to go," he wrote. The convention White Horse mentioned was Frank's October Convention, to be held in Portland, Oregon. "But I am asking the Life Spirit that we shall all receive benefit and the enlargement of our movement. May the Infinite Peace and Power abide with you. I am your friend and Student, Chief Moses White Horse."[32]

CHAPTER 43

Convention

Downtown Portland, Oregon, burned with fall colors as Frank and his entourage finished setting up for the evening's opening lecture at the Masonic Temple. It was familiar territory, as Frank had spoken there in the past, and so he would have felt at ease, by and large. The convention was ambitious, running from that Sunday, October 2, through Tuesday the 4th. It was both necessary and expensive. Still dogged by the lingering threat of a postal investigation, Robinson needed a jolt of energy and validation, something only a packed crowd of admirers could deliver. He needed a reset, but, more than anything, he needed money.

For months, Robinson had been advertising the convention in all of his student correspondence, urging his far-flung flock to attend. If there were real financial advantages to running a mail-order (and not bricks-and-mortar) religion, there were also challenges in sustaining a critical mass. A convention was the easiest way to get the students who—unlike Moses White Horse and so many others—could afford the travel, lodging, and meal expenses of attending a three-day event. Moreover, conventions served as recruiting events, aimed at drawing in the curious.

That evening, as the 7:00 hour approached, Robinson was relieved that he had in fact drawn a sizeable crowd. A local organist played soothing songs as the crowd streamed in and staked out their seats. Frank's duo of stenographers took their usual places on the stage, on either side of the illuminated PSYCHIANA sign. Per routine, volunteers handed out programs and donation leaflets. The only change for this particular lecture was that Dr. Tenney, Frank's aide-de-camp, was slated to speak as well.

Applause stole up over the crowd as Robinson took to the lectern, smiling. He basked for a moment until it grew quiet. "In every Movement," he began, "there is a head who does most of the talking and then there is a hidden power behind that Movement, so I want to introduce to you this gentleman, a Doctor of Laws, Dr. Tenney."[33] For the Psychiana loyalists, Tenney needed no introduction. After all, he had been the one with whom they had been corresponding for nearly two years. They had seen the photo of the strong-jawed man with pewter eyes. They knew his credentials as a former college president and director of religious education at the University of Idaho. So for the loyalists in the crowd that night, Frank's introduction of Tenney was superfluous. But for the uninitiated, Tenney's introduction validated Psychiana in a subtle but powerful way. A second, credentialed voice made Psychiana seem more legitimate, and less a one-man show.

Robinson yielded the lecturn to Tenney, and stood to the side. "When this meeting is over," Tenney said, looking at Frank, "I will have been with you, Dr. Robinson, for two years. I well remember that first day in the office when you tried to tell me something about this Teaching, though I knew I had read it more than I had studied it." Turning his attention back to the crowd, Tenney continued: "He said, 'Dr. Tenney, you ought to know that the Power which created man ought to be able to take care of him,' and my answer was, 'Doctor, you needn't worry about that part of it because I thought this thing through before I came to your office. Now, let's get to work.'"[34]

Tenney's short speech had four strategic objectives. The first was to address the elephant in the room, namely Robinson's trials and deportation. The second was to justify his own connection to Psychiana. Third, to lend credibility to the Movement. And the fourth, was to ask for money.

I learned something about Dr. Robinson because I attended a United States trial. Some people wonder why he needs money. Well, one day a man in that courtroom said to me, "Dr. Tenney, I don't see why you 'hobnob' with him." I said, "Please define your terms, what do you mean by 'hobnob'?" He said, "Well, I saw you talking to him." So I said, "I plead guilty, but if I had to take my place before my Maker, I would rather be in Dr. Robinson's shoes, innocent or guilty, than be in the shoes of any skunk who would do the best he could to put him in the penitentiary, break up his business, and destroy his home, simply because he did not happen to agree upon certain psychological, philosophical, or religious propositions just to get on the hot end of a small town row and religious discussion.[35]

Tenney then turned to the financial ask of his introductory remarks.

Last year we came to you here at Portland and held a convention. The convention cost about one thousand dollars and the collections covered about two hundred dollars. Dr. Robinson went to the bank and borrowed the money and, as far as I know, never told a soul. That is the reason for my asking you again to help so that he can come again—so that he can go to Seattle, Minneapolis, and I have so much faith in you that I am already saying to Chicago and Kansas City Students: I am trusting that you will have an opportunity to meet and hear him in your own part of the world sooner than you now expect.[36]

Teeing up Robinson's return to the lectern, Tenney, added, "Now I turn the meeting back to my chief, the man who gets up earlier, works faster, works longer, receives more letters from more people who experience more gratifying results, than I have ever seen in any other office or situation with which I have been connected: Dr. Robinson."

Frank stepped back to the podium while the applause receded. "I wonder," he said, gazing over his crowd, "who is here from the farthest distance?" One student shouted, "Cleveland, Ohio." Another cried out "Waterville, Maine." Others followed. Saskatoon, Canada. St. Petersburg, Florida. "Is someone here from Memphis, Tennessee? Where is that lady? Will you please come up here a moment?" All eyes swept toward the woman from Memphis as she made her way forward. "You know," Frank continued, "my telephone rang at the hotel this afternoon and someone said there was a Student of mine from Memphis downstairs, so I said to have her come up. She came up and I want this lady to tell you what the Power of the Spirit of God has accomplished in her life through the study of this Teaching." Robinson made it clear that everything was above board, that this woman wanted to speak of her own free will, and had not been induced by him or Tenney in any way. "I am going to ask our sister here to tell us whether or not she has found the Power."[37]

Taking her place on stage, the woman from Tennessee addressed the audience.

Dr. Robinson and members of Psychiana, I am glad to be here tonight. One reason is to thank Dr. Robinson for this wonderful Teaching. My life was a complete failure when I began joining churches to find satisfaction for my soul. But after reading in a magazine that man could talk with God, I tried that. I read these Psychiana Lessons for four months before I could understand what Dr. Robinson was talking about. Then after about twelve months, I found there was a Power—a Power coming over me which rocked and vibrated me so I called the doctor and I told him there was something wrong with me…I rocked back and forth and I knew that this was the Power I had been looking for. When I talked with God my fingers would pop and I knew I had found the Power of the true and living God.[38]

Robinson happily turned over the podium to several other students for the remainder of the first night of the Psychiana convention. His purpose seemed to be foster fellowship, encourage testimony, and collect money. After the student testimonials, Frank fleshed out the rest of his lecture with general statements about how vast the Movement was, and its seeming exponential growth. He talked about how many envelopes he had to buy and the costs of the operation. And of course, he delivered his origin story, which in many ways had become the core doctrine of Psychiana. Closing out the first night, he said, "That one man could go out of a drug store and put over a Movement of this size with ninety percent of the Students writing as these letters you heard tonight, there's something doing, isn't there? Now, who believes the Power of God is working on this earth?"[39] For the final time that night, applause echoed throughout the venue.

———◆———

The second night of the annual Psychiana Convention opened with the song "America." It was Monday, October 3. News that morning declared "Hitler Enters Sudetenland in Triumph."[40] The Nazi leader spoke to cheering masses: "In this solemn hour let us thank Almighty God that on our way thus far he has blessed us and pray that under His guidance our steps in the future may also be guided right."[41]

Again, Dr. Tenney delivered the opening remarks, informing the crowd that, just like encyclopedias and dictionaries, the Psychiana Lessons had to be revised and updated. Such revisions, Tenney said, cost money. He urged the crowd to donate or renew their subscriptions. Volunteers handed out order blanks while Tenney spoke. He read letters from students—one from St. Louis, another from Oakland, and yet another from Oudtshoon, South Africa. Then, wrapping up his remarks, Tenney talked about a tour he had done previously in Portland, visiting individual students in their homes and asking questions about their experience with the Lessons. ("I started out with the usual salesman talk," he confided wryly.) Of these meetings,

Tenney offered an example.

> I looked up a name in a phonebook and it had nothing but the initials
> before it and I naturally thought I was going to talk to a man but when
> the voice answered it didn't sound masculine at all. Then I went to the
> home and asked this lady the same questions, and she said, "Do you
> really want to know that?" And I said, "Certainly, that's what I came
> down here for." She said, "Dr. Tenney, before I found out about Dr.
> Robinson's Teaching, I was just one more Negro woman north of Mason
> and Dixon's line. I lived in that old house there and I had no hopes for
> anything better and thought no prospects for anything better could
> come my way. But I began to study these Lessons and the first thing I
> knew, the world looked different and the house in which you are now
> visiting is my own and paid for. Also this house next to it is mine and
> I am renting that and I am still working. Some of my friends wonder
> why I work when I have two houses and rent one of them, but it's lots
> of fun to work after you have studied Psychiana, Dr. Tenney."[42]

After Dr. Tenney concluded his remarks, Frank Robinson briefly revisited
his origin story of a humble drugstore clerk looking for God before riffing
on a favorite trope: numbers. 11,738 was the number of towns and cities
that were home to Psychiana students. 67 was the number of countries
to which Psychiana Lessons were mailed. $2.00 was the average cost for
a Psychiana Lesson. 1,400,000,000 was the number of people following
some kind of religious belief system worldwide. $50.00 was all that Frank
had when he started Psychiana. 15 was the number of people in the world
who truly knew God.[43]

Central to his talk that evening, though, was the core idea that God
was infallible. And an infallible God would not make a flawed human
doomed to spend his or her entire life atoning for some "original sin." A
student had inquired about this core idea, according to Frank.

> "But Dr. Robinson, I understand that when we find God we will have
> to repent, confess, and all that sort of thing." Repent of what? Your sins?
> Did you ask to come into this world? Do you believe that God cursed
> you? I don't. I give God credit for being able to, if there's anything
> wrong with your life, to take it out. And do you know how it's taken
> out? By recognizing the influence of the invisible Power of that life.[44]

Robinson's primary selling strategy was to convince his audience he was not selling anything. "I'm not selling Psychiana to you tonight," he said. "I am not interested in whether anyone takes it or not, but I am vitally interested in bringing to you, in my humble way, evidence of a Power which does exist."[45]

The following day, in an afternoon lecture, Robinson discussed the evidence of the invisible Power. He drew on his Lesson 10 analogy about planting seeds in the correct conditions. If the conditions are correct (i.e., soil, water, sun), the plant will grow because of the God Law governing it. "I take five acorns," he said that afternoon,

> and I plant one in Portland, Oregon, and I send another to South America and I plant it. Another I send to Eastern Canada and two more across the Atlantic, and plant them all and what do I find? Five blueberry bushes, or a blueberry bush in one country and another in a third? No, for the God-Law or the Realm of the Spirit which is God, operates with remarkable precision in any country, wherever the conditions are complied with, and you can't get away from that, and it means an oak wherever these conditions are complied with. So then, God responds to that phase and we have an oak.[46]

That night Tenney and Robinson closed out the annual Psychiana Convention. "I am telling you Beloved tonight," Frank said,

> that regardless of what your problem may be, the fact that you are what you are—God's highest creation—and the fact that the life of God, moment by moment is manifested in and through you is absolute assurance that all the Power of that Realm of God is available to you here and now, and if you wish to find it, keep off your knees, stand on your feet, look up to God and say, 'I believe—not in any organization's dogmas or creeds, but I believe in God.'[47]

Making one last pitch for people to donate or join his Movement, Robinson ended his three-day convention on a high note, with his volunteers collecting completed order forms throughout the hall.

CHAPTER 44

"The Meanest Swindler in the World"

On Wednesday, August 30, 1939, the front page of Missouri's *St. Joseph News-Press* was filled with dire headlines portending war and worse. "Hitler Demands Poland Give Up Areas Before Any Negotiations," read one. "Duce's Paper Says Versailles Treaty Must Be Scrapped," read another. And "Nazi Move Alarms." On the same page, below the fold, ran a partial map of the United States with a map of European capitals superimposed on top of it. Titled, "Crisis Dwarfed on United States Map," the info-graphic was attempting to minimize the scale of the conflict in Europe, geographically speaking. "Berlin is closer to London than Kansas City is to Denver," the paper rationalized. "The war, if it stays within Europe, won't be so big as far as miles are concerned."

On that same day, just forty miles due south in Leavenworth, Kansas, a fifty-one-year-old man named Fredrick Van Ness Person finished writing an essay titled, "The Fallacy of Fear," in which this line appeared: "I prefer the evil foreboding role of the Greek prophetess to that of a fatuous Pollyanna, dispensing shallow cheer."[48] Person's observation was not a rejoinder to the *St. Joseph News-Press's* vapid info-graphic, but it could have been. After all, Person was well read, culturally aware, incredibly intelligent, and insightful, especially when it came to the human condition.

At ten pages, the cleanly typed essay carried the epigraph, "The only thing we have to fear, is fear itself," along with attributive acknowledgments stating that the essay was dedicated to Frank Robinson.

———————◆———————

Two years older than Frank Robinson (their July birthdays were two days apart), Frederick Person had already lived a robust if enigmatic life. He was soft-looking, tall but paunchy, with a high forehead, good nose, a left eye with a slight yaw, and clean-shaven with a double chin. Like Frank

254

Robinson, Fred Person was a big man, a heavy smoker and coffee drinker. He either drank alcohol or he did not, depending on who was asking.[49] Talkative, charming, and charismatic, Person was born into a well-to-do and "comfortably situated" Chicago family in a "15-room well-furnished brick house." He was the third of five children, having two sisters and two brothers, and was raised by his doting English mother, Mary, and his father, David Van Ness Person, a New York-born publisher who made his fortune printing a trade magazine for the paint, oil, and varnish industries. A Silas Lapham-like figure of the nouveau riche, the elder Van Ness Person liked to flaunt his money, advertising once in 1907—widely and with great showmanship—that he was willing to pay "$10,000.00 a year and many perquisites for a maid who would serve his breakfast at 7 a.m. sharp every day in the year."[50] A year after placing his advertisement, the publishing magnate died of "apoplexy."[51]

While Person's mother Mary loved all her children, she favored Fred. According to one source, "he and his mother were deeply attached to each other," and he "stayed at home with his mother until he was 28 years of age."[52] While living at home, Person pursued his education and worked in the publishing company his father had founded, but was evidently dissatisfied with the work of printing news of the paint and varnish industry.

In January 1912, Person successfully convinced Marguerite Strong, the daughter of a colonel and insurance tycoon, to break off her engagement to a St. Louis reverend, and marry him instead.[53]

Within a couple of years of his marriage, Person had relocated to the San Francisco Bay area, settling into a modern cottage near the University of California campus in Berkeley, presumably to pursue advanced studies. (Marguerite likely joined him, although records are unclear.)[54] Fredrick Van Ness Person—who went variously by F.V. Person, Fred Person, Fredrick V. Person, etc.—excelled at mathematics, writing, and foreign languages. (He was fluent in Spanish, French, and German.) He transitioned easily into the elite circles of the university town.

Two years before Frank Robinson was freed from his prison term at Alcatraz and began prowling the Bay Area for odd jobs, Fredrick Person was roaming the same streets, formulating his own plans to make money. One plan entailed selling stock in the Allied Apartments Company of San Francisco. Representing the company's financial department, Person set up shop in the Modesto Hotel and advertised heavily.[55] But he also had other irons in other fires.

It was 1915 and the world of advanced engineering was fixed almost exclusively on aeronautics. Out of that technological fever, Person founded the Curtis Howell Aviation School across the bay in Richmond, California. "Plans for a building for the company are in the hands of a San Francisco architect," the *Oakland Tribune* noted of the start-up flying school. "And on completion of the structure, which is now practically assured, the manufacture of air craft will commence."[56] As the company's president, Person needed investors, and was able to convince a local songwriter named Walter Herzer to invest $1,500 into Curtis Howell Aviation. The school's revenue stream derived from the tuition of over sixty current students, totaling nearly $600 monthly. To further illustrate the lucrative nature of his company and his own personal success story, Person apparently procured a $5,000 showpiece French racecar, passing it off as his own.[57] Moved by Person's confidence, erudition, dress, and expensive car, Herzer handed over the cash, on the condition he be given a position at Curtis Howell Aviation. Person agreed to give Herzer a job, the two shook hands, and that was that.

Unfortunately for Herzer, Person was not the president of the company. In fact, there was no such thing as a Curtis Howell Aviation School of Richmond, California, or anywhere else for that matter. There were no sixty students, current or otherwise, and there certainly was not a $600 monthly tuition stream. The entire story was a con. Unable to recover his investment or find any tangible trace of this mysterious flight school, Herzer reported Person to the authorities, who launched an investigation. The *Oakland Tribune* followed up on the development, writing, "Berkeleyan is Accused of Fraud."[58] Exposed, Person hopped the first train back to Chicago, where he aimed to start over. But his past was not far behind.

———————◆———————

In mid-August of 1916, police in San Francisco had telegrammed Chicago law enforcement, alerting them of outstanding fraud charges against Person. Then, on August 22, Person was arrested at the Windy City's Edgewater Hotel. "Person said he would fight extradition," one paper confirmed.[59] Fred Person did fight both extradition and the fraud charges, and won, allowing some reprieve.

Like most able-bodied men of the era, Person, thirty-three, had signed his draft card in 1917, although the extent and details of his service, if any, are unclear. (By the end of the war, a passport application had him working as a broker in Chicago.) For the next couple of years, Person tried his hand at an array of occupations. He re-entered the publishing industry, studied law, pursued real estate, and eventually circled back to stocks and bonds.

Meanwhile, his personal life was in shambles. After detectives had discovered him in an apartment on a "day bed unclothed" with "two scantily-clad girls" and that "all three had been drinking," Marguerite filed for divorce, charging that Frederick V. Person had "undue intimacy with many unnamed women" and that he lacked the ability "to withstand the wiles of other women." The 1922 divorce was bitter and very public, bringing much shame and embarrassment on both families.[60]

Seven years later, on July 10, 1929, one week after his forty-fifth birthday, and some three months before the stock market crash, F.V. Person—then a broker for the Terrill Bond and Mortgage Company—was charged with selling fraudulent bonds in Indianapolis, and, having been found guilty, was ordered by a judge to pay nearly $50,000 in restitution within twenty-four hours or face imprisonment. While the *Muncie Evening Press* was able to unearth a previous grand jury indictment against Person "for using the mails to defraud," they evidently had not uncovered his fraud case in California. "Person has promised to return the money and cease operations in Indiana," the paper added.[61]

Person did neither. Instead, he fled. For nearly three years, Person remained in hiding. Then, in November 1932, a curious ad started appearing in regional newspapers, a few pages away from where one could find Frank Robinson's own Psychiana advertisements.

> UNUSUAL opportunity offered salesmen to sell proposition of merit. No experience necessary. Salary, commission, and expenses. No investment. Write details of your experience and references. Address: F.V. Person, 30 N. LaSalle St., Chicago.[62]

Person was busy advancing his most elaborate con of all: a swindle targeting a network of Catholic priests. A year later, news began leaking out: "Salesman Held in $580,000 Swindle," reported the *St. Louis Globe Democrat.*[63] The Illinois attorney general described Person as a "high-powered salesman," a term reporters and prosecutors had also used to describe Frank Robinson. The Illinois State Attorney's office further described Person as making a "specialty of victimizing Catholic priests, to whom he sold his securities for various parish endowment funds." Within the year, headlines about Person's illegal activities grew more acute.

"Catholics in Missouri Defrauded of Millions: Estimated Losses in Neighboring States by 'Investments', Likely to Run to $3,000,000."[64]

After posting a $5,000 bond, Person panicked and fled to Robinson's homeland of England. Authorities chased Person, one paper observed, "through several European countries and Canada."[65] Finally, Frederick Van Ness Person was arrested in New York on November 2, 1935. Newly married to a woman thirteen years his junior, Person gave up only when "he learned postoffice [sic] inspectors were threatening to hold his wife until he surrendered."[66]

It was the end of a long and sordid career. By the time he was taken into custody, Person was wanted by the state police in Charleston, West Virginia; the prosecuting attorneys in Cassville, Missouri and Point Pleasant, West

Arraigned on Mail Fraud Charge

FREDERICK VAN NESS PERSON

Associated Press Wirephoto.

LEAVING the Federal building in New York after being arraigned. He was indicted in Chicago and Kansas City in connection with an alleged $400,000 fraud scheme, and surrendered after a two-year search. Person is handcuffed to Frederick A. Tuttle (in foreground), formerly assistant chief inspector of immigration, who is under a two-year sentence for conspiracy to violate the immigration laws.

News item on Fred Van Ness Person's arrest on a mail fraud charge, in the *St. Louis Post-Dispatch*, November 5, 1935.

Virginia; and by the sheriff in Sibley, Iowa. All charges were for fraud and O.M.U.F.P.—Obtaining Money Under False Pretenses.[67] Ultimately, however, it was "mail frauds" that stuck, legally speaking, to Frederick Van Ness Person, the man prosecutors called "the meanest swindler in the world."[68]

◆

When Person wrote to Frank Robinson that August day in 1939, he was in legal limbo, having served his four-year prison sentence at Leavenworth only to await subsequent charges in another state. Outside on that particular Wednesday, the temperatures climbed to 97, making the Kansan flatlands shimmer in the distance. "My dear Dr. Robinson," Person began.

> I have just been released from the Penitentiary. A gracious friend forwarded to me, during my incarceration, the full course of PSYCHIANA Lessons, which prompted me to write the enclosed article which I have

dedicated to your work and entitled it "The Fallacy of Fear." I hope you will read it and pass it along to anyone that needs a "builder up."[69]

According to Fort Leavenworth records, Person was a prolific letter writer, maintaining an avid correspondence with a full roster of associates, legal advisors, clergy members, family, and friends.

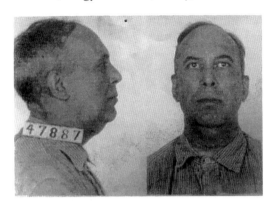

Ft. Leavenworth prison mug shot of Fred Van Ness Person, c. 1936. From the records of the Bureau of Prisons, Department of Justice.

As an inmate, Person was liked and seemed to get along with the other inmates and wardens. "This is a college man," the Ft. Leavenworth Admission Summary stated, "past middle age whose test intelligence is in the superior group."

He is a pleasant, cooperative, cultured man who is unusually well informed generally. He has been a broker for many years and apparently with considerable success and prominence. He is emotionally adequate, normally responsive and presents no findings of abnormal mental health. Our records show no previous conflicts with the law, which would indicate that for many years his activities have been entirely legitimate and would, in all probability, have continued so had it not been for adverse economic conditions and the legal restrictions instituted pertaining to banking and brokerage procedures.[70]

Despite a life of deceit and compulsive lying, and the long and tangled criminal career Person led, dating back decades to the formulation of a fictitious flight school, he had somehow managed to charm and cajole institution officials enough that even his personal narrative was laundered clean of nearly all blemishes and defects. Prison officials simply believed that "adverse economic conditions," and not a predilection to cheat or con, had led Person down this particular criminal path.

And if anyone could spin a narrative, it was Frederick Van Ness Person. To Frank Robinson, he continued:

I am sure, with your responsibilities, you have many lonely periods—sensing defeat for some of your plans and in those silent midnight hours feel that your strength is dependent upon the Supreme Commander. God will give you strength and courage to master all.[71]

Under "FAMILY DATA" the Ft. Leavenworth Admission Summary added that Person's "Father was born in New York [and] died at the age of 72 when subject was 21. Subject claims father had a university education and was a minister and publisher." While there is no evidence to support the claim that Person's father was cut from the same ministerial cloth as Frank Robinson's, the inclusion of this plot point says more, perhaps, about its source than its subject.

The question of Person's father and his ecumenical credentials notwithstanding, Fred Person was able to adopt the tone and cadence of a preacher's son, or, at the very least, the words and rhythms of the penitent in his letter to Frank Robinson.

We face grief with dismay—and usually in utter loneliness, and would be apt to lose our bearing, if it were not for the light ahead, and the Unseen Hand ever guiding toward that light. Please remember these inspired words which is [sic] the source of all human courage: "Wait upon the Lord, be of good courage, and He will strengthen thy heart."[72]

Of all the letters Robinson received from his students and followers, Person's is conspicuous in that it seems to be offering consolation rather than seeking it, and the fact that it comes from a prisoner makes it all the more curious.

According to his official prison file, Person liked movies, baseball, and football. "He smokes," the report stated, "but did not use liquor or narcotics. Attended church regularly and claims to have had many friends among nearly all occupations." Reports also note that he was proficient in "Salesmanship & Advertising" before his incarceration.

"During my forced exile from the outside world," Person wrote to Frank, "there seemed little chance of my rising to the surface of freedom again."

To me, however, an improbability is a direct incentive to make the improbably not merely probable, but certain. I hope the fates will be propitious and that I can again re-establish myself. At the present time I am confined in the County Jail—contesting my removal to West Virginia on indictments rendered many years ago—but a priest in that State still insists on having his "pound of flesh." But I hope to be successful in my efforts here.[73]

Person then explained his rationale behind including his ten-page essay, "Fallacy of Fear."

> If you feel your students or prospective students would be interested in how I "whipped fear" after reading 'PSYCHIANA' Lessons, you are at liberty to publish this article as a lesson or in booklet form. You also have my permission to edit, delete, or condense the article.

Then, closing out his letter, Person offered his services. "Being a former newspaper man, I am qualified to cover any subject and have had many years experience as a 'ghost writer,'" he wrote.

> Try me out; no obligation on your part. I have shed the prison past as a snake sloughs its skin. I will welcome criticism as well as commendation and will profit by both.
> May I hear from you.
> Sincerely yours,
> F. V. Person
> c/o County Jail
> 503 So. Third St
> Leavenworth, Kansas[74]

"The Fallacy of Fear" is an eloquent but meandering treatise arguing that human fear is a construct rather than a biological response to threats, real or perceived. Person hangs the entire essay from the solitary peg of his prisoner's perspective, a perch he views as privileged and therefore compelling.

> I have been unproductive and unashamed, devoid of evangelical fervor with no ambition to serve my fellow man, curious only to study him and am enormously amused when I observe lack of intestinal fortitude. Picture the mental reaction of a lone convict incarcerated in a penitentiary. I lived the life and I wrote it down. I wanted to see for myself and see I did.[75]

The piece is riddled with pithy one-liners that do not always add up to a unified whole, but are telling all the same. "An inexperienced narrator probably reveals more than is mannerly";[76] "Religion has been called the refuge of those with weak minds";[77] "Many of us suffer from the inability to forget the traditional";[78] "The object is not so much to ward off fear so that it shouldn't touch us; but to let it strike and rebound because it could make no impact and therefore no injury."[79]

While Person occasionally reaches high, summoning Emerson to the page, for instance—"Thought is the property of him who can adequately place it"—he also falls short with the odd cliché: "We have to pull ourselves up by the bootstraps."[80]

Still, it is difficult to divine the purpose of the essay and nearly impossible to guess its intended audience. Far from an article of atonement or absolution, the piece is alarmingly vacant of remorse or contrition. Allegedly aimed at current or prospective Psychiana students (though the religion is never explicitly mentioned in the text itself), the gist of the essay seems almost inwardly focused, as if Person was trying to cast fear from his own mind.

In rarer moments, the piece is like his letter in that it seems to offer—and not ask for—spiritual advice.

> It takes time to warm up, say we in extenuation. Remember that "eventually why not now" is a sound motto. Everybody assumed fear was an inevitable state. You were born subject to fear and that was the end of it, just as you were born subject to death. As daily dreads and fears confronted you, GOD was counted out…courage comes from God.[81]

Ultimately, it is impossible to know Person's true intentions behind writing and sending his letter and attached essay to Frank Robinson. Maybe he was genuinely stirred by the course of instruction. Or perhaps the Lessons, letter, and essay were mere entertainments, things to keep him occupied during incarceration. It may have been the case, too, that Person saw in Robinson and his religion a financial opportunity, a new mark or con. One conman conning another conman, in an age-old game of "it takes one to know one."

CHAPTER 45

Looking the Part

On Thursday, September 21, 1939—just three weeks after Hitler invaded Poland—Herman Forrest Edwards, a staff writer for *The Oregonian*, arrived at the Union Pacific train station in Moscow, Idaho. His train arrived on time at exactly 8:45 a.m.. He was in town to interview the self-help prophet of Psychiana. Edwards knew that Robinson had escaped imprisonment and that his Movement was, by all outward appearances, thriving. He decided to spend a couple of days in the small college town to get a sense of the man and Psychiana for a feature story.

Both Frank and Dr. Tenney met Edwards at the passenger station with hearty handshakes. Dr. Tenney, he later reported, was "66, according to 'Who's Who in America.'"[82] Tenney took the reporter's leather bag and stowed it in the back of Frank's new 1939 Cadillac 75. The enormous luxury car was considered a limousine at the time, seating seven comfortably. Sold in standard polished black, the Cadillac flaunted "suicide doors"— doors hinged at the rear rather than at the front—and over 1,000 pounds of chrome alone. That the car was far too much for just one man made it all the more obvious a choice for Frank Robinson.

The weather was warm and pleasant in the sleepy town as the three men drove a few short blocks to secure Edwards' lodging. Frank parked in front of the Moscow Hotel, and after Edwards checked into his room, they met downstairs in the restaurant for breakfast. "Robinson is a big man," Edwards wrote, "blond, blue-eyed, cordial; a vital, purposeful man, evidently in robust health." On the other hand, Edwards allowed, "critics call him an atheist, charlatan, faker, the modern Barnham of religion. They say he has grown rich at the expense of the gullible."[83] The critics Edwards mentions largely entailed clergymen, newspaper columnists, and outspoken members of law enforcement.

After breakfast, they took a "tour of the Robinson private enterprises." Frank showed Edwards the newspaper operation as well as the newly constructed Robinson Professional Building, a two-story brick building on the corner of Third and Jackson Streets. "We came to Psychiana's own build-ing," Edwards wrote, "a one-story brick which, Robinson said, already is outgrown." Inside the headquarters, he further noted, business "hums like a beehive." Touring Psychiana's hub of operations, Edwards continued on.

> From the hallway a door at the left opens into Dr. Robinson's comfort-able study, where he does most of his work. To the right are other offices, for Dr. Tenney, the business manager, secretaries, assistants. In the rear is Psychiana's 'workshop,' its mailing department, a big circular, revolving table where the lessons are assembled, [and] addressing machines.[84]

Such a thriving operation in small-town America seemed to fit the kind of man Robinson projected himself to be, even if the business of that operation was at odds with what small-town America was perceived to be in 1939. Robinson, Edwards astutely observed, "looks the part of the pros-perous business man, chamber of commerce committee chairman, service club member, home town booster."

Conspicuous in all of that projection, however, was Robinson's ego, the size of which was not lost on *The Oregonian's* reporter:

> Typical of him is the boast in advertising copy, as a sort of testimonial to the potency of this new "God Power," that "I own control of the largest circulating daily newspaper in my county; I own the largest office building in my city; I own my home, which has a lovely pipe organ in it."[85]

Robinson was a fighter, Edwards noted, one ready to strike back when attacked, especially by the clergy. "Robinson is no supine prophet," he added. "He attacks vehemently the institution he calls 'orthodox religion,' says it is built on fears and superstition and that it is decadent. He dispenses this unsolicited advice to churches: 'discard this story of Jesus Christ.'"

Had Edwards plumbed Robinson's biography more thoroughly, he would have seen the great and guiding conflict in Frank Bruce Robinson's life: all conventional religions represented his own father, Reverend John Henry Robinson, who had cast him out of his homeland when he was a boy. His retaliation against "orthodox religion" stemmed from a long-standing desire to retaliate against his father. He even said as much years later, in a telling passage from one of his books in which he substituted the word "religion" for his father:

I have seen lots of "religion" in my day. I have seen religion in action. I saw it nearly beat its own son to death. I saw it guzzling beer by the gallon. I saw it having illicit intercourse with members of its own church. I saw it lie under oath. I saw it steal. I saw it as it exists today. I do not want that sort of religion, for religion, or whatever masquerades as religion, has not changed for the better since my boyhood. [It] is a ghastly sham perpetrated on the world by the church in the name of God.[86]

Paradoxically, Frank hungered for his father's approval. As the leader of an iconoclastic religion, Frank Robinson got to have it both ways, if only in theory.

Wanting to know more about Psychiana and its beliefs, Edwards went out of his way to assure his impartiality in writing about the strange religion and its leader, whose reputations, for better or worse, had "skyrocketed into a position of international prominence." "Let me say now," Edwards averred, "that I shall not attempt in this article to discover proof of Dr. Robinson's statement that he talked with God. Nor shall I try to analyze Psychiana for its merits or lack of them, nor quarrel with Robinson's followers or critics." His interest, Edwards, wrote, was strictly "reportorial."[87]

✦

Edwards had arrived in Moscow on the heels of Psychiana's ten-year anniversary. Despite numerous investigations, a flagging economy, massive legal fees, attacks and allegations, Frank Robinson had not only kept his Movement afloat for over a decade, but he had expanded it. Like most operations, however, Psychiana had its slow periods, even after considerable expansion and having achieved mainstream status. When Edwards toured the offices, he witnessed Psychiana at the tail end of its "slack" season. "Advertising," he reported, "tapers off during summer months, and is resumed vigorously in the fall. Then the mail pours in and out, too."[88]

It was a good time, in other words, for Edwards to sit down with Robinson for an interview. "In the study, I asked Dr. Robinson to explain his theory of God."

Dressed in his usual attire—tie, shirtsleeves, vest, slacks—Robinson sat back in his desk chair, smiling.

We believe and teach that the invisible life which is in us is the Spirit of God dwelling in us, and that all may draw upon that supreme presence for everything needed in this life and in spiritual life forever more.

Psychiana changes God from an abstract theory to a living, vital power. No longer does God occupy a faraway throne in some mysterious realm in the heavens, but he is here, now, and everyone who becomes aware of his presence may talk with him.[89]

Edwards jotted down some notes and then turned the conversation to an inevitable topic. "'Let's hear something about the business end of things,'" he said. Robinson, Edwards wrote, "rang for a secretary, demanded records, marshaled figures, and offered this," he added. In 1938, Psychiana was carried on sixty-one radio stations nationwide, and by the time Edwards had sat down in Frank's study, the start-up religion was advertising in nearly 150 newspapers across the United States. "Advertising also is carried in seven magazines in England and in others in Canada and in Holland," Edwards wrote. "A branch office is maintained at The Hague."

Edwards broke down the basic pay structure of Psychiana Lessons for his readership. "The 20 Lessons in Advanced Teaching No. 1 sell for $20, fewer Lessons in Advanced Teaching No. 2 for $10, and 50 Lessons in No. 3 for $40," he explained. "The combination of the three courses lead to a degree of doctor of divinity, which Robinson says he is empowered to grant under his Idaho charter."[90] *The Oregonian* staff writer had singled out two significant developments in the Psychiana story. First, Frank had finagled a satellite office at The Hague. Second, he had laid the groundwork to legally confer "degrees" upon his students for a fee.

Having finished at the Psychiana offices, Edwards got a tour of the Robinson home on Howard Street. "I had a brief glimpse of the Robinson home life," he reflected. "Dinner at the fine brick home. A peep into the doll house of an 8-year-old Florence. Both Dr. Robinson and Alfred, high school athlete, played for me on the pipe organ. Mrs. Robinson who is active in lodge work was not home that day."[91]

Edwards finished his story "A Visit to the Man Who Talks With God," with a timely and telling observation. "Another world war, Dr. Robinson believes, will prepare the people all over the globe for a new religion," Edwards wrote. "He must, and says he will, be ready to meet that opportunity when conflict becomes universal."

CHAPTER 46

Winter War

Conflict was indeed becoming universal. On Thursday, November 30, 1939, some two million Soviet troops crossed the border into Finland and launched what would become known as the "Winter War." The scale of invasion was three times the size of the 1944 Allied invasion of Normandy. Finland, hopelessly small and isolated, had only 300,000 troops total, a handful of tanks, and a few clunky airplanes. The Soviets' aim was to crush the Finnish forces. Martha Gelhorn, one of the few international war reporters in Helsinki at the time, offered her first-hand account. "War started at 9 o'clock promptly," she wrote. "The people of Helsinki stood in the streets and listened to the painful rising and falling and always louder wail of the sirens. For the first time in history, they heard bombs falling on their city. This is the modern way of declaring war."[92] The invasion was so massive as to be grotesque. But the Finnish forces did not surrender as the Soviets had imagined they would. Instead, they dug in and fought. Franklin Roosevelt decried the attack as cowardly, calling Finland "a country so infinitesimally small that it could do no conceivable, possible harm to the Soviet Union." It was, he said, a "small nation that seeks only to live at peace as a democracy and a liberal, forward-looking nation at that."[93]

When Frank Robinson heard about the Soviet invasion of Finland, he immediately sent a message to the country's prime minister, Risto Ryti. He told the embattled leader that all of Psychiana's "God Power" would be fully focused on Finland in their fight against the encroachments of the Soviet Union. On Sunday, December 3, 1939—just three days after the invasion, while ash and smoke still filled the streets of Helsinki—Robinson, who was staying in Chicago's luxurious Stevens Hotel, received a return cable from the Prime Minister:

DR. FRANK B ROBINSON FOUNDER PSYCHIANA

HEARTIEST THANKS

VERY GREATFUL FOR EVERY HELP AND SUPPORT
GOD WILL SAVE MY COUNTRY
RISTO RYTI.[94]

Ryti's was more than just a perfunctory response to what could have easily been taken as a message from a crackpot. Frank's message may have resonated with the leader if only because Ryti was a devoted student of theosophy, an esoteric philosophy that probed such matters as the boundaries of human wisdom and the essence of the divine realm.[95] It was, in other words, a system of religion not radically different from much of Psychiana's derivative teachings. Ryti was known—famous even—for consulting clairvoyants and seers, and for his deep beliefs in the powers of fate. Why else would the leader of a country take the time to send a reply cable to a man he had never met while his country lay in ruins?

Psychiana mailer indicating Frank's plan for the Movement to begin establishing churches and ministries, c. 1940. University of Idaho Special Collections.

In January 1940, Frank Robinson, as a father, was encountering a different kind of war in his own home. Although Alf Robinson was by and large a good kid, smart student, able athlete, and excellent musician, he was not immune from the usual teenage temptations of the day. ("Drugs in our time consisted of beer and cigarettes!…[In] high school we could go downtown and order pitchers of beer as no I.D. was required in those days."[96])

Alf recalled the one time his father ever "physically abused" him. One night Alf and his friends had decided to skip their DeMolay International[97] meeting and instead went ice skating at Robinson Park, where they got drunk on sloe gin. "The night was cold, clear, and stimulating with six to eight inches of light snow on the ground and the lake," Alf recounted. "We had a ball, skating a while, then going back to my 1936 Chevy coupe for a 'belt' or two before returning to the ice. Fortunately, Dick and Don stayed sober, while Barney and I became plastered."

Later that night, Alf's sober friends leaned him against the front door of the Robinson home, rang the doorbell, "and ran like hell." Roused from their slumber, Frank and Pearl answered the door only to find an inebriated Alf at their feet.

> I remember he and Mother lifting me into the house, to the dining room, where Dad gave me a hard cuff on the side of my head, knocking me across the dining room table. I'm sure his frustration and past memories of his own childhood overcame him at this point.

This and similar episodes Frank never mentioned in his own writings, for such inclusions would have painted the picture of an average family, one which may not have had such a direct line to the God Power. Nor did Frank seem to dwell on domestic troubles. Instead, he worked, ensuring that his Movement was inextricably linked to world events. Of the Winter War, Frank wrote: "It begins to look as if our efforts against Hitler and Stalin are bearing much fruit, for the Finns have amazed the world in their stand against Red Russia. When a large nation like Red Russia attacks a peaceful little country like Finland, it brings down upon itself the indignation and the disgust of the whole world."[98]

His words appeared on the pages of *Psychiana Weekly*, a relatively new addition to his publication powerhouse. A compendium of brief lectures, organization updates, news items, testimonials, advertising for Frank's self-published books, and letters to the editor, *Psychiana Weekly* was popular among his students for its variety and, at ten cents, its relative affordability. But *Psychiana Weekly* was more than just Frank Robinson's mouthpiece to his Movement. It was the proving ground for his ideas, unbridled thoughts, pendulous moods, and fancies. He was often surprisingly candid in his writing, even showing vulnerability. But he could get cranky and impatient. In its pages, he often lashed out about the investigations into him and his Movement. It was also the place he went to boast and brag about his latest achievements, the growth of his Movement, the perfectness of his home and family. The *Weekly* was also Frank's schoolyard, where he argued with his enemies and shamed naysayers. But his retorts almost always said as much about their source than their intended targets, for Frank Robinson could credibly be charged with more than occasional projection onto others faults he himself showed.

Psychiana workers in the mailing department, c. 1940. Latah County Historical Society.

One of the favorite columns in the weekly was titled, "Questions & Answers," in which students could ask Robinson anything they like.

Q: "Why do you never mention the Bible in your writings or Lessons? Do you not believe it to be the Word of God?"

A: The Christian bible, I take it you refer to. You must remember that the eleven major systems of religion all have their 'bibles'which they consider just as much the Word of God as do Christians.[99]

Some student questions veered far from philosophical or theological topics, wading instead into current events and political matters.

Q: What do you think of the CIO [Congress of Industrial Organizations]?

A: I believe it to be communistic in essence. I have no use for communism, fascism, Nazism, or any other ism which is opposed to the fundamentals of Americanism.[100]

Despite a slowly recovering economy, labor strikes flared up around the country during this period. Talk about the American Federation of Labor (AFL) and CIO was commonplace, and therefore found its way into the *Weekly*.

Sometimes, Frank printed whatever was stuck in his craw at the time, even if it reflected poorly on him.

Q: Where do you get all the degrees you use after your name?

A: That's none of your business…You did not ask this question because you really wanted to know, you asked it to be smart, and sarcastic. It might interest you to know that, on account of having written *Gleams Over the Horizon*, I was recently given an honorary membership in the Eugene Field Foundation, and made an honorary member of the American Association of Authors and Publishers.

Q: Will Jesus Christ ever return to the earth in person?

A: No. Dead men have the uniform habit of staying dead. [101]

Driving home the necessity of Psychiana in an unstable world, Robinson also included a column titled, "Hitler and God," in which he wrote, "I notice a statement again today in which Hitler alludes to himself as 'God almighty and I.' Seems to me we heard that before. '*Gott mit uns*' was the battle cry of the old Kaiser, was it not? Yet *Gott* did not help him much."[102]

On the same page of *Psychiana Weekly* was an advertisement for Frank's book, *Secret of Realization*. "Many thousand copies of this famous little book have gone all over the world," the ad read. "It carries with it a message of dynamic power and brings peace to those who read it. The price of the book is only ONE DOLLAR."

In February 1940, the *Boise Capital News* featured a story on Frank Robinson, accompanied by a photo of the aging spiritual leader. Whereas Psychiana's leader had seemed the picture of health just a few months earlier when the *Oregonian* profiled him, he now was tired-looking. His eyes peered out above sunken dark rings, his fingernails were further burnished from nicotine. The story in the *Boise Capital News*—titled "Robinson Berates 'Radicals'"—focused entirely on the volatile situation on Europe, quoting Frank's predictions.

> He predicted that this spring the greatest—and the bloodiest—battle of history will start. Hitler, he believes, will start through Holland. Italy, in the meantime, according to Dr. Robinson's theories, will have joined Hitler. The Scandinavian countries will have joined with Finland for mutual protection. At the same time, England and France will start their defense. Thus the entire picture in Europe will change within the next two years.[103]

CHAPTER 47

"It Seems Terrible Hard at the Present Time"

Petersburg, Virginia
February 24, 1940

By all accounts, Evie Beeles had led a life of struggle, first in Nashville, her girlhood home, and then in Petersburg, Virginia, where she passed her days of toil in a ramshackle clapboard railroad house. The past two years had been especially hard. Her second husband, Jesse, died in 1938, at the age of forty-nine. A World War I veteran who had fought on the front in the 115th field artillery division, Jesse had been the sole proprietor of Beeles Market and Lunch Counter at 153 Terrace Avenue. But when he died, so too did his market.[104]

On that Saturday the 24th, when Evie finally took her daughter's advice and asked for Frank Robinson's help, the weather was cold, with rain in the evening forecast. News of Roosevelt's "Lend Lease" program filled the papers, announcing that the Allies would buy planes and other U.S. goods.[105] But things had gotten steadily worse lately for Evie. Her health was not good, even though she was just forty-five. But it was her daughter, Maydeen, and her son, Jerry, who caused her worry. "I received your *Psychiana Weekly*," she wrote Frank about the promotional copy of the newsletter, "and I enjoyed reading it. I would like to send in for this *Psychiana Weekly*, but my children work at the American Hardware Co. and they are all out on a strike."[106] Money was so scarce for Evie and her children that she could not afford the ten-cent newsletter. "I am doing everything in my power to help them win," she wrote. "But it seems terrible hard at the present time." Maydeen and Jerry were both members of the Luggage Workers Union Local 52, and alongside some 1,200 employees, the two had been on strike since January 30. "The law here does not

273

give the working people the rights for nothing," she wrote. For nearly a month, and in the grip of winter, the union strikers had been picketing American Hardware's plants in protest while their union representatives tried to negotiate better working conditions and pay for the employees. "It is awful the way the working people is treated," Evie added.[107] The standoff was an all too familiar narrative in the history of the American labor movement: tycoons making exorbitant profits on the backs of underpaid and overworked laborers. "Officials of the union," Newport News' *Daily Press* reported, "said only 100 workers entered the plant...but [American Hardware] officers said 300 to 400 went to work."[108]

Evie was tired of the constant struggle, the unfairness of it all. Why should some have so much, while others had so little? "The American Hardware co. can do anything," she despaired. But "if one of the strickers [sic] just do any little thing, the law will come along and pick him up and carry him down and fine him."[109]

The tycoons in this battle happened to be the blue-blooded Seward family of Petersburg. It was a family name Evie knew all too well. "Mr. Bernard Seward is one of the head men in this co.," she wrote. "The union met with American Hardware Co. last week, and while they were in conference Mr. Bernard Seward got up, walked out, and taken out another injuction [sic] against the stricking people." According to Evie, Seward was trying to "keep them away from the plant." She then added how Seward "tryes [sic] to keep the pickets from walking up and down the street." The situation was fraught as tensions ran high.

Four days after the strike started, "disorder broke out," resulting in several wounded demonstrators and the "arrest of three participants," according to one newspaper report.[110] Evie then asked Frank Robinson for some specific help. "My daughter ask me when I wrote to you to ask you if you would help the union to win so she could go back to work soon." Evie added, "When she drawed her first check, she would send you some money." Like so many people in similar circumstances, Evie Beeles felt her life was at the mercy of forces greater than her. "I am doing all I can for them," she confided. "But I feel like I need someone that has got more power than I have to help me."[111]

Nine days later, a response to Evie Beeles was generated inside the Psychiana hive. Erroneously addressed to "Eric" Beeles, the letter read:

Thanks for your brave report. Remember us to the splendid children. You know just as well as we do that the same God who created you can take care of you, and will do just this thing if you recognize his omnipotent, helpful, healing, loving Presence.

Do your best—with yourself, with your folks, with your associates, as well as all other [sic] who know you, believe in you, who will cooperate for you, or say a good word for you.

Count on us to help spiritually. Expect complete Victory. Never give up, and let us know just as soon as the new hope and better days begin to come your way.

Sincerely your friend and Teacher, C.W. Tenney.[112]

On March 15, 1940, ten days after Psychiana's response, local and regional newspapers were reporting on the latest developments with the strike. "Mass Picketing at Petersburg Denied," read one headline, summarizing the blow the Beeles children and their coworkers had sustained.[113] "Judge Richard T. Wilson refused to dismiss or modify temporary injunctions against violence and mass picketing issued in his court" after the strike began. Refusing the union's petition, Wilson said that the "terroristic activities of union members had threatened the safety of Petersburg citizens."[114]

In all, the strike against American Hardware lasted from January 30 through April 11, when negotiators finally reached a deal, under the darkening cloud of protest and widening public scrutiny. "Sources here attributed to Governor Price a big part in the ending of the strike," one paper noted.[115]

It is likely that Evie's children were able to go back to work, a point of relief for their worried mother, and a possible sign of Psychiana's God Power.

CHAPTER 48

"The Cobbler Mustn't Go Beyond His Last"

"PSYCHIANA"
HOOFDKWARTIER
Goudenregenplain, 55
DEN HAAG
24 February 1940

Evie Beeles was not the only Psychiana student seeking Frank Robinson's counsel on February 24, 1940. That same day, A.C. Plagge sat down at his desk, and rolled a sheet of official "Psychiana, Studie-Groep Nederland en Kolonien" letterhead into his typewriter. Plagge felt the matter at hand was urgent. "One of my Psychiana students here in town, a certain Miss C.H. Raket, is very badly handicapted [sic] by illness of her eyes," he wrote to Frank Robinson. The ill student wanted Plagge to contact Dr. Robinson directly for help in restoring her eyesight.

> I told her you have always been kind to thousands of people who were in distress…One of her eyes is as good as out of order and the other is very bad. Her heart-desire is to find through the Psychiana Lessons the power of the living God to cure her blindness…She is a nice and good old woman, and has a deep conviction in Psychiana. I am absolute [sic] sure that this good lady, who is unmarried, an ex-teacher with keen intellect, good education, good languist [sic], with a great erudition, would [have] been in different physical condition if she had the luck to had been a married woman and a mother of a dozen children.[116]

Almost nothing is known about Adrianus Cornelis Plagge, save that he was a Psychiana enthusiast, a man of leisure, polymath, trained architect, world traveler, and medical translator. According to later records, he stood just shy of six feet tall, had gray hair, blue eyes, and a fair complexion.[117]

Although he later made his home in The Hague, he had been born in the Dutch East Indies in 1876, and had spent a good deal of time traveling in modern-day Malaysia and Indonesia, and even more time in Australia. During his extensive voyages, Plagge had translated a number of Dutch medical articles into English.

It is unclear when A.C. Plagge became acquainted with Psychiana, though there are a few distinct possibilities. Like Geoffrey Peel Birley of Egypt, Adrianus Cornelis Plagge may have simply read an advertisement in a periodical gracing newsstands in The Hague or elsewhere. But it is also possible that Plagge may have also encountered Frank's religion through a strange and unsanctioned Psychiana lecture series occurring in Australia during his time there.

Unbeknownst to Frank Robinson, Psychiana was being advertised in Aussie newspapers under the "Medical Lectures" listings as early as June 1932, promoted by a man named John Applegarth. Calling himself a "medical psychologist, author, lecturer and practitioner of psychiana [sic]," Applegarth did not exactly take credit for inventing Psychiana, but neither did he credit Frank Robinson for creating it. An early ad read: "All Saints Hall, To-night at 8 o'clock, Psychiana: Conquering Nerves—Success. Written Questions Answered."[118] Not insignificant was this addendum in nearly all of Applegarth's advertisements: "A silver collection will be taken. Psychiana has helped thousands to be perfect health, happiness, and success."

John L. Applegarth. Undated photo. Ancestry.com.

John Lambton Applegarth was slightly dough-faced (a trait passed on from his mother), and neat in appearance, with a prominent part scoring the left hemisphere of his hair. His eyebrows came from his father and looked forever poised in a state of bemused self-assurance. If he were indeed an author, the titles, records, and remnants of his writings appear to have been utterly lost.

He was married twice: first to Ethel Mary Catherine Philomena Cane, who was two years older than he, with whom he had fathered two daughters, and later to Winifred Chapman, fifteen years his junior. During his first marriage, Applegarth worked as a draughtsman, but during the tenure of his second marriage, he switched professions, claiming "masseur" as his title. How, when, and by what means he became a "medical psychologist" is as unclear as the whereabouts of his supposed authored writings.

For the better part of a half decade, Applegarth spread the word of Psychiana to his fellow Aussies and Kiwis. The titles of his lectures, such as "The Pyramids and Ourselves," did not, however, seem to come from Robinson's own lectures, at least not explicitly. Applegarth also had the habit of splitting his audiences into two groups, based on gender. Advertisements promised how he planned to deliver a "special illustrated lecture to ladies only, 'Know Thyself,' and to men only, 'Rejuvenation.'"

By 1937, Applegarth had grown bolder with his advertisements, announcing, for instance, a Psychiana "world tour." For all its promotion, however, Applegarth's world tour does not appear to have left Australia. Nor does it appear that Applegarth was ever a student of Frank Robinson's. Moreover, by 1938, the year A.C. Plagge took up Psychiana, Applegarth ceased advertising the religion, presumably moving on to something else.

Another possibility of how Adrianus Cornelis Plagge came to hear of Psychiana was by way of visiting the United States. In 1935, Plagge docked in Seattle en route from Batavia (now Jakarta) to Holland. The details of his visit are lost, but he had planned to stay in the States for two months before sailing back to The Hague, giving him plenty of time to run across a Psychiana advertisement during that trip.

Although much remains unknown about Plagge, his involvement did extend far beyond that of the average student. As early as 1938, Plagge was copying and distributing materials in Europe on behalf of Psychiana. Operating out of his tidy brick row-house apartment at Edisonstraat,

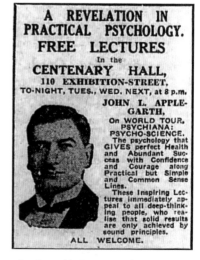

Applegarth's Psychiana Advertisement. *The Age* (Melbourne, Australia), July 26, 1937.

144, where the clinking and clanking trollies ran just feet away from his door, Plagge had secured permission from Robinson to work as the Dutch face of the Psychiana Movement in Europe. But in March 1938, one of Plagge's students, W.A.J. van Muers, went rogue, claiming that he—van Muers—was the sole authorized distributor of Psychiana's materials. On those specious grounds, he brought a suit against Plagge, effectively ordering him to cease and desist, and surrender all remaining printed materials at once. Van Muers also claimed what amounted to intellectual property rights over some of the materials.

Panicked, Plagge sent an urgent letter to Robinson back in Moscow, Idaho. "I know that time is of a priceless value to you," he began, "therefor excuse me that I trouble you with my own difficulties and affairs, but where it is for Psychiana, it is also of importance to you." In his letter, Plagge included recent legal correspondence, transcribed both in Dutch and English, pertaining to the present actions filed against him. Of his former student van Muers, Plagge was emphatic that he had severed all ties with the pupil.

> He was a man who always said, 'beware of the Jews' and now that he is between 'the divel [sic] and the deep sea' the first thing [he does] is run directly for help to an office of Jews, case-lawyers with 'some' reputation here in town.

In their official letter, van Muers' lawyer stipulated the terms of case.

> Under reserve of all rights, which my client moreover claims, I request you...immediately to deliver all copies of: a/ 20 Lessons of Psychiana-Course, b/ Brochures 'Who and What God Really Is,' c/ Several pamphlets, d/ Propaganda circulars, e/ the monthly Magazine. My client reserves for him all right against the pupils of the course, also the charges therefrom and also in the affair of the representation of Dr. Frank B. Robinson in Moscow, Idaho. If you do not follow my summons within 3 days after now, you can expect the lawmeasures [sic] will be taken against you.[119]

In his letter to Robinson apprising him of these developments, Plagge asked for written consent and acknowledgment of legal arrangements between Psychiana and Plagge.

Although it took ten days for Plagge's letter to make its way across the Atlantic, transit the continental United States, enter the Psychiana machine, and land in the hands of Robinson, the request bore fruit. Robinson cabled back: "A.C. PLAGGE ONLY HAS AUTHORITY

FOR PUBLISHING 'PSYCHIANA' COURSE UNTIL FURTHER
ORDERS. NO ONE ELSE HAS THIS AUTHORITY. FRANK B.
ROBINSON, FOUNDER 'PSYCHIANA'"[120]

———————◆———————

By the end of February 1940, however, when Plagge was asking Robinson for extra care for the elderly blind woman, he had moved his offices
a couple of blocks, from Edisonstraat 144, to Goudenregenplein 55, and
was evidently no longer being hassled by the former Psychiana student van
Muers. His present concern was Miss Cornelia Henriette Raket's eyesight.
"In whole her manner, action, in the way she expresses her feelings, her will
is…to become the things of her desire. I told her that the way to come in
contact with that great omnipresent Godpower [sic] of life, is the absolute
believing in that Power." But there was something else Plagge felt obliged
to tell Robinson. "This lady is of Jewish origins," he added.

> I tell you that regarding her chronical [sic] eye disease. Hoping that
> these informations will give some [help] if you will answer her letter.
> I am sure that you will try all that you be able to do for she is a very
> good lady and in her trouble is dependent on other assistance. I am, if
> I can in any way, willing to assist her, as a diligent pupil.[121]

Plagge closed the letter with some business ("I received *Psychiana Weekly* in
good order") and a word advising to stay out of political commentary, especially when it came to matters of Germany and Italy. "It seems a great pitty
[sic] that you are so often on the slippery road of the politics," he wrote.
"You brought the world a particular nice and beautiful message about the
Power of the Living God. My dear Dr. Robinson," he added, "'the cobbler
mustn't go beyond his last.'"[122]

Plagge's advice to Robinson to stay out of politics and stick with
teaching the God Power, may have stemmed, at least in part, from his
homeland's larger stance of neutrality as hostilities in Europe continued
apace. With the benefit of history, it is tempting to regard the failing eyesight of Henriette Raket—a retired Jewish teacher—as a cruel metaphor,
for it is unlikely that either one of these Psychiana students could have
foreseen Hitler's invasion of their country inside of three months.

CHAPTER 49
"This Imperishable Yardstick"

March 19, 1940
St. Thomas, Ontario, Canada

Five days after Psychiana processed Evie Beeles' erroneously addressed letter to "Eric Beeles," Ontario's *Windsor Star* filled its front page with large, black type: "CHAMBERLAIN WARNS NORWAY AND SWEDEN OF GRAVE PERIL." It was Tuesday, March 19, 1940, and the news that morning ran the gamut from Royal Canadian Mounted Police investigating anti-war propaganda, to the announcement that John Carradine would be playing Jim Casy in the upcoming film, *The Grapes of Wrath*.

In the otherwise idyllic and quiet city of St. Thomas, Ontario—a town known mostly as the site where Jumbo, the circus elephant, was struck and killed by a locomotive—a fifty-three-year-old man maneuvered his wheelchair to his typing station to begin the day's correspondence. Outside, the weather was fair, but a spring snow was in the forecast for the following day. Tall, of medium build with light hair, Bramwell Booth Saywell had been confined to his wheelchair since being stricken with polio over two decades earlier. Whatever Saywell may have lacked in physical ability, however, he more than made up for in written virtuosity and a surplus of opinions. Moreover, Bramwell Saywell's home-based business—Saywell Typewriters, Office Supplies, & Direct Mail—gave him the time, resources, and opportunity for his freewheeling correspondence.

Built in the 1830s, the elegant two-story Saywell home sat at 32 Talbot Street, some 300 feet from the spot where a life-sized memorial statue to Jumbo the elephant would stand decades later. Originally a medical clinic, the house once boasted a bay window in which Dr. Elijah Duncombe—the home's original owner—displayed a menagerie of bottles filled with "green and red fluids and live leeches."[123] A subsequent owner of the house, Charles Moore, modified one of the rear entrances to accommodate his wheelchair after having both legs severed in a railroad accident. Another former resident, Mrs. F.A. Fick, told a local paper about the improvements her family made to the home. "Lamps," she said, "had been used up to this time, but father had electric wiring put in, and I recall a workman saying, 'This place must have been built for elephants, it is so sturdy and substantial.'"[124]

Bramwell and Alexina MacDonald Saywell had been married just two years when he lost the use of his legs.[125] Desperate, the couple and the greater Saywell family sought the best medical care they could afford, eventually admitting Bramwell into a Chicago-area sanitarium to convalesce.[126] Saying goodbye to his wife, mother, father, and three sisters, Bram (as he was known) left St. Thomas, Ontario, for what would amount to nearly five years of ineffective care in Chicago.

After so many years with no improvement, in 1923 the family decided to move Bram back to Canada, where his parents—James and Eliza—had purchased the large home on Talbot Street for its spaciousness and wheelchair access. Bram and Alexina moved into the Talbot Street house with his parents, where they would live for the rest of their lives.[127]

———————◆———————

Any time an official document asked Bram Saywell to state his religion, he wrote down the same thing his father, James, did: Methodist.[128] A self-styled student of the world, Bram studied religion, faith, language, and metaphysics. He was an off-beat intellectual with spiritual, if eccentric, tendencies. His spiritual inclinations, however, seemed wholly driven by a desire to recover from his paralysis, and so he often gravitated toward healing-based literature. His desire, he wrote, "entailed an examination and for that matter application of healing philosophies from California to New York."[129] And it was in that sweep of philosophies that he chanced upon an American advertisement for Psychiana by Frank Robinson, an erstwhile Ontarian himself.

Bram had evidently been taking the Psychiana courses for some time when he dispatched a letter to Robinson on March 19, 1940. "Dear Doctor Robinson," he wrote:

> It was with a great deal of enthusiasm that I read the first half dozen of your lessons and started to apply them, but in getting your Weekly Magazine must confess my enthusiasm is not what it was at the beginning. For 23 years I have been paralyzed from the hips down from

polio, being unable to walk, and in this last year have had what I term a 'divine urge' to be healed.[130]

Saywell's "divine urge" led him in a roundabout way to study languages, specifically "the NT Greek." His in-depth study of New Testament Greek "revealed," he wrote, "truths that I know are almost completely hidden from the more accepted versions [of the Bible]." For Saywell, New Testament Greek was like a cipher, unlocking the Bible's coded messages. Every word was a potential doorway into new and revelatory understanding. Zeroing in on Robinson's casual use of the word "eternal" in many of his writings, for instance, Saywell flexed his critical muscles: "You have no real support for your use and implication of the word 'eternal.' Meaning 'without beginning and without ending' as it does, it is an impractical word, and really can convey no meaning to our practical finite minds."[131]

His quibble with Frank's breezy use of "eternal" notwithstanding, Saywell's sudden disinterest in Psychiana may have stemmed from the cover story of a *Psychiana Weekly* issue he would have received about a week earlier. Titled "Where Gods Come From," the article was provocative in the classic Frank Robinson manner: an upbeat attack on (in this case) the story of Christ. As he was wont to do, Robinson pointed out the mirrored aspects of the Christian creation story and that of other faiths. First promulgated in his luridly titled book, *Crucified Gods Galore*, the comparison was well-trod terrain for Frank. "The evidence is conclusive and overwhelming," Robinson wrote in the *Weekly*, "that the story of [Jesus Christ] is an absolute copy of the 'crucified god' of the Hindoo [sic]. Even the names are practically the same."

> No amount of church argument can refute this. On the one hand, Jesus Christ with a virgin-birth out of a woman called Mary, and on the Hindoo side, Jeseus Chrishna, with a virgin-birth out of a woman called Maia which means Mary. Both are born on the 25th day of December. Both considered the second person of a 'trinity.' Both crucified for the sins of the world and both coming to life three days later. Both are now in 'heaven' and both failed in their mission of saving the world incidentally.[132]

Skeptic and contrarian though he may have been, Bramwell Saywell was nothing if not a devoted Christian who believed in the divine nature of the Bible, especially as it pertained to Christ. "The crux of my objections to your development of theory," Saywell opined, "is your denial of the Christ—"

The biggest aspect of the scientific revelation of God's Word is the supernatural origin of these writings; greater-than-human construction. THEY BEAR WITHIN THEM THE EVIDENCE OF SUPER-NATURAL ORIGIN. An unbiased study of the infinite (I was going to say) interlocking of the word, the verse, the chapter, the book, will speedily convince any unprejudiced mind that there is something in its own way as remarkable as anything you describe of the nebulae, marvelous and true as they are.[133]

For Saywell, the text of the Bible in and of itself was irrefutable proof that the Christ story was not only true, but inviolable.

Robinson's full-throated dismantling of Christ's story, on the other hand, was theologically irreconcilable for Bramwell Saywell. It would have been a line in the sand. It was one of the only tenets in Psychiana's teaching that Saywell could not abide. "So what are we going to do?" He asked Robinson. "What and whom are we going to believe?"

> You say that God has no mind, is essentially not of a personality; you rule out the existence of our Lord, the Christ...What are we going to do with the plain statements, buttressed as they are by this internal proof of supernatural origin—what disposition are we going to make of them? The Scriptures say the sons were formed in Christ (incidentally the Greek word 'son' is mainly translated everlasting, eternal, etc. in the King James version). As a matter of fact it states that whole universe was headed up in Him.[134]

Frank Robinson was not the only one to receive the sharp end of a Saywell letter, nor was Psychiana the only religious system Saywell explored. Some fifteen years after writing Robinson, Saywell began a flurry of correspondence with the editors of *The Compleat Aberree*, a periodic newsletter billing itself as "the non-serious voice of Scientology."[135]

Much of Saywell's tenor and focus remained the same in his missives to the *Aberree* as they were in his communications with Psychiana. "Must say a word here about perhaps the most important repository of hidden healing data," he wrote, "one that has been significantly overlooked over the centuries: the Christian Scriptures, especially in their originals."[136]

His criticisms for both publications came in the guise of advice from a disappointed loyalist. Responding to a whimsical article on the efficacy of Eeman Circuits—"bioelectric" relaxation therapy involving copper screens and wires that complete one's body "circuitry"—Saywell wrote,

Alphia, why don't you consider a couple or so pages to be devoted to the serious side of this whole thing; a sick person, whether mentally or physically, is in not particular patience with the lighter, and perhaps indirect, type of healing suggestions. I have friends with cancer, heart trouble, mental, and all that, and know if they could be gotten interested in the background of what you people stand for, they would perhaps get interested and do something.[137]

Far from dismissing or ignoring the constant correspondence from Bramwell Saywell of St. Thomas, Ontario, the editors of *The Compleat Aberree* seemed more than happy to reprint and respond to his letters, even if mildly impatient with his irritability ("If Bramwell Saywell could sit at this desk for a week and see letters pouring in from all over the world, he would not be so cross," one editor groused).[138]

In reading Bramwell Saywell's raucous, contrarian, sometimes curmudgeonly, but always erudite letters, one is left with the unmistakable impression that, behind the rhetoric and bombast, the etymological swordsmanship and high-wire intellect, there was despair, grief, and anger. Saywell was a crusader looking to find the one system of spiritual revelation that would let him walk again. But each system of belief inevitably failed him, despite his incessant entreaties to their leaders to right their wrongs and correct their course of thinking.

In his parting shots to Frank Robinson, Bramwell Saywell took the Psychiana founder to task:

> To conclude, it seems a pity to me that you should confuse a man's actions with God's rock-like word. Pure human logic, which after all is a non-existing entity, would uphold you; those of us who revel in the unfoldings of God's revelations, exclaim inwardly as it were—"So THAT'S the course of His operations! I could never have reached that conclusion with my unaided intellect." It is at that point that you fall down so miserably to those of us who take up this imperishable yardstick.[139]

For twenty-three years, Bramwell Saywell had been looking for the miracle cure for his paralysis. And for eighteen of those years, he wheeled about the spacious family home on Talbot Street trying to decode the mystery of his affliction. For nearly two decades, he took up one philosophy after another, only to find that each was in its own way fatally flawed, inevitably so. And to Saywell, Psychiana's fatal flaw was Robinson's disavowal of Christ.

Doctor, I only wish you could see this; and what is perhaps of more importance, I wish you had not committed yourself so publicly and so violently; you have taken a stand so uncompromising that it would require almost a superhuman being to revoke it. You in all truth have become a veritable slave of your pronouncements. I say this in Kindness. Sincerely yours,

Bramwell Saywell.[140]

On March 29, 1940, C. W. Tenney dispatched a response to Bramwell Saywell of St. Thomas, Ontario. The letter was nearly word for word the same letter he had sent to Evie Beeles weeks earlier.

Thanks for your constructive criticism which we appreciate more than you know, and more than I will try to say. However, you and we agree that the same God who created us can take care of us, and will do just this thing if we recognize His omnipotent, helpful, healing, loving, living Presence...

We must then—do our best—with ourselves, with our folks, with our friends, with our associates, and with all others who know and believe in us, who will say a good word for us, or cooperate with us.

Count on us to help spiritually. Expect complete Victory. Never give up, and write again, when and whenever time and mood allow, for your good letter has helped me more than anything I could write today would help you.[141]

CHAPTER 50
Psychiana Blitzkrieg

As it happens, Finland's President Ryiti was not the only global leader to whom Frank had dispatched an unsolicited message in the early days of World War II. In fact, he sent three more telegrams to world leaders in May 1940. The first, dated May 15, was sent to Benito Mussolini. The premier is alleged to have previously corresponded with Frank about his work and Psychiana, although that correspondence, if it existed, has been lost. The Western Union cable that Robinson sent picked up from there.

Premier Benito Mussolini

Rome, Italy

Recalling your words of thanks for book some years ago, I am thinking of you today in your hour of perplexity. I am sure that you are too big a man to join in the ruthless shedding of human innocent blood so inhumanely being carried on today. Hundreds of thousands of our members the world over join with me in sending you our love, sympathy, and affection. If you follow the best instincts of your fine nature…you will be one of the best loved and most respected world leaders of today.[142]

Three days later, Robinson wired French Prime Minister Paul Reynaud. "Keep up the courage," Frank wrote. "Entire 'Psychiana' organization through which the Spirit of God is being manifested on this earth is throwing that power against your enemies. Consequently you cannot lose for power of God is more potent than tanks etc."[143]

The following morning, May 19, Robinson issued a final message to Winston Churchill, who had been named prime minister just nine days earlier. In the cable, Robinson wrote, "I am this day issuing instructions to our hundreds of thousands of members to throw the Power of God against your enemies four times daily…The Spirit which is God will bring you an everlasting victory. It cannot be otherwise."[144]

True to his word, Robinson set forth a series of instructions for the students of Psychiana. In order to bring down the "demon-possessed German leader," Frank advised his students on their role.

> What you can do is very simple. It is very dynamic. Do not look upon what I ask you to do merely as "an affirmation," for it is much more than that. IT IS A DIRECT TEST OF THE POWER OF GOD OVER THE POWERS OF EVIL…At 9 a.m., 12 noon, 6 and 9 p.m. (your time), I want you to get alone somewhere just for a few seconds; close your eyes, and quietly but earnestly repeat this statement three times. As you do, visualize and picture Hitler. Here is the statement: "THE SPIRIT WHICH IS GOD WILL BRING YOUR DOWNFALL."

Robinson then wrote, "Don't correspond with me about it, for I'm awfully busy here. Just do it, and keep it up. Then watch and see what happens."[145]

Frank called this Psychiana campaign of daily affirmations a "Spiritual Blitzkrieg." To make his campaign more visible and more lucrative, Robinson designed and ordered tens of thousands of buttons featuring Hitler's face and the words "PSYCHIANA SPIRITUAL BLITZKRIEG" over it. Beneath Hitler's face, the button read, "Believing that Right is Superior to Brute Force, I am Helping to Bring Hitlers [sic] Defeat by Repeating Hourly: The Power of Right (God) Will Bring Your Speedy Downfall." The faithful who purchased and wore their buttons could take heart in doing their part for the war raging in Europe.

Robinson sensed that the nation's worries were shifting away from the day-to-day Depression-era drudgery. After all, it was no longer a Depression, but a recession. There *had* been economic gains, thanks in large part to the New Deal. And the national picture *was* looking somewhat better. If people started to feel better and worry less, then the efficacy of Psychiana might wobble. It was therefore paramount for Robinson to link his Movement to the war, because Psychiana was a Movement tailored to, and dependent upon, its students' fears and vulnerabilities. That is why, when the rest of the world saw encroaching war as a thing of monstrous dread, Frank Robinson saw it as an opportunity.

Psychiana's spiritual blitzkreig button, 1940. University of Idaho Special Collections.

CHAPTER 51

"The Day I Answered Your Advertisement"

Titusville, FL
May 31, 1940

On the very day that British forces stranded at Dunkirk were facing their darkest hour, a muscular, twenty-eight-year-old Floridian man felt upbeat about his future. As of May 1940, Gordon Woodrow Fortenberry was a traveling salesman based out of Titusville, the Brevard County seat.[147] Born in Franklinton, Louisiana, Fortenberry had been raised along the waterfront ever since his family moved to Florida to homestead when Gordon—the oldest of the Fortenberry children—was just a toddler. He had an olive complexion, blue eyes, and a rug of brown hair on top of an otherwise perfectly shaved head. Military records indicate Fortenberry had permanent scars on his right eye and chin, and a crooked finger. At five feet, ten inches tall and one hundred seventy-five pounds, Fortenberry spoke with a thick southern accent (his father hailed from Mississippi)[148] and resided in Titusville, while his family lived some sixteen miles south in Cocoa. "Dear Dr.—So sorry not to have written or sent a payment sooner," he wrote in looping pencil.

> But I have been very busy on a new enterprise which I am confident will be a success due entirely to the acceptance and use of the God Law as you see it and teach. Truly it is a revelation to me and I know you must have put in many years of deep study to understand so well the workings of the Living God. I have studied your lessons earnestly and have accepted them fully as truth even though I am only twenty eight years old. I have searched and longed for an understanding which I did not get from the Bible or Methodist Church which I belonged to for about ten years. I was a steward of the church at twenty.

I know you must like to hear of the marvelous things these revelations are doing for your students. I have had a faulty kidney since I was about five years old and it has always hurt me. From the age of sixteen to twenty-five, I was a professional boxer and during this time I had it injured five times to the extent of bleeding for as much as ten days each time.[149]

Fortenberry's breezy mention of his career as a prize-fighter almost belies the spectacle of his time in the ring. Although Fortenberry was not internationally known like Tommy Burns, he was nationally known, especially amongst the sport's enthusiasts, and famous to Floridians and southerners alike. When he came to the nation's attention in 1929, it was not because of his pugilist prowess, however: it was because of his name. NEA sports writer William Braucher waxed whimsical in his nationally syndicated column when he wrote, "A reward is offered by this department for the discovery of a funnier fighting name than Gordon Fortenberry of Cocoa, Florida."[150] But Fortenberry's spry footwork and cleverness in the ring quickly tamped down the cracks about his name, refocusing fight-goers' attention on his skills.

Fortenberry's debut was on May 22, 1929, during Orlando's "Punch Bowl" fighting exhibition. Only seventeen years old, Gordon went up against a little-known fighter with the memorable name of the Sucarnochee Terror. Not only did Fortenberry win that match, but he went on to dominate, winning thirteen of seventeen matches, with the remainder being four draws.[151]

On May 19, 1931, nine years before Fortenberry sat down to write his teacher in Moscow, Idaho, Brooklyn's *Standard Union* highlighted the young fighter.

The first new talent shows in Madison Square Garden will take place tonight. In the semi-final bout, a lad named Gordon Fortenberry, who Matchmaker Martin says possesses great promise as a middleweight, will meet Allie Wolff, a former collegian. The bout will be eight rounds, if it goes the limit.[152]

Not yet nineteen, Gordon Woodrow Fortenberry found himself on the mat in the mecca of all prize-fighting: Madison Square Garden.[153] Battling in front of as many as 17,000 spectators, Fortenberry kept light on his feet, gloves up, and eyes open while the referee in his white shirt and slacks shadowed the boxers. Camera lights flashed white-hot in the periphery while cigar smoke hung thick and blue in the air. In the end, Fortenberry did not win the match (he was outpointed by Wolff in the eighth), but local papers went easy on him. "Fortenberry, a recent high school graduate, made a creditable showing."[154]

Fights Here Tomorrow

Gordon Fortenberry, 164, Merritt Island, who appears in main go at the Punch Bowl, tomorrow night.

Gordon Fortenberry boxing promotion in *The Palm Beach Post* (West Palm Beach, FL), September 23, 1930.

Weeks later, Fortenberry rallied, defeating Brooklynite Max Pinsker in the sixth round. "Pinkser," papers reported, "didn't know how to break through [Fortenberry's] peculiar defense."[155]

By 1933, Fortenberry's name was splashed in bold type across the sports pages nationwide, sharing news coverage with American icons like Max Schmeling, Babe Ruth, and Arnie Herber. In July that year, Fortenberry knocked out Martin Levandowski in Chicago, and two months later, also in Chicago, outpointed Fritz Heinz.

A year later, in February, Gordon Fortenberry fought John "Corn" Griffin in West Palm Beach, with the decision being a draw. In March, he was matched up against the world's light heavyweight champion, Maxie Rosenbloom.[156] The champion entered the ring "a trifle heavier after a vacation in Miami," the *Philadelphia Inquirer* noted.[157] His weight gain and possible sluggishness may have accounted for Fortenberry's ability to advance a significant lead in the first four rounds. But despite what the *Inquirer* called the "courage and aggressiveness of Fortenberry," Maxie Rosenbloom fought back, finally outpointing the "Florida boy" in the tenth round.[158]

Fortenberry fought his final match against Max Marek on March 23, 1936, in Miami Beach. Marek—known nationally as "the man who beat Joe Louis"—pummeled Fortenberry, knocking him down twice. By the fourth round, Fortenberry was bleeding severely from a gash above his right eye. Marek won by a technical knock out. It was one of only two knockouts delivered to Fortenberry. (He received the other from Pietro Georgi at San Francisco's Dreamland Auditorium.)[159]

In all, Fortenberry boxed in seventy-five fights, with fifty-two wins, fourteen losses, and nine draws. Of his victories, the Floridian delivered fourteen knockouts, winning the remainder on points. The final fight with Marek gave Fortenberry the permanent scar above his eye, and may have been one of the fights affecting his kidney. Whatever the outcome of that fight, it was Gordon Fortenberry's last.[160]

"A few months ago," Fortenberry added in his letter to Robinson, "I considered an operation for the kidney...on account of so much pain. I am happy to say the God Law, which you reveal, has as far as I can tell entirely cured this ailment."[161]

In closing his letter, Gordon Fortenberry reiterated his amazement at Psychiana's power to cure his kidney problems. "I think it is a wonderful faith that can cure an ailment over twenty years old." Psychiana seemed to have found Gordon—or he found it—at just the right time in his life. "I might say also I am happier than even before and success is coming to me. I could write many pages like this, but you are busy so I'll just say I'm grateful for the day I answered your advertisement. Sincerely, your student, Gordon Fortenberry."[162]

———◆———

By June 1940, Frank Robinson was almost fifty-three, and working harder than ever. He had put on weight and was smoking heavily. He rose early like always, ate breakfast, guzzled coffee, and attended to the demands of the *Psychiana Weekly*, punching out his standard 5,000 words daily, typing with two to three fingers. When he was not thundering away at his type-writer in a constant cloud of cigarette smoke, he was dictating lectures and articles, proofing copy, reading galleys of his books, and writing ads. The man who started the world's first mail-order religion, reading every letter that came in over the transom personally, now hardly read a single piece of mail himself. His troop of mail-room clerks worked on the front lines of the mail's daily inundation, sorting the letters into categories. Into one heap they placed letters pertaining to health and ailments. Into another, they stacked those asking for financial advice. Into yet another, they piled letters dealing with depression, sorrow, loneliness. Still another pile gathered letters related to the war in Europe. Letters that announced miracles, reported extraordinary fortune, or were otherwise conspicuous found their way to the tops of the various stacks, prioritized. From there, the letters eventually made their way to C.W. Tenney, who scanned them before assigning a boiler-plate response.

Only the most sensational letters were ever forwarded to Frank Robinson, and even then, he almost never replied personally, which is why it is surprising that he took the time to respond to Gordon Fortenberry's letter. "My dear Mr. Fortenberry," the June 14 correspondence reads. "Thank you very much for your good letter and the $2.25, enclosed, has been placed in your credit. I was happy indeed to hear from you, and glad to know that you are busy on a new enterprise and I trust that it will be very, very successful."

The Power of God in you is something like the power in a storage battery. To look at the battery you would not know that there is any power in it, for you cannot see it. But if you push the starter, making the connection, the hidden power in that battery instantly springs into action, and it can start the largest car. When you recognize the fact that this power does exist in you, it will not take you long to draw upon that power, and when you do. Your troubles will be over. For this Power is far greater than any Power you have ever known.

May the Spirit of Infinite Power be with you always and if we can be of further assistance to you with the Lessons, please let me know.

Cordially yours,

Frank B. Robinson[163]

CHAPTER 52

Drive

In June 1940, Frank made a grueling trip home from the Multnomah Hotel in Portland, where he often holed up to write. It was, Frank wrote, "a very fast trip. Some nine hundred and fifty miles."[164] The following day, a road-weary Frank rose from his slumber, dressed, and headed down to the kitchen. He was exhausted. Tired in his marrow. "I was so tired I could not eat my breakfast," he recalled. "Putting on my hat, I started for the door to go to the office for another day's strenuous work."

But something unusual happened.

"I never got as far as the door," he wrote. "On my way from the dining room to the front door, a very severe pain caught me in the middle of my chest. Usually, I can pass any pain off instantly. But I knew this was very serious pain."[165]

Frank B. Robinson was having a heart attack. "I sat in a chair and, the pain increasing in intensity, I asked Mrs. Robinson to call our family physician."

Within minutes, the doctor arrived with his bag and stethoscope, offering the diagnosis of "coronary thrombosis."[166] It was June 28, 1940. Leaving nothing to chance, the doctor called a specialist, who arrived from Spokane. "The next few weeks were precarious ones for me. I knew I should recover, but no one thought I would."[167]

Alf Robinson, senior year of high school, 1940. University of Idaho Special Collections.

Frank's children were especially shaken. Alf had just graduated high school that spring and was preparing to enter the Oberlin Conservatory to pursue his studies in piano. Florence, nine, was old enough to grasp the gravity of the situation. Pearl, just thirty-eight, was glimpsing the possibility of becoming an early widow. While Frank was recovering in the hospital, "hovering between life and death," as he called it, Pearl sat by his side "like the guardian angel she is."[168]

But despite constant care and Pearl's bedside vigil, Frank's condition worsened. In consultation with their physician and over the protests of others, the Robinsons determined that he needed to be transferred to Seattle for the most comprehensive, state-of-the-art treatment. After making a "bed" for Frank in the back seat of a car, a small entourage drove Psychiana's leader all day from Moscow to Seattle. "I nearly died on the trip," he later wrote, "for it really was a very foolish thing to attempt."[169]

Frank Robinson was admitted into Seattle's Virginia Mason Hospital, where doctors gave him a "thorough going over." Their assessment of his overall health was not good. Stubborn and driven, Robinson checked out of the hospital where he had been kept on a "strict diet" and checked into the New Washington Hotel. The next morning, Frank woke and decided to "celebrate" his release from the hospital by ordering room service. "I ordered ham and eggs, French fried potatoes, buttered toast, coffee and two pieces of custard, my favorite pie."[170]

Fully sated and evidently convinced he had the God Law behind him, Frank phoned his paper's editor, Bill Marineau, back in Moscow. "Bring the Cadillac," he instructed. "I'm coming home." Marineau obliged, driving over 400 miles to Seattle to fetch Dr. Robinson, only to drive back the same day. "I sat up in the front seat of that Cadillac," Frank wrote, "and rode 425 miles from Seattle to Moscow. And did not die either."[171]

Nor did he take it easy, as Alf later recalled. "He was advised to stay in bed, remaining quiet for at least six weeks while the heart and body were allowed to heal. This he did not do."[172] Despite his constant instructions to his students to "be quiet" and "be still," Robinson could not be held down any more than he could be muzzled.

Having faced death head-on, Frank changed nothing about his life except his drive to expand his Movement and boost his literary output, which he increased exponentially as if running out a clock. One of the most significant works Frank undertook during this time was a second memoir with the baiting title, *The Strange Autobiography of Frank B. Robinson.* Partially carved out of the American autobiographical tradition of Benjamin Franklin, which encourages its readers to emulate the author's life lessons, *The Strange Autobiography* is also a book of gripes, score-settling, vainglorious claims, and salesmanship. As books go, it is a wild read and to that end, the title does not disappoint. In some ways, the book shows Frank at his most vulnerable and endearing moments ("There are few moves I make today about which [Pearl] is not consulted, and her good judgment, which is instantaneous, is seldom wrong"[173]) and in other ways it is classic Robinson. When he is not bemoaning the many "persecutions" he has had to endure, for instance, or trying to get even with his old rival, George Lamphere, the newspaperman he nearly put out of business ("He's a chronic drinker"[174]), he spends his time tracing the genuinely remarkable and improbable rise of Psychiana. Readers get the impression that Frank himself could hardly believe his mail-order religion had actually worked.

When taking a break from his *Strange Autobiography*, Frank threw his new-found energy into drafting new ads and new issues of *Psychiana Weekly*, which, despite his health troubles, ran a faithful 52 issues in 1940. Not counting his book projects, lectures, radio addresses, ad copy, and new material, Frank turned out nearly a half-million words by the end of the year just for *Psychiana Weekly* alone. It was an enormous, incessant undertaking.

In the September 7, 1940, issue, Frank led the newsletter with the words, "The Coming Peace" emblazoned on the front. The gist of the feature was that good would triumph over evil, and that Psychiana was at the core of all the good in the world. "Underlying our American civilization are principles far stronger than Hitler. In the hearts of Americans is a strength, a faith, and an invisible Power against which Hitler, who is only a flash in the pan, cannot survive."[175]

The Questions & Answers section offered readers a fresh round of back and forth:

Q: Do you know what the best school of music in the United States is? I want to send my daughter there to study music.

A: Oberlin College at Oberlin, Ohio, is not outrated by any school of music in America. It is generally conceded to be tops. My son goes there.

Q: Is there a Psychiana branch here in New York?

A: We have no branches anywhere except in The Hague, Holland.

Q: When are you on the radio? I can't ever hear you any more.

A: Radio in my opinion has passed its peak and is losing its usefulness as an advertising medium. We are confining our efforts to newspapers and magazines exclusively. I doubt if we shall ever go on the air again—the results last year were not very good.

Q: Why did you go to Moscow, Idaho instead of coming here to New York where more people are?

A: I just happened to be in Moscow when this Movement started. Had I been in your city, I would have started there. But I would not like to live in New York. You find more of God out here in these wide open spaces, don't you know. I am never more lonesome than when in New York. I feel like a lost soul in that town. Too much of everything, and not enough of anything worth while. Give me Idaho.[176]

In another issue, two weeks later, Frank wrote another article about his contention that the Bible's stories were apocryphal, never meant to have been taken literally, and that each time church officials promulgated those stories, they were, in effect, spreading lies. "Adolph Hitler recently said that 'If you get a lie big enough, tell it often enough, you can get millions of people to believe it.'"[177] His critics may have balked at such a quotation coming from the founder of Psychiana.

Further along in the newsletter, Frank began reflecting on the present-day political scene in America. "As I write this, the radio is grinding out the proceedings of the Republican National Convention in Philadelphia," Frank wrote under the header, "Responsibility."[178] Robinson continued on:

It is a great thing to be President of the United States in these dangerous times. It is a great honor to be a Representative or Senator from any state at any time. Many a time, your Leader has been literally begged to enter politics. It has been pointed out that he could be of much use in Washington. I remember that grand old Senator from Idaho [William Borah] who, shortly before his death, told me that there was one thing which would make him supremely happy, and that was to see me sitting in his chair in Washington D.C. after he passed on. He evidently knew death was near.[179]

CHAPTER 53

The Poet

Feeling revitalized, Frank Robinson doubled up on his writing projects, broadening his scope and reach, but at the expense of focus and clarity. The sheer number of unpublished and half-finished manuscripts from this period show the inner workings of a restless mind. To handle the workload and to take pressure off of Frank, C.W. Tenney convinced Robinson to hire William Walter DeBolt, another front man who could help answer the letters and write for the *Weekly*.

Tenney had his own reasons for hiring another assistant, however. After having served Robinson loyally for four years, Tenney was facing a personal crisis brought about exclusively by his affiliation with Psychiana. After having attended a Methodist conference in southern Idaho, Tenney learned of a new measure the state leadership was enacting. "The Conference then passed a resolution condemning any Methodist who had anything to do with me," Robinson wrote, "threatening excommunication to any member of that Church who did have anything to do with this Movement. (That is what they did to Jesus, too.)"[180] As loyal as Tenney had been, excommunication was not a consequence he wanted to face, and he began disentangling himself from Psychiana at once. The first step was installing a replacement.

A few years earlier, a thin, intelligent pastor named William Walter DeBolt had appeared in Moscow to preach for the Church of God. The forty-year-old pastor had brown wavy hair and his blue eyes peered out through the lenses of his thin-framed glasses. For the previous five years he had been traveling, preaching at revivals around the country, including stops in Florida, Alabama, Oklahoma, Nebraska, Utah, and Montana.[181]

Born into a poor farming family in Springhill, Pennsylvania—a wooded backwater up against the West Virginia border—DeBolt was one of five children. Although his father, Wiley, could not read or write,[182] William developed a passion for reading early on, eventually finding his way to poetry. During World War I, when DeBolt, at nineteen, had registered for the draft, his listed occupation was not "pastor" but "poet."[183]

Over the years, DeBolt had published his poetry in small literary and religious magazines and newspapers. By the time he arrived in Moscow, Idaho, in September 1936, he had published two slim volumes of his work, and was preparing a manuscript for what would be his third book, *Vials of Verse.* (He would go on to publish over a dozen books in his lifetime.)

Newly married, DeBolt made a paltry $35 a month as the pastor for the Church of God in Moscow, which was hardly enough to live on. His wife, Gwendolyn, secured work downtown styling hair at a salon, and when he was not busy writing sermons, DeBolt wrote poetry. While a good amount of his poetry fell along religious topics, much of it engaged daily subjects. A student of poetry and its craft, DeBolt experimented with closed forms, haiku, and blank verse alike. Some of his best poems were almost epigrammatic: short, wry pieces that often surprise. Others were overly concerned with rhyme, or were bogged down in sentimentality.

One of DeBolt's poems appeared the *Spokane Chronicle* in the summer of 1938.

The Postman

He is the only Memnon of our world
Brought to the wars of tired society
With armor as gaudy as a lovely bee
To all who have their yesterdays unfurled
And dissipation, flaglike, have uncurled
To memory's breeze, or have the weary
Knee
Bowed as low as fallen oak to throned
Ennui
Which cherub-like is never earthward
hurled
How very precious does the dear man look!
His blessings outpile Jacob's! He commands
The treasures of the east, the gold of
the book
The gorgeous plunder of a pirate band

And diamonds digged from a distant nook
Which he distributes with impartial hands.[184]

DeBolt's later poems took full advantage of brevity.

Littered Trail
He left behind him
a string of disappointments
longer than his life.[185]

Trifle
My shoe rubs a toe
and gets more attention
than how I should live.[186]

Eureka
Paucity of words
is the philosopher's stone
seekers might have found.[187]

Hoping to share his poetry regularly and earn a little extra money on the side, DeBolt had approached Robinson about publishing a series of poems in Robinson's daily newspaper. Frank agreed. In that exchange, Robinson got to know DeBolt and his wife Gwendolyn, and the two men talked often on matters of religion and literature.

In late summer 1938, the Debolts moved to Libby, Montana, where he took up a better-paying post as pastor for the local congregation of the Church of God. Their stay was short-lived, and the couple returned to Moscow. When Frank learned that Tenney had to resign from his Psychiana duties in late 1940, he paid a call to William Walter DeBolt, offering him the job with a handsome salary. DeBolt accepted at once.

"Dr. DeBolt stepped into Dr. Tenney's shoes, and filled them admirably," Frank wrote. "He is not the man Dr. Tenney is. He is much younger, and has an altogether different aspect on life. He is one of the young, up-and-coming type who is very apt to go places."[188]

Soon it became DeBolt's job to answer stacks and stacks of letters, and to assist in the daily operations of Psychiana. His talents as a writer were especially useful in producing content for the *Weekly* and for proofing

William Walter DeBolt, Psychiana's new #2 in his office at Psychiana Headquarters, c. 1938. University of Idaho Special Collections.

Frank's copy. He was religious but evidently had a broad enough view of God that his affiliation with Psychiana did not conflict with his ecumenical beliefs. At least not at first. "As I suspected however," Frank wrote, "all would not be well for long."[189]

Three days after Christmas 1940, Frank Robinson received a letter from the Church of God with ominous news.

To Whom It May Concern:

The following statement concerning W.W. DeBolt and his wife, Gwendolyn DeBolt, of Moscow, Idaho was passed at the last business meeting of The Inland Empire Ministerial Association of the Church of God: 'We heartily endorse the action of the ministers of the Northern Rocky Mountain District of the Church of God in the rejection of W.W. DeBolt as a minister of the Church on the basis of his rejection of the fundamental doctrines of the Bible. Neither do we consider him a member of the body of Christ. We wish to do all that is in our power, however, to restore him to God and the fellowship of the Brethren…We also endorse the rejection of his wife, Gwendolyn DeBolt, as a gospel worker and as a member of the body of Christ. We will do our utmost in her restoration. Signed, Alrey D. Skinner, Secretary.[190]

A couple weeks later, the Church of God's clergy informed the rest of the ranks of their decision to defrock DeBolt. "Because of W.W. DeBolt's association with Dr. Robinson and the 'PSYCHIANA' Movement of Moscow, Idaho, the brethren found it necessary to add their renunciation to that of the Rocky Mountain District of the Church of God."[191]

✦

Like Tenney, DeBolt faced the same decision: stay with Psychiana or be defrocked. On the one hand, DeBolt was making about five times the amount of money he had been making as a pastor for the Church of God.

On the other, pastoring (along with poetry) had been his calling. Making matters worse, his wife Gwendolyn was guilty by association, which was enough for the Church of God to excommunicate her.

"DeBolt took an entirely different attitude from that taken by Dr. Tenney," Frank wrote. "I cannot use his absolute words when he received his official 'de-frockment' from the Church of God."

When DeBolt received the letter, he went to Frank and said, "To hell with them."[192]

The poet was not going anywhere.

DeBolt was not the only Psychiana officer with literary aspirations at the time. Topping Robinson's writing project list for 1941 was his second memoir, *The Strange Autobiography of Frank B. Robinson*, along with two slim volumes, *For Rent: A Cross*, and *Blood on the Tail of a Pig*. At fifty-five, Frank was also finishing a novel titled, *God...And Dr. Bannister: This War Can Be Stopped*, his first foray into fiction, writing most of the material during his periodic stints in the Multnomah Hotel suite in Portland.

William Walter DeBolt (left) with Frank Robinson and unidentified office worker at a sorting machine in the Psychiana offices, c. 1940. University of Idaho Special Collections.

As a novel, the book is bad, written more as an alternative media vehicle by which to deliver Psychiana's message (although Psychiana does not itself occur in the plot). Frank decided—wisely, perhaps—to set the book in the Bay Area rather than in Idaho, and to name the central religion "All Souls Church." The protagonist, Howard Bannister, is an amalgam of Frank's actual life story and his self-invented biography, making for a strange narrative that is oddly consistent with much of what he had been saying about himself for years. In one way, fiction gave Frank Robinson license to say overtly what he had wanted to say "truthfully" for years.

"Howard Bannister had been pastor of All Souls Church since its inception. Brilliant of intellect, keen of mind, a handsome earnest man, his reputation had gone far and wide," Frank wrote.[193] "He was considered the most brilliant preacher in the United States...He was a little over six feet tall and weighed about two hundred pounds. His age was fifty-five, although he looked nearer forty than fifty-five."[194] It is clear that Frank's imagination did not wander too far to unearth names for his characters. The protagonist's first name, Howard, came from the street on which the Robinsons lived. Another character in the book, Dr. Bowers, was named "Alfred," and had "earned his Doctorate in Music at the famed Overland Conservatory of Music."[195]

Like the real Frank Robinson, Howard Bannister also had a family.

His family consisted of his ten year old daughter, Margie, and eighteen year old son, Bruce, who was following in the footsteps of Dr. Bowers and studying pipe organ at Overland Conservatory. Bannister was passionately fond of his family. He lived for just two things. One was to make God a living reality to the world and the other was—his family. With him, church work was a passion. Paid a ten thousand dollar a year salary with a drawing-account the same size, Bannister would not have hesitated to exchange the finery and prestige of All Souls for a waterfront mission job if he thought by taking the waterfront job he could do more towards making God real to humanity.[196]

Conspicuously absent from the ostensible praise of Bannister's family (which ends with a focus on money) is his wife. The opening section of the book functions both as a weird biographical revision and fantasy of Frank Robinson's life to that point, echoing impulses he first indulged in Klamath Falls when dropping false news stories in the paper about his father's and brothers' valor and deaths.

Readers glimpse a vignette of young Howard Bannister's life in New York City shortly after his parents' deaths (from tuberculosis, we're told) when he is but a ten-year-old street urchin hustling a soda jerk for food in a drugstore. Through charm and grit alone, Howard Bannister eventually got a job as a druggist, saving enough money to enter the theological seminary years later, where he would earn a Doctor of Divinity degree with honors. Years later, while riding in his stretch limousine across the Bay Bridge to Oakland, Dr. Bannister reflected on his graduation day from the theological college when he was called into a conference meeting by the deans.

The final conference…was held in the executive office of the seminary. All the Deans were there. The executive Board was there, for Bannister had made a record at that seminary. He had been loved by all. His deeply religious nature had won them. His innate natural ability on the platform and in the pulpit had begun to manifest early…And so recognizing the depth of character in young Bannister, the Deans had decided to call him in for one final word.[197]

The reason for this conference, Frank wrote, was it had become clear to the seminary's leadership that Howard Bannister was the Chosen One. "We feel that God has chosen you to bring this world some great message."[198]

God…And Dr. Bannister is revelatory not in what it conveys about Robinson's conception of God or of the evolution of Psychiana at the dawn of World War II, but because it is one more example of a man at pains to reinvent himself and control the perception of his life and its meaning. That, after all, was the primary message of Psychiana. It was not a reactive religion whose congregants prayed for good things to happen, and then waited to see if those things came to pass. It was an active religion that prodded its followers to tap into the God Power *now* in order to improve their conditions. That was a powerful message for an entire generation of people caught between the Great Depression and another world war. Still, reading the pages of Robinson's novel demands the same kind of dual awareness readers need when perusing any of Psychiana's materials: where does the real Frank end, and the fictional Frank begin?

When, in *God…And Dr. Bannister*, we are finally introduced to Howard Bannister's wife, it is jarring because it is so thinly veiled as to be reportage. Bannister's chauffeur has just dropped him off at his house, and Banister enters after a long day of work.

> Seated in a comfortable armchair, his wife, Pearl Bannister, was awaiting his arrival as usual. Almost to the minute every Sunday night she could count upon her husband to be home…Mrs. Bannister was loved by all who knew her. Her husband had a knack for making enemies. Many people were just jealous of his success. But Mrs. Bannister, well, she just did not make enemies.[199]

Robinson advertised *God…And Dr. Bannister* as "The Sensation Novel of the Year." Self-embellishments notwithstanding, the book did contain sensational aspects, such as forecasting Hitler's demise. In the scene, newsies are barking out the stunning developments:

'WUXTRY! WUXTRY! HITLER COMMITS SUICIDE! HIT-
LER COMMITS SUICIDE! WUXTRY! WUXTRY! THE WAR
IS OVER! HITLER COMMITS SUICIDE! PAPER! PAPER!
READ ALL ABOUT THE FALL OF HITLER!'[200]

But as of 1941, Hitler was anything but dead, and war was very much active. Just as the world itself was changing, ever taking darker and more cynical turns, so too did the tone of Robinson's other writings. In *For Rent: A Cross*, for instance, Robinson revised the language he used describing God. Instead of referring to the "God Law," "Great Spirit," or "Creative Spirit," Robinson now called it "The Scientific Principle," a moniker more suited perhaps for a time of accelerated technology and war. "The Scientific Principle—God—has existed from time immemorial. It had no creator. It is, and always was, self-existent."

Always one to up the ante, Frank also began laying the foundation on his ideas of immortality, something he had teed up previously, but now believed to be part of the Scientific Principle. "What the average American wants to know is why, if God lives, is death necessary?"[201]

CHAPTER 54
"What Do You Want?"

Kokomo, Indiana
April 9, 1941

It was a fair Wednesday morning in Kokomo, Indiana, when Ella Louise Newcom sat down at her typewriter to write Frank Robinson in Moscow, Idaho. The spring morning was chilly but the temperature would hit a high of 71 by midday. At fifty-four, Ella was the same age as Robinson, and a devoted Psychiana student.

Ella lived with her husband Harlan Henry Newcom in their comfortable brick bungalow-style home at 616 South Indiana Avenue. She and "Harl," as he was called,[202] had moved into the home some years earlier, from a much smaller house four blocks away, where they raised their three boys: Harlan Jr., Thurston, and Lloyd. Her new neighborhood on Indiana Avenue was exactly what you might expect from small-town, middle-America: neat and Norman Rockwell-esque with prim lawns and swept sidewalks; crisp American flags adorning the prouder homes in the neighborhood. Ella's home had a wide and spacious front porch that provided plenty of shade on hot summer days, and the home sat back from the street a fair distance with a long sidewalk and a few steps running up the gentle slope of the lawn to the porch stairs.

A master mechanic and later a foreman, Harl Newcom worked at Continental Steel, a massive mill that employed some 1,500 employees in Kokomo. Continental Steel was a revered institution in town, providing good-paying jobs to its employees and playing a vital role in the community at large. On a daily basis, Continental workers rolled out miles of steel fencing wire along with tons of nails and other building materials that were central to an industrial economy.[203] Ella and Harl's second son, Thurston, also worked at Continental, taking after his father. Continental Steel was a quintessentially American factory employing quintessentially American workers in a quintessentially American town.

306

For her own part, Ella stayed busy working with the Order of the White Shrine of Jerusalem[204] and in various civic clubs and organizations. She hosted parties and chicken dinners, and appeared as much or more on the *Kokomo Tribune*'s society page as any one of her friends did. Harl was deeply involved in the Freemason's affiliate, the Knights Templar, where he served as Eminent Commander. When they were not occupied with club dinners and balls, Ella and Harl attended Continental parties and company picnics where they toasted retirements and promotions of neighbors and coworkers. They were members of several local civic clubs, one for which Ella was recently hostess, entertaining "an all day meeting" of twenty-four ladies at their brick bungalow on South Indiana Avenue.[205]

By all accounts, Harl and Ella were happily married. In January 1930, while still living in their tiny home on 747 South McCann Street, they had celebrated their 25th wedding anniversary in grand style, inviting "a large number of guests."[206] They received from family and friends—some of whom had traveled from out of town—many "cards and gifts of flowers and silver." The local paper noted that "Mr. and Mrs. Newcom have spent their entire married life in Kokomo."[207] And in 1955, when they celebrated their 50th anniversary, that occasion also made the pages of the *Kokomo Tribune* (although by that time, they were spending their winters in St. Petersburg, Florida). "Wedding cake and ice cream were served to 140 guests following a mock wedding ceremony."[208]

Kokomo, Indiana's population in 1941 was about 44,000, give or take, and the quaint but vibrant downtown was like something off the cover of a *Saturday Evening Post*. Boys and girls would have flocked to Charlie Sullivan's Victory Bicycle and Hobbies store, while their mothers might have shopped at F.W. Woolworth's five and dime store, or at the Big Shoe Store next door. At the Fox Theater on Mulberry Street, families routinely took in popular movies of the day such as *Citizen Kane*, *The Maltese Falcon*, and *Sergeant York*. In April 1941, Kokomo was still the kind of town where bakeries like Dietzen's, Omar's, and Joy Ann's dispatched their delivery men, each donning uniforms fit for policemen—blue suits with ties and peaked service hats—to deliver their daily bread.[209]

But beneath that thin veneer and magazine gloss of American exceptionalism, there lurked a much more troubling side of Kokomo, Indiana. Eighteen years earlier, when Harl was forty-five and Ella thirty-seven, Kokomo had pulled out all the stops for its July 4th celebration. That year, upwards of two hundred thousand people flocked to Kokomo. What had made the 1923 Kokomo July 4th celebration so significant was that it had been organized by and for the Ku Klux Klan. That year, Klansmen from every county in Indiana and from around the country arrived by car and train. One regional paper reported, "Great Day for the Klansmen: Tri-State Meeting at Kokomo Wednesday Draws Enormous Crowd."[210] Events entailed a massive parade and fireworks; an airplane boasting an enormous white cross circled above. "The giant gathering made its participants feel part of something vast, patriotic, and noble—a celebration of Americanism," one historian wryly wrote. *The Kokomo Tribune* advertised the event on its front page under the "What's Doin" section.[211]

To read the society page of the *Kokomo Tribune*, you get the sense that Ella Newcom led a carefree life. But beneath that public narrative existed a woman filled with worry. Ella Newcom had always maintained a strong connection to religion, even from a young age, but her connections had varied over time. As early as 1918, Ella and her family had been active Quakers.[212] But by 1941, she was a Psychiana devotee, and it was her mail-order religion that had brought some calm to her worried days. "I am so happy to be able to write you this morning, and tell you my life has changed and the God Law is really working for me," she wrote to Frank Robinson.[213] "I have had so many wonderful manifestations of Its power, in the past few days. The other evening [I felt] a very strong drawing in my very being to write and tell you a few of them, I do not know where to begin, and do not wish to tire you, as I know you are very busy."[214]

Despite her outwardly appearing demanding social schedule, Ella Newcom confessed to Frank Robinson that she was not as social as some might think. "I am alone most of the day," she reported.[215] Although Harl was sixty-three, he evidently was still working at Continental, and all of their sons were grown with families of their own. That left Ella at home by herself to do housework and to reflect. In the days leading up to that Wednesday morning when she finally decided to sit down and write her teacher, Ella had experienced something rather strange. "I was doing my work," she wrote, "and all at once it sounded like some one was in the room with me." That is when she heard a voice call out to her: "'What do you want?'"[216]

"You will remember I told you I had centered my thoughts on health as without health, one cannot be really happy," she wrote. "I visited my Dr. last Jan 3rd and each week sense [sic] then I have noticed a change for the better, and today my health seems perfect," Ella added. "I have no fear in my mind at all, but a sweet peace. I used to have a headache often," Ella continued. But since reading her Psychiana Lessons, even her headaches were gone. "Now if I have one, I just don't keep it at all and do not take pills eather [sic]. Such little things as that are taken care of in short order. I cannot begin to tell you how much these lessons have ment to me, and I spend one hour each day with the lessons on hand." In wrapping up her letter to Frank, Ella confessed a feeling that she had been keeping to herself.[217]

> Last Saturday night, I did not go to sleep till after three in the morning. Just thought these words over and over again: The Living God is makeing [sic] me whole. I did not want to sleep. It seems foolish to tell you about it, but is the truth just the same and sense [sic] then I have had such a wonderful happy feeling in my whole being, maybe you will understand. I can not tell any one else as they would think me very foolish, but I know better.

> Sincerely your friend and student, Ella L. Newcom,
> Kokomo, Ind.
>   616 South Indiana Ave.[218]

Eight days later, on Thursday, April 17—a day after London had suffered its worst air raid to date—William Walter DeBolt dispatched a form letter to Ella Newcom of Kokomo, Indiana. "Thank you for the names of your friends which you were kind enough to send in."[219] Psychiana often asked their students to submit the names and addresses of friends and relatives they think might be interested in learning about the power of the God Law. When students like Ella Newcom submitted these names and addresses, the mailing department at Psychiana's headquarters converted them into actionable marketing leads. The rest of DeBolt's letter, however, read like every letter sent back to Psychiana students.

> It was very nice of you indeed to tell me about the many things that God has done for you of late. My heart rejoices with you because of these great victories which you have won. If you knew how many thousands of people write us as you did, you would know that at long last the actual truths of God are being made known to men and women on this

earth. May the Spirit of Infinite Power be with you always. If we can be of any further assistance to you with the Lessons please let us know.[220]

Although only two of Ella Newcom's letters with Psychiana survive, her hurried note five months later, on September 5, makes clear that she was a Psychiana devotee who wrote often to Frank Robinson. "I do hate to bother you again," she wrote. "But I must explain to you some things that have happened to me during the study of these lessons."

> Last Tuesday when I wrote you such a worried letter I did not understand what was wrong, but I believe I have found the answer. Yesterday morning I still felt depressed and something told me to go see a lady down the street, and I took her some of the messages you sent me in the begining [sic] of this course and left them for her to read. We talk[ed] about this course and she noticed the great change that has taken place in me in the last few months. I think I have been too timid to talk about it to others. After I left her house I felt like I was walking on air.[221]

Ella went on to discuss how she had read Lesson 16, which included an Associated Press clipping about the 1932 discovery of a particle called a "neutron," calling it the "Embryo of Matter." Robinson had pointed to this discovery as proof of the invisible God Law. "While this is, of course, going into the realm of physics," Frank wrote in his original Lesson, "I think that all my students will see the principle behind it all, and will know by this time that the important and controlling forces of this universe are spiritual or unseen forces. This is exactly what I have claimed and what I still claim."[222]

But it was Robinson's discussion of the "still small voice" of this unseen God Law that most moved Ella Newcom.

> Back to the first Lesson, I heard the still small voice but have kept it to myself for fear of others not beleiving [sic] me or thinking me crazy. I was alone at the time and had been studing [sic], it asked me very plain, "What do you want?" I just looked up but did not seem surprised to not see any one and I knew it had to be God or the Life Spirit it could not be anything else. I have told those that I have talked to that this course is the most wonderful thing that ever came in my life, I have received wonderful experiences that money could not buy.[223]

When Psychiana's mailing department received testimonials that were particularly poignant, moving, or seemingly miraculous, they flagged them with a note and filed them to be used in marketing materials later. If letters contained some bit or line that could be used as ad copy, they were likewise flagged and filed. On Ella Newcom's September 5, 1941, letter, someone penciled across the top "Money could not buy. File."

Five days later, on September 10, William Walter DeBolt wrote back to Ella Newcom: "Thanks for your good letter. I was happy to hear from you. I have been expecting to hear from you with a good report. So I am not surprised therefore that you have written such a fine letter. If you knew how many thousands of people write us as you did, you would know that at long last the actual truths of God are being made known to men and women on this earth. May the Spirit of Infinite Power be with you always. If we can be of any further assistance to you with the Lessons please let us know."[224]

CHAPTER 55

Vision Quest

A set of scattered notes—partially handwritten on Davenport Hotel stationery, partially typed on onionskin paper—reflect Frank's mind in a freewheeling state in 1941. One can see him casting about to find something to grab on to, something substantive that might move him forward in his ever-pressing quest to keep Psychiana not only solvent, but relevant in such a changing world. The handwritten notes are difficult to parse on account of their arrangement and Frank's hurried penmanship.

> Psychiana. 5 yrs ago. 67 countries—1000000 enve[lopes] 8 tons paper. March. Shall speak plainly. Orthodox noise hasn't respect[ed] everyone's beliefs…What I am after is truth in realm of religion. Not interested in what is told me if cannot be proven or if not reasonable. I search for truth old dogmas found false & therefore discarded. Shall speak very plainly. Want to hurt noone's [sic] feelings.

The typed pages in this batch of notes present a more cohesive narrative thrust, but show how Frank was still searching for Psychiana's next campaign.

> I.
>
> Prov. 29:18 –"WHERE THERE IS NO VISION THE PEOPLE PERISH." And judging by the conditions of the world today, not only people, but nations are on the verge of perishing. Look all around you, Germany—France—England—Russia."
>
> (Paint picture of world conditions)
>
> Picture our own United States – communism, atheism, infidelity, socialism, revolutions, etc.
>
> Germany claims it must lead the world.
>
> Great Britain adopts the attitude of European mediator.
>
> France says Germany Is about to attack her—Germany says same of France.
>
> Italy goes to Africa—slaughters, Lyon of the Tribe of Judah helpless.

II.

If there is any vision, I would like to know what it is.

Visions of fear, of attack, of disaster—all material visions if any at all. NO VISION OF GOD.

With all due respect to religious organizations, they are powerless to stem the tide of atheism and infidelity which is sweeping the U.S.

They hold out a hope for the future—but none for today.

They do the best they can.

They are absolutely honest.

They are following their vision.

III.

WHERE DID THEY GET THEIR VISION OF GOD?

Let's talk plainly—Let's not mince words.

I GO INTO DETAIL WHERE THE CHURCH VISION CAME FROM. IT'S A VISION OF THE PAST—Men are looking 2000 years back for their inspirations and not to the present or future.

The GOD VISION HAS ACCOMPLISHED NOTHING YET, for in spite of the earnestness of the churches, and in spite of their philiosophy, the world is in a worse mess today than it ever was.

Therefore, I say we need A NEW VISION OF GOD.

Now what VISION would best meet the needs of the world today?

What are the Nations clamoring for?

What are individuals clamoring for?

IV.

HOW IS NEW VISION ATTAINED? – Turn your eyes from the past to future, and see the existing Spiritual Truth.

This Truth has always existed, but you couldn't see it.[225]

In June 1941, Frank took a break from work, and joined Pearl on a train trip east to visit Alf at Oberlin College in Ohio. By then, Alf had settled in, met friends who were just as passionate about music as he was, and was enjoying college life. "My folks came [at] the end of second semester," he later remembered. "They remained a few days and then we all went on to New York City for a short vacation."

The vacation may have been precisely what an anxious, cast-about Frank Robinson needed at the time, for when he returned, an unexpected path forward for Psychiana presented itself.

Chapter 56
"Frankly Speaking"

Los Angeles
September 21, 1941

On a warm Sunday afternoon, a well-dressed man in a pressed suit left his modern ranch home, and drove fifty-four miles into Los Angeles to do a friend a favor. The man was Sidney P. Dones, a high-profile, multi-talented real estate impresario and civil rights activist. The favor that afternoon entailed giving his friend a ride to a lecture that had been widely publicized.[226]

Born in Marshall, Texas, on February 18, 1892, Sidney P. Dones enjoyed an upbringing by parents who cherished education and encouraged Sidney to pursue mathematics. After three years at Wiley College in Marshall, Dones heeded the call heard by so many young people of the time, and moved to Los Angeles. There, he married Bessie Williams, a renowned violinist, and, in 1916, launched his career, opening the Booker T. Washington Building on Central Avenue, headquarters for the Sidney P. Dones Company.[227] Specializing in real estate, loans, and insurance, the upstart business stood next door to the African American-owned *California Eagle* newspaper. With plenty of allies, capital, and a powerful newspaper on his street, Dones quickly became a key figure in establishing a thriving African American community along Central in Los Angeles.[228] A year earlier, *The New Age* reported that Sidney P. Dones was "enjoying the greatest real estate and insurance business of any race man in the West."[229]

Sidney P. Dones. Photo from Pragmatic Obots Unite; accessed on blackcinemaconnection.com.

314

Not one to be bound by the parameters of his job description or the color of his skin, Dones got into acting, and starred in three early Hollywood films: *Loyal Hearts* (1919); *Reformation* (1920); and *The Ten Thousand Dollar Trail* (1921), making him one of the first-ever African American film stars.[230] His celebrity as an actor boosted his visibility in the increasingly competitive Hollywood real estate market, earning his young family of four a comfortable living. At the exact same time a young Frank Robinson was across town, selling stocks to Hollywood celeb Tom Mix, Sidney P. Dones was diversifying his own business a few blocks away, brokering property sales and handling investments.

As early as 1920, Dones began placing ads in African American newspapers such as the *Dallas Express*, the *Pittsburgh Courier*, and the *Neighborhood News*, hoping to lure Black buyers to California, the land of plenty and opportunity. "CALIFORNIA WELCOMES YOU," one Dones ad read.

FAIR TREATMENT, LEGAL EQUALITY, GOOD POSITIONS.

SIDNEY P. DONES, Real Estate. Buy a home in California. Beautiful homes on easy terms. Before you come to Los Angeles, write and let me look after your interest.

SIDNEY P. DONES[231]

When his name was not accompanying one of his investment ads, it very often appeared on the theater and motion picture pages around the country. One advertisement from October 26, 1921, in Vicksburg, Mississippi, featured a typical Dones theatrical promotion.

PRINCESS THEATER

Showing Today

SIDNEY P. DONES

With All Star Colored Cast in

"LOYAL HEARTS"

A 5-reel thriller

Showing the Colored Doughboys

in Action in the World War

In 1924, Dones and a small group of investors launched his greatest project yet: Eureka Villa, a 1,000-acre development in Santa Clarita Valley marketed exclusively to African Americans as a premier destination resort. Later named "Val Verde," the resort featured cabins, tennis courts, golf course, club house, and hiking trails, and was enjoyed by guests from across the country who wanted to vacation without racial harassment. Later, an Olympic-sized swimming pool was installed, and Val Verde became known as the "Black Palm Springs."[232]

By 1941, Dones was actively engaged in local, state, and national politics while still working the real estate market. "Find Your Future in Southern California," was the hook in one of his most current ads. "The Garden Spot of America...All Races Welcome."[233] When Dones was not selling and promoting a multi-cultural Eden, he was writing "Frankly Speaking," a nationally syndicated column running primarily in the African American newspapers he so often advertised in. His column took on a range of subjects, big and small, often related to success in business. In one column, for instance, he talked about buying a copy of Dale Carnegie's *How to Win Friends and Influence People*, touting its merits.

Carnegie's classic self-help book for entrepreneurs squared, in some ways, with Dones' abiding interest in New Thought and its many evangelists. But his interest in Carnegie's work and New Thought spoke to a larger motivation for Dones: he was always looking to leverage unconventional thinking to profitable effect. He was as astute a student of business as he was of human nature.

That confluence of business motivation and spiritual interests is part of what drove Dones on that September afternoon in 1941 to make the trip from his ranch home into the city for a lecture. "Sometimes a bad start makes a good finish," Dones wrote in "Frankly Speaking" a few days later.[234] "On Sunday, I made a special trip from the ranch to attend a lecture at the Philharmonic Auditorium at 3 p.m. I probably would have missed the lecture but I had promised a friend I would go.

> I was attracted to the lecture because of the two eminent religious leaders who sponsored this joint series of meetings, Dean Ernest Holmes of the Institute of Religious Science, whom I know and admire very much, and Dr. Frank B. Robinson, founder of Psychiana, whom I never met but have been a student of the wonderful philosophy he teaches.
>
> As I say, a bad start makes a good finish because when I arrived in Los Angeles, I was disappointed that my friend had ignored the appointment, although I had ridden 54 miles to keep it. However, I attended the lecture alone.[235]

Frank Robinson had been back in Hollywood once or twice, meeting with Ernest Holmes, the diminutive man who had founded "Religious Science" in Los Angeles during the 1920s when Robinson and Dones were getting their respective starts there. In the early summer of 1941, Holmes and his wife, Hazel, traveled to Moscow, Idaho, to visit with the Robinsons. Alf—who was home from Oberlin that summer—remembered the event. "Mother prepared one of her fabulous 'everything included' dinners," he wrote. "Creamed onions, white and sweet potatoes, two kinds of meat, pie and plum pudding. Of course the entire meal was served on the 'good' black Chinese print china with the 'best' silverware."[236]

It turned out that Holmes and Robinson had more in common than just their beliefs and mutual desire to teach the power of the Living God. Born within six months of one another, each came from a family of boys. Where Frank was the oldest of four; Ernest was the youngest of nine. That Ernest's father was from Canada meant that they each had ties to that country, and they had both traveled from the east to the west to seek their respective fortunes. Each was charismatic, charming, and intelligent, and both were prolific writers and lecturers.[237]

At dinner in the Robinson home, Frank had confessed a personal failure. His plans to build the Psychiana Temple in Hollywood had fallen through, due to the overwhelming costs of his legal defense from 1936 to 1937 during the passport fraud and deportation trials. He did not have the funds to build what he had envisioned as a "twenty-story" headquarters. Holmes then suggested that they join forces. After all, their basic philosophies were the same. They appealed to the same demographic. And by combining Psychiana and Religious Science, they would double their flock, and therefore, their profits. It was, to Holmes' mind at least, a win-win scenario.

Despite their similarities and dovetailing interests, the men were also a study in contrasts. "Both men had similar beliefs," Alf wrote, "but used different promotion methods."[238] While Robinson relied on shock value, sensationalism, and baiting tactics in advertising Psychiana, Ernest Holmes used more conventional and strategic methods to promote Religious Science. But there was a more significant difference, one that would ensure the longevity of one and the end of the other. "Holmes had planned and organized his institute to carry on its work over time," Alf recalled. "This, my father did not do with Psychiana."[239]

Indeed, Religious Science was a long-term organization with a leadership structure, "Parent Institute," and Board of Trustees. Holmes had always viewed his work as extending beyond his own life and had laid sufficient groundwork to achieve it. "A plan for the establishment of adequate funds for the work was divided into five parts," Holmes's brother, Fenwicke, wrote, "a fund to provide land and buildings for the central chapter; an extension fund for organizing and administering new chapters; an educational fund for assisting the training of leaders, particularly the younger generation; a literature fund; and finally an endowment fund, the income to be used for designated purposes."[240]

Psychiana had none of that. Why Frank did not put into place a succession plan remains one of the great mysteries of Psychiana, and underscores the extent to which it was inextricably and fatally bound to its founder.

------◆------

Still, when the two men came together, as they did for their lectures at the Los Angeles Philharmonic in September 1941, they stirred the crowd. "The American Spiritual Awakening," as they called it, drew some 3,500 attendees, one of whom was Sidney P. Dones.[241]

Inside the Philharmonic, the seats were filled with spectators. On stage stood a single lectern and two chairs in which were seated the men of the hour: Holmes and Robinson. That is how Frank had framed his advertisements for the event: "The HOLMES-ROBINSON Spiritual Awakening."[242]

The Sunday meeting opened with the entire audience singing "America the Beautiful," and then Robinson addressed the crowd. "Let us remain quiet for a few minutes so that we may draw inspiration and power from the Divine source of all power."[243]

After two more songs ("Lead Kindly Light" and "My God to Thee"), Ernest Holmes took his turn at the podium. "I wish to explain the purpose of these meetings," he said. "We believe that there is a spiritual force which can destroy this action of evil, no matter through whom or what such action takes. We are gathered together here, probably from all races, from all religions, and from those who have no particular religious viewpoint."[244]

On these points, Holmes was correct. The audience was as theologically mixed as it was ethnically and racially diverse.

"Dr. Robinson calls his work 'Psychiana' which means bringing Spiritual Power to the world. I happen to belong to a movement called 'Spiritual Science,' which means the same thing," Holmes added.

Some of you may go to a Jewish Synagogue; you may be a Methodist, Baptist, Catholic, but there is but one God. We meet here today not on a theological background, but upon the foreground of a spiritual conception, the common meeting ground of every race, every creed, every color, every philosophy, and every religion on the face of the earth.[245]

Robinson echoed those sentiments later in his own address. Looking over the crowd of 3,500, Frank began:

Beloved, when the Almighty created the human race, He created black, white, yellow, and every other color which exists on earth, in one creation. He did not make three or four special jobs of creation, nor did He make several different attributes, one for each nation. He made them all flesh and blood...We are all brothers, regardless of our religious affiliation, our race, or nationality.[246]

These calls for cultural inclusivity in 1941 were decades ahead of their time. While often identifying as a political conservative, Frank Robinson was far more socially progressive than many of his contemporaries, speaking his mind on matters of race even when—or especially when—it was unpopular to do so.

The spirit of unity was not lost on the crowd, nor was it lost on Sidney P. Dones. Reporting later in his "Frankly Speaking" column, Dones wrote, "Dr. Robinson and Dean Holmes are asking the American people to pledge themselves in a unit to ask God to bring peace to the world. They are asking the American people to reiterate and reaffirm that they believe in the power of the living God."[247]

"In my years of business," Dones continued,

I have spent some profitable days. I have been paid well for my services, but there is not one time in my life that I believe I received as high a compensation as I did by sitting in at this meeting at the Philharmonic Auditorium last Sunday.[248]

Dominating the tenor and tone of the Holmes-Robinson Spiritual Awakening was the ever-present concern of war. Both Holmes and Robinson preached peace over war, tolerance over hate, and unity over divisiveness. Their lectures that week of September 1941 resonated on both geo-political and national/cultural levels. "Dr. Robinson and I are neither isolationists nor pacifists," Holmes said on the matter. "We are not so simple minded as to believe that in a world of force our nation should remain unprepared

...We are merely saying this: in the midst of all this uproar, carnage, strife and slaughter there must arise a voice, telling us of the Power of God, and that voice, we believe, will arise here in America."[249]

Those words especially resonated with Dones.

I was gratified to know that they are preaching a doctrine that I, myself, spoke of in this column some months ago. That is, that this war will never completely cease, no victory will ever be won until victory is predicated upon love triumphing over hate, and peace of mind and consciousness triumphing over selfishness and creed.[250]

If Dones—as a self-identifying student of Psychiana—ever wrote to Robinson directly, the whereabouts of that correspondence is unknown. But as one who refused to be conscripted by social norms, as someone who cut against the grain and with great success, Sidney Preston Dones saw tremendous value in the message Robinson and Holmes were broadcasting, especially in such troubling times. At the dawn of his fiftieth year, Dones embodied the essence of the American Dream. He had been a Hollywood movie star, a super-successful businessman, a political operator, a writer, civic leader, and activist. And add to that list, a Psychiana student. Dones had nothing to gain or lose by promoting the Holmes Spiritual Awakening. "Today is Thursday," he wrote, wrapping up his "Frankly Speaking" column. "Tonight is the last night of these meetings. I wish many of my friends would attend this meeting. If it does for you what it has done for me, you would not take a hundred dollars for attending this meeting."[251]

Chapter 57

The Pilot

When Alfred Robinson stepped out of the Apollo Theatre on East College Street in Oberlin, Ohio, on Sunday afternoon, December 7, 1941, the news had already spread across town.[252] Across the state. The nation. The world. A swarm of Japanese fighter planes—the so-called "Zeroes"—had attacked Pearl Harbor in Hawaii. Total devastation. Alfred was eighteen, tall, lean and handsome like his father. He was in his second year at Oberlin College Conservatory. Not unlike the fictional Bruce Bannister of his father's "novel," Alf was becoming a gifted pianist. He had the raw musical talent his father possessed, but he was earning a formal education, something his father lacked. On hearing the news of Pearl Harbor, Alfred—like so many young men at the time—enlisted.

Alfred had wrapped up his studies early that spring of 1942 with plans to complete his degree at Stanford after the war. Before shipping out, however, Alf moved back home to reunite with his family. Like his father, he chose the Navy. Unlike his father's, Alfred's enlistment would not only be completed and honorable, but it would be one of distinction. Before shipping out, he became a Navy pilot and began his flight training, first at the University of Idaho in Moscow, then transferring to Pasco, Washington, and finishing at Pensacola, Florida.[253]

Before he left for college in Ohio, Alfred had been dating a local Moscow High School girl, Eva Annette Hamer. The two had an on-again, off-again relationship. "Between the fall of 1937 and the spring of 1939," Alf recalled, "we went 'steady,' and were involved in all those adolescent behaviors indigenous to the times: cruising in our cars, attending school and other parties and dances, having sex (we had been virgins), talking on the telephone for hours on end, being possessive and jealous, [and] swaying in and out of break-ups and reconciliations."[254] But when he finally left for Oberlin, their relationship wandered into uncertain territory. While he was at school, they "kept up a desultory long-range correspondence."[255]

But by Christmas of his first year, the relationship broke with "emphatic finality." So when he returned home to announce to Frank and Pearl that he had decided to join the Navy, he was decidedly single, free to go to war unencumbered by romantic attachments back home.

But by January of 1943, Annette (as she was called) and Alf had rekindled their affair through letters. It was an altogether unexpected reunion, a "bizarre rejuvenation and resuscitation of an expired relationship," he wrote.[256] This time, however, they were serious. For once and for all. They planned to be married on March 25, 1943. They stumbled through the wedding plans by phone and through letters. The son of Psychiana's founder would be married, it was determined, in a Presbyterian Church. And before she knew it, Annette was a Navy bride living with her husband on a base in Florida.

The marriage seemed doomed from the outset. Although young, Annette was already drinking heavily and often. Alf, by his own admission, "used passive-aggressiveness a great deal" to get his way.[257] The newlyweds were deeply unhappy. Annette drank more and more, and Alf did not hide his resentment and animosity. "[M]y behavioral repertoire," he recalled, "began to exude an insidious layer of devastating control over Annette."[258]

Alf was pinned between a failing marriage at home and a raging war overseas. Instead of turning to drink (although he would later in life), the young pilot "would withdraw from Annette to read Psychiana literature; or go jogging."[259]

At the time, war was the one and only thing on the minds of people in America. In August 1943, First Lieutenant Alf Robinson was stationed on the famed aircraft carrier USS *Hornet*, where he piloted TBM Avenger torpedo bombers on campaigns over the bloody South Pacific. Back home, Frank Robinson let his daughter-in-law rent the house he owned next door, and gave her a job at Psychiana. She was in every way irrevocably tied to the Robinson family and to the Movement. Frank Robinson—the Archbishop of Psychiana—had become her father-in-law, neighbor, landlord, and, now, her boss.

CHAPTER 58

Prophet and Mystic

With their son deployed, Frank and Pearl were shouldering the daily dread of so many parents across the country in 1942 and 1943. Although questions have long lingered over whether or not Frank Robinson really believed in Psychiana, there can be little doubt that the leader of Psychiana needed to believe in *something* with his son flying missions in the South Pacific. His writing in this period reveals a lurking conflict in his thinking. On the one hand, national fear and worry created a need for belief and the kind of assuring voice so many people got from Psychiana. On the other hand, he now had his own real fears and worries, which placed him in the position of becoming his own student in a way he may not have anticipated.

Like so many of his students before, Frank Robinson needed, now more than ever, something to believe in.

After Alfred enlisted, Robinson set to work on a new book: *What This War Really Means: With a Prophecy Concerning the Outcome of the Present Conflict.* Dedicated to his son, the book opens with an "Introductory Message by W.W. DeBolt, D.D."

DeBolt had been working diligently for Frank Robinson and the greater Psychiana machine for two years when his boss asked him to write the introduction to his new book. Whenever possible, Robinson relied on others to boast on his behalf, especially if those people had some level of clout or standing. In DeBolt the poet, Frank saw not only a faithful employee of religious conviction, but also a writer and wordsmith. For his own part, DeBolt was more than happy to oblige. He respected Frank and his family, even if he quibbled here and there with some of Robinson's bombast. Not only had Frank stood by DeBolt when he was defrocked, but he paid him a generous salary and provided him with a publishing outlet for his poems. DeBolt's allegiance would have made agreeing to Frank's request of writing an introduction easy, even if the content of his introduction bore the heavy-handed imprint of Frank's own ego. "The author of this book," DeBolt wrote, "is a true mystic. He is, perhaps, the greatest mystic of all times."

> Those privileged to work with him know that he lives in a state of almost constant inward and spiritual communication with his Maker. Contemporaries, friends, and enemies have generously called him 'the greatest spiritual genius of all times.'[260]

One of the "tells" in DeBolt's introduction that reveals Robinson's considerable influence is the incessant messianic attribution, painting Frank as the most brilliant mystic in history on the one hand, and a simple servant of God on the other.

> Perhaps his most outstanding characteristic is simplicity. He is, too, the most normal, business-like individual it has ever been my privilege to meet…Keen of mind, a very shrewd business executive, kind-hearted to a degree—this is Frank B. Robinson.[261]

Of the many words that can aptly describe the inventor of Psychiana, simplicity is not one of them. But it was that kind of dual messaging—the simple genius and shrewd executive messiah—that most ably softened the ground for the book's thesis: Frank Robinson could predict the future. "Those who know him best," DeBolt wrote, "are sometimes rather awed at his uncanny ability to predict the future along religious lines…If I were a gambling man, I'd gamble that no matter how strange and preposterous the spiritual predictions of my friend may seem—they will come true. For this man is a true mystic."[262]

No book or piece of Psychiana-sanctioned literature would be complete without Robinson's trademark confrontational posturing or "baiting style," as Alf once called it. "There will be consternation," DeBolt wrote, "among those millions of followers of orthodoxy as a result of this book. But one thing is sure—there exists on the earth today no theological organization, or no religious belief which can actually demonstrate the invisible superhuman Power of God."[263]

In *What This War Really Means*, Frank Robinson's presiding theme was that the world was a mess because the current systems of religion were hollow, devoid of God, and therefore had created a moral vacuum in which war could thrive. "I have repeatedly made the statement after many years of research," Robinson wrote, "that every system of theology on the face of the earth is either man-made or church-made, which amounts to the same thing."[264] Because those systems of religion were man-made, they were false, and did not contain the power of the Living God. "Christianity cannot save humanity," he added, "because it cannot disclose the Power of God to humanity. Not being able to do that, humanity is not interested in it."[265]

Only Frank B. Robinson and Psychiana could save humanity, for only Robinson—the true mystic and prophet—could disclose the Power of God. The efficacy and legitimacy of his claims hung, in part, on his new-found ability to see the future.

> I do not see the present world conflict ending in victory for either side. What I do see is the most horrible, ghastly wholesale shedding of human blood the mind of man can conceive. In fact, the American mind is not capable of conceiving the horrors of the Japanese mind.[266]

Like so many mainstream Americans in post-Pearl Harbor America, Robinson was shocked and devastated by that attack, but was also susceptible to the propaganda circulated at the time about the Japanese.

> It is quite possible that these insane devils will drop bacteria and plague germs from the skies into our reservoirs and other water supplies. They may drop "suicide squads," enveloped in flame into our forests. There is nothing their vile minds are not capable of conceiving in order that the true knowledge of the Power of the Spirit of God may be kept from coming to the earth.[267]

Echoing the sentiments set forth in *God...and Dr. Bannister*, Robinson returned to his prediction about the leader of the Third Reich. But at the same time, he allowed for a more nuanced view of the people beholden to world despots. "I see Adolph Hitler committing suicide," he wrote.

> I see the German people, the Japanese people, and the peoples of every nation, turning from war to God when the true conception of God is brought to them. I see the Power of the Spirit of God completely dethroning, not the German or the Japanese people, but those leaders in authority over them who have dragged them into this inhuman conflict entirely against their wishes.[268]

At worst, *What This War Really Means* is a rehash of Robinson's other writings and a vehicle for propaganda common in America in the early 1940s. At best, the writing shows one man trying to make sense of a rapidly changing world and of a war his son was now fighting. It shows a man both vilifying and humanizing the same swath of people within pages of each example. It shows a man who is grasping for hope in the dire face of the unknown, desperate to pin down some kind of answer that is more concrete and satis-factory than platitudes of the "invisible Power of God." It is, in other words, the work of a mere mortal, not a mystic or prophet, but a man at pains to convince himself more than anyone else that everything would be okay.

---------------◆---------------

As usual, Frank B. Robinson was feverish, nearly maniacal, in his literary out-put, publishing nine books over a two-year period. He typed, one reporter later wrote, "in a hunt and peck system," turning out countless pages every day.[269] The work was so taxing that Robinson taped his overtaxed fingertips up to spare himself pain. His work during this period reflected the trance-like state of his life at the time, verging on the surreal, preposterous, and strange.

One of the strangest titles to emerge out of this manically prolific period was his pocket-sized volume, *Blood on the Tail of a Pig*. Not only was it the most bizarre in some ways, but it also became one of his most popular. Robinson spent the first third of the brief text establishing more than just his credibility and importance (the first two pages entail an alleged meeting he had with President Roosevelt, for instance); he went to great lengths to establish his sanity (while revealing his inflated ego). "There are some people who, after reading this book, will say 'the man's crazy,'" Frank wrote. "Let us see."[270] Rob-inson pointed to examples of his success to preempt and thwart any attacks on the book. "Speaking with no thought whatsoever of egotism," he added, "let me say that perhaps more eyes are upon my religious Movement than are upon any other religious organization or movement in existence. I have been written up by such outstanding magazines as *Time, Newsweek, Magazine Digest, The Editor and Publisher, Advertising Age* and literally scores of other internation-ally known periodicals."[271] Not one of these magazines, Frank pointed out, had ever even "hinted" that he might be "mentally unbalanced." It was critical that Robinson establish himself as both stable and a genius. Exhibit B in his sanity defense entailed the end-of-life plea Senator William Borah is supposed to have made of him. It was an anecdote Frank was given to repeat: "'Doctor Robinson, there is one thing that would make me supremely happy, and that is for me to have the assurance that after I pass along, you will be sitting here at my desk in Washington'...I do not believe the late Senator would have made such a statement had there been the faintest suspicion in his mind that 'that man's crazy'." Robinson then assured his readers that Borah's wish was not merely a one-off: "I have been begged to run for the U.S. Senate, and may do so some day."[272]

Robinson wrote *Blood on the Tail of the Pig* while staying encamped in a "suite of rooms in the Roosevelt Hotel in New York City," where he enjoyed fine dining, room service, and live entertainment by "Guy Lombardo and his magnificent orchestra." Lest he come off as a braggart, Robinson was quick to tamp down any lingering feelings of envy his readers might harbor. "Let none envy the path of the spiritual pioneer," he instructed. "For whatever truth is gleaned from the Realm of the Spirit of God these days, is gleaned at a terrible cost." His path had been one of "bloody sweat," he wrote, filled with grief and "heartaches."[273]

> Many a time have I looked up into the face of God and asked to be taken away from this scene of human misery and horror. For I detest it. I despise it. My whole being revolts at it. Oh God—here in this Roosevelt Hotel in New York, give me strength to write vividly and truly the message you have to bring to this world.[274]

The inspiration for the book's odd title came from a trip Frank had taken from his home in Moscow to Seattle, Washington, to meet with his advertising agency. He was driving, he wrote, "a large Cadillac 75"[275] —the same car his newspaper editor Bill Marineau had used to fetch him from Seattle following his heart attack. It was "a reasonably fast car," Frank allowed. On that particular trip he had come upon a farmer hauling a pig to market. "Usually," Robinson admitted, "I pass everything on the road when making a trip on business. This morning, however, at sight of that truck I deliberately seemed to dawdle along."

When his large chrome bumper drew nearer to the back of the hog truck, Frank noticed that the giant pig was bleeding a great deal from its tail. Stepping on the gas, Robinson whipped into the oncoming lane, pulling alongside the farmer, and signaled for the man to pull over. "I carry a deputy sheriff's badge and I am a regularly commissioned deputy sheriff in Latah County, usually carrying a siren on my car," he boasted. "Although I was out of my jurisdiction, I sirened the car to stop."[276]

According to Frank's account, the farmer was of German descent. When Robinson asked the man about the bleeding pig, the farmer was alleged to have said, "'Vat piznessh is dot off yourss?'" Explaining, the farmer told Frank that the pig had refused to board the truck, so he struck the "'gottdam pick'" in the backside using a board with a nail stuck through it, causing it to bleed.[277]

Robinson was furious that anyone would treat an innocent animal so cruelly, even if it was off to the slaughterhouse. (At this point, the farmer evidently moved on down the road.) "But to torture the animal in that manner made me see red," he wrote. "And then I remembered Europe."[278]

Roadside, Frank was distraught and began speaking directly to God, asking why so much bloodshed and cruelty was allowed. After a short while along the rural highway, amid rolling fields of wheat, Frank climbed back into his limousine, and floored it.

When he caught up to the farmer, though, he noticed something strange. The pig was no longer bleeding. In fact, Frank could spot no trace of blood at all. So he pulled the German farmer over again to inspect the pig, and found that indeed, the wounds were gone all together. "Instinctively, the thought came to me—*'Your sympathy and your uttered word have healed the tail of that pig'*" [italics original].[279]

Although the alleged incident comprises the core narrative in the book, it is not the only one involving miracles and the animal world. After the tale of the pig, Frank introduced his readers to "Ching," the Robinson family dog. Ching, he wrote, slept "in a box in the basement," but often would bound upstairs when he saw Frank's office light burning at night. One night, however, this mundane ritual took a surprising turn. "The door leading from the hall to my study was closed," Frank wrote. After calling for Ching, Robinson watched in amazement as his dog came "*through* both closed doors." Defying all physics, Ching left Frank's office the same way: by passing *through* closed doors.[280]

Robinson's rationale behind these grand stories of miracles in a turbulent world was made clear in this small book. "I did not know how long this amazing experience would last," he added.

> I did know that I wanted it to last forever. But I knew it never would. I knew why the experience had come to me. I knew that God had chosen me to be the medium through which the whole world could be made conscious of the presence of God, even though that Presence is invisible to mortal eyes.[281]

Robinson's posturing as a mystic and prophet took a somewhat inevitable turn when he began writing more declaratively about immortality. He had started drafting a new course of study titled, "The League of Eternal Life," which laid the groundwork for immortality through Frank's pay-to-pray religion. Robinson had started this work in a previously published slim volume titled, *Shall We Know Each Other Beyond the Tomb?* At one point in the booklet, Robinson attempted to disrupt the reader's reality, or his or her sense of reality. "At this point in our little discussion," he instructed, "I want you to remember that the seen things of life are the unreal things, while the unseen forces are the real things."[282] For proof of his assertion, Frank pointed to love as an unseen reality. He cited thoughts as unseen, but real phenomena. And lastly, he called his reader's attention to life itself as something real but unseen. Of course, the ultimate unseen reality, according to Robinson, was the God Law itself.

Circling back to one of his favorite topics—the Cosmic Ray—Robinson handily connected his seen and unseen reality observations to that phenomenon. "Just think of it," he implored. "A dynamic energy which is called an electric energy, permeat[es] the entire universe, through all interstellar space…I wave my hand through these Cosmic Rays. I have looked through a powerful telescope at planets millions of light years away, and I know that even there, exists this phenomenon of nature or phenomenon of God called the Cosmic Ray."[283]

It was important to Robinson that his students and readers understand that the Cosmic Ray was comprised of "electric energy," precisely because of its relevance to the human body, particularly in light of recent strides in cardiology. Pointing to a 1937 article that had appeared in *The American Mercury* magazine, Robinson offered up Dr. Albert S. Hyman's contribution to science as a possible direct connection between the Cosmic Ray (or the God Law) and the human body. Hyman, Frank wrote, "has invented an artificial heart-pacer, and has dramatically demonstrated by this electrical contrivance that THE DEAD CAN BE BROUGHT BACK TO LIFE."[284]

It was Dr. Albert S. Hyman, famed and pioneering cardiologist, who invented the world's first cardiac pacemaker and who gave us its name. Although his breakthrough—which was tested on animals and at least one human—was publicized as early as 1937 and on into the early 1940s, it would not be until the mid-1950s that this device would be fully accepted and integrated into the world of medicine.

"The staggering thing I want to bring to you," Robinson wrote, "is the fact that it is an electrical current, or electrical energy, generated by the heart itself, which causes your heart and mine to beat."[285] It was electricity, and not the whim of an Old Testament God, keeping humans alive. The God Power, in other words, was based in science and had nothing whatever to do with sin or guilt, salvation or redemption. Instead, it was a dynamic force that everyone could access if they only knew how. If they only had Psychiana.

CHAPTER 59

A Mad World

The effect of WWII was felt everywhere and by everyone, and the operation of Psychiana was no exception. A return to Depression-era frugality settled across America as rationing became the law of the land. Nearly all Americans did their part to scrimp, save, and reign in excess use of materials that were needed for the war effort. This climate of rationing may explain, at least in part, the absence of student letters during the war years.

But the Psychiana literary output continued, with Frank generating original content, new slogans, urgent designs, and timely campaigns. Typescripts—some published, some not—reveal Frank's wartime worries and preoccupations. One such typescript was originally titled, "The Discovery of God," but that was crossed out in pencil and replaced with a new handwritten title: "God vs. the Axis."[286] The typescript's content is not just stylistically raw, but is emotionally charged, too. It is a rare instance where we see Frank relatively unfiltered on personal matters. While much of the manuscript is a regurgitation of previous Psychiana materials (e.g., the virgin birth is not an original story, nor is the crucifixion, etc.), the most salient parts deal explicitly with the war and his son, Alf.

> A prophet is not needed to tell us that this world knows nothing whatsoever about God. The broken bodies of our sons, lying suffering in our hospitals which are jammed to the doors, speak very eloquently—they testify silently to this fact. For they have seen the hell-holes of Guadalcanal, and they know God was not in those hell-holes. They looked in suspense to the skies which contain beautiful stars, and from those skies came death—horrible, mutilating death and destruction.
>
> They have seen their buddies—high school boys who played football with them on the home squad—writhing and dying in indescribable agony. They have seen disease emaciate and finally pull down the curtain on lives they knew so well back home. Many of them have seen death… as the torpedo crashed its way into the side of their ship—the ship

which was ploughing its way through the black night, carrying them
to some foreign land, there to kill, maim, and destroy fellow human
beings whom they had never seen before.[287]

Passages like these in "God vs. the Axis" also lend some insight into the
fragility of Frank's state. By 1942, his words had taken on a dark, pessimis-
tic tone while he wrestled with the reality of his son's enlistment. The tenor
of the typescript is a far cry from that of the heroic tales he told in *The
Evening Herald* two decades earlier about the supposed Victoria Crosses
his family members had won in combat. Nor do these words contain the
glibness prevalent in the scattered reminisces of his own spotty military
service. For the first time in his life, war was a reality that carried unfath-
omable consequences for Frank B. Robinson.

Of Alf's current status, Frank wrote, "Now he's an ensign, and God
help the Jap who runs into him in combat. He's scheduled for a Grumman
Avenger at this writing, and I expect before too long he'll be on a carrier,
dropping his 'tin fish' against the side of every Jap ship he can find."[288]

Frank's patriotic confidence in his son's abilities gives way, slightly, to
a more cynical view.

The boy is a typical American boy. Loved by most who know him, he
never was a killer. Left-guard on the local high school football squad,
he took a leading in the annual high school plays. A refined, sweet little
fellow who would not hurt a fly unnecessarily. But he's a killer now.[289]

✦

"A Mad World." That was the red-inked opening for one packet Frank dispatched during those turbulent days. It continued: "Reeking In the Stench
of Human Blood, and Saturated With Misery—Begs For An Answer."[290]

Of course the answer was Psychiana.

The four-page packet contained material of well-trodden Robinson
terrain: "The world has never known the Power of the Spirit of God. Today
it is sweltering in the maze of a welter of systems of theology. Priests,
preachers, rabbis of all brands of theology flounder round in a maze of
superstitions of their own creating, and the more they flounder, the deeper
into the mire they go."[291]

While physical copies of student letters are non-existent from the
war years, plenty of testimonial excerpts show up in an array of Psychiana
promotional materials, circulars, and packets like "A Mad World." In this
packet, one such testimonial from a man—known only as "T.R.F." of

Baltimore—told the story of unemployment, and having to move his wife and baby in with his parents on account of having no income. "Things were getting worse," he wrote. "One day I read your ad in our Baltimore papers, and decided to enroll. To do this, I had to borrow the money from the few friends I had at the time. My first Lessons convinced me I had the key. My folks frowned up it at first, but gradually they fell in line." Dated June 7, 1942, the testimonial reports that T.R.F. went from living with his parents to living in a "modern apartment," after becoming a licensed pilot and working in an airplane factory.[292]

Another from August 1942, attributed to "F.I." of Jacksonville, Florida, appears under a red-lettered banner reading, "God Cures Cancer Very Easily."

I WROTE YOU LAST WINTER ON BEHALF OF A FRIEND WHO HAD CANCER, AND KNOW YOU WILL BE DELIGHTED TO HEAR THAT HE HAS COMPLETELY RECOVERED, CONSIDERED A MIRACLE BECAUSE THE DOCTORS HAD GIVEN HIM A VERY SHORT TIME TO LIVE, BUT NOW CONSIDER THAT HE IS COMPLETELY WELL.[293]

Tellingly, Frank was as quick to advertise this miracle-cure story as he was to distance himself from it by way of what appears to be a disclaimer. "Note: There is nothing we can do except point to the Power of the Spirit of God, which can cause any cancer to disappear. The Power that created the human body, is abundantly able to heal it."[294]

Psychiana literature in the early days of World War II largely fell into two campaigns: inward-facing messaging, and outward-facing messaging. In the former, the literature was preoccupied with reaffirmation and retention of students and fees. The latter campaign focused more on recruitment, outreach, and growth. The packet, "A Mad World," for instance, falls into the former campaign, using testimonials to reassure students that the God Power is real and to encourage them to stay the course. The latter campaign, comprised primarily of strategically placed advertisements, blended Frank's success story, purported powers of prophecy, and wartime themes, making for strange and tonally discordant copy.

Even as Frank continued his robust literary and advertising output, and tried to expand the Psychiana footprint (he bought another building in downtown Moscow in early 1943), he was still struggling. "World War II brought with it major life-changes," Alf later observed. "The business

Advertisement from 1942 claiming that Frank had predicted the bombing of Pearl Harbor. University of Idaho Special Collections.

world struggled to cope with material and labor shortages...I feel at this time, a gradual retrenching of Psychiana operations was taking place," he added. "Probably because of Dad's worsening physical condition. Another factor may have been the war and its restrictions upon goods and services for the private sector."[295]

If ever there was a perceptible wobble in Frank's Movement, this time may have been it.

Part V
REQUIEM FOR A PROPHET
1946–1952

CHAPTER 60
Psychiana in the Nuclear Age

Frank Robinson (right) with governor of New York and then presidential candidate
Tom Dewey (left) with unidentified pressman in the middle, 1943. University of
Idaho Special Collections.

After the United States dropped atomic bombs on Hiroshima and
Nagasaki in 1945, the grim possibility of nuclear annihilation at the
hands of a bad actor haunted everyone's thoughts worldwide. While Russia
was racing to become a nuclear power, fears of espionage abounded, even as
world leaders clamored to impose controls on this new weapon that could
end the human race. At the same time, bureaucrats and technocrats were
trying to sell atomic energy as a marvel of modernity, something to have
faith in rather than to fear. "Atomic Energy May Be Future Rainmaker,"
read one headline in the *Iowa Press Citizen*. "Successful experiments both
in the United States and Australia have proved that both rain and snow

can be created artificially under proper atmospheric conditions."[1]

For Frank Robinson, the spectacle of atomic energy fit neatly in his bailiwick. Not only was it literally "an invisible power" and clear evidence of "the God Law," but it was that rare phenomenon that allowed Robinson to play the Janus-like role of fear-monger and savior, both of which were good for a business like Psychiana.

World war and the atomic age induced Robinson to disseminate a new wave of circulars capitalizing on these bipolarities. Advertised under the title of "The New Psychiana," one red and black ink flyer was eye-catching for its bold lettering, if not for its content.

THIS CIVILIZATION IS DOOMED.

THE NEXT WAR WILL BE AN ATOMIC WAR. FEW WILL SURVIVE...THIS MAY BE YOUR LAST CHANCE TO LEARN OF THE ACTUAL POWER OF GOD. DO NOT LET IT SLIP BY...LET'S NOT FOOL OURSELVES. IT IS COMING.[2]

The reverse side of the flyer read, "GET READY. THIS IS GOOD NEWS." The Psychiana flyer then attempted to synthesize these whipsaw claims—a doomed planet on one hand, and good news on the other—in an apocalyptic prediction.

> But on the wreck of this civilization there will rise a very much grander [sic] structure. There will be no illness, no pain, no labor, no toil, no misery in that new civilization, but all shall live FOR EVER [sic] WITH THE GREAT SPIRIT WHICH IS GOD.[3]

Despite lingering fears of atomic war, Americans were by and large optimistic on the heels of World War II. A December 1946 *Fortune Magazine* poll found that this optimism held true across race, age, and class lines as well. "Nearly seventy men out of every hundred think they have better opportunities than their fathers had...Men between 17 and 25 are considerably more optimistic about their own chances than are men over 40... Negroes, most significantly, are more optimistic about their own opportunities."[4]

While this was good news for America, it was bad news for Psychiana. The upbeat attitude of the masses helps explain Robinson's hard turn toward end-of-times language, imagery, tones, and themes in his ads and writing. After all, American self-help relied on a paying consumer base

Florence Robinson and family dog Ching, who allegedly walked through solid doors, c. 1942. University of Idaho Special Collections.

that needed—or perceived that they needed—help. Of course, Psychiana's utopian promises of a pain-free and misery-free existence would effectively nullify the efficacy of Robinson's Movement all together, but that promise was the carrot, with fear being the stick of this recent campaign.

One of the more interesting images that Robinson began using in the late 1940s to convey this apocalyptic forecast was a volcano. Frank had touched briefly on the image of the volcano—that ultimate icon of dormant doom and impending disaster—as early as 1932 in Lesson 5 ("This old world is trembling, even as I write this, on the brink of a volcano. We do not know at what moment it will blow us into a terrible conflagration"), but he did not fully seize upon the image and its power until after the war.[5] One of the first of these flyers took the image a step further, connecting the volcano with atomic weapons.

WHEN THE VOLCANO ERUPTS
CHANCES ARE YOU WILL GO WITH IT

Yes—the chances are that out of the darkness of the night, shocking, horrifying, terrible death, instant death will descend without warning upon this beloved country of ours…A recently returned ambassador to Russia made the statement a few days ago that if Russia had the atom-bomb she would have dropped it on America long ago. But there is no proof that this God-hating nation has not the atom-bomb.[6]

Another flyer was far more visually arresting, showing an illustration of the planet Earth sitting atop a volcano. "This World is Sitting on Top of a Volcano. It May Erupt Momentarily." Written across the volcano's slope are the words, "The Atom-Bomb | Fission of the Cosmic Ray | Poison Gas | Bacteriological Warfare." Robinson's use of the volcano as an image and metaphor was not arbitrary. He liked it so much that he had used it regularly over the previous three-year period. In a workplace memo, Frank gave one of his managers specific directions relating to that campaign. "If I recall correctly," Frank wrote, "There is a mailing to go to the [Psychiana] grads after the old names have been circularized by the VOLCANO circular...It will go to the 1944-5-6 names exactly as the VOLCANO did."[7]

It is notable, perhaps, that Robinson was not the only self-help religious leader to use the volcano as a metaphor. L. Ron Hubbard would go on to use it as a central piece of his own Church of Scientology movement. (The cover of his 1950 book *Dianetics* features a volcano, for instance.)

On the one hand, Robinson was pushing out large text quotes like "INSIDE OF FIVE YEARS, 95% OF THE AMERICAN PEOPLE WILL BE DESTROYED BY THE ATOM BOMB,"[8] while on the other, he promoted counterintuitive messages such as "SCIENCE SAYS THAT THE VALUE OF THE ENERGY IN YOUR BODY IS MORE THAN 96 BILLION DOLLARS." The latter quote appears inside of a mushroom cloud on a widely distributed flyer. "The above is a staggering statement," the flyer continued, "but at long last the human race, through the discovery of atomic energy and atomic radio-activity, is enabled to come closer to the answer of the God problem than ever before."[9]

These contradictory campaigns ultimately showed Robinson's strategic uncertainty in an uncertain time. As with most Americans, Frank Robinson's view on the atomic age vacillated wildly from salvation to annihilation. Unsure of which direction the winds were blowing on the matter, he directed his advertising in both directions, waiting to see, it seems, which got traction.

CHAPTER 61

The Gathering Storm

It was in his office in the Chrysler Building in New York that Edward L. Greene, general manager of the Better Business Bureau, first became aware of Psychiana and its prophet's promises. It was 1947. Greene was two years' Robinson's senior, and had been nationally known as a one-time All-American football star. The New Haven, Connecticut, native made a name for himself at the University of Pennsylvania as both student and athlete, and later became head football coach at the University of North Carolina and the North Carolina College of Agriculture and Mechanic Arts (now North Carolina State University).[10]

With a mind for business, a nose for truth, and the investigative prowess of a detective, Greene could not have come of age—professionally speaking—at a better time. In 1911, just after he finished college, an American consortium of advertising organizations formed a commission with a singular charge: "Truth in Advertising." This charge and the committee that carried it out eventually evolved into the National Vigilance Committee. In 1925, however, when fraudulent stocks and bonds were flooding the market, the committee was reconfigured into the National Better Business Bureau, and entrusted to the leadership of Edward L. Greene. Known in the industry as "Big Ed," Greene had made a name for himself in the Cleveland branch with his codifying credo, "Before You Invest, Investigate," making him the clear leader of the new watchdog group.[11]

As general manager of the Better Business Bureau, Greene had battled an array of businesses, including Lucky Strike Cigarettes and the American Cigar Company, and worked tirelessly to keep close watch on suspicious operations.[12] And it was in this role that Greene quickly came to see Psychiana and its leader as a racket and racketeer, and immediately launched a sweeping investigation.

First, Greene put out a bulletin to the bureau branches to watch for any and all Psychiana advertisements. Among others, he specifically contacted

341

Homer McEldowney of the Detroit branch, Lyle Janz of the Portland, Oregon office, and Bob West of the Tacoma, Washington office.[13] Green's team dispatched a series of letters to their respective media outlets, dissuading them from running subsequent advertisements from Frank Robinson's self-help religion.

A few weeks later, Robinson received word through an employee that *The Detroit News* had, on counsel from the Better Business Bureau, declined to run a Psychiana advertisement. Robinson could not afford to be blocked, and being shut out of such a large media market was both insulting and injurious. Soon it became clear to Robinson and those in Psychiana's advertising department that *The Detroit News* rebuff was not merely an isolated event. More and more newspapers and magazines were discontinuing current Psychiana ads or refusing to run new ones.

In a fiery six-page letter to Edward Greene, Robinson insisted that the Better Business Bureau was a "SUBVERSIVE UN-AMERICAN ORGANIZATION [THAT] HAS ATTEMPTED TO SUPPRESS RELIGION IN THE UNITED STATES, THE PSYCHIANA RELIGION TO BE EXACT." Robinson stormed on—

> If all the fraud and dishonesty you have widely proclaimed has really been going on—if we are so bad that our advertising should not be allowed to appear in newspapers and magazines, is not our Federal Government being very lax, Mr. Greene? We have operated exclusively by mail for about twenty years, and neither you nor anyone else has been able to give to any government agency the slightest scintilla of evidence that there is either dishonesty or fraud connected with us.[14]

Robinson dared Greene to bring the matter before a federal court where, he assured Greene, the case would be seen as one of religious persecution. "But you won't do that—will you, Mr. Greene?" He wrote. "You are afraid to. Besides, your attorneys won't let you, will they Mr. Greene?"[15]

In response, Greene only stepped up his efforts. He demanded that Robinson send him copies of Psychiana's tax-exempt records, which Robinson refused to do. To complicate matters even more for Frank, Greene alerted the Securities and Exchange Commission to Psychiana's advertisements selling shares in the "non-profit" religion, and, as Frank's son, Alf put it, the SEC was "breathing down dad's neck." At the same time, a Mr. McIntyre from the Internal Revenue Service was holed up in the Psychiana Headquarters, auditing their books.[16]

Once again, Frank felt surrounded.

———————◆———————

By early spring of 1948, Robinson was encumbered with health problems and pending investigations, so he decided to take a month-long vacation at the expansive and palatial Mission Inn in Riverside, California. He was run-down and paunchy. He needed to clear his head so he could get back to the work. He had just brokered what would be Psychiana's final real-estate deal, purchasing an entire city block in Moscow, near the post office. Frank "wished for a large Psychiana complex," something akin to what he had envisioned in Hollywood, Alf later recalled.[17]

Frank was able to take such a long vacation because Alfred, who had by this point finished his degree at Stanford, had moved back to Moscow. "Dad was ill—more ill than not in '47 and '48, and the reason we trekked back to the town of our youth," Alf recalled. It was, he and Annette reasoned, "a good place to raise kids." In Moscow, you did not "need to lock the house or car doors."[18] In what he described as "flow writing," a technique of journaling he learned from counseling later in life, Alf added a few more details about their moving back. "To help Dad with Psychiana—my duty—then to enter the cultural parade to have house on block, have job, and raise kids—and it would all work out. It didn't."[19]

Making that "unilateral decision to return to Moscow and become active in Psychiana," Alf continued, "became the third major mistake of my life and was to greatly inhibit my individuation or maturation process in the years following."[20]

Alfred was the closest thing Frank had to a successor, but his fidelity to the Movement was based entirely on a passing interest and familial obligation. Still, he played the part, even though it meant being absent from his own family. "Did all I could to keep busy so I wouldn't have to relate to my family," he confessed. He joined all the right groups, too. "Boy, could I join! The Masonic Lodge, service clubs, airport board—all in the name of 'PR' for Psychiana and the newspaper."[21]

When Robinson returned to Moscow from his vacation at the Mission Inn Resort, he felt refreshed and driven, although lingering health problems nagged at him.

On an unremarkable warm summer morning in 1948, Frank Robinson, sixty-two, gaunt-faced and wispy-haired, woke with a lump in his chest. Pearl insisted he have it looked at. Frank refused, dressed for the day, and

Robinson family c. 1948, shortly before Frank's death. From left: Florence, Alf, Pearl, and Frank. University of Idaho Special Collections.

made a pot of black coffee. That afternoon, he received a phone call from Professor Charles Braden at Northwestern University. Dr. Braden, who had been writing a book on cults in America, wanted Frank to pay a visit to Chicago for an interview before he finalized his chapter on Psychiana. Robinson agreed, booking his train ticket to Chicago. The interview, however, was "terminated," as Alfred put it. Frank "began suffering a great deal of pain in [his] Chicago hotel." Pearl asked Alfred to fly to Chicago and bring his father home. "As we were returning on the train," Alfred recalled, "Dad may have been questioning his faith." Perhaps sensing his own mortality, Frank turned to Alfred and said, "'There *must* be a God, a law which I can draw upon to lick this physical problem.'"[22]

Frank's emphatic "must" alarmed Alfred. "It was the first time I had heard him make such a statement."

On the evening of October 13, 1948, Frank was at home with Pearl, Forence, and Alfred, when he began hemorrhaging blood out of his mouth. Panicked, Pearl telephoned Dr. Wilson at once. The doctor arrived within ten minutes and looked him over thoroughly. He insisted that Frank undergo an X-ray the following morning, an order Frank evidently refused. Instead, he lay in bed drifting in and out of consciousness. Six days later, just after noon, Dr. Frank B. Robinson died. He was sixty-two.

Pearl called long-time family friend Sophia Marineau, who arrived and took over details. She alerted Dr. Wilson. Sophia contacted the funeral home. She saw to it, in other words, that Pearl need only to sit by her Robbie's bedside. Alf also stepped in to help, although he sought to "cover up [his] grief" by "coldly help[ing] mother with all the arrangements."[23]

Alf then drove to the Psychiana Headquarters to alert the staff. "When I met E.J. Kass, our auditor, and the girls in the mailing department, I simply said, 'Dad died about an hour ago.'" On hearing this announcement, Mr. McIntyre, the IRS investigator, "quietly gathered his papers together and departed." Everyone was stunned, and fell silent. Marjorie, Frank's personal secretary, sobbed.[24]

In the weeks and months following Frank's death, Pearl and Alfred found themselves in an increasingly awkward situation. Everyone knew that, with the death of the Mail-Order Prophet, the death of his Movement could not be far behind. Alfred and Pearl's obligations were to their community and their employees, not necessarily to the students. As for their own welfare, their share in the newspaper was sufficient income to live on.

The business of Psychiana marched on, although it took on a wooden, rote feel, as evidenced in the literature and student responses. Alf assumed the role of responding to the student letters himself, relying almost exclusively on the form letter and its stock language. The Psychiana staff repackaged much of Frank's original work, and shipped it out in new containers, one in magazine format titled, *The Way*, and another in newsletter form, titled *The Psychiana Bulletin*. To fill these publications and give them a fresh feel, Alf invited theologians sympathetic to—but not members of—Psychiana to contribute articles that loosely fit beneath the umbrella of the God Power.

While Alf was busy with Psychiana and serving on the board of directors for the newspaper (then called *The Idahonian*), as well as participating on a number of other committees and organizations, his home life was spiraling out of control. His wife Annette struggled with prescription drug and alcohol addiction. Alf became depressed. Tensions were rising among the rank and file of *The Idahonian*, causing some friction between the Marineaus and the Robinsons, who had been friends ever since Frank bought the printing press and moved it to Moscow from Elk River.

Eventually, it all became too much.

On October 30, 1952, four years after Frank's death, Pearl and Alfred made a public statement. In an article titled, "Mounting Costs Cited as 'Psychiana' Ends Activities," they stated the following: "We regret to announce the suspension of work of the Psychiana Movement."[25] They cited increased postal rates and a "heavy payroll" as the leading factors for the ultimate dissolution.

One month later, *Newsweek* reported "The Death of Psychiana." Although Alfred had stated that he hoped the Movement would continue on its own, *Newsweek* predicted rightly that, "without the dynamic personality of the founder or the continuing spreading of his word by mail, Psychiana seemed to be doomed to death."[26] Alf and Pearl "closed the doors," he later wrote, with no desire or motivation to continue, and no regrets."

In the end, even the God Law could not save Psychiana.

Florence, who had stayed out of the family business affairs, had by this point married her high school sweetheart, Raoul Ashby, a soon-to-be military professor and high-ranking Army officer. His career uprooted the couple from Moscow, eventually landing them in Wichita Falls, Texas. Alf and Annette eventually divorced, and even Pearl left the confines of Moscow for Monterey, California, where, at seventy-one, she remarried. In her final years, she had moved in with Florence and Raoul in Texas, where she eventually died in 1982.

It was if Frank had been the rock against which everyone in his orbit had either hardened or broke, and now he was gone.

Epilogue:
"A Fortune to Share with the World"

May 12, 1978
Toledo, Ohio

From Apartment 609 in the dilapidated six-story brick Kenmore Manor, Paul Harsch scribbled off another in a series of letters to Moscow, Idaho's resident historian, Keith Petersen. Keith was new on the job as the director of the Latah County Historical Society, and one of his side projects in those days concerned gathering all existing materials related to a strange religion started by Frank B. Robinson. Because the Robinson family had donated all of Frank's materials to the University of Idaho, with the stipulation that they remain sealed for twenty-five years after his death, few materials existed outside of the university vault. But Paul Harsch had been studying Psychiana, he wrote, "for 25 years," and had collected a full set of Frank's Lessons. He was happy to make copies for Petersen's archive. Petersen was thrilled of course, but what he did not know was that Paul Harsch had mistaken Petersen's archival work for an interest in reviving Psychiana.[27]

Harsch first came across Robinson's work, he wrote, by "chancing upon three bound volumes of PSYCHIANA in the Detroit Public Library." The brother of Joseph C. Harsch, the famed *Christian Science Monitor* journalist,[28] Paul had grown up as a Christian Scientist in Toledo, following the faith, he wrote, "entirely all my life until one specific, dire need was not satisfied." While he was vague about what that need was, he was clear that Psychiana fulfilled it.

But it was on that rainy and blustery May evening, that Paul—aged seventy-two—made a life-changing decision. He was going to move to Moscow, Idaho, and assist Petersen in the re-launch of Psychiana. "Dear Latah County (ALL of you)," Paul wrote, "Since you have in Legacy of

347

Frank B. Robinson a fortune to share with the world, I'm casting my lot in with you."[29]

When Keith Petersen received the scribbled note, he became alarmed. On May 16, 1978, the young historian rolled a sheet of typing paper into his typewriter and carefully wrote his reply. "I just received your letter explaining that you are planning to move to Moscow," he typed. "Such a move seems to me to be a rather drastic and disruptive action," he warned, "and should not be undertaken without careful thought and planning. I hope we have not misled you into believing that any semblance of the Psychiana movement still exists in this area. It most definitely does not... In no way am I personally, or is the Historical Society, attempting to revive the Psychiana movement...I should further add that, if you are interested in reviving this religion, Moscow is probably the worst place to begin from. The feeling here is generally very negative, and you could no doubt accomplish more where you are presently."[30]

Paul was unfazed. "Hope you've overcome the shock of reading my late-threat to Latah County of invading your fair little city," he replied. "Surely that rich, productive [area] can afford to republish Psychiana in one form or another."[31] His "invasion" of Moscow, he noted, "may be a year or so away—if that's a relief to any of those proud Moscovites." After all, he had to plan. "In leaving my apartment here in Toledo," Harsch wrote, "I must dispose of everything possible."[32]

In the late 1970s, it was customary for the director of the Latah County Historical Society to live in the McConnell Mansion, a Victorian home owned and maintained by the society. Keith was relaxing one evening in the mansion after work. It had been a year since his curt exchange with Paul Harsch, and Petersen had all but forgotten Harsch and his threat to move to Moscow. Then the doorbell rang. When he opened the door, an elderly man stood before him. It was Paul. He was driving, Keith recalled, a station wagon covered with slogans that read "God-Guides, Unlimited." When Petersen made it absolutely clear to Paul that he would play no part in a revival, Paul got into his station wagon, and drove away. The two never spoke again.

While Paul's hopes for a Psychiana revival may have been dashed, he stayed true to his faith. His nephew, Jon, remembered clearly Paul's devotion to Psychiana. "I was certainly aware that Uncle Paul was a passionate follower of Frank Robinson," he wrote.[33]

In the years after Psychiana's demise, the faithful few tried, like Paul Harsch, to advance their religion in various ways. Mrs. Orrin Kurth of Chippewa Falls, Wisconsin, for instance, felt empowered to freelance, taking out an ad in her local paper. "What 'Psychiana' Teaches," it read. "All men are living reflections of God. The invisible life Impulse, which gives you the power to move, think, work, and live, is in essence the very same life as the life of God."[34] A man in Jacksonville, Illinois, placed an ad in his paper stating, simply, "Psychiana members, please call or write Wilford Smith, Illinois Hotel."[35] In the *Los Angeles Times*, there appeared another ad, reading, "WANT PSYCHIANA lessons 1 thru 6 & 38 thru 40. Pls. wr. Raymond Hill."[36] In March of 1978, Baltimore's *Evening Sun* published a brief notice, "WANTED 'Wealth & Achievement Programs' by Herb Jahn Also Psychiana Lessons by Frank B. Robinson."[37] Even today, someone has uploaded Robinson's Lessons to YouTube and there is a website devoted to his following.

These individuals were just a few of the thousands whose self-help faith lived beyond the life of their teacher, and who knew the power of belief, no matter the optics, facts, or criticism. For it was the power of belief that had shepherded them through the good times as well as the bad.

Acknowledgments

A project of this scope is not possible without the help, advice, and encouragement from a vast network of trusted readers, friends, associates, good Samaritans, and family members. But in particular, I need to thank my wife, Kelli, and children, Mason and Madeline, for their ironclad faith in this story. And to my parents, who never lost faith, I say thanks. I would also like to thank a number of folks who helped guide and shape the narrative along the way including Beth Deweese, Keith Petersen, Ben George, and Matt McGowan. Most of all, I have to thank my editor, Linda Bathgate, who had a vision for the story from the outset, and whose editorial guidance has made me sound so much smarter than I actually am. And to Caryn Lawton and everyone else at WSU Press, I owe a great debt of gratitude.

Numerous are the groups, organizations, and individuals who provided resources, time, and valuable assistance: Rick Ardinger and the Idaho Humanities Council for providing a vital and generous grant early in the stages of my research; the University of Idaho for granting much needed funds and resources; Zachary Wnek at the Latah County Historical Society; Gregory Schmidt at the National Archives at Kansas City; Brita Merkel and Ken House at the National Archives at Seattle; Bill Manny at Idaho Public Television; Chris Robinson for his insights into the Robinson family dynamic; Glenda Hawley for her recollections of the Psychiana operations; Jon and Paul Harsch; Barbara Wolff at the Albert Einstein Archives, Hebrew University, Jerusalem; Joanna Friel at the Chislehurst Society (UK); Marie-Delphine Martellière at the Centre d'Études Alexandrines (Egypt); Chewikar Abdel Aziz at the University of Alexandria (Egypt); Michael Haag; John Black for his valuable online Psychiana resources; Chuck Simmons; Becker J. Gutsch; Dan McCaffery; Lynn McCreight; Agnes Rivers-Moore, Hanover Public Library, Hanover, Ontario; Bill Doucet at the *Cambridge Times* (Canada); Susan R. Petersen at the Latah County Clerk's office; Olivia Ma; David Menary; Cecelia Carter Smith; Dan Crandall; Dusty Fleener; Edith Atkins; Michael Rebman at the Artesia Museum and Historical Center (New Mexico); Randy Ema for his help identifying Robinson's Duesenberg; the staff at the University of Idaho Library, but especially Jesse Thomas, Julie Monroe, and Amy Thompson; as well as the staff at Washington State University's Holland & Terrell Library. Finally, I'd like to thank my friends and colleagues at Washington State University whose support I depend upon more than they know.

Appendix

Psychiana Lessons followed more or less the same formula with a prefatory letter, the primary text of the Lesson, usually ending with "Points to Remember" and/or "Examination Questions." While revised and expanded over time, the first run of Lessons are essentially Psychiana's blueprints, offering the surest insight into Frank's teachings. Core excerpts from those Lessons are as follows:

Lesson 1   This course of instruction is entirely different from anything ever put into print before. Probably that is the reason for its remarkable success.
        It is advisable, if you possibly can, to have some definite hour and definite place in which you can give full attention to these studies without interruption from the outside.[1]

Lesson 2   Any God that you need to be afraid of, is no God for you…Most of that "fear" proposition, however, is a relic of the dark ages, and is not believed in any more.[2]
        Close your eyes. There always is, in every man's closed eyes, a certain area which, when you learn how to find it, is the very thin veil between you and the God Law of the Universe…You will not have so much trouble in finding that "bright spot" or "white spot."[3]

Lesson 3   So keep an expectant attitude—expect the best—and be ready for it when it comes. Don't do these exercises nor go ahead with this course unless you PREPARE YOURSELF TO EXPECT, AND REALLY DO EXPECT BETTER THINGS TO COME TO PASS IN YOUR LIFE.[4]

Lesson 4   I am writing for the man on the street—the man who needs [this] most. I want THAT fellow man to grasp what I am talking about.[5]
        Had the church left [Christ] as a man, as HE claimed to be, and not tacked onto Him the nonsensical resurrection from the dead, and the equally nonsensical and unprovable ascension into a place called heaven, what a difference it would have made…By introducing a story that He was God, and therefore possessing a power which no one else can possess, they just simply took Him away out of reach of the common folks like you and me, and placed Him on a pedestal where He never belonged.[6]

Lesson 5   Throughout all this marvelous interstellar space, and surrounding all these mighty suns and stars and planets, there is, like a belt of living electricity, the famous "cosmic ray."[7]

Lesson 6   [Repeat these affirmations]: I AM MORE AND MORE SUCCESSFUL—I AM MORE AND MORE SUCCESSFUL.
        THE LIVING GOD IS MAKING ME WHOLE. THE LIVING GOD IS MAKING ME WHOLE.[8]

Lesson 7　POINTS TO REMEMBER:

1. There is in existence throughout the ether, a thinking substance which is spiritual in its essence.

2. Your thoughts are the things that draw from this Spiritual Realm the things you need.

3. Don't limit the power of the God-Law. Expect great things—then go after them.[9]

Lesson 8　I think it might be interesting however to tell you the names of a few of the "world's crucified Christs," and I know of no better book to quote than the wonderful volume written by Kersey Graves [*The World's Sixteen Crucified Saviors*, 1875.] So I quote the names of these saviors:

"Krishna of India was supernaturally born and crucified in 1200 B.C.

Sakia the Hindoo [sic] 'god' was crucified in 600 B.C.

Thammuz of Syria was crucified in 1160 B.C.

Wittoba was crucified in 552 B.C.

Iao was crucified in 622 B.C.

Hesus of the Celtic Druids was crucified in 834 B.C.

Quexalcote of Mexico was crucified in 587 B.C.

Quirinus of Rome was crucified in 506 B.C.

Indra of Thibet [sic] was crucified in 725 B.C.

Alcestos was crucified in 600 B.C.

Atys of Phrygia was crucified in 1170 B.C.

Crite of the Chaldeans was crucified in 1200 B.C.

Bali of Orissa was crucified in 725 B.C.

Mithra of Persia was crucified in 600 B.C."

I do not mention these names to get into any religious controversy at all...but I do mention them in proof of my statement that Christ was not the only "world savior" to be crucified—he was the most recent.[10]

Lesson 9　Now it must be a fact, that a universal GOD must be a GOD who appeals to ALL NATIONS AND RACES, and one who CAN BE UNDERSTOOD BY THEM ALL. This teaching that only ONE system of religion has the truth and all the rest are damned is an utterly false teaching, and the very brand of falsity is stamped on it by such a teaching.[11]

Lesson 10　The power behind it all .. IS A LAW OF ABSOLUTE CONFIDENCE.

FIRST: Confidence in the Law itself

SECOND: Confidence in one's self to use the LAW.

THIRD: Confidence in one's fellow men and women.

That will bring the Law into play. That will make you an overwhelming victor in life—and don't you forget it brother or sister.[12]

Lesson 11　And it is my contention that no really true religion can have its basis in fear of anyone or anything. Yet they all have.[13]

Lesson 12   No prayer of any kind ever enters into my life—there is no need of it. My knees are never bent at the bedside. That would be idolatry and pagan superstition. For I know that the God-Law knows better than I know the thing for which I am best suited. And I know also that there is absolutely no need for me to beg and implore God to do this for me, or that for me. I KNOW A FAR BETTER WAY. I KNOW THAT GOD IS.[14]

Lesson 13   As a matter of fact there is far more evidence that Plato lived than there is that Christ lived. However—I am not questioning His birth at all, for history gives us enough indirect evidence that a person called Jesus Christ probably lived on earth. Where I differ with "supernaturally-revealed" religion is on the point of His "immaculate birth," His "resurrection" and other impossible things attributed Him. Those who gave us these pagan yarns little knew the harm they were doing to humanity when they gave them.[15]

Lesson 14   The Spiritual Law cannot operate to the full as long as death reigns supreme on earth. It was NOT meant that it should so reign, and beloved student, hear me well when I say to you that THE FULL UNDERSTANDING OF THE SPIRITUAL LAW OF GOD WILL ABSOLUTELY BANISH DEATH.[16]

Lesson 15   Any religion, whether it be "orthodox" or whether it be "psychological" must be a religion pure in intent. It must teach a PURE God, or a PURE God-Law. Hence, I should be untrue to both you and myself if I did not call your attention also to the finer things of life as well as the material things.[17]

Lesson 16   Too many of us look upon the good things of life as the exceptions whereas they should be the natural things. It is natural—divinely natural—for you to have a strong physical body. It is also divinely natural for you to be successful in everything you undertake. It is divinely natural for you to be supremely happy.[18]

Lesson 17   Those who want to be successful in life will go chasing this rainbow and that rainbow. They will search here and they will search there. They will buy this theory and they will buy that theory. They will follow every psychological faker that comes along…Some charlatan or other comes along, and these good earnest souls are to be found following in the band wagon.[19]

Lesson 18   You will find as you progress in this Realm of God that the master key which unlocks all the other locks in this great mansion may be called the KEY OF PEACE. Perhaps TRUST would be a better name for it.[20]

Lesson 19   The poverty which perhaps has dogged your footsteps is not due to the power of "Satan" or anything on that order. It is due but to the ABSENCE of the God-Law in your own life. Many people write and tell me about the "power" of "sin," and the "power" of "Satan"…THERE IS NO POWER IN THE UNIVERSE OTHER THAN THE POWER OF THE LIVING GOD-LAW.[21]

Lesson 20   EXAMINATION QUESTIONS FROM LESSON 20

      … What would be the consequence if the presence of the God-Law were to be, even for one instant, removed from this world?

      … What is a light year?

      … Compare the penetrating force of the Cosmic Ray with that of the Gamma Ray, which ranks next to the Cosmic?[22]

NOTES AND SOURCES

Prologue

1. It is difficult to overstate just how over-the-top this car was for the period in general, much less for a small town in Idaho. At a time when a new sedan cost close to $600, the Duesenberg sold for about $13,500 or more. Curious as to the fate of Robinson's "Duesy," I called Randy Ema, the world's foremost expert on Duesenbergs, to see if I might track it down. Ema, who has restored Duesenbergs for Jay Leno, knew the exact car I was asking about. "He sold it to Mae West," he said. This squared with my own research, which also showed that West then sold it to her butler for $500, who later sold it to a psychiatrist named Donald Vessley in Tampa.

2. This was a trope Robinson used often in his media releases. See, for instance, *Psychiana Quarterly*, "The Persecution," September 1936, or "Govern't Not Persecuting," *The Latah Journal* (undated). It is important to note that *The Latah Journal*, a small newspaper printed at the time in Deary, Idaho, was actively antagonistic toward Frank Robinson and Psychiana.

3. "Death of Psychiana," *Newsweek*, November 24, 1952. Frank Bruce Robinson Papers, 1929–1951, University of Idaho Library Special Collections and Archives (hereafter Robinson Papers, UI), Box 6, Folder "Magazine Articles."

4. "Court Jammed as Defendant Repeats Story," unattributed clipping. Psychiana Archives, Box 1, File 3, Latah County Historical Society, Moscow, ID.

5. Background on Edward Robertson is gleaned from a number of sources including "Captain Robertson is Commander," *Spokane Chronicle*, February 6, 1919, 2; WWII draft registration card; "E.W. Robertson, Former Resident, Dies in Spokane," *State Times Advocate*, Baton Rouge, LA, May 29, 1961, 3; the application for Robertson's headstone (June 26, 1961) proved useful; and Frank Robinson's own recollections which, among other things, provides some personal color and characterization of Robertson's southern accent (i.e., "Gennelmen of the joowy... ah've been called most everything a lawyer can be called"), *The Strange Autobiography of Frank B. Robinson*, Metropolitan Press, Portland, OR, 1941, 255.

6. Alfred Robinson, "A Family Trilogy, Book II: Frank Bruce Robinson," unpublished manuscript, 100–102, Latah County Historical Society. A striking revelation in my early research was that Frank's son, Alfred, was as puzzled by the real story of his father as everyone else who knew or knew of him. That Alfred loved his father is without question. But it is also fair to say that their relationship was complicated, and part of that complication, I think, had to do with Frank's unknowableness.

7. Ibid., 109.

8. Pearl Robinson, "Statement by Mrs. Robinson," *The Strange Autobiography of Frank B. Robinson*, 13.

CHAPTER 1 No Man Knew His History

1. Copy of birth certificate in Alfred Robinson, Exhibits, "A Family Trilogy, Book II," author's private collection.

2. Family background taken from the exhaustive research done by Alfred Robinson for his three-volume family history.

3. Frank Robinson (hereafter FBR), *The Strange Autobiography*, 31.

4. Alfred Robinson, "A Family Trilogy, Book I: John Henry Robinson." Untitled clipping, *Halifax Courier*, 1873.

5. FBR, *The Strange Autobiography*, 38.

6. Arthur Robinson to Frank Robinson, November 8, 1938, 2. Latah County Historical Society.

7. Fawn Brodie, *No Man Knows My History: The Life of Joseph Smith* (New York: Vintage Books, 1995), vii.

8. Alfred Robinson, "Death of Mrs. J.H. Robinson," *Halifax Courier*, February 13, 1897; "A Family Trilogy, Book I," 58.

9. FBR, *The Strange Autobiography*, 39.

10. Alfred Robinson, A Haigh Family Picture Taken Near the Time of Marriage, "A Family Trilogy, Book I."

11. FBR, *The Strange Autobiography*, 41.

12. Ibid.

13. Ibid., 42.

14. Archibald S. Hurd, "How Blue-Jackets are Trained," *The Windsor Magazine*, 321–328.

15. Frank Bruce Robinson Royal Navy Discharge record, Catalogue record ADM/188/381, Image Reference 331, British National Archives.

16. FBR, *The Strange Autobiography*, 43.

17. FBR, *The Strange Autobiography*, 44.

18. John Pry Royal Navy, Catalogue record ADM/188/381, Image Reference 81, British National Archives.

19. Royal Navy Discharge record.

20. "Dr. Robinson's Brother Says Psychiana Is a Fake," *The Latah Journal* (Deary, ID), August 12, 1937, Latah County Historical Society.

21. House of Commons, Health, Minutes of Evidence, https://publications.parliament.uk/pa/cm199798/cmselect/cmhealth/755/8052025.htm, August 10, 1998.

22. Ibid.

23. "Children from the Older Lands," *Detroit Free Press*, January 11, 1903.

24. FBR, *The Strange Autobiography*, 60.

Chapter 2 Vagabond

25. "'Home Children' Remember: Forced Child Emigration Shameful Shadow of Past," *The Ottawa Citizen*, August 26, 1985, 41. See also Joy Parr, *Labouring Children: British Immigrant Apprentices to Canada 1869–1924* (Toronto: University of Toronto Press, 1994).

26. House of Commons, Health, Minutes of Evidence.

27. In *The Strange Autobiography* and other writings, FBR mistakenly refers to Robert Wallace as "Henry."

28. "For Ernie Urban…" *The Windsor Star*, November 19, 1981.

29. FBR, *The Strange Autobiography*, 75.

30. "Honorably Acquitted," *The Windsor Star*, January 12, 1906.

31. Incident is recounted both in *The Strange Autobiography*, 37, and later in the transcript of the federal trial, 50–52.

32. "Dr. Robinson's Brother Says Psychiana Is a Fake," *The Latah Journal* (Deary, ID), August 12, 1937. Psychiana Archives, Box 1, File 3, Latah County Historical Society, Moscow, ID.

33. FBR, *The Strange Autobiography*, 89.

34. Ibid., 127.

35. Alfred Robinson, Exhibits, "A Family Trilogy, Book II."

36. Duane Colt Denfield, "Naval Hospitals in Washington," https://www.historylink.org/File/10144.

37. FBR, *The Strange Autobiography*, 158.

38. Alfred Robinson, Exhibits, "A Family Trilogy, Book II," U.S. Navy discharge record.

39. FBR, *The Strange Autobiography*, 163.

40. Ibid., 169.

41. Ibid., 169–170.

42. "Govern't Not Persecuting…" *The Latah Journal* (Deary, ID) clipping (undated), Psychiana

Archives Box 1, File 3, Latah County Historical Society. *The Latah Journal's* bias against Robinson notwithstanding, their mention of Alcatraz is corroborated in other sources including a May 7, 1979, letter from Frank S. Nooney (a federal agent who had been assigned to Robinson's case) to Keith Petersen of the Latah County Historical Society. Unfortunately, his military records from this period were destroyed in the 1973 National Archives fire in St. Louis.

43. FBR, *The Strange Autobiography*, 177.

44. Pearl Robinson, "Statement by Mrs. Robinson," *The Strange Autobiography*, 13, and in Alfred Robinson, "A Family Trilogy, Book II," 78.

45. A significant amount of Leavitt family history can be found in Alfred Robinson's "Family Trilogy."

46. Alfred Robinson, "A Family Trilogy, Book II," 74.

47. Ibid., in Exhibits.

48. Ibid., in Exhibits.

49. Ibid.

50. A number of these ads ran in the Klamath Falls newspaper *The Evening Herald*.

51. *Los Angeles Times*, October 1, 1924.

52. *Los Angeles Evening Express*, June 9, 1925.

53. Alfred Robinson, Exhibits, "A Family Trilogy, Book II."

54. Ibid., 89.

55. FBR, *The Strange Autobiography*, 180.

56. Ibid., 190.

57. Robert Collier, *The Secret of the Ages in Seven Volumes* (1926; repr., Rough Draft Printing, 2013), 66.

58. FBR, *The Strange Autobiography*, 190.

59. Ibid.

60. Ibid., 193.

61. Ibid., 194.

62. Ibid.

CHAPTER 3 From the Ashes

1. Clifford M. Drury to Keith Petersen, January 23, 1978, Latah County Historical Society.

2. Alfred Robinson, "A Family Trilogy, Book II," 93.

3. Charles Haanel, *The New Psychology* (Wilkes-Barre, PA: Kallisti, 2006), 166.

4. Ibid., 37.

5. FBR, *The Strange Autobiography*, 196.

6. Alfred Robinson. "A Family Trilogy, Book II," 93.

7. FBR, *The Strange Autobiography*, 215.

8. Ibid., 196.

9. FBR, "Psychiana (The New Psychological Religion), Introductory Lecture," 1929, 2. Robinson Papers, UI, Box 4, Folder 21.

10. Ibid.

11. Charles Haanel, *The New Psychology*, 78.

12. FBR, "Psychiana (The New Psychological Religion), Introductory Lecture," 2.

13. Charles Haanel, *The Master Key System*, 28.

14. FBR, "Lesson No. 2," *Psychiana: The Advanced Lessons* (Cabin John, MD: Wildside Press, 2007), 21.

15. Charles Haanel, *The New Psychology*, 44.

16. Frank Robinson, "Lesson No. 1," *Psychiana: The Advanced Lessons*, 17.

17. FBR, "Psychiana (The New Psychological Religion, Introductory Lecture)," 6.

18. Ibid.

19. Ibid.

20. Ibid.

21. FBR, "Psychiana: The New Psychological Religion, Lesson No. 1," 1. Robinson Papers, UI, Box 4, Folder 2.

22. Ibid.

CHAPTER 4   Ad Man

23. FBR, *The Strange Autobiography*, 199.

24. FBR, "Success or Failure…" promotional booklet. Robinson Papers, UI, Box 5, Folder 25.

25. FBR, *The Life Story of Frank B. Robinson (Written by Himself)* (Moscow, ID: Review Publishing Co., 1934), 149.

26. Ibid., 150.

27. Ibid., 151.

28. Ibid., 153.

29. Ibid.

30. Ibid., 154.

31. Fitzgerald quoted in Robert S. McElvaine, *The Great Depression*, 17.

32. Roland Marchland, *Advertising the American Dream: Making Way for Modernity, 1920–1940* (Berkeley: University of California Press, 1985), 1.

33. Sinclair Lewis, quoted in *The New York Times*, April 18, 1943.

34. Stephen Leacock, *Garden of Folly* (New York: Dodd, Mead, and Company, 1924), 123.

35. Charles Rappleye, *Herbert Hoover in the White House: The Ordeal of the Presidency* (New York: Simon & Schuster, 2016), 115.

36. Morton Walker, *Advertising and Promoting the Professional Practice* (Ann Arbor: University of Michigan Press, 1979), 51.

37. Drury to Petersen, 2. Latah County Historical Society.

38. FBR, *The God Nobody Knows* (Moscow, ID: Review Publishing, 1930), ix-x.

39. Ibid., 42–43.

40. Ibid., 101.

41. Ibid., 132, 141.

42. Ibid., 147.

43. FBR, *The Life Story*, 158.

CHAPTER 5   "Keyed Up to a High Pitch"

44. Michael Haag's definitive works on Alexandria (*Vintage Alexandria: Photographs of the City 1860–1960* [Cairo: American University in Cairo Press, 2008]; *Alexandria: City of Memory* [New Haven, CT: Yale University Press, 2004]); along with personal correspondence with Mr. Haag proved foundational in capturing the contours and details of Alexandria at the time Birley resided there. Also of significant value was Lawrence Durrell's sweeping and lyrical book series *Alexandria Quartet* (New York: Faber and Faber, 1968).

45. Biographical information on Geoffrey Peel Birley and his family is scant, but *Le Mondain Egyptien (The Egyptian Who's Who 1943)* was particularly helpful. Sahar Hamouda and Colin Clement, *Victoria College: A History Revealed* (American University of Cairo Press, 2002); *The Killearn Diaries: 1936–1946*, ed. Trefor Evans (London: Sidgwick & Jackson, 1972); and Hanna F. Wissa, *Assiout: The Saga of An Egyptian Family* (London: Book Guild, 1994) also provided family background and context. Several clippings from *The Times* (March 24, 1900;

November 18, 1908; November 13, 1963) and various records from Ancestry.com helped to fill in many blanks.

46. "The Situation in Egypt," *The Guardian*, October 24, 1930, 8.

47. Geoffrey Peel Birley (hereafter GPB) to FBR, October 24, 1930. Frank Robinson Papers, Box 1, File 7, Latah County Historical Society, Moscow, ID.

48. FBR, "Psychiana: Lesson No. 4," 3. Robinson Papers, UI, Box 4, Folder 1.

49. Ibid.

50. GPB to FBR, Frank Robinson Papers, Box 1, File 7, Latah County Historical Society.

51. "Wave of Business Optimism Sweeps Nation," *Altoona (PA) Tribune*, October 24, 1930, 1.

52. "Bowers Calls Hoover Regime Utter Failure," *The Scranton (PA) Republican*, October 24, 1930, 14.

53. FBR, *The Strange Autobiography*, 216.

54. Headlines from the front page of *The Brooklyn Daily Eagle*, December 15, 1930.

CHAPTER 6 Occult Appeal

55. "New York Bank Troubles," *The Guardian*, December 12, 1930, 12.

56. "Nation Greets New Year Gaily," *Binghamton (NY) Press and Sun-Bulletin*, December 31, 1930, 1.

57. "500 Hungry Farmers Storm Shops," *The Capital Times* (Madison, WI), January 4, 1931.

58. Amity Shlaes, *The Forgotten Man: A New History of the Great Depression* (New York: Harper Perennial, 2007), xiv.

59. Bob Feeney, "Homade [sic] Hooch," *Quad-City Times* (IA/IL), January 23, 1931, 2.

60. Ibid.

61. Alfred Robinson, "A Family Trilogy, Book II," 104.

62. Photo referenced at Library of Congress digital archives, https://www.loc.gov/item/2016832910/.

63. Harvey F. Lovejoy to Postmaster of Moscow, Idaho, May 14, 1931. Frank Bruce Robinson Papers, Box 1 File 7, Latah County Historical Society.

64. FBR, *Psychiana Monthly*, December 1931, cover and 1. Robinson Papers, UI, Box 4, Folder 23.

65. Ibid., 17.

66. Gary Lachman, *Aleister Crowley: Magick, Rock and Roll, and the Wickedest Man in the World* (New York: Tarcher/Penguin, 2014), 231–232. Lachman's work was especially valuable in providing context for Russell and the Chorozon Club. I never suspected that research into Psychiana would take me down the strange and baffling corridors of the occult in the 1930s wherein séances and mediumships were as common as sporting events. Also useful in this context was Mitch Horowitz's *Occult America: White House Seances, Ouija Boards, Masons, and the Secret Mystic History of Our Nation* (New York: Bantam, 2009). Horowitz includes a decent chapter on Robinson and Psychiana, "Mail Order Messiah."

67. The word "magick" in the world of the occult differs from the familiar "magic" (i.e., sleight of hand, tricks, illusions, etc.) in important and complex ways. While Crowley offered his own somewhat convoluted definition of magick, a serviceable definition can be found in John L. Stedman's *H.P. Lovecraft and the Magickal Tradition* (Newburyport, MA: Red Wheeler/Weiser, 2015), 2–3: "the use of language, gestures, symbolic objects, and stylized settings for the purposes of establishing contact with. . .gods or deities."

68. Ibid., 244, 253.

69. https://psi-encyclopedia.spr.ac.uk/articles/american-society-psychical-research#Personnel_and_Main_Events.

70. "Adrift in the Spirit World," *Hartford (CT) Daily Courant*, August 24, 1930.

71. "Séance to Communicate With Valentino's Spirit Described," *The San Francisco Examiner*, February 17, 1931.

72. "Queer Disclosures," *The Miami News*, November 22, 1931.

73. The magazine also provides a complicated and somewhat contradictory portrait of FBR's racial views. On page 14, under a section on prayer, Robinson uses several racial epithets when referring to African Americans. The instance bears noting because it stands in contrast with the more inclusive views he espoused in subsequent literature.

74. FBR, "How the Church Heals," *Psychiana Monthly*, December 1931, 5.

75. Ibid., 6.

76. Ibid., 31.

77. "Hoover Urges Adoption of His Program," *The Brownsville (TX) Herald*, January 4, 1932.

78. Robert S. McElvaine, *The Great Depression* (New York: Times Books, 1984), 80.

79. Ibid.

80. James Ledbetter and Daniel B. Roth, eds., *The Great Depression: A Diary, by Benjamin Roth* (New York: PublicAffairs, 2009). This volume proved indispensable in corroborating daily events as they related to the Great Depression and to the lives of Psychiana students generally. I've relied on Benjamin Roth's capable and inestimable account for context, color, and unflinching candor.

81. Ibid., 47.

82. "Psychiana Elects New Officers," Unattributed clipping. Psychiana Archives, Box 1, File 3, Latah County Historical Society.

83. Ibid.

84. Roth, 48.

85. Alfred Robinson, "A Family Trilogy, Book II," 95–96.

86. Drury to Petersen, January 23, 1978. Psychiana Archives, Box 1, File 1, Latah County Historical Society.

87. FBR to Mary Cunliffe. Alfred Robinson, Exhibits, "A Family Trilogy, Book II."

88. "New Waukegan Bank Receiver is Appointed," "Name Suspect in Kidnapping of Lindy Baby," *Chicago Tribune*, May 24, 1932.

89. FBR to Mary Cunliffe. Alfred Robinson, Exhibits, "A Family Trilogy, Book II."

90. Alfred Robinson, "A Family Trilogy, Book II," 96.

91. Richards and Higgins financial statement. Frank B. Robinson Papers, Folder 10, Latah County Historical Society.

92. Howard Zinn, *A People's History of the United States 1492–Present* (New York: Harper Perennial, 1995), 381–382. Also useful for information and history of the Bonus Army March was Amity Shlaes, *The Forgotten Man: A New History of the Great Depression* (New York: Harper Perennial, 2007).

93. "Doctor With New Idea Puts Little City on Map," *Spokane Press*, November 24, 1932. Robinson Papers, UI, Box 7, Folder 2.

Chapter 7   "The Shackles Are Off"

94. Nancy Dunn, *Artesia* (Images of America series) (Mt. Pleasant, SC: Arcadia, 2011). Useful text in getting a historical sense of nearby Hope, NM.

95. Family, biographical, and physical descriptions derived from Ancestry.com census records, immigration records, and WWII draft registration card (February 16, 1942). John Klassen Obituary, *El Paso Times*, June 17, 1998. Photograph found in "Baccalaureate Speaker," *The Santa Fe New Mexican*, May 25, 1962.

96. Special thanks to Michael Rebman, Museum Supervisor of the Artesia Historical Museum & Art Center, for his assistance in identifying the location of the Methodist Church in Hope, New Mexico. Google Maps also provided visual details.

97. Rev. John Klassen to FBR, University of Idaho Special Collections. MG 101, Robinson Papers, UI, Box 7, Folder 23.

98. Ibid.

99. "City Pay Cuts, Effective Dec. 1, Are Predicted," *Albuquerque Journal*, December 4, 1932.

100. Frank Robinson, *Psychiana: The Advanced Lessons* (Cabin John, MD: Wildside Press, 2007), 81.

101. Ibid.

102. Ibid.

103. McElvaine, 134.

104. "The Dangerous Decline of the Church," *Literary Digest,* July 5, 1930, 20–21.

105. FBR, *The God Nobody Knows,* 37.

106. T.H. Watkins, *The Hungry Years: A Narrative History of the Great Depression in America* (New York, NY: Holt, 2000), 88.

107. Population census data gathered from three government reports: "Thirteenth Census of the United States Taken in the Year 1910: Statistics for New Mexico," ftp://ftp.census.gov/library/publications/decennial/1910/abstract/supplement-nm.pdf; the decennial report for 1940 (which gives 1930 data), https://www2.census.gov/library/publications/decennial/1940/population-volume-1/33973538v1ch07.pdf; and the decennial report for 1950 (which provides 1940 data), https://www2.census.gov/library/publications/decennial/1950/population-volume-2/26082967v2p31ch1.pdf.

108. Klassen to FBR, 1.

109. KOB advertised their regular program schedule on page 4 of the *Albuquerque Journal,* e.g., December 2, 1932, edition.

110. Franklin D. Roosevelt to FBR, Frank Robinson Archives, Box 1, File 7, Latah County Historical Society.

111. Klassen, 1.

CHAPTER 8 Toil

112. Roth, 83.

113. Ibid.

114. "The Church Invites You," *The Journal News* (Hamilton, OH), January 7, 1933.

115. Franklin D. Roosevelt, First Inaugural Address, March 4, 1933. National Archives, https://catalog.archives.gov/id/197333.

CHAPTER 9 "Does the LAW Work?"

116. Information pertaining to the Beeching home, address, ages, residential occupants, and Beeching's occupation culled from federal census data sheet, April 8, 1930.

117. Leslie Beeching to FBR, April 12, 1933. Robinson Papers, UI, Box 7, Folder 21.

118. Ibid.

119. Ibid.

120. FBR, "Psychiana: The Advanced Course, Lesson No. 17," 1932. Introductory Lecture. Robinson Papers, UI, Box 4, Folder 2.

121. Ibid., 1.

122. Ibid., 2–3.

123. Phillip R. Hastings, "T & N.O. Junction," *Railroad Magazine,* February 1952, 34–45. Author's private collection.

124. Ibid., 37.

125. Ibid., 37–38.

126. Beeching, 1.

CHAPTER 10 "At the Hour You Took Command"

127. Address and neighborhood information taken from 1930 census record, California voter registration card.

128. "Industries, Labor, Farmers Join in Cry for Inflation," *Oakland Tribune,* April 16, 1933.

129. Linda Gordon, *Dorothea Lange: A Life Beyond Limits* (New York: W.W. Norton, 2009), 115.

130. Information taken from Ethel Cone's Funeral Record, April 7, 1949. Ancestry.com.

131. "In the Supreme Court of the New South Wales, Matrimonial Causes Jurisdiction. No. 7864 Between Sarah Ann Cone, Petitioner and Percy Cone, Respondent," *The Sydney Morning Herald,* August 5, 1911, Trove Digitised Newspapers. Article details the nature and charges of Cone's separation. Cone's Petition for Citizenship record (October 13, 1932) provides his immigration information and other vital statistics. An article titled "Harry and Brother William Cone," which appeared in Sydney's *Sunday Times* on May 20, 1917, provides photographs of the brothers and their service in WWI. Trove Digitised Newspapers and various ship manifests track Cone's career in the merchant marine. See for instance the manifest for the SS *Flying Dragon,* July 15, 1952. The death of Cone's son, Albert, was reported in the *Sydney Morning Herald,* October 4, 1928, "Fatal Cycling Accident," Trove Digitised Newspapers. Both of Cone's draft registration cards detail his physical traits including weight, height, hair color, and the like.

132. FBR, "Psychiana: Advanced Course, Number Two: Lesson 1," 4. FBR's correspondence with Percy and Ethel Cone is included and referred to within the lesson itself. Robinson Papers, UI, Box 4, Folder 4.

133. Ibid.

134. Ibid., 6–7.

CHAPTER 11 Faith Factory

135. FBR, *Psychiana Quarterly,* June 1933, 13. Robinson Papers, UI, Box 4, Folder 22.

136. "Canadian Doctors are Working Hard," *Vancouver Daily World,* April 1, 1916.

137. "Magee Jury Failed to Agree," *Vancouver Daily World,* November 21, 1914.

138. "Did Not Appear," *The Ottawa Journal,* September 20, 1919.

139. "Re-Hearing Given Malpractice Case," *The Ogden Standard-Examiner,* August 7, 1928.

140. Data collected from the 1930 U.S. census.

141. FBR, *Psychiana Quarterly,* June 1933, 16. Robinson Papers, UI, Box 4, Folder 22.

142. Ibid.

143. Ibid., 20.

144. FBR, *The Strange Autobiography,* 234.

145. Clifford M. Drury, "Psychiana: A New Religion," *The Presbyterian Banner,* August 3, 1933. Robinson Papers, UI, Box 6, Folder Scrapbook, 8.

146. "Moscow to Have New Newspaper," *The Spokesman Review,* June 8, 1933.

147. Alfred Robinson, "A Family Trilogy, Book II," 105.

148. "Our Introduction," *Moscow Review and Shopping Guide,* June 30, 1933. Robinson Papers, UI, Box 6, Folder Scrapbook, 10.

149. Mildred Hensley to Keith Petersen, January 28, 1978. Psychiana Archives, Box 1, File, 1, Latah County Historical Society.

150. Juanita Tisdall's photo and job title listed in *The Life Story of Frank B. Robinson,* 96–97.

151. Hensley to Petersen.

152. Ibid.

153. Beulah Herrmann, interview by Sam Schrager, November 9, 1976, Latah County Oral History Collection, University of Idaho Digital Initiatives.

154. Ibid.

155. Ibid.

156. Ibid.

157. Robinson Papers, UI, Box 6, "Lists of publications used for Psychiana" Folder. Using this list of magazines, I was able to cross-reference specific titles with those in which L. Ron Hubbard published, as a way of drawing parallels between the two figures, but more importantly, as a way of identifying their respective target audiences. For instance, Hubbard published his first short story, "The Green God," in *Thrilling Adventures,* February 1934.

158. Herrmann, interview.

CHAPTER 12 "The Magic Wand"

159. "Hitler's Latest Edict," *Western Morning News* (Southwest UK), July 15, 1933.
160. GPB to FBR, July 16, 1933. Frank B. Robinson Archives, Box 1, File 7, Latah County Historical Society.
161. Ibid.
162. Ibid.

CHAPTER 13 Under the Banner of Advertising

163. Clifford M. Drury, "Psychiana: A New Religion," 8.
164. Ibid.
165. Ibid.
166. Ibid.
167. Ibid.
168. Ibid.
169. Ibid.
170. Ibid.
171. Ibid.
172. Ibid.
173. Ibid.
174. Roth, 125.
175. FBR, *Psychiana Quarterly*, December 1933, 7. Robinson Papers, UI, Box 4, Folder 20.
176. FBR, Psychiana letter to students, 1933. Robinson Papers, UI, Box 7, Folder 24.
177. Ibid.

CHAPTER 14 No Narrow Creed

178. FBR wrote of his own work habits, and they were often corroborated by first-hand reports such as that found in Herman Forrest Edwards' later account. "A Visit to the Man Who Talks With God," *The Oregonian*, September 24, 1939. Robinson Papers, UI, Box 7, Folder "Clippings About Robinson."
179. Details about FBR's office, secretary, and general layout taken from photographs and Edwards' article that described his tour through the spaces.
180. John Kobler, "The Shepherd of Moscow," *Colliers*, February 20, 1943. Robinson Papers, UI, Box 6, Folder "Magazine Articles."
181. Ibid.
182. Alfred Robinson, "A Family Trilogy, Book II," 101.
183. FBR, "Psychiana: Visitors Week, May 12–17" 2. Booklet. Robinson Papers, UI, Box 4, Folder 22.
184. Ibid., 3.
185. Ibid.
186. "Dillinger and Hamilton Escape Trap," *Dixon Evening Telegraph*, April 2, 1934.
187. "Slew All Six in Bloodlust Fury," *The Spokesman Review*, April 2, 1934.
188. "Half Million Workers Promised Increase in Wages," *The Post-Register* (Idaho Falls, ID), April 1, 1934.
189. FBR, Easter Sunday Lecture, 2. Robinson Papers, UI, Box 5, Folder 29.
190. Ibid., 3.
191. Ibid.
192. Ibid., 4, 6.
193. Ibid., 8.

194. Ibid., 11. The transcripts of FBR's lectures are often filled with scenic details including when the audience breaks into applause.

195. Ibid., 14.

196. Ibid.

CHAPTER 15 Passport To Trouble

197. "James Doran is Given Promotion," *The Post-Star* (Glens Falls, NY), June 13, 1933. See also, "Inspector is Inspected," *Fort Worth Star-Telegram*, October 11, 1947. Article features large photograph of an older Doran auditing the records of a subordinate inspector.

198. "'G' Men Break Insurance Plot," *The Spokesman-Review* (Spokane, WA), August 8, 1938.

199. FBR, *The Strange Autobiography*, 245.

200. Dialogue and details taken from trial transcript, 28–29, 67–68. Frank B. Robinson Archives, Box 1, File 11, Latah County Historical Society.

201. FBR's passport application obtained from the National Archives in Seattle, WA.

202. FBR trial transcript, 28–29.

203. Alfred Robinson, "A Family Trilogy, Book II," 107.

204. FBR, "To My Students," letter included with mailers, 1934. Author's private collection.

205. "Papen Stirs Germany By Rap at Nazis," *Alton (IL) Evening Telegraph*, June 18, 1934.

206. "Mussolini, Impressed by Hitler Meeting, Will Repay Call," *Indianapolis Sunday Star*, June 17, 1934.

207. Roth, 155, 156, 157.

208. Weather according to reports in *The Brooklyn Times Union*, July 1, 1934.

209. SS *Hamburg* American Line manifest, July 1, 1934, Ancestry.com.

210. "Hitler Crushes Revolt by Nazi Radicals," *The New York Times*, July 1, 1934.

211. For details on period ocean liners including menu cards for voyages in 1934, see the Gjenvick-Gjonvik online archives at www.gjenvick.com.

212. See, respectively, "A Victory of the Right," *The Guardian*, July 2, 1934; "Battle Rages as S.F. Opens Port," *Oakland Tribune*, July 3, 1934; "Safeguarding Nation's Soul," *Los Angeles Times*, July 2, 1934.

213. "Safeguarding," *Los Angeles Times*, July 2, 1934.

214. Arthur Robinson to FBR, August 11, 1934. Robinson Papers, UI, Box 3, Folder 1.

215. Donald Sturrock. *Storyteller: The Authorized Biography of Roald Dahl* (New York: Simon & Schuster, 2010), 133.

216. Haag, *Alexandria: City of Memory*, 133.

217. "Von Hindenburg Dies at 86," *The New York Times*, August 2, 1934.

218. "Palouse Welcome View to Traveler," *News Review* (Moscow, ID), undated. Robinson Papers, UI, Box 6, Folder "Clippings About Robinson."

CHAPTER 16 "There Will Be No Peace in Our Household"

219. "Yarn Prices: Egyptian Section and a New Agreement," *The Guardian*, September 22, 1934.

220. GPB to FBR, September 22, 1934. Frank B. Robinson Archives, Box 1, File 7, Latah County Historical Society.

221. Ibid.

222. Ibid.

CHAPTER 17 American Spectacle

1. Alfred Robinson, "A Family Trilogy, Book II," 104, 107.

2. Ibid.

3. *Los Angeles Times*, January 6, 1935.

4. Ibid.

5. Ibid.

6. FBR, "Lecture Delivered at Trinity Auditorium, Los Angeles, California," 1. Robinson Papers, UI, Box 5, Folder 12.

7. Ibid., 4.

8. Ibid., 10.

9. Ibid., 14.

10. Ibid.

11. Ibid., 15–16.

12. "Temple Fete Commences," *Los Angeles Times*, January 6, 1935.

13. "Cult to Build Temple Here," Unattributed news clipping. Frank B. Robinson, Box 1, File 10, Latah County Historical Society, Moscow, ID.

14. Ibid.

15. "Tabernacle to Be Built," *Los Angeles Times*, January 17, 1935.

16. Radio program listings lend great insight into public interest at the time. Robinson's "Flashes of Truth" was broadcast on Sundays and advertised in the newspapers in sections like "On the Air Today," *Stockton Independent*, January 19, 1935.

17. "Flashes of Truth No. 2" transcript, 1. Most of Robinson's radio programs featured the same format with a "Guide" introducing Psychiana and its leader to the audience. Robinson Papers, UI, Box 5, Folder 31.

18. Quote comes from caption on Lange photo, Library of Congress, https://www.loc.gov/item/2017759801/.

19. To capture the sense of the scene and the people of the time, I pored over countless period photographs from Lange, as well as other Farm Security Administration photographers. A useful repository of such images can be found at Yale's Photogrammar, which has some 170,000 photos from 1935 to 1945, all searchable by county. http://photogrammar.yale.edu.

CHAPTER 18 "That We Should Enter Again into Our Partnership"

20. Seven Trees has a fascinating history, including its status as a safe haven for refugee children from Central Europe in 1939. A brief account of its history is detailed in Joanna Friel and Adam Swaine's history, *Secret Chislehurst* (Stroud, UK: Amberley Publishing, 2015), 74–77. I was also fortunate enough to glean further information from Joanna Friel in personal correspondence.

21. GPB to FBR, Frank B. Robinson Archives, Box 1, File 7, Latah County Historical Society.

22. Ibid.

23. *The Guardian*, July 9, 1935.

24. FBR, "God and the World Mess," *Psychiana Quarterly*, December 1935, 16. Robinson Papers, UI, Box 4, Folder 20.

25. "Britain's Attitude," *The Honolulu Advertiser*, November 15, 1935.

26. FBR, "God and the World Mess," 21.

27. Ibid.

CHAPTER 19 "The Suffering of Humanity"

28. Return address on Baity's correspondence and census records—cross referenced with Google maps—provided details and images of Baity's residences.

29. Andrew D. Young, *St. Louis and Its Streetcars: The Way It Was* (Archway Publishing 1996). In researching this chapter, I found Young's book to be especially informative. The historic photos and descriptions reveal rich details about the streetcars, the city's "motormen," and the routes Baity would have worked. It also provided excellent context for the period in which Baity was writing to Frank Robinson.

30. Edgar Giles Baity to FBR, January 8, 1936. Letter was published under the title "Once More—

God" in *Psychiana Quarterly*, March 1936, 21–22. Robinson Papers, UI, Box 4, Folder 20.

31. E.G. Baity, "A Sadder and Madder Man," *The Motorman and Conductor* 35, (1926): 33.

32. C.C. Wylie, "Fireballs Reported to the University of Iowa," *Monthly Report to the University of Iowa*, October 21, 1930, 555. "Eight bright meteors…have been reported to the Department of Astronomy . . . from June 12, 1930, to October 10, 1930, inclusive…Professor E.B. Frost, of the Yerkes Observatory, forwarded a letter from E.G. Baity of St. Louis with an observation…"

33. Baity to FBR, 21.

34. Ibid., 21–22.

Chapter 20 Prosecution

35. Robinson Park still remains a popular recreation spot, though the reservoir has long since been drained. Few locals know the history of the park's name or the man who donated the land.

36. FBR notes to staff. Robinson Papers, UI, Box 3, Folder 1.

37. "Wire Here for Postcard: Sent By Hauptmann: Dr. F.B. Robinson Asked to Send Postcard He Received Here From Bruno," *News Review*, January 10, 1936. Robinson Papers, UI, Box 6, Folder "Scrapbook."

38. FBR, *The Strange Autobiography*, 243.

39. Ibid.

40. Ibid., 244.

41. *History of the Bureau of Diplomatic Security of the United States Department of State* (E-Book), 2. https://2009-2017.state.gov/documents/organization/176705.pdf.

42. FBR, *The Strange Autobiography*, 245.

43. "The Bannerman Years," *History of the Bureau*, 18.

44. FBR, *The Strange Autobiography*, 247.

45. "U.S. Jury Lands on Moscow Man," *Spokesman Review*, February 14, 1936, 9.

46. Biographical information on Stephen Howard Morse was taken from an extensive newspaper profile, "Meet S.H. Morse, Who First Came to Bay as Postal Official in 1908," *The Coos Bay Times*, November 23, 1936. Other details derived from a story on Morse's retirement ["Postal Inspector S.H. Morse Will Retire March 31," *News Review* (Roseburg, OR), March 27, 1943, 2] and Morse's obituary (*Eugene Herald*, March 10, 1946, 16) along with census data and numerous newspaper clippings spanning several decades of his career, also provided key insights into his background. To wit: "Postoffice Inspector Gives Testimony Damaging to Lumber Company," *Philadelphia Inquirer*, March 27, 1913, 4; "Holly Hearing Today," *Harrisburg Telegraph*, August 13, 1908, 11; "Blackhand Case May Be Retried: Postoffice Inspector Dissatisfied with Acquittal of Paul Terusa," *San Francisco Chronicle*, March 3, 1916.

47. "Stephen H. Morse Dies at Seattle," *Eugene Herald*, March 10, 1946.

48. Letter from Stephen Howard Morse to Clerk, United States District Court, Boise, ID, February 14, 1936. *United States v. Frank B. Robinson*, Case C-3781. National Archives, Seattle, WA.

49. Alfred Robinson. "A Family Trilogy," 112–113.

50. For biographical background, see "E.W. Robertson, Former Resident, Dies in Spokane," *State Times Advocate* (Baton Rouge), May 29, 1961; "Captain Robertson Is Commander," *Spokane Chronicle*, February 6, 1919. A photograph of Robertson from Historical Images helped with physical description. See also FBR's personal account of Robertson in *The Strange Autobiography*, 254–255.

51. Background on Morgan: "Guest Tonight," *The Post-Register* (Idaho Falls), October 27, 1937, 1; "Bar Head Makes Plea," *The Post Register*, October 28, 1937, 1; "Morgan Head of Bar Association," *The Twin Falls News*, July 24, 1937. See also FBR's own description in *The Strange Autobiography*, 252.

52. FBR, "At Last," *Psychiana Quarterly*, March 1936, 3. Robinson Papers, UI, Box 4, Folder 20.

53. Ibid.

54. Ibid.

55. Ibid.

56. Ibid., 4.

57. Ibid., "Life After Death," 14.

58. "Visions Man Keeping Alive for Centuries: Dr. Carrel Believes Humans May be Put in 'Cold Storage.'" *Des Moines Register*, December 13, 1935.

59. Ibid.

60. FBR, "Life After Death," 14.

CHAPTER 21 On Trial

61. "Govern't Not Persecuting Moscow Psychist [sic] Is Claim," *The Latah Journal* (Deary, ID) undated. Psychiana Archives, Box 1, File 3, Latah County Historical Society.

62. Ibid.

63. For background on Erle Hoyt Casterlin, see "Mason Boy Goes to Porto Rico [sic] to Teach History to Natives," *Detroit Free Press*, August 22, 1908, 6.

64. FBR, *The Strange Autobiography*, 254–255.

65. Ibid.

66. All dialogue in the following court scenes section is taken directly from the transcript of Robinson's trial. Frank Robinson Papers, Box 1, File 11, Latah County Historical Society (hereafter Transcript).

67. Transcript, 1.

68. Transcript, 3.

69. Transcript, 4.

70. Transcript, 5.

71. Transcript, 6.

72. Transcript, 7.

73. Transcript, 8.

74. Transcript, 9.

75. Transcript, 10.

76. Transcript, 11.

77. Transcript, 12.

78. Transcript, 13.

79. Transcript, 14.

80. Transcript, 19–20.

81. Transcript, 20–21.

82. Transcript, 22.

83. Transcript, 22–23.

84. Transcript, 24–25.

85. Transcript, 26.

86. Transcript, 27.

87. Transcript, 33.

88. Transcript, 34.

89. Transcript, 35.

90. Transcript, 44.

91. Transcript, 45.

92. Transcript, 46.

93. Transcript, 46–47.

94. Transcript, 48.

95. Transcript, 48–49.
96. Transcript, 50.
97. Transcript, 52.
98. Transcript, 57.
99. Transcript, 58.
100. Transcript, 59.
101. Transcript, 62.
102. Transcript, 64.
103. Transcript, 65.
104. Transcript, 65–66.
105. Transcript, 66. N.B. I have slightly altered the wording of sentence only for clarity of the narrative.
106. Transcript, 67.
107. Transcript, 68.
108. Transcript, 69.
109. Transcript, 70.
110. Transcript, 71.
111. Transcript, 71–72.
112. Transcript, 72–73.
113. Transcript, 75.
114. Transcript, 76.
115. Transcript, 78.
116. Transcript, 79–80.
117. Transcript, 81.
118. Transcript, 82.
119. Transcript, 83.
120. "Acquitted by Jury," *News Review*, May 20, 1936.
121. See *United States v. Frank B. Robinson*, Case C-3781. National Archives, Seattle, WA. See also "Acquitted by Jury," *News Review*, May 20, 1936.
122. There are multiple clippings about Robinson's acquittal. Robinson Papers, UI, Box 6, Folder "Clippings About Robinson."

Chapter 22 "Psychiana is With Me"

123. One of the briefest but most striking pieces of correspondence from Psychiana students is the postcard from someone known only as Mrs. Pfeffer who was touring Nazi Germany in 1936, when political tides were shifting dramatically. Student Correspondence K-Z, 1936. Robinson Papers, UI, Box 1, Folder 6.

Chapter 23 The Marksmen

124. "30 Years' Service Finished for Immigration Officer," *Spokane Chronicle*, December 1, 1955, 34.
125. See, for instance, "Old Man Bear is Target," *The Semi-Weekly Spokesman Review*, October 2, 1947. Nooney is listed as "president of the Spokane Rifle Club." Several articles detail Nooney's marksmanship.
126. Photos from newspaper articles helped with physical description (e.g. "Inspector Nooney Drives New Studebaker From Factory," *Spokane Chronicle*, November 2, 1938. 19.
127. Emma Markley to FBR, August 8, 1936. Robinson Papers, UI, Box 7, Folder 21.
128. "Postmasters Await Opening of Convention," *Eugene Register-Guard*, July 12, 1936, 1.
129. "Psychiana Man Arrested Here," *Spokesman Review*, August 10, 1936, 18.

130. FBR, *The Strange Autobiography*, 260.

131. Ibid.

132. "Havre Man Gets Inspector's Job," *The Independent-Record* (Helena, MT), April 15, 1926. The article describes Stewart's promotion and his recent mandate to "make arrests for violation of any federal laws, including smuggling and liquor running."

133. See Stewart's WWI draft registration card, June 5, 1917; 1900 U.S. Census; 1920 U.S. Census. Photos and vital records obtained from Ancestry.com.

134. See "Elks All Ready for Big Minstrel Show," *The Havre (MT) Daily News*, February 7, 1926.

135. "Dicks Shoot Man and Woman in Border Booze Run," *The Independent-Record* (Helena, MT), July 1, 1926. See also "Woman is Arrested in Smuggling Deal," *The Billings Weekly*, February 15, 1927.

136. "'Psychianist' Faces Charge," *The Ogden (UT) Standard Examiner*, August 8, 1936.

137. "Psychiana Founder Faces Deportation," *Twin Falls (ID) News*, August 8, 1936. Robinson Papers, UI, Box 6, Folder "Clippings About Robinson."

138. Ibid.

139. Ibid.

140. "Robinson Faces Deport Hearing," *Boise Statesman*, August 22, 1936. Robinson Papers, UI, Box 6, Folder "Clippings About Robinson."

141. "Deportation of Idaho Mystic is Request of U.S.," *Wenatchee (WA) World*, August 14, 1936. Robinson Papers, UI, Box 6, Folder "Clippings About Robinson."

142. U.S. Department of Labor, Immigration and Naturalization Service, Spokane Washington. File No. 9012/7424, Under Department Warrant No. 55916/995, Latah County Historical Society. The deportation hearing file (hereafter Hearing), like the trial testimony, contains a trove of case details, legal exchanges, first-hand testimony, and context. Page 9. Frank B. Robinson Archives, Box 1, File 11, Latah County Historical Society.

143. Hearing, 1.

144. Hearing, 22.

145. Hearing, 28.

146. Hearing, 29.

147. Hearing, 31.

148. Hearing, 14.

149. Hearing, 35–36.

150. Robinson Papers, UI, Box 6, Folder "Clippings About Robinson."

151. "Robinson Data to Washington," *Spokesman Review*, August 23, 1936. Robinson Papers, UI, Box 6, Folder "Clippings About Robinson."

152. Ibid.

CHAPTER 24 "A Pack of Bloody Hounds"

153. *Psychiana Quarterly*, September 1936, 35. Robinson Papers, UI, Box 4, Folder 20.

154. GPB to FBR, Frank B. Robinson Archives, Box 1, File 7, Latah County Historical Society.

155. Alfred Robinson. "A Family Trilogy, Book II," 108.

156. GPB cable to FBR, Frank B. Robinson Archives, Box 1, File 7, Latah County Historical Society.

157. "Dr. Tenney Accepts 'Psychiana' Position" *News Review* (Roseburg, OR), October 2, 1936. Robinson Papers, UI, Box 6, Folder "Clippings About Robinson."

158. "Both Sides of the Curtain," *Brooklyn Times Union*, 10.

CHAPTER 25 "Out in these By-Ways and Hedges"

159. Baity/FBR/C.W. Tenney correspondence. Robinson Papers, UI. "Correspondence Samples."

160. Ibid.

161. Tim O'Neil. "A Look Back: 5,000 Settle in Shacks…" *St. Louis Post-Dispatch*, January 10, 2010.

162. Baity/FBR/C.W. Tenney correspondence. Robinson Papers, UI. "Correspondence Samples."

163. Ibid.

164. "'Philosophy of Soul' Lecture Series Nears," *Citizen News* (Hollywood, CA), October 24, 1936. Robinson Papers, UI, Box 6, Folder "Clippings About Robinson."

165. "On Way to Egypt," *News Review*, November 3, 1936. Robinson Papers, UI, Box 6, Folder "Clippings About Robinson."

166. "Roosevelt Plan Fine for Egypt," *The Spokesman-Review* (Spokane, WA), November 3, 1936. Birley's comments on FDR's handling of the American cotton industry was likely a reference to the president's Agricultural Adjustment Act of 1933.

CHAPTER 26 "Redeemed from the Jaws of Doubts and Agnosticism"

167. "Philippine Farm Valley Turned into Graveyard Today," *Corsicana Semi-Weekly Light*, December 11, 1936, 11.

168. Physical description taken from his passport photo via Ancestry.com.

169. *The Filipino Student*. United States: Filipino Students in America, 1912. See "My Christmas Retrospection," wherein star-crossed lovers confess their love to one another on the eve of the protagonist's departure for another country. "The rhythmical midnight song of the crickets and the faint throbbing chords of the distant *cutibeng* fall upon the evening air and intensify the quietude of the place. Above us, intermingling the green foliage of the tall trees are fireflies exhibiting their glow in its most exquisite splendor. 'Your father forbids our love,' the protagonist says, 'because I am poor and beneath you; but tomorrow I will go in search of wealth to become your equal.'"

170. "Philippino Concert and Lecture," *Marble Rock (IA) Journal*, April 13, 1916.

171. N.B. Dalao to Albert Einstein, December 5, 1938. Albert Einstein Archives, Hebrew University of Jerusalem, Micro Reel 53, File 11 (a) 52-811–52-841. Notes and additions by J. Stachel. Thanks to Barbara Wolff at Hebrew University for her help in tracking down this letter.

CHAPTER 27 Criminal Action

172. FBR to Edgar Giles Baity, December 23, 1936. Robinson Papers, UI, Box 1, Folder 2, "Correspondence Samples."

CHAPTER 28 "The Child is the Father of Man"

173. See "Burns Hates Negro Because Gans Made Him Hand Over 80 Per Cent," *The Buffalo Commercial*, May 15, 1908. So dogged by the question of his sympathy toward black pugilists, Burns penned a letter attempting to correct this assumption. "This letter," he argued, "will show the public that I am no nigger lover." See also McCaffery, 4. It is worth noting that Burns would go on to marry Irene Peppers, an African American woman.

174. Dan McCaffery, *Tommy Burns: Canada's Unknown World Heavyweight Champion*, (Toronto: Lorimer, 2000), 4. McCaffery's biography is the best book on Burns and is, at present, the definitive authority on the life and career of Tommy Burns. This book proved indispensable to me as I gathered details about Burns' nearly forgotten story. Dan McCaffery was also kind enough to answer my questions via email while I was investigating the Burns chapter.

175. Joyce Carol Oates. "The Man with the Golden Smile," *The New York Review of Books*, November 18, 2004.

176. McCaffery, 212.

177. "Winter Sporting Dope From Everywhere," *Chicago Day Book*, January 20, 1914, 24.

178. McCaffery, 50–51.

179. *The New York Times*, October 18, 1930.

180. McCaffery, 232.

181. "Tommy Burns Speaks," *Psychiana Weekly*, October 19, 1940, 2. Robinson Papers, UI, Box 4, Folder 28.

182. Tommy Burns to FBR, March 29, 1937. Robinson Papers, UI, Box 7, Folder 9.

CHAPTER 29 The Lion of Idaho

183. Alfred Robinson, "A Family Trilogy, Book II," 113.

184. Pearl Robinson, "Statement by Pearl Robinson," *Strange Autobiography*, 14.

185. Order of the Eastern Star is a branch of Freemasonry that inducts both men and women into its order. Founded in 1850, it is organized on a number of biblical principles.

186. Alf Robinson, 113.

187. William Borah to Judge Hodgins, May 8, 1937. Frank B. Robinson Archives, Box 1, File 10, Latah County Historical Society.

188. Ibid.

189. "Negress Wins Her Freedom at Boise," *The Post-Register* (Idaho Falls, ID), April 8, 1937.

190. Borah to Hodgins.

CHAPTER 30 Letter from Bledington

191. GPB to FBR, Frank B. Robinson Archives, Box 1, File 7, Latah County Historical Society.

CHAPTER 31 Loyalty

192. "Postal Inspector Will Be Honored," *The Eugene Herald*, April 9, 1937.

193. Seattle Washington City Directory, 1938; King County Washington Census, April 16, 1940.

194. Stephen Howard Morse to Psychiana students, July 7, 1937. Robinson Papers, UI, Box 1, Folder 4.

195. Guajardo to Morse, July 19, 1937. Robinson Papers, UI, Box 1, Folder 4.

196. Moore to Morse, August 18, 1937. Robinson Papers, UI, Box 1, Folder 4.

197. Perkins to Morse, August 2, 1937. Robinson Papers, UI, "Correspondence Samples."

198. Pettis to Morse, September 15, 1937. Robinson Papers, UI, Box 1, Folder 3.

199. Ramsey to Morse, July 29, 1937. Robinson Papers, UI, Box 1, Folder 3.

200. FBR to Psychiana students, Undated. Robinson Papers, UI, Box 1, Folder 4.

201. Sweet to FBR, July 27, 1937. Robinson Papers, UI, Box 1, Folder 3.

CHAPTER 32 Havana

202. "Science and Demonism United," Robinson Papers, UI, Box 6, Folder "Clippings About Robinson."

203. Ibid.

204. Compton White to R.G. Bailey, June 19, 1937. Frank B. Robinson Archives, Box 1, File 10, Latah County Historical Society.

205. Ibid.

206. See "Labor Bureau Demands Frank Robinson Leave This Country by July 1," Robinson Papers, UI, Box 6, Folder "Clippings About Robinson."

207. FBR, *The Strange Autobiography*, 251.

208. Nooney to Petersen, May 7, 1979. Psychiana Archives, Box 1, File 1, Latah County Historical Society.

209. FBR, *The Strange Autobiography*, 268–269.

210. "Labor Bureau Demands Frank Robinson Leave This Country," *Boise Pioneer*, September 1, 1937. Robinson Papers, UI, Box 6, Folder "Clippings About Robinson."

211. Ibid.

212. A number of the details from FBR's stay at Hotel Nacional in Havana are listed in his lodging receipt. Frank B. Robinson Archives, Box 1, File 10, Latah County Historical Society.

CHAPTER 33 "It is Terrible Discouraging Here"

213. One of the most illuminating and instructive works that I came to rely on in studying the Dust Bowl—and Kansas particularly—was Timothy Egan's *The Worst Hard Time*, Mariner Books, New York, 2006. Egan's references to Liberal, Kansas, (including photos) were also immensely salient to the crafting of this chapter.

214. Nettie Long to FBR, 1. August 2, 1937. Robinson Papers, UI, Box 1, Folder 3.

215. C. Robert Haywood, "The Great Depression: Two Kansas Diaries," *Great Plains Quarterly* (Winter 1998): 27, 34.

216. Long, 1.

217. Ibid.

218. "Hutchinson Greets Neighbors…It's an Empire of Riches: Not Only Great in Wheat Production, But in Livestock," *The Hutchinson News* (Kansas), May 12, 1928.

219. Long, 3.

220. Long, 2.

221. Long, 3.

222. Long, 2.

223. Donald Worster, *Dust Bowl: The Southern Plains in the 1930s* (Oxford UP, 2004), 20.

224. Haywood, 34.

225. FBR, *Psychiana: The Advanced Lessons* (Cabin John, MD: Wildside Press, 2007), 23.

226. Long, 7.

227. FBR, *Psychiana*, 17.

228. Long, 3.

229. FBR, *Psychiana*, 26–27.

230. Long, 5.

231. Long, 6.

232. Long, 7–8.

233. Long, 8.

234. Long to Morse, August 2, 1937. Robinson Papers, UI, Box 1, Folder 3.

235. Reynolds to Long, August 7, 1937. Robinson Papers, UI, Box 1, Folder 3.

CHAPTER 34 Return

236. FBR, *The Strange Autobiography*, 270.

237. "Robinson Leaves the United States: Reported to Be in Cuba Preparing to Re-enter Through the Coal Hole," *The Latah Journal* (Deary, ID), August 19, 1937. Psychiana Archives, Box 1, File 3, Latah County Historical Society.

238. Ibid.

239. FBR, *The Strange Autobiography*, 270.

CHAPTER 35 "Through the Bright Spot, Out Into Somewhere"

240. Mildred C. Gage to FBR, September 6, 1937. Robinson Papers, UI, Box 1, Folder 4.

241. Ibid.

242. Ibid., 1.

243. Ibid.

244. Ibid.

245. Ibid., 2.

246. Ibid.

247. Ibid.

248. Moon phase calendars for September 16, 1939, show that it was a waxing crescent moon that shone that night. See https://mooncalendar.astro-seek.com/moon-phases-calendar-september-1939.

249. "Scandia Woman Takes Own Life with Revolver," *Warren (PA) Times Mirror*, September 18, 1939.

CHAPTER 36 "My Road is Pretty Rocky"

250. "17 Marriage Ties Severed," *Reading (PA) Times*, June 6, 1917.

251. Anna Ernst to FBR, October 16, 1937, 4. Robinson Papers, UI, Box 1, Folder 4.

252. Ibid.

253. Roth, 201.

254. Ernst to FBR.

255. Ibid.

256. Ibid.

257. FBR, *Psychiana*, 127.

258. Ibid.

259. Ernst to FBR.

260. Ibid.

261. Ibid.

262. Ibid.

CHAPTER 37 Be Quiet

263. C.W. Tenney to Anna J. Ernst, October 25, 1937. Robinson Papers, UI, Box 1, Folder 4.

CHAPTER 38 Fallout

264. Alfred Robinson, 114–115. See also subhead, "Wife of 'Psychiana' Founder Passes Federal Exam to Become Citizen," *The Semi-Weekly Spokesman Review*, November 24, 1937.

CHAPTER 39 Radio Psychiana

1. "Psychiana Transcription #1," September 28, 1937. Robinson Papers, UI, Box 5, Folder 32.

2. Ibid., #2.

3. Ibid., #3.

4. Ibid., #4.

5. "Money-Back Religion," *Time Magazine*, January 17, 1938. Robinson Papers, UI, Box 6, Folder "Magazine Articles."

6. Ibid.

7. Ibid.

8. "Radio Psychiana" transcript #2. Robinson Papers, UI, Box 5, Folder 39.

9. Ibid.

10. "Ex-Envoy Dodd Calls Hitler Killer," *Daily News* (New York) January 14, 1938, 130.

11. Susan J. Douglas. *Listening In: Radio and the American Imagination* (New York: Times Books, 1999), 161.

CHAPTER 40 "You Are God's Moses to Me"

12. Reverend Charles Sidney Burke to FBR, February 4, 1938. Robinson Papers, UI, Box 1, Folder 5 ("Correspondence Samples").

13. Ibid.

14. Ibid.

15. Ibid.

16. Ibid.

17. *The Idaho Statesman* (Boise), February 13, 1938.

18. FBR to Burke. February 14, 1938, Robinson Papers, UI, Box 1, Folder 5 ("Correspondence Samples").

CHAPTER 41   "On the Ether Waves and the Cosmic Rays"

19. "Sarnia Marriages," *The Times Herald* (Port Huron, MI), December 28, 1906.

20. A.J. Carter to FBR, March 31, 1938. Robinson Papers, UI, Box 1, Folder 5 ("Correspondence Samples").

21. Carter's full military record can be viewed on Ancestry.com: https://www.ancestry.com/imageviewer/collections/61084/images/b1538-s041-001?pId=646433.

22. A serviceable gloss of the Bear Wood Convalescent Hospital can be found at http://www.arborfieldhistory.org.uk/WW1/WW1_Bearwood.htm.

23. "Who'll Live Should England Die?" *The Windsor Star*, June 3, 1939. Strangely, while researching Alfred John Carter and his writing, I came across another Ontarian writer named Alfred J. Carter who published at least three short stories, two of which centered on men in war; "Black Men of War" (*Veterans Magazine*) and "The Man with the Glass Jaw" (*American Legion Magazine*) with the third being a kind of hard-boiled love story, titled "Two in Love" (Canada's *Maclean's Magazine*). Because two of the stories were published a year after A.J.'s death, it seems possible, though unlikely, that they were written by the same man.

CHAPTER 42   "I Used to Go to the Hills and Pray to that God in the Sky"

24. Chief Moses White Horse to FBR, August 28, 1938. Robinson Papers, UI, Box 1, Folder 5 ("Correspondence Samples"), 1.

25. See Jacqueline Fear-Segal and Susan D. Rose, *The Carlisle Indian Industrial School: Indigenous Histories, Memories, and Reclamations* (Lincoln: University of Nebraska Press, 2016), 45. Another extremely valuable resource is Dickinson College's Carlisle Indian School Digital Resource Center. Not only did this repository provide a trove of relevant materials about the school during the time in which White Horse attended, but it also contains some of his personal records. http://carlisleindian.dickinson.edu.

26. White Horse, 1.

27. "Wounded Eagle Gives Captor Stiff Battle," *Great Falls (MT) Tribune*, December 3, 1925.

28. "White Horse Fights for Indian Rights," *Great Falls (MT) Tribune*, May 20, 1928.

29. Ibid.

30. White Horse, 1–2.

31. Ibid., 2–3.

32. Ibid., 3.

CHAPTER 43   Convention

33. FBR and C.W. Tenney, "1938 National Convention Speech, Lecture 1," Masonic Temple, Portland, OR, October 2–4. Robinson Papers, UI, Box 5, Folder 38, 1.

34. Ibid.

35. Ibid., 1–2.

36. Ibid., 3.

37. Ibid.

38. Ibid., 4.

39. Ibid., 12.

40. From *The Capital Press* (Madison, WI), October 3, 1938, 1.

41. "Hitler Enters Sudetenland," *The Indiana Gazette* (Indiana, PA), October 3, 1938.

42. FBR and Tenney, "1938 National Convention Speech, Lecture 2," Robinson Papers, UI, Box 5, Folder 38, 4–5, 12.

43. Ibid.

44. Ibid., 15.

45. Ibid.

46. FBR and Tenney "Lecture 3," October 4, 1938. Robinson Papers, UI, Box 5, Folder 38, 2.

47. Ibid.

CHAPTER 44 "The Meanest Swindler in the World"

48. Fredrick Van Ness Person, "The Fallacy of Fear," Unpublished Essay. Robinson Papers, UI, Box 1, Folder 6.

49. I have to thank Gregory M. Schmidt at the National Archives Kansas City for tracking down F.V. Person's complete Leavenworth prison record. The record turns out to have been lengthy and included his photograph, personal correspondence, a narrative on family background, and scores of processing documents that reveal the traits and quirks of a fascinating man. Record Group 129, Records of the Bureau of Prisons Department of Justice, Bureau of Prisons. U.S. Penitentiary, Leavenworth. Inmate Case Files, 1895–1957. National Archives Identifier 571125. Inmate #47887.

50. "May Menzies," *Chicago Tribune*, December 7, 1907.

51. "Trade Paper's Editor Dies," *Chicago Tribune*, January 3, 1908.

52. "Parole Progress Report: Social Services Unit," December 4, 1936. National Archives Kansas City.

53. "Wife Accuses Erstwhile Broker and Many Women," *Chicago Tribune*, April 8, 1922.

54. "Berkeleyan Is Accused of Fraud," *Oakland Tribune*, June 6, 1915. Article lists Person's address as 2712 Darby Street.

55. See for instance, "OPPORTUNITY: An Initial Offering, Subject to Prior Sale, of the Treasury Stock of the ALLIED APARTMENTS COMPANY OF SAN FRANCISCO...for further particulars apply to F. Van Ness Person, Modesto Hotel, Modesto, CAL," *Modesto Evening News*, February 11, 1915.

56. "Richmond May Have School of Aviation," *Oakland Tribune*, June 26, 1914.

57. Ibid.

58. See subhead: "F.V. Person Charged With Obtaining Money Under False Pretenses," *Oakland Tribune*, June 6, 1915.

59. "Broker Taken On Warrant: Fredrick Person of Evanston [IL] Charged with False Pretense in San Francisco," *Chicago Tribune*, August 22, 1916.

60. "Mrs. Person Given Divorce After Judge Hears About Parties," Chicago Tribune, April 22, 1922. See also note 53.

61. "Orders Firm to Turn Back Bond Sales," *Muncie Evening Press*, July 10, 1929.

62. See for instance, *The Star Press* (Muncie, IN), November 6, 1932.

63. Subhead: "Chicagoan Accused of Specializing in Victimizing Catholic Priests," *St. Louis Globe-Democrat*, November 11, 1933.

64. Subhead: "Operations of Indicted Chicago Securities Dealer, F. Van Ness Person, a Fugitive, Began in 1929," *St. Louis Globe-Democrat*, April 2, 1935.

65. "Held for Mail Frauds," *Times Union* (Brooklyn, NY), November 3, 1935.

66. "2-Year Fugitive Gives Up Gladly," *The Des Moines Register*, November 3, 1935.

67. Record of Court Commitment, United States Penitentiary, Leavenworth, Kansas, November 18, 1935. Record Group 129, Records of the Bureau of Prisons Department of Justice, Bureau of Prisons. U.S. Penitentiary, Leavenworth. Inmate Case Files, 1895–1957. National Archives Identifier: 571125. Inmate #47887.

68. See column, "Late Flashes," *The Muscatine (IA) Journal*, April 5, 1934.

69. Person to FBR, August 30, 1939. Robinson Papers, UI, Box 1, Folder 6.

70. Admission Summary, 3. Record Group 129, Records of the Bureau of Prisons Department of Justice, Bureau of Prisons. U.S. Penitentiary, Leavenworth. Inmate Case Files, 1895–1957. National Archives Identifier L 571127. Inmate #47887.

71. Person to FBR, 1.

72. Ibid.

73. Ibid.

74. Ibid.

75. Person, "Fallacy of Fear," 1.

76. Ibid.

77. Ibid., 2.

78. Ibid., 4.

79. Ibid., 7.

80. Ibid.

81. Ibid.

CHAPTER 45 Looking the Part

82. Herman Forrest Edwards. "A Visit to the Man Who Talks With God," *The Oregonian*, September 24, 1939. Robinson Papers, UI, Box 6, Folder "Clippings About Robinson."

83. Ibid.

84. Ibid.

85. Ibid.

86. FBR, *The Strange Autobiography*, 56.

87. Herman Forrest Edwards. "A Visit to the Man…"

88. Ibid.

89. Ibid.

90. Ibid.

91. Ibid.

CHAPTER 46 Winter War

92. Martha Gelhorn, *The Face of War* (1959; repr., New York: Atlantic Monthly Press, 1988), 53.

93. "Roosevelt Assails Soviet Dictatorship," *The Burlington (VT) Free Press*, February 17, 1940.

94. Cable from Ryti. Latah County Historical Society, Moscow, ID. See also: "Dr. Robinson Gets Cable from Finnish Premier Who Solicits 'Psychiana' Aid in Russ War," Unattributed clipping, Frank B. Robinson Archives, Box 2, File 4, Latah County Historical Society.

95. Martii Turtola, *Risto Ryti: Elämä isänmaan puolesta* (*Risto Ryti: A Life for the Fatherland*), Helsinki, 1994.

96. Alfred Robinson, "A Family Trilogy, Book III," 36.

97. Established in Kansas City, Missouri, in 1919, DeMolay International is a fraternal order for youths aged 12-21 that teaches leadership. The organization is named after Jacques de Molay, the last Grand Master of the Knights Templar.

98. FBR, "The Finns," *Psychiana Weekly: A Movement of the Spirit of God on Earth*, January 27, 1940, 3. Robinson Papers, UI, Box 4, Folder 28.

99. Ibid., 4.

100. Ibid.

101. Ibid.

102. Ibid., 3.

103. "Robinson Berates 'Radicals,'" *Boise Capital News*, February 12, 1940.

CHAPTER 47 "It Seems Terrible Hard at the Present Time"

104. See obituaries for Evie Beeles, *The Tennessean*, December 19, 1945, and Jesse Lee Beeles, *The Tennessean*, December 31, 1938.

105. "Allies to Push Plane Buying in America," *Richmond (VA) Times-Dispatch*, February 24, 1940, 1.

106. Beeles to FBR, February 24, 1940. Robinson Papers, UI, Box 1, Folder 7.

107. Ibid.

108. "Strike at Petersburg," *Daily Press* (Newport News, VA), January 31, 1940.

109. Beeles to FBR, 1.

110. "Hurt in Strike Melee," *Daily Press* (Newport News, VA), February 3, 1940.

111. Ibid., 2–3.

112. Tenney to Beeles, March 5, 1940. Robinson Papers, UI, Box 1, Folder 7.

113. "Mass Picketing at Petersburg Denied," *The Bristol (VA/TN) News Bulletin*, March 15, 1940.

114. Ibid.

115. "Settle Strike at Petersburg; Men to Return," *The Bee* (Danville, VA), April 11, 1940.

CHAPTER 48 "The Cobbler Mustn't Go Beyond His Last"

116. A.C. Plagge to FBR, February 24, 1940. Robinson Papers, UI, Box 1, Folder 8.

117. The National Archives at Washington, DC, Manifests of Alien Arrivals in the Seattle, Washington District, NAI 2953576; Records of the Immigration and Naturalization Service, 1787–2004, Record Group 85, Series A4107, Roll 033.

118. "Lectures," *The Brisbane Courier*, June 20, 1922.

119. A.C. Plagge to FBR, March 1938. Robinson Papers, UI, Box 3, Folder 1.

120. Ibid.

121. Plagge to FBR, February 24, 1940.

122. Ibid.

CHAPTER 49 "This Imperishable Yardstick"

123. "About the House Which is to Become Elgin Museum," *St. Thomas (Ontario) Times Journal*, April 9, 1955.

124. Elgin County Historical Society: https://elginhistoricalsociety.ca.

125. Saywell and MacDonald Marriage Certificate, November 19, 1915.

126. Sanitarium Registration Card, DuPage County Local Board, Wheaton, IL, September 12, 1918.

127. "About the House."

128. Ancestry.com; https://www.ancestry.com/imageviewer/collections/7921/images/ONMS932_334-0429?pId=2085829.

129. Saywell to FBR, March 19, 1940. Robinson Papers, UI, Box 1, Folder 8.

130. Ibid.

131. Ibid.

132. FBR, "Where Religions Come From," *Psychiana Weekly: A Movement of the Spirit of God on Earth*, Robinson Papers, UI, Box 4, Folder 28.

133. Saywell to FBR, 1.

134. Ibid.

135. Published by Agnes and Alphia Hart—the former editor of the *Dianetics Journal* and the *Journal of Scientology*—*The Compleat Aberee* eventually published a variety of fringe material ranging from "UFOs to psychic phenomena." Several issues of *The Compleat Aberee* can be found at https://www.aberree.com, including those in which Bramwell Saywell's letters and opinions appear.

136. Saywell to FBR, 1–2.

137. Ibid.

138. "Dear Editor," *The Compleat Aberee*, March 1959. https://www.aberree.com.

139. Saywell to FBR, 2.

140. Ibid.

141. Tenney to Saywell, March 29, 1940. Robinson Papers, UI, Box 1, Folder 8.

Chapter 50 Psychiana Blitzkrieg

142. FBR to Benito Mussolini, "Three Cables," Robinson Papers, UI, Box 7, Folder 31. Archives contain both the copies and originals of the various cables Robinson sent to world leaders.

143. Ibid.

144. Ibid.

145. Instructions printed in red ink on a circular sent out to students including the telegram to Mussolini. Robinson Papers, UI, Box 7, Folder 31.

Chapter 51 "The Day I Answered Your Advertisement"

147. Based on 1940 federal census.

148. References to the Fortenberry dialect can be found in articles such as Ewart Hendry's "Merritt Island's Fortenberry..." *Orlando Sentinel,* October 22, 1939.

149. Gordon Fortenberry to FBR, May 31, 1940. Robinson Papers, UI, Box 1, Folder 7.

150. William Braucher, "Hooks & Slides," *The Decatur (AL) Daily,* August 1, 1933.

151. Stats taken from Boxrec.com, "Boxing's Official Record Keeper," https://boxrec.com/en/proboxer/34993.

152. "Garden Goes in for New Talent," *Standard Union* (Brooklyn, NY), May 19, 1931.

153. As it happens, Gordon Fortenberry's father, Andrew Fortenberry, would become even more famous (or infamous, perhaps) than his son, the prizefighter. A. Fortenberry, as he was known, was the Brevard County commissioner and owner of Merritt Island Lumber Company. By turns lauded and despised, A. Fortenberry was the driving force behind establishing Port Canaveral. Creating a viable shipping port was a vision of Andrew Fortenberry ever since he homesteaded his property in 1913.

154. *The Standard Union,* May 20, 1931, 11.

155. Charles Vackner, "Allie Wolff Wins," *Brooklyn Times Union,* June 2, 1931.

156. boxrec.com/en/proboxer/34993.

157. "Rosenbloom Beats Gordon Fortenberry," *The Philadelphia Inquirer,* March 13, 1934.

158. Ibid.

159. boxrec.com/en/proboxer/34993.

160. Ibid.

161. Fortenberry to FBR, Robinson Papers, UI, Box 1, Folder 7.

162. Fortenberry to FBR, 3.

163. FBR to Fortenberry. Robinson Papers, UI, Box 1, Folder 7.

Chapter 52 Drive

164. FBR, *The Strange Autobiography,* 275.

165. Ibid., 276.

166. Ibid.

167. Ibid.

168. Ibid.

169. Ibid.

170. Ibid.

171. Ibid., 277.

172. Alfred Robinson, "A Family Trilogy, Book II," 118.

173. FBR, *The Strange Autobiography,* 179.

174. Ibid., 237.

175. FBR, "The Coming Peace," *Psychiana Weekly,* September 7, 1940, 1. Robinson Papers, UI, Box 4, Folder 28.

176. Ibid., 3.

177. FBR, "Believing Lies," *Psychiana Weekly*, September 21, 1940, 1. Robinson Papers, UI, Box 4, Folder 28.
178. Ibid., 4.
179. Ibid.

CHAPTER 53 The Poet

180. FBR, "We Read an Amazing Story," chapter 5, unpublished manuscript, 158. Robinson Papers, UI, Box 5, Folder 1.
181. Church announcements in various newspapers track DeBolt around the country as he preached his way west. See *Latrobe (PA) Bulletin*, June 1, 1929; *The Kinmundy (IL) Express*, July 24, 1930; *Beatrice (NE) Daily Sun*, August 31, 1934; *Great Falls (MT) Tribune*, September 27, 1936, etc.
182. According to federal census.
183. Draft registration card, September 12, 1918, Waynesburg, PA.
184. William Walter DeBolt, "The Postman," *Spokane Chronicle*, June 10, 1938.
185. DeBolt, *Gates and Trails* (Dexter, MO: Candor Press, 1975), 31.
186. Ibid.
187. Ibid., 28.
188. FBR, "We Read an Amazing Story," 162.
189. Ibid.
190. Ibid., 162–163.
191. Ibid., 163.
192. Ibid.
193. FBR, *God...and Dr. Bannister* (New York: American Book-Stratford Press, 1941), 4.
194. Ibid.
195. Ibid.
196. Ibid., 4–5.
197. Ibid., 10.
198. Ibid., 11.
199. Ibid., 20–21.
200. Ibid., 296.
201. FBR, *For Rent: A Cross* (Moscow, ID: Psychiana, Inc., 1941), 11.

CHAPTER 54 "What Do You Want?"

202. The Newcom's local paper, the *Kokomo Tribune*, regularly referred to Harlan as "Harl."
203. Thomas Hamilton, *Kokomo, Indiana* (Images of America), (Charleston, SC: Arcadia Publishing, 2002), 28–30.
204. The Order of the White Shrine of Jerusalem is an appendage of the Freemasons open to men and women. Its mission is to espouse Christian ideals.
205. "Society," *Kokomo (IN) Tribune*, February 17, 1939.
206. *The Kokomo (IN) Tribune*, January 13, 1930.
207. Ibid.
208. "50th Anniversary Observed in South," *Kokomo (IN) Tribune*, January 21, 1955.
209. Hamilton's slim volume on Kokomo was very useful in capturing the businesses and establishments of the era.
210. "Great Day for the Klansmen," *The Fairmount (IN) News*, July 6, 1923.
211. Linda Gordon, *The Second Coming of the KKK: The Ku Klux Klan of the 1920s and the American Political Tradition* (New York: Liveright, 2018), 1.
212. Ella, Harl, and their boys appear on the rolls of three separate U.S. Quaker meeting records (1918, 1921, and 1927).

213. Newcom to FBR, Robinson Papers, UI, Box 1, Folder 9.
214. Ibid.
215. Ibid.
216. Ibid.
217. Ibid.
218. Ibid.
219. DeBolt to Newcom, April 17, 1941. Robinson Papers, UI, Box 1, Folder 9.
220. Ibid.
221. Newcom to FBR, September 5, 1941.
222. FBR, *Psychiana: The Advanced Lessons*, Lesson 16, 203.
223. Newcom to Robinson.
224. DeBolt to Newcom.

Chapter 55 Vision Quest
225. Robinson Papers, UI, Box 5, Folder 36.

Chapter 56 "Frankly Speaking"
226. Sidney P. Dones, "Frankly Speaking," *The Neighborhood News* (Los Angeles), September 25, 1941. Robinson Papers, UI, Box 6, Folder, "Clippings About Robinson."
227. Delilah Leontium Beasley, *The Negro Trailblazers of California: A Compilation of Records from the California Archives in the Bancroft Library at the University of California, in Berkeley...* (1919; repr., Whitefish, MT: Kessinger, 2010), 205.
228. Douglas Flamming, *Bound for Freedom: Black Los Angeles in Jim Crow America* (Berkeley: University of California Press, 2006).
229. Ibid., 121.
230. Sidney P. Dones (1888–1947), IMDb, https://www.imdb.com/name/nm0232452/.
231. *The Dallas Express*, March 6, 1920.
232. Lawrence Culver, *The Frontier of Leisure: Southern California and the Shaping of Modern America* (New York: Oxford University Press, 2010), 244. See also Allison Rose Jefferson, *Living the California Dream: African American Leisure Sites During the Jim Crow Era* (Lincoln: University of Nebraska Press, 2020).
233. *The Pittsburgh Courier*, October 4, 1941.
234. Dones, "Frankly Speaking."
235. Ibid.
236. Alfred Robinson, "A Family Trilogy, Book II," 120.
237. Fenwicke L. Holmes, *Ernest Holmes: His Life and Times* (New York: Dodd Mead, 1970), 1–11.
238. Alfred Robinson, "A Family Trilogy, Book II," 120.
239. Ibid., 119–120.
240. Holmes, *Ernest Holmes*, 254.
241. FBR, "The Holmes-Robinson American Spiritual Awakening" (hereafter "Holmes-FBR Typescript"), Typescript, Lecture 1, September 21, 1941. Los Angeles, CA. Robinson Papers, UI, Box 5, Folder 18.
242. This "branding" was used on a variety of materials including mailers, flyers, and campaigns. See for instance mailer including a photo of Holmes and Robinson at the Philharmonic in Los Angeles, Robinson Papers, UI, Box 7, Folder 1.
243. Holmes-FBR Typescript, 1.
244. Ibid.
245. Ibid.
246. Holmes-FBR Typescript, September 22, 1941, 2.

247. Dones, "Frankly Speaking."

248. Ibid.

249. Holmes-FBR Typescript, 2.

250. Dones, "Frankly Speaking."

251. Ibid.

CHAPTER 57 The Pilot

252. Alfred Robinson, "Echoing Memories of World War II, Pacific Theater" (unpublished manuscript), 3. This brief handwritten autobiographical account of Alf's time leading up to, and throughout, his enlistment as a pilot is fascinating from both personal and historical contexts.

253. Ibid., 4–9.

254. Alfred Robinson, "A Family Trilogy: Book III," 135.

255. Ibid., 136.

256. Ibid.

257. Ibid., 138.

258. Ibid.

259. Ibid.

CHAPTER 58 Prophet and Mystic

260. William Walter DeBolt, "Introductory Message," in Frank B. Robinson, *What This War Really Means (With a Prophecy Concerning the Outcome of the Present Conflict)* (Portland, OR: Metropolitan Press, 1942), 9.

261. Ibid., 10.

262. Ibid., 11, 14.

263. Ibid., 16.

264. FBR, *What This War Really Means*, 36.

265. Ibid., 153.

266. Ibid., 141.

267. Ibid.

268. Ibid., 28.

269. John Kobler. "The Shepherd of Moscow," *Colliers*, February 20, 1943. Robinson Papers, UI, Box 6, Folder "Magazine Articles."

270. FBR, *Blood on the Tail of a Pig* (Portland, OR: West Coast Binding & Printing, 1941), 8.

271. Ibid.

272. Ibid., 8–9.

273. Ibid., 25.

274. Ibid.

275. Ibid., 28.

276. Ibid., 29.

277. Ibid.

278. Ibid., 30.

279. Ibid., 32.

280. Ibid., 48–49.

281. Ibid., 45–46.

282. FBR, *Shall We Know Each Other Beyond the Tomb?* (Moscow, ID: News Review Publishing, 1937), 34.

283. Ibid., 56.

284. Ibid., 59.

285. Ibid.

CHAPTER 59 A Mad World

286. "God vs. the Axis," Robinson Papers, UI, Box 5, Folder 8.

287. Ibid.

288. Ibid.

289. Ibid.

290. "A Mad World," Robinson Papers, UI, Box 7, Folder 26.

291. Ibid.

292. Ibid.

293. Ibid.

294. Ibid.

295. Alfred Robinson, "A Family Trilogy, Book II," 120-121.

CHAPTER 60 Psychiana in the Nuclear Age

1. "Atomic Energy May Be Future Rainmaker," *Iowa City Press-Citizen*, February 14, 1947.

2. "This Civilization is Doomed," Psychiana flyer. Robinson Papers, UI, Box 7, Folder 31.

3. Ibid.

4. Walter Lippman, "Color Optimistic," *The Pantagraph* (Bloomington, IL), December 31, 1946.

5. FBR, *Psychiana: The Advanced Lessons*, 74.

6. "This World is Sitting on Top of a Volcano," Flyer mailed to students and advertising outlets. Robinson Papers, UI, Box 7, Folder 4.

7. Typed memo from FBR to employee, E.J. Kass. Robinson Papers, UI, Box 7, Folder 33.

8. Robinson Papers, UI, Box 7, Folder 4.

9. FBR, "Science Says..." flyer. Robinson Papers, UI, Box 7, Folder 4.

CHAPTER 61 The Gathering Storm

10. "Honored at Silver Anniversary Luncheon; Greene Honored as BBB Leader," *New York Times*, March 16, 1950. See also *The Agromeck*, North Carolina State College yearbook, 1912, 145.

11. "Business: Better Business," *Time Magazine*, March 24, 1930.

12. Ibid.

13. The whereabouts of the communications between Greene and his agents is unknown, but FBR refers to this investigative correspondence in his own undated letter to Edward Greene. "Letter from Robinson to Better Business Bureau," Robinson Papers, UI, Box 3, Folder 1.

14. FBR to Greene.

15. Ibid.

16. Alfred Robinson, "A Family Trilogy, Book II," 123, 126.

17. Ibid., 124.

18. Alfred Robinson, "A Family Trilogy, Book III," 102.

19. Ibid.

20. Alfred Robinson, "A Family Trilogy, Book II," 123, 126.

21. Alfred Robinson, "A Family Trilogy, Book III," 103.

22. Alfred Robinson, "A Family Trilogy, Book II," 125.

23. Alfred Robinson, "A Family Trilogy, Book III," 103.

24. Alfred Robinson, "A Family Trilogy, Book II," 126.

25. *Daily Idahonian*, October 30, 1952.

26. "Death of Psychiana," *Newsweek*, November 24, 1952. Robinson Papers, UI, Box 6, Folder "Magazine Articles."

EPILOGUE   "A Fortune to Share with the World"

27. Paul Harsch to Keith Petersen. Psychiana Archives, Box 1, File 1, Latah County Historical Society, Moscow, ID.

28. Joseph C. Harsch's *At the Hinge of History: A Reporter's Story* is an absolutely fascinating tale of Harsch's uncanny knack for being at the right place at the right time, scoop-wise. The book was also useful as it features a photo of Joseph and his brother Paul in Paris during the war when the brothers were both in uniform.

29. Harsch/Petersen correspondence.

30. Ibid.

31. Ibid.

32. Ibid.

33. Personal correspondence, April 24, 2016.

34. "What 'Psychiana' Teaches," *Chippewa (WI) Herald Telegram*, August 1, 1952.

35. *Jacksonville (IL) Daily Journal*, June 23, 1953.

36. *Los Angeles Times*, December 9, 1955.

37. *The Evening Sun* (Baltimore, MD), March 24, 1978.

Appendix

1. Frank Robinson. *Psychiana: The Advanced Lessons*, Lesson No. 1, 8.

2. Ibid., 21.

3. Ibid., 26.

4. Ibid., 46.

5. Ibid., 50.

6. Ibid., 53.

7. Ibid., 69.

8. Ibid., 89.

9. Ibid., 98–99.

10. Ibid., 103–104.

11. Ibid., 118.

12. Ibid., 129–130.

13. Ibid., 141.

14. Ibid., 159.

15. Ibid., 166.

16. Ibid., 181.

17. Ibid., 199.

18. Ibid., 204.

19. Ibid., 214.

20. Ibid., 229.

21. Ibid., 239.

22. Ibid., 264.

Bibliography

Bach, Marcus. *They Have Found a Faith*. Indianapolis: Bobbs-Merrill, 1946.

Baity, Edgar Giles. "A Sadder and Madder Man." *The Motorman and Conductor* 35 (1926): 33.

Beasley, Delilah Leontium. *The Negro Trail Blazers of California: A Compilation of Records from the California Archives in the Bancroft Library at the University of California at Berkeley*.... Los Angeles: 1919. Reprint, Whitefish, MT: Kessinger, 2010.

Braden, Charles Samuel. *These Also Believe: A Study of Modern American Cults and Minority Religious Movements*. New York: Macmillan, 1949.

Brodie, Fawn M. *No Man Knows My History: The Life of Joseph Smith*. New York: Vintage Books, 1995.

Cahill, Richard T. *Hauptmann's Ladder: A Step-by-Step Analysis of the Lindbergh Kidnapping*. Kent: Ohio State University Press, 2014.

Carnegie, Dale. *How to Win Friends and Influence People*. New York: Simon & Schuster, 2011.

Collier, Robert. *The Secret of the Ages in Seven Volumes*. New York: Robert Collier, 1926. Reprint, Seaside, OR: Rough Draft Printing, 2013.

Crowley, Aleister. *The Book of the Law*. San Francisco: Weiser Books, 1976.

Culver, Lawrence. *The Frontier of Leisure: Southern California and the Shaping of Modern America*. Oxford: Oxford University Press, 2010.

Dalao, Nicolas B. "My Christmas Retrospection." *The Filipino Student* 1, no. 4 (March 1913).

DeBolt, William Walter. *Gates and Trails*. Dexter, MO: Candor Press, 1975.

Dickstein, Morris. *Dancing in the Dark: A Cultural History of the Great Depression*. New York: W.W. Norton, 2010.

Douglas, Susan J. *Listening In: Radio & the American Imagination*. Minneapolis: University of Minnesota Press, 2004.

Dunn, Nancy, and the Artesia Historical Museum and Art Center. *Artesia: Images of America*. Charleston, SC: Arcadia Publishing, 2011.

Durrell, Lawrence. *The Alexandria Quartet*. New York: Penguin, 1991.

Ehrenreich, Barbara. *Bright Side: How Positive Thinking is Undermining America*. New York: Picador, 2009.

Flamming, Douglas. *Bound for Freedom: Black Los Angeles in Jim Crow America*. Berkeley: University of California Press, 2005.

Fried, Richard M. *The Man Everybody Knew: Bruce Barton and the Making of Modern America*. Chicago: Ivan R. Dee, 2005.

Friel, Joanna, and Adam Swaine. *Secret Chislehurst*. Gloucestershire, England: Amberley, 2015.

Egan, Timothy. *The Worst Hard Time: The Untold Story of Those Who Survived the Great American Dust Bowl*. New York: Mariner, 2006.

Gelhorn, Martha. *The Face of War*. New York: Atlantic Monthly Press, 1988.

Gill, Gillian. *Mary Baker Eddy*. Radcliffe Biography Series. New York: Perseus Books, 1998.

Gordon, Linda. *Dorothea Lange: A Life Beyond Limits*. New York: W.W. Norton, 2010.

———. *The Second Coming of the KKK: The Ku Klux Klan of the 1920s and the American Political Tradition*. New York: Liveright, 2017.

Grosser, Philip. *Uncle Sam's Devil's Island: Experiences of a Conscientious Objector in America During the World War*. Boston: A Group of Friends, 1933.

Haag, Michael. *Alexandria: City of Memory*. New Haven: Yale University Press, 2004.

———. *Vintage Alexandria: Photographs of the City 1860–1960*. Cairo: American University in Cairo Press, 2008.

Haanel, Charles F. *The Master Key System in Twenty-Four Parts with Questionnaire and Glossary*. St. Louis: The Master Key System, 1941.

———. *The New Psychology*. Self published, 1924

Hamilton, Thomas. *Kokomo, Indiana*. Images of America. Charleston, SC: Arcadia Publishing, 2002.

Hamouda, Sahar, and Colin Clement. *Victoria College: A History Revealed*. Cairo: American University in Cairo Press, 2002.

Harsch, Joseph C. *At the Hinge of History: A Reporter's Story*. Athens: University of Georgia Press, 1993.

Hastings, Philip, R. "T & N.O. Junction." *Railroad Magazine* (February 1952): 34–45.

Haywood, Robert C. "The Great Depression: Two Kansas Diaries." *Great Plains Quarterly* 18 (Winter 1998): 27–37.

History of the Bureau of Diplomatic Security of the United States Department of State. 2009-2017.state. gov/documents/organization/176705.pdf.

Holmes, Fenwicke L. *Ernest Holmes: His Life and Times*. New York: Dodd, Mead, 1970.

Horowitz, Mitch. *Occult America: White House Seances, Ouija Boards, Masons, and the Secret Mystic History of Our Nation*. New York: Bantam, 2010.

———. *One Simple Idea: How Positive Thinking Reshaped Modern Life*. New York: Crown, 2014.

Hubbard, L. Ron. *Dianetics: The Modern Science of Mental Health*. Los Angeles: Bridge Publications, 2007.

Hurd, Archibald S. "How Blue-Jackets Are Trained." *The Windsor Magazine: An Illustrated Monthly for Men and Women* 4 (July 1896): 321–328.

Jefferson, Allison Rose. *Living the California Dream: African American Leisure Sites During the Jim Crow Era*. Lincoln: University of Nebraska Press, 2020.

Jenkins, Philip. "The Great Anti-Cult Scare 1935–1945." Paper presented at the 1999 conference for the Center for the Study of New Religions.

Kennedy, David M. *Freedom From Fear: The American People in Depression and War, 1929–1945*. New York: Oxford University Press, 1999.

Kyvig, David E. *Daily Life in the United States: 1920–1940*. Chicago: Ivan R. Dee, 2002.

Lachman, Gary. *Aleister Crowley: Black Magick, Rock and Roll, and the Wickedest Man in the World*. New York: Tarcher-Perigee, 2014.

Lampson, Sir Miles (Lord Killearn). *The Killearn Diaries: 1934–1946*. Edited by Treford Evans. London: Sidgwick & Jackson, 1972.

Larson, Erik. *In the Garden of Beasts: Love, Terror, and An American Family in Hitler's Berlin*. New York: Crown, 2014.

Ma, Olivia. "The Profiteering Prophet: Frank B. Robinson and the Selling of Psychiana." Unpublished senior thesis, history and literature, Harvard University, 2006.

McCaffrey, Dan. *Tommy Burns: Canada's Unknown World Heavyweight Champion*. Toronto: Lorimor, 2000.

McElvaine, Robert S. *The Great Depression: America 1929–1941*. New York: Times Books, 1993.

McGee, Micki. *Self-Help, Inc.: Makeover Culture in America*. New York: Oxford University Press, 2005.

Miller, David, Joseph R. McGeshick, Dennis J. Smith, James Shanley, et al, eds. *The History of the Assiniboine and Sioux Tribes of the Fort Peck Indian Reservation, 1600–2012* (2nd ed.). Helena, MT: Montana State Historical Society Press, 2012.

Monroe, Julie R. *Moscow, Idaho*. Images of America. Charleston, SC: Arcadia, 2006.

Norman, Michael, and Elizabeth M. Norman. *Tears in the Darkness: The Story of the Bataan Death March and its Aftermath*. New York: Farrar, Straus and Giroux, 2009.

Oates, Joyce Carol. "The Man with the Golden Smile." *The New York Review of Books*, November 18, 2004.

———. *On Boxing*. New York: Harper Perennial, 2006.

O'Neil, Tim. "A Look Back: 5,000 settle in shacks along the Mississippi during the Great Depression." *St. Louis Post-Dispatch*, January 3, 2010. www.stltoday.com/news/local/a-look-back-settle-in-shacks-along-the-mississippi-during/article_795763a0-affc-59d2-9202-5d0556860908.html.

Parker, Roy. *Uprooted: The Shipment of Poor Children to Canada 1867–1917*. Bristol, UK: Policy Press, 2010.

Parr, Joy. *Labouring Children: British Immigrant Apprentices to Canada 1869–1924*. Toronto: University of Toronto Press, 1994 (reprint).

Petersen, Keith C. *Psychiana: The Psychological Religion*. Moscow, ID: Latah County Historical Society, 1991.

Reitman, Janet. *Inside Scientology: The Story of America's Most Secretive Religion*. New York: Houghton Mifflin, 2011.

Robinson, Alfred. "A Family Trilogy, Book I: John Henry Robinson." "A Family Trilogy, Book II: Frank Bruce Robinson." "A Family Trilogy, Book III: Alfred Bruce Robinson an Autobiography." Unpublished manuscripts.

———. "Echoing Memories of World War II, Pacific Theater." Unpublished manuscript.

Robinson, Frank B. *America Awakening*. Moscow, ID: Psychiana, 1931.

———. *Before the Dawn* (Posthumous). Moscow, ID: Psychiana, 1951.

———. *Blood on the Tail of a Pig*. Portland, OR: West Coast Printing & Binding, 1941.

———. *Crucified Gods Galore: Or, Christianity Before Christ: Containing Shocking New, Startling, and Extraordinary Revelations in Religious History, Which Disclose the Oriental Origin of All Doctrines...* Moscow, ID: Psychiana, 1933.

———. *For Rent: A Cross*. Moscow, ID: Psychiana, 1941.

———. *Gems of Spiritual Truth*. Moscow, ID: Psychiana, 1947.

———. *Gleams Over the Horizon*. Portland, OR: Metropolitan Press, 1939.

———. *God...and Dr. Bannister*. New York: American Book-Stratford Press, 1941.

———. *God in the Dark*. Moscow, ID: Psychiana, 1948.

———. *The God Nobody Knows*. Moscow, ID: Psychiana, 1930.

———. *Is the Story of Jesus Christ Fact or Fiction?* Moscow, ID: Psychiana, 1935.

———. *The Life Story of Frank B. Robinson (Written by Himself)*. Moscow, ID: The Review Publishing Co., 1941.

———. *The Name of the Beast 666*. Moscow, ID: Psychiana, 1935.

———. *Pathway to God*. Moscow, ID: Psychiana, 1943.

———. *A Prophet Speaks*. Moscow, ID: Psychiana, 1943.

———. *Psychiana: The Advanced Lessons*. Cabin John, MD: Wildside Press, 2007.

———. *Secret of Realization*. Moscow, ID: Psychiana, 1932.

———. *Shall We Know Each Other Beyond the Tomb?* Moscow, ID: Psychiana, 1937.

———. *The Strange Autobiography of Frank B. Robinson*. Portland, OR: Metropolitan Press, 1941.

———. *Through War to God*. Portland, OR: Metropolitan Press, 1943.

———. *The Wanderer: A Novel*. Moscow, ID: Psychiana, 1947.

———. *What God Really Is*. Moscow, ID: Psychiana, 1937.

———. *What This War Really Means: With a Prophecy Concerning the Outcome of the Present Conflict*. Portland, OR: Metropolitan Press, 1942.

———. *Ye Men of Athens*. Moscow, ID: Psychiana, 1940.

———. *Your God Power: With Twenty Lessons Showing How to Find and Use It*. Moscow, ID: 1943.

Roth, Benjamin. *A Great Depression Diary*. Edited by James Ledbetter and Daniel B. Roth. New York: PublicAffairs, 2009.

Shlaes, Amity. *The Forgotten Man: A New History of the Great Depression.* New York: Harper Perennial, 2007.

Sturrock, Donald. *Storyteller: The Authorized Biography of Roald Dahl.* New York: Simon & Schuster, 2010.

Suggs, Jack M., Katherine Doob Sakenfeld, and James R. Mueller, eds. *The Oxford Study Bible: Revised English Bible with the Apocrypha.* New York: Oxford University Press, 1992.

Watts, Steven. *Self-Help Messiah: Dale Carnegie and Success in Modern America.* New York: Other Press, 2013.

Willoughby, Laura E. *Petersburg, Virginia.* Then and Now. Charleston, SC: Arcadia, 2010.

Wissa, Hanna F. *Assiout: The Saga of an Egyptian Family.* Sussex, England: Book Guild, 1994.

Worster, Donald. *Dust Bowl: The Southern Plains in the 1930s.* New York: Oxford University Press, 2004.

Wright, Lawrence. *Going Clear: Scientology, Hollywood, and the Prison of Belief.* New York: Vintage Books, 2013.

Young, Andrew D. *St. Louis and Its Streetcars: The Way it Was.* St. Louis: Archway Publishing, 1996.

Zinn, Howard. *A People's History of the United States: 1492–Present.* New York: Harper Perennial, 1995.

Index

Numbers in italic indicate illustrations.

391

About the Author

B randon R. Schrand is the author of *The Enders Hotel: A Memoir*, and *Works Cited: An Alphabetical Odyssey of Mayhem and Misbehavior*. His work has appeared widely in popular and literary magazines such as *Sports Illustrated*, *The Utne Reader*, *The Georgia Review*, *The Missouri Review*, *The North American Review*, and others. He has won Shenandoah's Carter Prize, the Pushcart Prize, and has received a residency at Yaddo. He lives in Moscow, Idaho, with his wife and children.